UNIVERSITY OF NORTH CAROLINA AT CHAPEL HILL
DEPARTMENT OF ROMANCE LANGUAGES

NORTH CAROLINA STUDIES
IN THE ROMANCE LANGUAGES AND LITERATURES

Founder: URBAN TIGNER HOLMES

Editor: CAROL L. SHERMAN

Distributed by:

UNIVERSITY OF NORTH CAROLINA PRESS

CHAPEL HILL

North Carolina 27515-2288

U.S.A.

NORTH CAROLINA STUDIES IN THE
ROMANCE LANGUAGES AND LITERATURES
Number 276

SAVAGE SIGHT/CONSTRUCTED NOISE

POETIC ADAPTATIONS OF PAINTERLY TECHNIQUES
IN THE FRENCH AND AMERICAN AVANT-GARDES

SAVAGE SIGHT/ CONSTRUCTED NOISE

POETIC ADAPTATIONS OF PAINTERLY TECHNIQUES IN THE FRENCH AND AMERICAN AVANT-GARDES

BY

DAVID LeHARDY SWEET

CHAPEL HILL

NORTH CAROLINA STUDIES IN THE ROMANCE
LANGUAGES AND LITERATURES
U.N.C. DEPARTMENT OF ROMANCE LANGUAGES

2003

Library of Congress Cataloging-in-Publication Data

Sweet, David LeHardy, 1961-
    Savage sight, constructed noise: poetic adaptations of painterly techniques in the French and American avant-gardes / by David LeHardy Sweet.
    p. cm. – (North Carolina Studies in the Romance Languages and Literatures; no. 276).
    Includes bibliographical references.
    ISBN 0-8078-9281-5 (pbk.)
    1. French poetry–20th century–History and criticism. 2 Apollinaire, Guillaume, 1880-1918–Knowledge–Art. 3. Reverdy, Pierre, 1889-1960–Knowledge–Art. 4. Breton, André, 1896-1966–Knowledge–Art. 5. O'Hara, Frank, 1926-1966–Knowledge–Art. 6. Ashbery, John–Knowledge–Art. 7. Art and literature–France–History–20th century. 8. Art and literature–United States–History–20th century. 9. Avant-garde (Aesthetics)–France. 10. Avant-garde (Aesthetics)–United States. I. Title. II. Series.

PQ443.S875 2003
841'.91209357–dc21   2003044214

Cover design: Heidi Perov

ISBN 0-8078-9281-5

IMPRESO EN ESPAÑA

PRINTED IN SPAIN

DEPÓSITO LEGAL: V. 5.415 - 2003

ARTES GRÁFICAS SOLER, S. L. - LA OLIVERETA, 28 - 46018 VALENCIA

TABLE OF CONTENTS

LIST OF ILLUSTRATIONS

INTRODUCTION

> To employ her
> construction ball
> Morning fed on the
> light blue wood
> of the mouth
>   cannot understand
> feels deeply)
>
> from "Europe"
> in *The Tennis Court Oath*

J OHN Ashbery's early collection of poems *The Tennis Court Oath* elicited extreme reactions from literary critics, most significantly Harold Bloom, who had elsewhere hailed Ashbery as the spiritual heir to Wallace Stevens and the American romantic tradition. Bloom described *The Tennis Court Oath* as "calculated incoherence," and stubbornly assumed Ashbery was employing an alien technique–a painterly or musical manipulation of language–that disqualified it as poetry: "Poems may be like pictures or like music, or like whatever you will, but if they *are* paintings or musical works they will not be poems. The Ashbery of *The Tennis Court Oath* may have been moved by De Kooning or Kline, Webern or Cage, but he was not moved to the writing of poems."[1]

It is interesting that Bloom did not say whether it was painting or music he found in *The Tennis Court Oath,* thereby suggesting that although it was not poetry, the book's musical or painterly properties were not mutually exclusive. Thus both were available to Ashbery as means to radicalizing his work. Given the examples Bloom lists, it would appear to be the avant-garde features shared by the two media that had effectively spoiled Ashbery's poetry for

---

[1] Harold Bloom, "John Ashbery: The Charity of the Hard Moments" in Harold Bloom (ed.), *John Ashbery* (New York: Chelsea House, 1985), p. 53.

him. Such features (i.e., of emphasizing process over product and allowing aleatory factors into that process) were indicative of a more general breakdown of boundaries between media, genres, and forms that art critic Michael Fried, responding to a similar phenomenon in the plastic arts, decried as "theater." [2]

It should be noted, however, that Bloom's absent-minded equation of painting and music for their "corrosive" properties vis-à-vis poetry conversely reflects a change in attitude among experimental poets themselves, who had, earlier in the Twentieth Century, tended to prefer painting to music as an exemplary modernist medium. It was a preference based on their own impatience with an aesthetic hierarchy, articulated by Walter Pater, which idealized music as the condition to which all arts should aspire. [3] By the time of Ashbery's work, however, it was clear that music had availed itself of the very techniques which had made the plastic arts such a conspicuous vehicle of the Avant-Garde in the first half of the century. It is a premise of this study, then, that experiments in the plastic arts were central in affirming, suggesting, influencing, and sometimes defining avant-garde practice in French and American poetry (although Symbolist poetics strongly influenced the artists as well). A corollary of this premise is that such influences on poetry sometimes thwarted, sometimes combined with the literary traditions from which avant-garde poetry emerged as a correction or affront. Thus, in accordance with Derridean notions of the truth in painting or poetry vis-à-vis the essential detachment of their elements from proprietary claims, no exclusive restitution of avant-garde poetry to avant-garde painting is asserted here. [4]

Whatever the restitutional stakes or mistakes might be, other literary critics have responded more enthusiastically than Bloom to what they see as the painterly qualities of avant-garde and postmodern poetry, citing the influences of painters and their apologists on Ashbery and Frank O'Hara, the so-called "painterly poets" of the New York School (according to Fred Moramarco, who wrote one

[2] Michael Fried, "Art and Objecthood" in *Aesthetics Today*, eds. Morris Philipson and Paul J. Gudel (New York: New American Library, Meridian, 1961).
[3] Walter Pater, "The School of Giorgione" (excerpt) in *Victorian Poetry and Poetics*, Second Edition, eds. W. Houghton and G. R. Stange (Boston: Houghton Mifflin, 1968), p. 733.
[4] Jacques Derrida, "Restitutions" in *The Truth in Painting*, trans. Geoff Bennington and Ian McLeod (Chicago: University of Chicago, 1987), pp. 272-273.

of the first interdisciplinary studies of their work).[5] Marjorie Perloff remains the foremost of these critics. In four landmark studies, *The Poetics of Indeterminacy, Frank O'Hara: A Poet Among Painters, The Futurist Moment,* and *Radical Artifice: Writing Poetry in the Age of Media,* Perloff revealed that there was, if not a causal relationship, at least a functional symbiosis between avant-garde poetics and painterly techniques. *The Poetics of Indeterminacy* provided a blueprint for an alternative history of modern poetry by identifying literary processes–as opposed to finished works–as the defining features of a radical modernist sensibility. If certain works were representative of this sensibility, it was due, according to Perloff, to the exemplary way in which writing process, strategy, or technique interfered with (or imposed itself as) subject matter or meaning, and thus gave the works their character of indeterminacy. Such interference exposed and exploited the arbitrary relationship, posited by De Saussure,[6] between the verbal signifier and signified and thus between form and content. In this way she suggested that the divorce between these components was less characteristic of all literature (as Derridean scholarship would claim) than of a specific body of literature that self-consciously utilized such strategies: an "other tradition" that ran from France to America, from Arthur Rimbaud to Ashbery and Cage.[7]

More significantly, many of these strategies were derived from painterly ones–particularly the cubist and surrealist techniques of fragmenting familiar objects and juxtaposing others through chance combinations in order to contradict or undermine the logic of illusionism and its premise of a "Universal Visual Experience."[8] In this way avant-garde technique infiltrated traditional portraits, landscapes, still-lifes, and other genres in Western art that seemed to affirm this "perceptual"[9] conception of painting, a conception challenged in the modern context through overt de-familiarization. In poetry a similar baring of the device had gotten in the way of

---

[5] Fred Moramarco, "John Ashbery and Frank O'Hara: The Painterly Poets" in *Journal of Modern Literature,* 5:3 (September 1976), pp. 436-462.

[6] Ferdinand de Saussure, "Nature of the Linguistic Sign" in *Critical Theory,* ed. Dan Latimer (New York: Harcourt Brace Jovanovich, 1989), pp. 3-5.

[7] Marjorie Perloff, *The Poetics of Indeterminacy: Rimbaud to Cage* (Princeton: Princeton University, 1981), p. 18.

[8] Norman Bryson, *Vision and Painting: The Logic of the Gaze* (New Haven: Yale University, 1983; reprinted 1997), p. 6.

[9] *Ibid.,* p. 5.

mimetic transparency (the systematic revelation of meaning through disguised techniques that make the meaning seem natural), a quality maintained through traditional narrative and other rhetorical devices in much nineteenth-century poetry. Thus, in structural and procedural terms, the new poetry assumed an *iconic* [10] relation (i.e., structurally similar) to experimental painting–allowing, of course, for the necessary semiotic substitutions appropriate to the verbal medium. But more important is whether or not such practices in poetry can also be seen as Peircean *indices* [11] of their plastic correlatives–i.e., causally effected in terms of intellectual influence, and not merely similar in terms of structure and method. In order to answer this question, certain "plastic" practices in poetry must be distinguished from other verbal ones evolving on their own under pressure of modern demands. Thus, if an indexical relation is to be credited, the collagist component of the new techniques in poetry, for instance, must be distinguished from another textual strategy with a rich genealogy: the practice of citation, a discursive phenomenon from which collage may not be entirely dissociable insofar as citation may indeed exemplify the entire process of linguistic iteration from the standpoint of semiology. (It has also had the advantage of being, perhaps, exhaustively described in Antoine Compagnon's *La Seconde Main*.) [12] Yet to the extent that literary collage may be effected as much by painterly experiments as by the modern morphologies of citation itself, my thesis also reflects the view that literary style is as much a product of historical and sociological changes external to literature as of technical changes internal to the medium itself. As art historian Norman Bryson has argued: No noumenal basis of reality can be determined or agreed upon; therefore, experience can only be judged on the basis of how competing semiotic systems reconfigure themselves and what kinds of recognizable behaviors people exhibit in response. [13] Painting is one such system that has the advantage of competing with literature as a primary channel of socio-cultural formation and poets have responded in distinctive ways.

---

[10] C. S. Peirce, "Logic as Semiotic: The Theory of Signs" in *The Philosophy of C. S. Peirce: Selected Writings* (New York: Harcourt, Brace & Company, 1950), p. 102.
[11] *Ibid.*
[12] Antoine Compagnon, *La Seconde Main, ou le travail de la citation* (Paris: Éditions du Seuil, 1979), pp. 15-19.
[13] Bryson, pp. 39-41.

Given Perloff's own emphasis on "de-familiarizing" techniques in literature (Shklovsky's term), [14] it is interesting that Ezra Pound figures so prominently in her survey. Even though Pound made full modernist use of such techniques, his aims–as revealed in his editorializing influence on Ernest Fenollosa's *The Chinese Written Character as a Medium for Poetry*–were rather to bridge the gap between representamen and object, [15] between literary forms and the modern contents they were supposed to express–but to do so in a new way, as the famous Poundian dictum of "make it new" makes clear. Insofar as the Chinese "ideogram" visually resembled, according to Pound, its meaning or referent, meaning presumably inhered, naturally, in the sign for it–not as a positive correspondence but as an instance of the actual functioning or recognition value of signs. [16] In a way, then, the medium was now the message, and any other message was purely rhetorical, a matter of persuasion, illusionism.

This interpretation of the Chinese written character provides an analogy for the way certain painterly techniques functioned, in part, as an attempt to yoke contents more closely to form by incorporating into the art work or poem a kind of physical evidence of the real at the level of the sign itself: as manifest process, as iconic resemblance, or by evoking the aleatory, circumstantial character of physical adjacencies through a similar textural clash of semiotic entities. Such evidence of aleatory action on a material medium removed it from any locus of the sacred and distinguished it from the auditory medium of music, the immateriality of which provided an idealizing aura of pure, intellectual structuralization. Paintings and poems, on the other hand, now conveyed their physical conditioning in material circumstances–as evidenced by residues of the "real" (or the social) in the form of collage or found elements (or, in poetry, "found" language: overheard bits of conversation, advertising copy, technical jargon, clichés, or even unconventional typography or handwritten phrases). Thus, the signifier and its referent were closely joined at the surface level, the level of the sign itself as a material fact or facet. The verbal collagist sign did something compa-

---

[14] Viktor Shklovsky, "Art as Technique" in *Twentieth-Century Literary Theory*, ed. K. M. Newton (London: Macmillan, 1997), p. 4.

[15] Peirce, p. 99.

[16] Ernest Fenollosa, *The Chinese Written Character as a Medium for Poetry*, ed. Ezra Pound (San Francisco: City Lights, 1983), pp. 8-9.

rable as a fragment of discourse retaining residues of its previous *énonciation*, its fractured state and tenuous grafting onto a verbal structure of other such grafts tending to frustrate the "interdiscursivity" of textual citation. [17] Through fragmenting, tearing, appending, and framing identifiable elements of an ordinary world onto a painterly or textual surface, the works of avant-garde painters and poets called attention to their own materials and modes of production–against all traditional requirements of a coherent discursive or symbolic function.

But a clear distinction must continue to be made between the collagist resources available to painters and to poets. For painters, the collage element is always a physical index or synecdoche of its source that can be utilized only once (even when the materials used are mass-produced). Except in instances when poets have created actual collages that survive as unique artifacts, the basis of literary collage is primarily semiotic, hence virtual or simulated (though spacing, paper, typeface and ink, all straddle the border between sign and material, i.e., reveal the material vehicles commandeered, as it were, by the sign). Poetry's collagist features, then, must also be determined on the basis of their enunciative or "physical" usage as *parole* [18] (implying a non-literary, token, anonymous, or random instance in the fluid present), instead of the signatory or proprietary *énoncé* of discourse (which is always cited in some fashion in explicit conformity with the urge to preserve the past and uphold the idea of the *énoncé* as an unchanging, abstract system: *langue*). Nevertheless, both resources, the physical and the abstract, are deeply imbricated in avant-garde works, making the process of discriminating between them a highly meticulous one involving painstakingly close reading.

If Perloff's first book never fully elaborates the modernist motives behind calling attention to artistic technique and thus thwarting certain signifying processes, *The Futurist Moment* offers a corrective by discussing collage technique in the context of the futurist discourse of simultaneism. In describing pictorial collage as a "contrast of materials" in which "the alterity of assembled elements" is never entirely suppressed, [19] Perloff reveals the "exem-

---

[17] Compagnon, p. 54.
[18] Saussure's terminology, "Nature of the Linguistic Sign," p. 12.
[19] Perloff, *The Futurist Moment* (Chicago: University of Chicago, 1986), pp. 46-47.

plary" [20] way in which collage technique demonstrates the simultaneism of modern experience. The work's modernist content *is* the
simultaneous contrasts of its different elements, elements that frustrate discursive resolutions and even impede the seductive deferral
of meaning along chains of signifiers that otherwise "solicit" [21] the
reader. Because these assembled elements retain qualities of their
former, supposedly un-artistic or utilitarian sources, art and literature's opposite (life, the world) seems to infiltrate their otherwise
self-defining procedures. Indeed, in combining elements from different media, the Futurists wanted to create a collective, all-encompassing aesthetic event that was indistinguishable from life and politics themselves as an arena of competing productive and social
forces.

Thus collage represents a vital first step in a broader avant-
garde program of incorporating non-art elements to art itself and,
in this way, of changing its character as a closed technical system.
Yet in later "synthetic" works, non-art elements and procedures begin to reveal their own aesthetic potential, a potential initially disguised by the shock value of technical appropriations from one art
or medium to another. What initially represents a form of provocation or critical protest against artistic boundaries (even against art
itself) becomes an expansion of technical means, a recuperative
process, culminating–especially for the Futurists–in the aestheticization of everything as a form of dynamic, even violent spectacle.
It involves both a loss and a potential rediscovery of formal identi-
ties at a new level. Parallel with this alternation is a kind of techni-
cally-engineered violation of the artistic personality and its potential
rediscovery as a technologically improved or empowered being
(Rimbaud's *je est un autre* becomes normative). The cyborg character of the modern creator complements the collagist disavowal of
citation as a "canonical metonymy" [22] of famous subjects and its re-
definition as a structure of frustrated interdiscursivity between participants whose individual proprietary claims are partially annulled
in the interest of fostering a sense of either collective identity or
corporate entitlement.

---

[20] My use of the terms "exemplary" and "exemplification" are derived from
Nelson Goodman's use in his *Languages of Art: An Approach to a Theory of Symbols*
(Indianapolis: Hackett Publishing Co., 1976), pp. 50-57.

[21] Compagnon, pp. 23-25.

[22] *Ibid.*, p. 55.

Although various critics have viewed inter-media influences and other avant-garde innovations as a way of always just evading this recuperation of life by art and "directing aesthetic experience . . . *toward* praxis of life" [23] in a way that implies the end of art practice as such, there is always also this recuperative potential that institutionally and interpretively validates that earlier quality of shock or protest. Radical, inter-media transgressions in poetry and art, then, seem to be modeled, in their modernist impulse toward self-revolution and "originality," on technological revolutions as much as social ones, revolutions that quickly render their immediate predecessors obsolete while fostering consensus about the cumulative ubiquity of technology itself. The difference is that art and literature lend themselves, even in their quality of protest, to a particular interpretive status premised on their own social and technological irrelevance or expendability. Thus inter-media innovations *ironically* emulate technological revolutions, their advances being purely parodic, rhetorical, seductive, while giving the lie to any over-serious faith in social or technological teleologies. In borrowing from the painters, then, avant-garde poets reveal a tendency to "outsource" from a companionably disenfranchised medium, even as that medium borrows from other, technologically advanced media (such as photography, video or computers) with greater commercial viability–a situation that would render the visual image increasingly suspect for certain poets writing in the postmodern era, according to Perloff). [24]

The great risk in making aesthetic comparisons between one medium and another in respect of avant-garde technique is that, without some alternative system of verification, technical analogies can become too ambitiously self-confirming. With the claim that technique provides a basis for associating poetic and painterly experiments, a whole taxonomy of such techniques, their sources and interdisciplinary modes, and a history of their development should, ideally, be elaborated. Techniques, however, are invaluable to creators in all media because of their simplicity, adaptability, variation,

---

[23] Peter Bürger, *Theory of the Avant-Garde*, trans. Michael Shaw (Minneapolis: University of Minnesota, 1984), p. 34.

[24] See Perloff's chapter, "Against Transparency" in *Radical Artifice: Writing Poetry in the Age of Media* (Chicago: University of Chicago, 1991) for her discussion of the effect of advertising and advertising images on postmodern poetry.

and disposability. They are protean in nature, modifying themselves in the hands of talented individuals for diverse applications. In the context of poetry, then, variations of technique may be at least as numerous as the poems in which they appear. For this reason this study will use the more practical approach of focusing on particular poets who have demonstrated a high level of engagement with the plastic arts in their writings and personal connections with the art world. In this way, comparisons between poetry and painting can be made in the context of discussions about individual or idiomatic stylistic development, inter-individual semiologic exchange, and, where relevant, the broader historical milieu.

Interpretive biography provides one example of how the specifics of technical appropriations can be critically elaborated. In *Frank O'Hara: A Poet among Painters,* Perloff places O'Hara at the apex of a sporadic literary tradition of borrowing from painters after a close examination of his personal and professional associations with Jackson Pollock, Larry Rivers, Norman Bluhme, and other artists. O'Hara's metonymical "poetics of attention" are compared to painter Hans Hofmann's dictum that the painted surface is "the creation of forces in the sense of *push and pull*," [25] a comparison Perloff then corroborates by citing O'Hara's writings on artists and his attempts to articulate the relation between his own poetic practice and various aesthetic imperatives propounded by Harold Rosenberg and Clement Greenberg apropos of Abstract Expressionism. Furthermore, by stealing the subtitle from biographer Francis Steegmuller's *Apollinaire: Poet among the Painters* (1963) Perloff suggests a practical historical framework for the study of this kind of interaction and the importance of taking a patiently documentary, historicist approach. Unfortunately, like Steegmuller's book, Perloff's literary biography is so meticulously anecdotal it implies that the relations between poetry and painting are mostly a matter of glittery social intercourse. The evidence supporting her analogy between the arts becomes, perhaps, too circumstantial; the push and pull of biographical details distracts one from the primary issue, not of what effect painters have on the poet among them, but of what procedural effect their work has on his or her poetry and what new hermeneutic conditions they help consolidate. One wish-

---

[25] Perloff, *Frank O'Hara: A Poet among Painters* (New York: George Braziller, 1977), p. 22.

es the historical framework implied in the subtitle of Perloff's study had a firmer historical, theoretical, and textual grounding. [26]

Intellectual history, unlike biography, reminds us that hierarchical notions of painting and music were ideologically charged for most poets of the early Twentieth Century. But if, as we have seen, the post-war American Avant-Garde did not discriminate on any such basis, this development should not obscure the fact that the initial impulse to transgress artistic boundaries between media exposed certain internalized ideological constructs–depending upon the medium (painting or music) preferred. As much as possible, then, this study attempts to trace the theoretical implications of poets turning to the plastic arts as a source of innovative techniques and how those implications changed in the course of the century.

Apollinaire and other "cubist" poets of the French Avant-Garde provide a useful starting point because they identified painting not simply as another art form to emulate but as an activity that had become aesthetically and ideologically opposed to aspects of Symbolism and its idealization of music. ("De la musique avant toute chose . . . et tout le reste est littérature," as Verlaine wrote in his poem "Art poétique.") In essence, music–abstract, aural, and temporal– represented a pure art form, which painting–representational, material, and spatial [27]–did not. In a celebrated letter to Villiers de l'Isle-Adam, Stéphane Mallarmé articulated the requirement of pure poetry "to divorce itself from dreams and chance and link itself to the idea of the universe." [28] Thus, only pure notions of objects (the signifieds) and not the objects themselves (the referents) were to be represented by words, and by implication, pure *langue* as system, not messy *parole* as instance; the unimpeachable *énoncé*, but not the dubious *énonciation*. Mere instantiation or objecthood,

---

[26] Perloff does manage to satisfy this requirement in her final study *Radical Artifice*, but only by confining her discussion to neo-avant-garde and postmodern poets whose responses to visual culture can no longer be said to derive chiefly from painting as an art form.

[27] The distinction between painting and music on the basis of the metaphysical categories of space and time reflects on a similar distinction between painting and poetry that was most fully elaborated by Gotthold Lessing in his treatise *Laocoön*. For an overview of the philosophic tradition of comparing notational and plastic arts, see W. J. T. Mitchell's *Iconology: Image, Text, Ideology* (Chicago: University of Chicago, 1986).

[28] Stéphane Mallarmé, letter to Villiers de l'Isle-Adam, September 24, 1866, in *Correspondance* (Paris: Gallimard, 1985). My translation.

the circumstantial or material manifestation of an otherwise disembodied thought, was subject to all the hazards of material existence that had nothing to do with the idea of the universe–only with its temporary, fragmentary, and heterogeneous configurations.

Modern painters, on the other hand, had seized on precisely these aspects of their chosen medium–the plastic–as a way of shattering any complete, coherent idea of the universe. As E. H. Gombrich stated in *Art and Illusion,* Cubism was the first painterly aesthetic to insist upon contradictory evidence to prevent any coherent image from forming, or at least the illusion of one.[29] But Gombrich discusses Cubism and Abstraction at the very end of his seminal study because they clearly pose problems for his theory of art by breaking away from the illusionistic function he proposes for painting. His emphasis on illusionism, visual coherence and the laws of perspective, all spring from his idea of painting as a method for testing psychologico-visual schemata against the evidence of the senses in order to create a sort of ideal reproduction of reality (even though he mostly contests the so-called "copy theory" of art in this early book,[30] only making the case for "natural resemblance" later in order to counter what he considered the over-sophistication of symbol theorists[31]). But this theory, as Norman Bryson has complained, depends upon assuming the existence of an unchanging, de-historicized viewer for whom painting provides direct entry to an otherwise unattainable noumenal reality rather than providing a configuration of signs the viewer may or may not recognize, decode, and respond to with appropriately recognizable behavior patterns.[32] While Bryson's own historico-semiological theory of painting offers a way of moving beyond the reality/illusion, correct/erroneous oppositions of Gombrich's theory, his notion of paintings as semiotic agglomerations of the social formation (which only the historical subject is technically

---

[29] E. H. Gombrich, *Art and Illusion* (Princeton: Princeton University, 1969), pp. 281-282.

[30] *Ibid.,* pp. 86-88.

[31] Gombrich, who once argued that visual signs were as conventional as those of language, would later argue for "the commonsense distinction between images, which are naturally recognizable because they are imitations, and words, which are based on conventions." Gombrich, "Image and Code: Scope and Limits of Conventionalism in Pictorial Representation" in *Image and Code,* ed. Wendy Steiner (Ann Arbor: University of Michigan Studies in Humanities, No. 2, 1981), p. 11. See also: Mitchell, *Iconology,* p. 77.

[32] Bryson, pp. 31-33, 39-43.

competent to decode, according to Bryson) seems no less stumped by the problem of Cubism and so avoids it altogether. While modern art frustrates Gombrich's need for illusionistic consistency as an index of true representation over idiomatic stylistic approximation, it also complicates Bryson's requirement of sign-recognition within the so-called "habitus" of different societies or cultures. [33] The exact social significance of Cubism's signs is not easily determined because of their quality of fragmentation or abstraction. In some measure these broken signs represent themselves alone, thus fueling a whole critical discourse, anti-establishment in outlook, "against interpretation." [34]

Because these partial-signs open up a work to a surplus of critical ambiguity through extreme detachment and semiotic discontinuity, their effect on other denotative systems attempting to simulate their operations is inherently corrosive, fostering an abstract, equivocal hermeneutics. It is this notion of painting as a corrupting influence on poetry that interests me, but also as an influence on its own terms, i.e., by virtue of its plasticity and not its traditional function of visually rendering literary themes. It should be pointed out, then, that cubist and futurist experiments had helped artists shed the traditionally narrative or figurative functions in painting; but in emphasizing painting's compositional, self-referential aspects, Cubism was partly a continuation of symbolist prerogatives and thus set the stage for painting's own leap of faith into abstract art–another form of aestheticism or purism, according to Meyer Schapiro. [35] Thus, although Cubism's use of collage suggested a critique of the Avant-Garde's earlier aestheticist assumptions, cubist discourse itself veered toward a new aestheticism of its own in both its "synthetic" and "Orphist" manifestations (the latter of which revealed, according to Apollinaire, an impulse among modern painters toward abstraction and pure color). The first strenuous resistance to this tendency came with Dada and Surrealism. The surrealist reintroduction of figurative or literary elements into painting provided a form of insurance against "pure painting" by insisting on the representative function of painting–provided what was represented was unheard of (i.e., *jamais vu*, surreal).

---

[33] *Ibid.*, p. 53.

[34] Susan Sontag, "Against Interpretation" in *Against Interpretation* (New York: Farrar, Straus Giroux, 1966), pp. 3-14.

[35] Meyer Schapiro, "The Nature of Abstract Art," in *Modern Art: Nineteenth and Twentieth Centuries, Selected Papers* (New York: George Braziller, 1978), pp. 185-211.

One must clearly discriminate, then, between the kinds of art to which poets respond, the different uses to which poets put these alternative sign systems, and the theoretical implications of their appropriation. At the same time, a consistent yet flexible theory of symbolization is necessary to negotiate these differences and to establish grounds for interpretive comparison. Nelson Goodman's *Languages of Art* offers a useful and encompassing analysis of symbolic systems and his discussion of such terms as "representation," "expression," "denotation," and "exemplification" has informed this study.[36] W. J. T. Mitchell's *Iconology* takes Goodman's work a step further by examining the ideologically gendered character of philosophic discourse on the arts beginning with Gotthold Lessing's *Laocoön*, in which painting and poetry are respectively associated with female and male by way of Kantian *a priori* intuitions of space and time.[37] This study partly challenges and partly follows on this philosophical discussion about the relations between the arts and their relevant sense perceptions, but always in the context of examining specific modern works.

The strict boundaries between any two artistic media, by which technical appropriations once engendered a sense of transgression, lost considerable sway in the postmodern context. So far, all attempts to historicize this development have been limited to the most rudimentary historical analyses in the form of biographies or influence studies. Works of cultural criticism that have attempted to convey the dialectical tensions of modern artistic and literary developments (works such as Peter Bürger's *Theory of the Avant-Garde*) have been limited to outlining developments without the inconvenience of applying the dialectic to specific technical issues of inter-media appropriations. Clearly, one of the dangers of doing so would be the debilitating effect such technical hybrids have on historical theorizing: they tend to invite competing, contradictory, or paradoxical interpretations. Yet, as David Carrier has shown in his own studies of "artwriting," important art works always generate multiple interpretations, even where consensus exists among critics about what formal, technical or stylistic issues ultimately matter.[38]

---

[36] Goodman, chapters I & II.
[37] Mitchell, pp. 109-111.
[38] David Carrier, *Principles of Art History Writing* (University Park, PA: Pennsylvania State University, 1991), pp. 237-241.

So despite these risks, the present study will attempt just such a comparative history, paying close attention to the poets' critical responses to contemporaneous plastic works and how those responses are translated into avant-garde writing processes. The value of closely scrutinizing a poet's writings on the plastic arts is in recognizing that they often constitute a proto-poetics and thus provide a historical index not only of relations between the arts but of how those relations affect the idea of modernity in poetry. The poets included have been chosen as much for the vigor of their responses to the arts as for their success in adapting painterly techniques to poetry, if only in certain exemplary instances (revealed in specific poems to be analyzed for their "plastic" properties). In this way, the "artwriting" of poets reveals a consensus among them about the relevance of art criticism to poetic innovation, even if individual poets differ over how best to apply it.

My investigation, then, focuses on the French poets Apollinaire, Pierre Reverdy, and André Breton, and the Americans O'Hara, and Ashbery (although shorter discussions of Baudelaire, Mallarmé, and William Carlos Williams are also included). In choosing these poets, I do not assert the existence of a direct chain of influence between them, nor do I affirm, with respect to the American poets, the primacy of an avant-garde, internationalist tradition over an Anglo-American one. What I want to demonstrate is a kind of reverberating or ricochet influence between disciplines and the epistemological dispersions (as Michel Foucault describes them in *L'Archéologie du savoir*) of technical and theoretical concepts promoted and exemplified in the plastic arts. Furthermore, my decision to link the French and American Avant-Gardes in this way and, thereby, to divert attention from the more obvious channels of literary influence on the Americans, is to show how they responded to France as a source of ideas that ran against the grain of the American romantic tradition, yet which insinuated or grafted themselves on to that tradition. (Part and parcel of this grafting is the influence of Cubism and Surrealism on Williams, Pound, Gertrude Stein, and Wallace Stevens and how it affected O'Hara's and Ashbery's reception of their work.)

My study is divided into two parts, the French and the Americans. With respect to the modern tradition of poets responding to contemporaneous developments in the arts, the French influence on the Americans seems paramount, particularly insofar as that tradition pertains to the more conspicuous features of avant-garde practice in literature. The programmatic way in which the French addressed the relation between the two arts also helps to clarify the attitude of the younger Americans, who tended to avoid making theoretical pronouncements or of seeing themselves as part of an organized movement. Furthermore, the French provided O'Hara and Ashbery with a modern counterweight to the giants of their own modernist tradition (Eliot and Pound), a counterweight that distinguishes the younger poets' work as more than simply "late modern," but as "postmodern." In this way, the New York poets extended the avant-garde critique of high modernism by challenging and parodying the notion of a complete, unified, and original artwork, the surface fragmentation of which masked a deeper structure.

In all five cases, a considerable body of critical writings on art and artists is available because each poet wrote copiously for contemporary periodical or gallery publications. This study has been facilitated, however, by the fact that most of these writings are now assembled in individual anthologies. In the case of Apollinaire and Breton, these collections have been translated into English as *Apollinaire on Art* and *Surrealism and Painting*. Reverdy's early writings can only be found under the French title *Nord-Sud, Self-Defense et autres écrits sur l'art et la poésie*. O'Hara's numerous catalogue essays for the Museum of Modern Art are combined with articles he wrote for *ArtNews* in *Art Chronicles 1954-1966*; and Ashbery, who worked as arts editor for the Paris edition of *The New York Herald Tribune* and later for *ArtNews* in New York, has had his writings collected under the title *Reported Sightings: Art Chronicles, 1957-1987*. More important to this study, however, is the fact that each poet has written significant poems that either demonstrate or refer to specific painterly procedures or combinations thereof. Sometimes a certain ekphrastic preoccupation with a particular painting has prompted these demonstrations and in this way facilitated my efforts to reveal influence. But for the most part I have had to rely on formal literary analyses combined with more circumstantial evidence gleaned from the sources mentioned above. I have avoided discussing poems that seem to be merely about or addressed to painters whose work the poet admired.

In many respects, Apollinaire is the most exemplary poet for this study, both for the breadth of his curiosity about avant-garde art movements and in his aspiration to create an encompassing, "synthetic" poetry that would combine all the resources of the different arts, especially of poetry and painting. In attempting this, he made use of different avant-garde trends among contemporaneous painters, whether cubist, simultaneist, futurist, machinist, or Orphist. This desire to create a more plastic, almost proto-"concrete" poetry culminated in his calligrams, poem-paintings that oscillate between verbal and visual form in a way that defies oral presentation. In presenting language as varied typographic textures abutting at different angles, the calligrams draw attention to the spatio-material qualities of their medium. But in disrupting the sequential organization of lines, an initial sense of randomness, even chaos, is created for the reader. The elements of the calligram meet the eye with a provocative, "simultaneist" impact, making one aware of the total surface of the page. In this way Apollinaire produces a feeling of cognitive overload in a genre that seems to demand an accelerated receptivity. Only gradually does the reader come to recognize visual patterns that suggest possible orders of reading. Nevertheless, a constant adjustment between verbal and visual levels of reception is required.

Frustrating as it may be for the reader, this constant oscillation also reveals the limits of Apollinaire's formal transgressions because the verbal aspect of the work never entirely loses a lyrical resonance. Furthermore, it retains an idea of a coherent poetic persona or voice, a voice that surfaces now and again with a nostalgic aside, as if in remembrance of things past (or "tout ce que j'aime encore" as he writes in "Liens"). But although Apollinaire is one of the few who make this quality of a nostalgic subjectivity explicit, it is subtly indicated–in different ways and in different degrees–in the work of each of the poets to be examined.

The most rigorous aesthetician among them is Reverdy, who backs away from Apollinaire's exuberant aspiration to create a poetico-plastic hybrid. Instead, like the Symbolists before him, Reverdy insists on the purity of the poetic medium for the purpose of creating an aesthetically autonomous object. But he also finds a compelling plastic example of such purity in the case of synthetic Cubism. In such circumstances, the two arts represent parallel but autonomous regions whose distinctness fosters vigorous communication about what constitutes true creativity. In this respect, Reverdy is a kind of avant-garde conservative. Little trace of new-

age optimism infects his modest temperament. His compact, geo-
metrically constructed poems seem introverted yet strangely impersonal, acquiring an air of mystery through the elegant simplicity of
his technique: a grid-like intercalation of fractured images. His
compositional devices are more purely cubist than Apollinaire's
(which are more eclectic), yet his constructions lend an almost surreal glow to the humble, sensory fragments he assembles. Kenneth
Rexroth has distinguished Reverdy from both Apollinaire and the
Symbolists on the basis of their narrative and syntactical cohesion
as against Reverdy's "conscious, deliberate dissociation and recombination of elements into a new artistic entity made self-sufficient
by its rigorous architecture."[39]

Yet in backing away from simultaneism and the aesthetic confusions risked by Apollinaire, Reverdy seems to spread a veil between
the arts–and between art and life as well. Nowhere is this differenti-
ation more evident than in his rejection of the role of accident or
chance in the creative process. For Reverdy, art was a deliberate
and distinct activity from other "praxes" of life, and therefore
techniques that made use of chance were simply depriving art of its
true being, of its ability to compete on equal footing with ordinary
reality and its petty, commercial preoccupations. Indeed, it is the
question of the role of chance that finally distinguishes Reverdian
poetics not only from Apollinairean experimentalism, but from
Bretonian Surrealism as well. This distinction persists despite both
the surrealist aura of Reverdy's conscientiously constructed poems
and the contribution of his famous definition of the image to surrealist thought.

With the advent of Dada and Surrealism, Apollinaire's urban
scavenger hunts for random poetic images began to seem both
prophetic and provincial. Partly as a consequence of simultaneist
discourse, chance operations and free association came into their
own as creative principles in the dadaist and futurist performances
held in Zurich and Italy before resurfacing in Paris and Berlin after
World War I. The first artists to employ chance operations in the
plastic arts were Jean Arp, Francis Picabia, and Marcel Duchamp,
each of whom were important influences on Breton. Certain dada
and surrealist collages, including ones by Breton, demonstrate the

---

[39] Kenneth Rexroth, introduction to *Pierre Reverdy: Selected Poems* (New York:
New Directions, 1972), p. vi.

literal appropriation of a plastic procedure by poets. Words and phrases in these works are actual cut-out, material objects, found and displayed for both visual and verbal effects. Thus chance operations with language qualify as plastic procedures insofar as language is treated less as a system of reference than a kind of undifferentiated, printed matter subject to physical, even violent, manipulations.

Such experiments also set the stage for Breton's promulgation of automatism as a poetic procedure involving the chance association of verbal elements through speeding-up the writing process. In automatic writing, unlike collage, chance and speed become "invisible" plastic functions evidenced only by the initial illogic of their productions. What chance and speed make possible is the intellectual estrangement of the poet from his creation by submitting the poetic process to physical laws, in this case acceleration. Thus, a certain Viconian principle of knowledge-via-fabrication that is still operative in Reverdy's cubist poetic surrenders to a Rimbaldian one of blind visionarism (as Breton describes it in the essay "Le Message automatique"), of an unknowable and unknowing creative process whose only "reasoned" (raisonné) dimension is a technical adherence to high velocity. In this way, a new, unmediated expression of the unconscious was presumably made possible. Thus, Breton's identification of automatism as the unmediated expression of the unconscious turned Rimbaud's discovery into a technique; the first Manifesto of Surrealism became the how-to manual of anti-literary inspiration.

The earliest surrealist paintings of De Chirico and Ernst, however, reveal that the technical means of expressing the unconscious could also be highly structured. When Breton distinguished Miró as one of the greatest surrealist painters, he did so because of Miró's absolute adherence to painterly automatism. Although Miró acknowledged that his works began as automatic exercises, he also admitted that their secondary phases of production were "carefully calculated." [40] Indeed, many surrealists relied on an almost academic illusionism for the purpose of visually conveying unconscious realities. Like academic illusionism, surrealist illusionism finds its literary counterpart in the syntactical, narrative, and even prosodic

---

[40] William S. Rubin, *Dada, Surrealism, and their Heritage* (New York: Museum of Modern Art, 1977), p. 68.

devices that found their way back into surrealist poetry despite the automatist prerogatives of Breton's program. It is to this extent that the relation between surrealist poetry and painting is often more ekphrastic or descriptive than procedural in any radically plastic way.

In turning to the Americans, it should first be noted that Ashbery and O'Hara enjoyed personal and critical associations with Abstract Expressionists such as Jackson Pollock, Willem de Kooning, and Franz Kline, but also with such "pop" or "new realist" artists as Robert Rauschenberg, Jasper Johns, and Larry Rivers. In respect of these painters, Ashbery's and O'Hara's distinct poetic sensibilities personalize the competing theoretical postures of the two camps. In turn, these postures reflect two modes of avant-garde discourse issuing from France that are closely connected yet vibrantly antagonistic and which resituate the drama of those earlier aesthetico-ideological divisions among the Symbolists, Cubists, and Dada-Surrealists as described. The divisions have transposed themselves, through the mechanisms of discourse, into ever more esoteric arguments that might broadly be categorized in terms of formalist and immediatist sensibilities, sensibilities implied in the contradictory tendencies of Surrealism toward both academicism and automatism.

Immediatist sensibilities try to suspend the formal or mimetic structures through which experience is organized to create an illusion of coherence or legibility. Their works attempt to convey a kind of blind, unknowing interaction with the world as if in advance of conscious, rhetorical formulations, even if in so doing they resort to techniques that imply at least a minimum of conscious control (e.g., the use of syntax in automatic writing). Immediatist sensibilities thrive in a presumably un-self-reflective present; formalist sensibilities are always belated, always self-reflective, and always mediated by a culturally inculcated reference system (if often with a sense of ludic irony). At the same time, expression in either mode involves a complex negotiation with their opposites, a negotiation that can sometimes be revealed through critical analysis. Interestingly, Ashbery's and O'Hara's own poetry manages to incorporate these opposing tendencies in forms so ideologically etiolated, so mannered, as to yield a congenial, pluralist outlook one can only call American postmodern.

The rival claims of automatism and academicism are central when considering the surrealist influences on Ashbery and O'Hara, apropos of painterly sources. Sometimes those influences were effected through American intermediaries, most significantly Jackson Pollock whose monumental "action" paintings gave automatism an American bigness. It was O'Hara's craving for a kind of poetic seriousness that drew him to Abstract Expressionism for an aesthetic credo; at the same time, his jaunty Apollinairean sensibility drew him into the streets of New York on his lunch hour in pursuit of a more syncopated, highly enjambed, "all-over" (the term is Clement Greenberg's) [41] texture of writing to accommodate that credo. O'Hara's automatism was more "queer" than "unconscious," more social than private. Thus the big and the small, the serious and the trivial all entered the fabric of his poems by virtue of their accidental proximity to the poet.

Unlike Apollinaire's urban meandering, however, O'Hara's ambulatory search for poetic images was concentrated more closely with the writing body and its physical relations to its surroundings. "The scale of the body," [42] which defined for him the altered relation of the painter to the painting in the work of Jackson Pollock, was also an important criterion for what constituted the poetic utility of chance proximities. Urban rambling condensed into occasional poems written on the spot, to lunch poems written between 12:00 and 1:00 P.M., to F.Y.I. poems written on the job. Anything physically present at the scene of writing was a potential found object since the magnetic field of poetic transformation was simply the poet's own alertness to his immediate environment. Yet O'Hara's technique is by no means reducible to an Abstract Expressionism of words. It remains to be determined whether O'Hara's oeuvre is truly expressive of such an aesthetic or whether it merely constitutes an appreciation of Pollock's and De Kooning's paintings. In this respect, the poet's relation to Larry Rivers provides an important corrective.

As opposed to O'Hara's more additive, "all-over" approach, John Ashbery relied on what he called a "leaving-out business" [43] in his poetic application of chance. For example, in his long poem

---

[41] Clement Greenberg, "The Crisis of the Easel Picture," in *Art and Culture* (Boston: Beacon Press, 1965), pp. 154-157.

[42] Frank O'Hara, *Jackson Pollock* (New York: George Braziller, 1959), p. 28.

[43] John Ashbery, "The New Spirit," in *Three Poems* (New York: Viking, 1972), p. 3.

"Europe," Ashbery cut up and reassembled a girls' adventure book–a found object–in an almost literal application of Tzara's famous description of how to write a poem. [44] Yet the Eliotic title he gave it and the hundred and eleven sections into which he divided it, suggest a distended Dantesque vision or ironic academicism. Ashbery's formal effects are more disjunctive, more staged, more parodic than O'Hara's, which strive, rather, for personal sincerity apropos of physical surroundings ("I am needed by things," [45] as the poet once wrote).

The leaving-out business is like an overly intricate editorial process that complicates instead of clarifies. In poems like "The Skaters," Ashbery alternately juxtaposes and overlaps different poetic voices, producing an effect of interlocking or inter-penetrating rhetorical frames, a formal device with strong analogies to modern painting. In painting, the physical frame is never just a support but a theoretical structure that concretizes the metaphysical relations between art and life as well as the aesthetic ones between illusionism and objecthood. The problem of the frame is beautifully illustrated by De Chirico's painting *The Double Dream of Spring* [fig. 1], which was also the title of another Ashbery collection. Thus, the surrealist resuscitation of illusionism in the Twentieth Century has relevance for the study of Ashbery's parodic academicism.

This combination of academicism and dadaism is what constitutes Ashbery's own "new realism," an attitude with general implications for the postmodern American situation. In light of Ashbery's considerable critical output on postmodern and realist painters in America, it is indicative of his pluralist breadth of vision that he chose Parmigianino's *Self-Portrait in a Convex Mirror* as the basis for his long poem by the same name. Something had happened in the culture that allowed a sixteenth-century masterpiece to emblematize postmodern ruminations about pictorial and literary forms of representation. At the same time, the choice seems deviant and ironical in ways that evoke conceptual and pop art (Jasper Johns's three-tiered American flag, for example, similarly establish-

[44] See Tristan Tzara's "Manifesto on feeble love and bitter love, part viii" in *The Dada Painters and Poets*, ed. Robert Motherwell (Cambridge, Massachusetts: Belknap Press, 1989), p. 92.
[45] Frank O'Hara, "Meditations in an Emergency" in *The Selected Poems of Frank O'Hara* (New York: Random House, 1974), p. 87.

es a physical vanishing or tapering-off point in front of the painting instead of illusionistically establishing one behind it). Thus, while seeming to deviate from contemporary art discourse, Ashbery coolly reiterates and enhances it.

What I hope to have shown in this discussion of the different poets are the historical and theoretical reversals that warrant consideration when exploring aesthetic assimilations between media– their appropriations, their exclusions, and where possible, their ideological ramifications. In pursuing these questions further, I hope to contribute some historico-theoretical depth to the comparative study of avant-garde poetics and, more specifically, to the study of French avant-garde influences on O'Hara and Ashbery.

CHAPTER I

GUILLAUME APOLLINAIRE

I N his analysis of the Avant-Garde, Peter Bürger claims that reciprocal influences between the arts depend on technical innovations external to the arts; but he also recognizes "non-synchronies in the evolution of various arts," [1] implying that certain technical advances may be media-specific. Thus, technical influences between media are subject to directional shifts inspired by recognized innovations and innovators in different fields. When a surge of new methodologies in a particular medium or art tips the balance of influence in a certain direction, that shift is nevertheless expressive of a general ambiance of innovation among all the arts, where creators are necessarily attentive to developments affecting their production. At the same time, technical influences from different media blur the boundaries between internal evolution and external influence.

In many ways the era of the Avant-Garde constitutes a historic phase in which such shifts occurred with unprecedented intensity. But one of the most conspicuous shifts, in which literary production was more strongly influenced by developments in the plastic arts than at any other time, took place at a particular stage in the evolution of the Avant-Garde. The radical break with the formal traditions of painting effected by Picasso and Braque after the turn of the Nineteenth Century had far-reaching consequences not only in the plastic arts, but in literature as well. And although many poets and writers, from Blaise Cendrars to André Gide, were affected by these developments, none was more responsive than Guillaume Apollinaire.

---

[1] Peter Bürger, *Theory of the Avant-Garde.* Theory and History of Literature, Vol. 4 (Minneapolis: University of Minnesota, 1984), p. 33.

The object of this study is to show how a non-verbal medium such as painting may undergo a number of critical decodings before resurfacing in the context of literary art. By focusing on the work of poets like Apollinaire, the complex maneuvers involved in translating innovations in one art or medium to another can be examined with greater specificity. But before embarking on a three-tiered study of art criticism, poetics, and poetry, it will be necessary to consider that broader milieu of reciprocal influences suggested above.

The problem of inter-arts influence in the early Twentieth Century cannot be isolated from a modern tradition among poets–beginning with Baudelaire–of writing on the different arts for literary purposes. Elements of this tradition have been regularly recycled and reinvested in newer, individualized forms, whether by poets or artists in turn. They have also been completely reinterpreted, as Carrier's study of artwriting demonstrates, albeit in the framework of critical consensus between poets and painters about the relevance of certain issues to their production. As a result, the question of influences between the plastic arts and literature is complicated by instances of literary discourse on the arts influencing both poets and artists and then feeding back through a cultural loop system to yield technical innovations in poetry, putatively derived from the arts. Thus any reliance on a poet's art criticism as a way of detecting influences from the arts raises the question of how much he or she has borrowed from earlier poets whose pronouncements in this genre were often well known. Is a poet's critical examination of art works of his time a direct response to the new, or simply an allegory of reading-about-the-new, a reference to previous responses to art? No definitive answer exists, but to whatever extent the latter condition applies, a restatement of those earlier responses seems appropriate, the general features of which conform to what can best only be described as "symbolist aesthetics."

SYNAESTHESIA AND THE IDEAL OF MUSIC: BAUDELAIRE AND MALLARMÉ

Nineteenth-century symbolist aesthetics derived largely from a deep concern about the autonomy of the various arts and their relation to corresponding senses, especially optical and auditory perception. The precise formulation of that concern can be found in the discourse of *synaesthesia,* Baudelaire's theory of "reciprocal analogies" between the senses that express the "complex, indivisible totality" of the universe. [2] In poetry this preoccupation manifests itself in verbal analogies between various sensory experiences as demonstrated in the familiar stanza from "Correspondances":

> Comme de longs échos qui de loin se confondent
> Dans une ténébreuse et profonde unité,
> Vaste comme la nuit et comme la clarté,
> Les parfums, les couleurs, et les sons se répondent. [3]

> (As far-off echoes from a distance sound
> In unity profound and recondite,
> Boundless as night itself and as light,
> Sounds, fragrances, and colours correspond.) [4]

As Jean-Paul Sartre informs us in his study of the poet, Baudelaire's borrowing of the Swedenborgian notion of correspondences did not mean he adhered to its mystic hermeneutics; "it was rather because he wanted to find in each reality a fixed non-satisfaction, an appeal to another thing, an objectified transcendence. . . . Ultimately these acts of transcendence would extend to the whole world. The world as totality would have meaning. . . ." [5]

A technical analogue for Baudelaire's idea of universal correspondences can be found in Eugène Delacroix's formulation and application of color theory, which the poet himself elaborated in articles on the artist long before the publication of *Les Fleurs du mal.* [6] In Baudelaire's description of Delacroix's system, color is defined as a balance of tones, each of which can never exist in and of itself,

---

[2] Charles Baudelaire, "Richard Wagner and *Tannhäuser* in Paris," in *Baudelaire: Selected Writings on Art & Artists,* trans. P. E. Charvet (Cambridge: Cambridge University, 1972), p. 331.

[3] Baudelaire, "Correspondances" in *Les Fleurs du mal* (Paris: Librairie Générale Française, 1972), p. 16.

[4] Baudelaire, "Correspondences," in *Selected Poems,* trans. Joanna Richardson (New York: Penguin, 1975), p. 12.

[5] Jean-Paul Sartre, *Baudelaire,* trans. Martin Turnell (New York: New Directions, 1950), p. 178.

[6] It should be noted that Baudelaire's own insights to the art of Delacroix were fueled by literary antecedents, notably Hoffmann's *Kreisleriana,* in which "colors, sounds, and scents" are said to "unite in a wonderful concert." Hoffmann quoted by Baudelaire in "The Salon of 1846" in *Selected Writings,* p. 58.

but only in relation to the others. [7] Color, then, represents a total scale of tonal relations–not unlike those of music–which reflects or gives the illusion of an ideal order. For many nineteenth-century poets, music came closest to this ideal order, an order that presumably motivated creative production. Unfortunately, this privileging of music often depended on the poets' own lack of technical expertise in that field. But even when musical terminology was effectively employed (as in Baudelaire's use of "melody," "harmony," "tone," and "scale"), music's prerogative was rarely challenged in discussions of the other arts, while features of those arts that lent comparison to music were emphasized. Color, therefore, easily accommodated the concert of musical analogies Baudelaire utilized in his critical writings on art because its qualities seemed fleeting and im- material–like sound itself and not like the material objects or environments with which it could be mistaken.

Furthermore, as Baudelaire learned from his musical idol Richard Wagner, the arts, too, were situated in a scale of relations–or rather, they occupied specific territories in an aesthetic geography where artistic borders were cooperatively maintained through aesthetic alliances. Wagner explains:

> I recognized in fact that at the precise point where one of these arts reached limits beyond which it could not go, there began at once with rigorous precision the sphere of action of the other; that, consequently, by the intimate union of these two arts, it would be possible to express with wholly satisfying clarity what each of them could not express separately. [8]

Thus, whenever a "gap" in one art had to be "bridged by the imagination," [9] the imagination would be assisted by the action or memory of another art. Not surprisingly, Wagner occupies a special place in Baudelaire's system insofar as the composer of *Tannhäuser* conceived of the dramatic art as "art in the fullest sense of the term, the most all-embracing and the most perfect." [10] But the complete success of the dramatic art depended on the harmonious interaction of

[7] *Ibid.*, p. 56.
[8] Richard Wagner quoted by Baudelaire in "Richard Wagner and *Tannhäuser* in Paris" in *Selected Writings*, p. 336.
[9] *Ibid.*, p. 328.
[10] *Ibid.*

distinct arts whose limits were recognized by the sensitive spectator. Where specific boundaries were not observed, the illusion of wholeness broke down, as Baudelaire, quoting Wagner again, reveals: "Any attempt to express with the means of one [art] what could be expressed only by the two together, must inevitably lead to obscurity and confusion first of all, and then to the decay and corruption of each art individually." [11]

Thus, the assumption of one art's means by another was risky business. Baudelaire himself offered a caveat about synaesthetic interactions that applied above all to language: "There is in words, in the Word itself, something sacred that forbids our turning them into a game of chance." [12] An instance of this was when words assumed the character of plastic elements, the significance of which were bound to material circumstance. Not surprisingly, the one art that came closest, in Baudelaire's view, to the inertia of materialism or the inconsequentiality of accident, was sculpture, which he dismissed as "a bore" [13] precisely because he believed it was too close to nature, the realm of physical extension and pure contingency.

By contrast, Mallarmé seems less dismissive of nature's capacity to climb in the scale of the various arts with intent to molest (or partake of) the purity of their universal idea–perhaps because he premised so much upon that purity. As the self-designated father/protector of Poetry, Mallarmé acutely sensed the delicacy of the poet's charge insofar as the very tissue of poetic textuality seemed positioned for its own preservation/destruction with every reading. For Mallarmé, Nature, or Chance, represented the possibility of literary mishandling–i.e., misreading by hermeneutic closure, a kind of forcing of the text to a condition of semantic servitude. But for Poetry's pure ideality to be true, it had to be constantly "tested," the ambiguity of this word suggesting the poet's own ironic position: he imposed on language strict codes of conduct (prosodic, metaphoric, etc.) which enhanced the possibility of its aesthetic liberation, but also its intellectual misapprehension. Literary composition, then, became an act of presentation and withdrawal, exposure and disguise, as the text–virgin with each new reading–awaited the One reading.

---

[11] *Ibid.*, p. 336.
[12] "Théophile Gautier" in *Selected Writings*, p. 272.
[13] "Why Sculpture is a Bore" in *Selected Writings*, p. 97.

In his essay "Crise de vers" Mallarmé employs a musical conceit to suggest that, of all the arts, music comes closest to their universal idea by virtue of its rigorous composition in which nothing is left to chance. For Mallarmé, great music writes itself as an attribute of cultural necessity: "Whether willed or not by the musician, the meteor of modern times, the symphony, approaches thought." [14] This is the reason poets must "investigate the art of transposing the symphony to the book." (*S*, p. 9) And, like musical composition, the "structure of a book of verse must arise throughout from internal necessity–in this way both chance and the author will be excluded." (*S*, p. 8) This internal necessity would seem to be inviolate, free of any "material constraint," (p. 8) or specific manifestation. In short, it should only exist as an abstraction. Nevertheless, it bears a name: Language.

> Les langues imparfaites en cela que plusieurs, manqué la suprême: penser étant écrire sans accessoires, ni chuchotement mais tacite encore l'immortelle parole, la diversité, sur terre, des idioms empêche personne de proférer les mots qui, sinon se trouveraient, par une frappe unique, elle-même matériellement la verité. [15]

> (Languages being imperfect because they are so numerous, the supreme one is missing: Since thought is writing without accessories or whispering without the Immortal Word, the diversity of idioms on earth prevents anyone from producing words which would bear the direct imprint of Truth incarnate.) (*S*, p. 5)

It seems then that mere languages can only approximate the Music beyond their means. Through prosody, versification, and other devices, language can simulate musical composition, but its basic medium remains the drab, utilitarian, and material signifier of the word. But this condition is not the stumbling block to truth it

---

[14] Stéphane Mallarmé, "Crisis in Verse" in *Symbolism: An Anthology*, ed. and trans. T. G. West (London: Methuen, 1980), p. 7. All subsequent references to "Crisis in Verse" will refer to this edition and will be cited in the text with an *S*, followed by the page number.

[15] Stéphane Mallarmé, "Crise de vers" in *Oeuvres Complètes*, Henri Mondor & G. Jean-Aubry, eds. (Paris: Bibliothèque de la Pléiade, Gallimard, 1945), pp. 363-364. Subsequent citations to "Crise de vers" will refer to this edition and will be indicated in the text by *OC* followed by page numbers.

would at first seem to be for Mallarmé. After all, music must rely on various instruments to produce its idea; so too, poetry depends on individual languages to evoke the idea of Language in its essence. Like Hegel's concept of the *notion*, Mallarmé's pure aesthetic idea must be conscious of itself through its concrete manifestations. Thus, all the arts express their idea in a sensuous way and in so doing constitute restless, yet mutually reinforcing analogies for each other.

For Mallarmé, both music and poetry exist on a continuum between ideality and its negation through chance, contingency, and diversity. Each artistic embodiment involves imperfection or an almost Gnostic degradation of the ideal, an ideal that is nevertheless premised upon that degradation; therefore, no necessary hierarchy among the arts exists except insofar as one may provide a propaedeutic for another's evolution. This exception explains Mallarmé's deployment of musical analogies in "Crise de vers." With respect to language, musical phenomena are situated in the same sense category of sound, yet they transcend, in terms of receptive ease, the plurality of linguistic and phonological sign systems that constitute language's actuality. Cultural differences, historical developments, individual styles, even the diversity of sounds themselves are downplayed in Mallarmé's essay in order to establish Music as the analogue of purity that language must strive, poetically, to restore. The dialectic of purity and impurity (or perfection and imperfection) in music is largely repressed in order for the reader to conceive of music as an idea instead of as concrete works, as the latter would vitiate music's heuristic function in a discussion of language, the only medium through which Mallarmé understands music: "For Music must undeniably result from the full power of the intellectual word, not from the elemental sounds of strings, brass and woodwind: it must be a full, manifest totality of relationships." (*S*, p. 10)

It is through his sustained disquisitions on language, not the suggestiveness of his metaphors of music, that Mallarmé explores the complexities of the dialectic he pronounces. Language, in its existential modifications of the "supreme one" he imagines, both produces and devalues its potential ideality. Language–especially as poetry–is always in and out of itself, aspiring toward a purity too often confused with its opposite–transparent meaning. Mallarmé's search for a supreme language does not represent an attempt to cut language off from history, but to focus it on its own history as language, to condense that explicit history or etymology into a more resonant linguistic configuration similar to myth–or what Mallarmé called the Orphic explanation of the universe. But, unlike the linguist's concept of a proto-Indo-European language, Mallarmé's aesthetic formulation is not reductive, an ideological expedient, but an open hypothesis in order to enrich one's responses to and uses of language. Thus, the notion of Pure Language emits an almost sonorous polysemy that gives "un sens plus pur aux mots de la tribu" (a purer sense/meaning to the words of the tribe). [16] This purity has a sensuous appeal precisely because its significance is inexplicit and–for Mallarmé–universal. As he wrote to Villiers de l'Isle-Adam in 1866: "I discovered the idea of the universe through sensation alone." [17]

Clearly then the "sense" attributes of any medium do not represent barriers to the ideal but provide a vehicle for it. Yet the statement's implications for any medium besides language and music are not elaborated in "Crise de vers." By confining his aesthetic analogizing to musical figures, Mallarmé dismisses the visual arts as an adequate paradigm for his own aesthetic speculations. One word, however, conveys Mallarmé's attitude toward painting: at one point the word "color" is used to describe the music of the human voice. (S, p. 5) Although the word already had specific musical applications at that time, Mallarmé, by conflating the idea of color with voice in this single reference, dissociates it from the studio and the palette to resituate it in the conservatory.

Yet the word synaesthetically evokes the sole property by which painting was considered among the Symbolists to participate in the universal–as a scale of visual tones. In identifying color with sound, Mallarmé further refines it by liberating color from physical objects–of which paintings themselves form a part. Beyond any critical advocacy of Impressionist experimentation with color, [18] Mallarmé's

---

[16] Mallarmé, "Le Tombeau d'Edgar Poe" (trans. M. A. Caws) in *Selected Poetry and Prose*, ed. Mary Ann Caws (New York: New Directions, 1982), p. 50.

[17] Mallarmé, letter to Villiers de l'Isle-Adam, September 24, 1866 (trans. Bradford Cook), in *Selected Poetry and Prose*, p. 86.

[18] In "The Impressionists and Edouard Manet," this advocacy assumes the form of identifying open-air painting (almost exclusively) with the "search after truth" that Impressionism promises. For Mallarmé, open-air painting allows the subject in painting to "palpitate with movement, light, and life" in being "com-

dictum that artists should "paint not the thing, but the effect that it produces" [19] underscores his antipathy for the object of representation and the representational object–the commercial product the plastic work of art is destined to become. It would seem, therefore, that Mallarmé severely limits the importance of plastic expression in his primary statement of aesthetics because he finds its main attributes as material objects to be at odds with his aspirations for language, to be reminders of what he considers impure with respect to Language.

Mallarmé's discomfort with the material contingencies of the creative act (a throw of the dice, as it were) has less to do with the sensuous properties of those "material constraints" than their venality apropos of utilitarian or exchange values. Nowhere is language more corrupt than in the form of "ordinary communication": "Speech has only a commercial interest in the reality of things." (S, p. 8) Its most pervasive print form is journalism, the narrative discourse of which must be transcended by poetry:

> Un désir indéniable à mon temps est de séparer comme en vue d'attributions différentes le double état de la parole, brut ou immediate ici, là essentiel.
>
> Narrer, enseigner, même décrire, cela va et encore qu'à chacun suffirait peut-être pour échanger la pensée humaine, de

---

posed of a harmony of reflected and ever-changing lights" by means of "simple color, fresh, or lightly laid on." Color, once again, is a system of tones reflecting nature as a whole, but only to the extent that the artist "endeavour[s] to suppress individuality for the benefit of nature." At the same time, the truth that such painting yields is somewhat different in aspect to that of poetry, inasmuch as Manet and the Impressionists, in re-educating the public eye, usher in the day when "the graces which exist in the bourgeoisie will then be recognised and taken as worthy models in art." Although in the hands of these modern masters, modern painting will indeed, like poetry, achieve the purity of its own idea, Mallarmé seems to suggest that its idea is of a somewhat lower grade than poetry's insofar as painting is so closely bound to the education of the public eye: "The noble visionaries of other times, whose works are the semblance of worldly things seen by unworldly eyes (not the actual representations of real objects), appear as kings and gods in the far dreamages of mankind; recluses to whom were given the genius of a dominion over an ignorant multitude. But to-day the multitude demands to see with its own eyes; and if our latter-day art is less glorious, intense, and rich, it is not without the compensation of truth, simplicity, and child-like charm." Stéphane Mallarmé, "The Impressionists and Edouard Manet" in *Mallarmé, Manet, and Redon* by Penny Florence (Cambridge: Cambridge University, 1986), pp. 11-18.

[19] Mallarmé, letter to H. Cazalis, October 1864, quoted in translation by Wallace Fowlie in *Mallarmé* (Chicago: University of Chicago, 1953), p. 125.

prendre ou de mettre dans la main d'autrui en silence une pièce
de monnaie, l'emploi élémentaire du discours dessert l'universel
reportage dont, la littérature exceptée, participe tout entre les
genres d'écrits contemporains. (*OC*, p. 368)

(One of the most undeniable desires of my age is to separate the
functions of words with the result that there is a crude and immediate language on the one hand and an essential language on
the other.

The former use of language in narration, instruction, and description–necessary of course, though one could get by with a
silent language of coins–is reflected by the ubiquitous journalism
which attracts all forms of contemporary writing except literature.) (*S*, p. 10)

Be that as it may, Mallarmé saw the work of various symbolist
poets as evidence of a poetic revival that was, by his own account,
"taking place publicly." (*S*, p. 3) Yet the public nature of this revival
was the source of more anxiety than celebration, which is why his
own poetry assumes the portentous tones it does, particularly in
"Un Coup de dés." Far from being revived, poetry seems on the
brink of extinction here (another Hegelian *topos*) as it enters the
public sphere. The blank spaces, those painterly voids negatively
contoured by the wayward trace of a poetic line, foretell the intrusion of the poetic space of language by public speech and the complicity of the latter with commodity exchange.

Such is the extreme risk run by pure language whenever poets
attempt its public transcription–as Mallarmé does in "Un Coup de
dés" where the distribution of words on the page mimics his aesthetic wager. Such a transcription is a modern gamble, the rarified
signifiers of each line yielding a lucky or unlucky number depending on whether they add up, whether they invite interpretation. Yet
poetry's greatest peril is no reception at all, the mute hostility of a
public that no longer has time for its mystery, that sees only a pure
void (its own image) in the white spaces between lines. Such a reception is Chance realized in its inconsequentiality, not its surprising coincidence.

Mallarmé disdains the ideologues of commerce who can only
ask of poetry, "What purpose?" Yet his pure idea is premised on
risking all to avoid empty abstraction. Thus the white spaces in
Mallarmé's poem also act as a kind of sensuous matrix through

which the ever-receding message of words can compose itself, splinter, regroup, and resonate in memory. To the demand, "What purpose?" poetry offers pure imagination: both nothing ("Rien, cette écume") and everything–verbal constellations for the infinite expansion of meaning. But to preserve its exquisite insubstantiality, Mallarmé banishes ordinary communication from his gossamer pantheon of sense where his faith in eternal values is ritualized in an almost silent, almost invisible language.

In their critical writings Baudelaire and Mallarmé extend the domains of the different arts to what they believe to be their respective limits. Only upon reaching those limits can the artist achieve sensuous purity in his medium through the establishment of a definitive (yet suggestive) border between it and what is foreign to it. In this way, both poets adhere ideologically to a vitally important notion of purity–however precarious they may want it to seem. Any lapse or transgression of aesthetic means is interdicted in their systems, systems that nevertheless obscure such interdictions through a seductive discourse of sense and sensuosity. Hence, the exact contours of the different arts are never unanimously declared, and one wonders if Baudelaire would not have greeted Mallarmé's typographic innovations in "Un Coup de dés" as just such a transgression. Where they clearly agree, however, is on the urgent need to prevent the total collapse of language into modes of mere communication, instruction, or anecdote. Above all else, this disdain for what was considered a bourgeois "language of coins" [20] sets the nineteenth-century avant-garde poets apart from their successors. A later wave of French poets, emerging after the turn of the century, reinvested everyday, utilitarian language with a poetic significance the Symbolists denied it. Yet the consequence would be an even stronger barricade against the bourgeois appropriation of language through acts of creative misappropriation. Apollinaire was among the first to resacralize, in a sense, the reified language of modern life on the basis of collage techniques.

---

[20] *Ibid.*, p. 10.

MATERIAL CONTINGENCIES OF THE WORD: APOLLINAIRE,
SIMULTANEISM AND COLLAGE

Perhaps more than any other, the discourse of simultaneism
helps explain the procedural and ideological shift from a unified
symbolist aesthetics to the splintered, discontinuous ones of the later Avant-Garde. Simultaneism–the cubo-futurist strategy of presenting multiple and contradictory aspects of modern life in a single
composition–was nurtured on the paradox of symbolist "purism"
to yield the very "obscurity and confusion in the arts" Baudelaire
had warned against. By moving beyond prescribed limits in the arts
and beyond presumed tolerance levels of most "sense" receptors,
simultaneist works administered a formal shock to the senses,
which were still attuned to traditional aesthetic ideals of harmony,
order, universality. Simultaneism represented the spectacle of conflicting sensory data impinging on their separate domains and disrupting any sense of cohesion in individual works that might have
been attained through more harmonious combinations. The ideological thrust of this war of nervous systems was the quest for technological hegemony–technology being the only force that could
successfully yoke together and overcome, presumably, the aesthetic
claims of each, merely human, sense (i.e., senses geared to the older,
hierarchical technologies of the book, the painting, the orchestra, as
opposed to the newer, "popular" ones of cinema, photography, and
radio through which the older ones were framed as contents).
    Symbolist aesthetics thus contributed to the incipient anti-aes-
thetics of simultaneism, fueled as Symbolism was by the contradictions of synaesthetic discourse. In its tendency to promote each art
as a living body of sense-relations, synaesthesia gradually yielded a
notion of culture as a competitive arena where each art attempted
to appropriate the other's means according to certain rules. But the
rules gave way to spectacle just as musical organization of tones
gave way to plastic contrast of values as the pre-emptive metaphor of
modern poetic discourse. Plasticity was less spiritual, less nostalgic,
less idealizing than music; it was more feasible as a modus operandi
of alienated production in the modern metropolis. The plastic arts
were more readily adapted to the modern scene–its secularism,
commercialism, de-humanism–primarily because plasticity materially exposed the violence of this adaptation. Hence, plasticity pro-

vided a kind of ideologizing vortex to be described in hysterical manifestoes by Marinetti, Apollinaire, and Pound. Collaged, hand-written, or typographically-enhanced elements of language helped to satisfy the initial impulse toward creating, or *transliterating*, a virtual plastic poetry in a way that quotation and citation of acknowledged literary sources, in their quality of "accommodation" [21] to conventional reading postures, no longer seemed to do.

Among these three major proponents of the plastic sensibility in poetry, Apollinaire represents the most ambivalent attempt to remake one's creative sensibility into something "inhuman" as a way of competing in the age of mechanical reproduction. The key to this ambivalence can be found in his divers writings on art and in certain of his poems. Perhaps more than anything else, his attempt to explain Picasso, Delaunay, Braque, Gris, Léger, Chagall, De Chirico, and others provided the impetus for this remaking, which culminated in his famous *Calligrammes* (1918), in many ways the fruit of his earlier meditations on Cubism, Futurism, and Orphism. As informal elaborations of plastic concepts, Apollinaire's critical writings reveal his extraordinary acumen in determining the poetic potential of specific plastic operations. Yet his initial response to these innovations was refracted through the lens of symbolist assumptions that only gradually ceded to the new poetics, where they occur, of *Calligrammes*. Indeed, those assumptions are never entirely absent in that work and sometimes surge forth, fully intact.

As one of the first defenders of Cubism, Apollinaire makes frequent, lyric evocations in his writings of the purifying "flame" of artistic genius. What at first seems a late romantic reiteration of the divine nature of creativity, however, becomes more complicated because Apollinaire discovers this divine spark within the plastic itself. His speculative essay on art, "Les Trois Vertus plastiques"

---

[21] As Antoine Compagnon writes: "La citation est un lieu d'accommodation prédisposé dans le texte. Elle l'intègre dans un ensemble ou dans un réseau de textes, dans une typologie des compétences requises pour la lecture." And elsewhere: "La citation est un élément privilégié de l'accommodation car elle est un lieu de reconnaissance, un repère de lecture." But note also: "C'est sans doute la raison pour laquelle aucun texte, si subversif qu'il se veuille, ne renonce à toute forme de citation. La subversion déplace les compétences, embrouille leur typologie, mais elle ne les abolit pas en principe, ce qui reviendrait à se couper de toute lecture." Antoine Compagnon, *La Seconde Main, ou le travail de la citation* (Paris: Éditions du Seuil, 1979), p. 23.

("The Three Plastic Virtues"), which first appeared in an exhibition catalogue in 1908 when Picasso and Braque were creating Cubism, defines the plastic virtues as purity, unity, and truth. Fire is used as the symbol of plasticity, which "suffers the existence of nothing foreign to itself." [22] Thus Apollinaire describes the plastic in almost the same way that Mallarmé describes music. And, like pure music, pure painting involves the disappearance of the creator's personality as he succumbs to the logic of his medium:

> Le tableau existera inéluctablement. La vision sera entière, complète et son infini au lieu de marquer une imperfection fera seulement ressortir le rapport d'une nouvelle créature à un nouveau créateur et rien d'autre. Sans quoi il n'y aura point d'unité et les rapports qu'auront les divers points de la toile avec différents génies, avec différent objets, avec différentes lumières ne montreront qu'une multiplicité de disparates sans harmonie. [23]

> (The painting will exist ineluctably. The vision will be whole, complete; its infinity, instead of signaling an imperfection, will only accentuate the relationship of a new creature to a *new creator* [italics mine] and nothing else. Otherwise there will be no unity and the relationships that will exist between various points of the canvas and various essences, objects, and kinds of light will produce only a multiplicity of disparate and unharmonious parts.) (*AA*, p. 49)

A purificatory process—whereby a particular medium defines its constitutive elements—is here posited so that art, as a new creature, may rise to the challenge of its new creator, both of whom exist ineluctably above the inconsequentialities of unorganized or merely tendentious expression and ordinary "human" existence. The need for such self-definition was particularly acute in painting because "resemblance" had long been considered one of its constitutive fea-

---

[22] Guillaume Apollinaire, "The Three Plastic Virtues" in *Apollinaire on Art: Essays and Reviews 1902-1918,* ed. Leroy C. Breunig, trans. Susan Suleiman (New York: Da Capo, 1988; Viking, 1972), p. 47. Subsequent citations in English of Apollinaire's essays and reviews will refer to this edition and will appear in the text and notes as *AA* followed by the page number.

[23] Apollinaire, *Chroniques d'art: 1902-1918*, L. C. Breunig, ed. (Paris: Gallimard, 1960), p. 73. Most citations in French of Apollinaire's essays and reviews will refer to this edition and will appear in the text and notes as *CA*, followed by the page number.

tures–just as "verisimilitude" had been in writing. But, like those who had endeavored to elevate language above its merely communicative functions, Apollinaire wanted to liberate plastic representation from "the state of a pictorial writing designed simply to facilitate communication between people. . . ." (p. 49) Such pictorial writing strives, through slavish imitation, to represent "the too-fugitive present, and what for an artist can be only the mask of death: Fashion." (p. 48) Clearly, in this instance, Apollinaire wants to see the plastic arts eternalized, in the spirit of Symbolism, as a pure medium.

Yet it was the plastic arts' representational function itself that rendered purification an ironic gesture–just as it had in language. But in the case of the plastic arts, representation was premised on iconic resemblance–the plastic sign's physical similarity to its concept, as Peirce has shown–and not the conventional association of sign-to-concept on which linguistic representation was premised. Thus, the materiality of plastic representation, in a certain measure, only facilitated the communicative function, incurring a peculiar prejudice against it–as if its surface appeal made meaning transparent, hence, trivial. Surface was the essence of the "too-fugitive present," while purity lay at the core of reality as a kind of logical necessity. If such criteria were to be upheld, it would be at the expense of the art objects Apollinaire admired. Thus, his modes of critical celebration were still aesthetically incompatible with the objects of that celebration.

One senses that a nostalgic cooptation of the new painting by an outmoded aesthetic jargon was being attempted here. To overcome this problem the "too-fugitive present" would have to be recognized in some way as a feature of plastic purity. Henri Bergson's concept of pure duration "in which the past, always moving on, is swelling unceasingly with a present that is absolutely new" [24] provided just the philosophic modulation needed to accommodate the "fugitive present" to Apollinaire's plastic aesthetics. To do this, Apollinaire injected an apocalyptic tone into his Mallarméan precepts, thus undermining their delicate sense of purity, since Mallarmé considered eschatology a compromise between myth and vulgar history. The plastic virtues Apollinaire celebrated involved the fren-

---

[24] Henri Bergson, *Creative Evolution*, trans. Arthur Mitchell (New York: Random House, 1944), p. 219.

zied, turbulent swell of creative power in its present conditions, threatening to up-end all familiar human values, let alone the rarefied, "musical" ones that formerly exemplified purity, unity, and truth. This possibility becomes explicit in the essay when Apollinaire exhorts the painter to be "inhuman," to be a visionary hero instead of a resigned and gloomy hermit, and thus, to "take in at a single glance the past, the present, and the future." (*AA*, p. 48) In this way, all things are subsumed in a kind of Bergsonian *duré* of plastic insight in which the first evidence of simultaneist feeling is discovered. Simultaneist discourse was the full elaboration of an insight whereby the impurity imputed to the plastic via symbolist aesthetics would be the basis for its ascendancy as herald of the new.

Certain poems in *Calligrammes*, including "Les Collines," "Le Musicien de Saint-Merry," and "Un Fantôme de nuées," reflect this earlier, transitional stage in Apollinaire's poetics and are closely allied to Picasso's own pre-cubist art. Three years before the appearance of "Les Trois Vertus plastiques," Apollinaire wrote an enchanting and lyrical description of some works by Picasso included in a group exhibition at the Galérie Serrurier. The works, from Picasso's "Rose Period," depict *saltimbanques*, harlequins, and acrobatic girls somberly rehearsing in forgotten landscapes [fig. 2]. Yet, as Apollinaire describes them, these disenfranchised celebrants of "wordless rites" inspire awe just as the ideal painter should, for they have shed their humanity (and in some cases their sex) for the sake of some vast, unutterable vision:

> Les soeurs adolescents, foulant en équilibre les grosses boules des saltimbanques, commandent à ces sphères le mouvement rayonnant des mondes. Ces adolescents ont, impubères, les inquiétudes de l'innocence, les animaux leur apprennent le mystère religieux. Des arlequins accompagnent la gloire des femmes, ils leur ressemblent, ni mâles ni femelles. (*CA*, p. 38)

> (The adolescent sisters, treading and balancing themselves on the great balls of the *saltimbanques* impart to those spheres the radiant movement of the planets. These girlish adolescents, children still, have the anxieties of innocents; animals teach them the religious mysteries. Some harlequins accompany the aura of the women and resemble them, neither male nor female.) [25]

---

[25] Apollinaire, "Young Artists: Picasso the Painter" in *AA*, p. 16.

Years later, while assembling articles for his collection, *Médita-*
tions esthétiques: Les Peintres cubistes (1913), Apollinaire redacted
elements of this passage into the poem "Un Fantôme de nuées." [26]
As if to concretize the suggestion of sexual interchangeability that
he attributed to Picasso's figures, Apollinaire transformed the adolescent girl into a boy juggler who emerges from under the barrel
organ of an old grinder:

> Une jambe en arrière prête à la génuflexion
> Il salua ainsi les quatre points cardinaux
> Et quand il marcha sur une boule
> Son corps mince devint une musique si délicate que nul
>   parmi les spectateurs n'y fut insensible
>
> Un petit esprit sans aucune humanité
> Pensa chacune
> Et cette musique des formes
> Détruisit celle de l'orgue mécanique
> Que moulait l'homme au visage couvert d'ancêtres
>
> (One leg back ready to kneel
> He saluted the four points of the compass
> And when he balanced on a sphere
> His thin body became such delicate music that none
>   of the onlookers could resist it
>
> A small inhuman sprite
> Each of them thought
> And that music of shapes
> Destroyed the music of the mechanical organ
> That the man with the ancestor-covered face was grinding out)
>   (*C*, pp. 84-85)

In these lines Apollinaire acknowledges both the contribution
and insufficiency of symbolist aesthetics, which, by the time of *Cal-*
ligrammes, could be symbolically linked with the demented repetition of musical progressions. The last line above would seem to be
an indictment of Paul Verlaine whose "Art poétique" extolled the

---

[26] Apollinaire, *Calligrammes: Poems of Peace and War* (1913-1916), trans. Anne
Hyde Greet (Berkeley: University of California, 1980), p. 390. Subsequent citations
of this edition, both the poetry and the notes, will appear in the text as *C*.

music of the poetic line (its rhythm and nuance) above all things. And although Verlaine's intention was to discourage the mechanical use of rhyme and verse, the alternative he offered was, in Apollinaire's view, just "l'ancien jeu des vers" (the old game of verses). [27] The charming, but still mechanical line of Verlaine has given way to vers libre here.

But, as Claude Debon shows in his study of Apollinaire after Alcools, the new "music of forms" that replaces the old one is still bound to the past insofar as the juggler evokes not the clarity, but the "mystère des temps modernes" (mystery of modern times). [28] And mystery, even the most modern, is nostalgically inflected. Indeed, Apollinaire invests the svelte juggler with a Dionysian aura. Furthermore, a hypnotic musical ambiance envelopes the whole scene, as Philippe Renaud reminds us in Lecture d'Apollinaire: "Au moment où la formule musicale du poème disparaît, le poème commence à être hanté par l'esprit, le fantôme de la musique" (At the moment when the musical formula of the poem has disappeared, the poem begins to be haunted by the spirit, the phantom of music). [29] This "phantom" has supplanted the music produced by the barrel organ of traditional verse. But does Apollinaire emphasize the resurrection or the death? the new incarnation or the old spirit?

Apollinaire's enunciation of a music of forms, as well as the purely narrative aspects of the poem, subtly allude to his own descriptions of Picasso's painting and in so doing suggest that painting itself represents the new incarnation of the old spirit. Yet painting as an art form–unlike music–is never explicitly cited in the poem; rather, it is invisibly alloyed with the narrative props of the poem. In a way, then, painting is united with the purely circumstantial, mimetic elements that encode the "fugitive present." In other words, it is barely present as a concept; its manifestation is purely sensuous, swelling up and fusing with the memory of music. Thus, memory and sense are the agents of a temporal coalescence of the two arts, which blend in a modern ritual of sheer aesthetic potentiality. In this way, the poem demonstrates a Bergsonian modulation

---

[27] From Apollinaire's "Les Fiançailles," in Alcools, trans. Anne Hyde Greet (Berkeley: University of California, 1965), pp. 174-175.

[28] Claude Debon, Guillaume Apollinaire après "Alcools" (Paris: Minard, 1981), p. 68.

[29] Philippe Renaud, Lecture d'Apollinaire (Lausanne: Éditions l'Âge d'Homme, 1969), p. 279.

of traditional synaesthetic interactions through an ideological identification of music with memory and tradition, painting with the
senses and the new.

Analytic Cubism

This swelling of past and present in an act of imagination seems
comparatively benign in view of later, radical developments in the
arts. But for Apollinaire, these tentative steps helped defuse an
abiding symbolist prejudice against the present. The popular street
performance he describes in "Un Fantôme de nuées" has a mimetic
cogency that suggests how far the poet had come toward accepting
the modern condition *per se*, as a set of lived circumstances with its
own aesthetic potentiality. On this basis, critic James Lawler has
distinguished Apollinaire from Mallarmé: "Whereas Mallarmé
wanted salvation as if in spite of the world, Apollinaire sought the
ideal music through his contact with outer reality. It is possible,
then, to consider his attitude as a personal dialogue with Symbolism
which continued the ambition of his predecessors to wed poetry
and music, but which rejected the temptation of angelism for the
shock and tension of external phenomena." [30] But the shock and
tension of external phenomena could only divorce poetry from music–the very aura of angels–through an adulterous association with
plastic forms. Apollinaire himself announced the total divergence of
sensibility in 1914:

> Nous connaissons quelques peintres, nous connaissons un petit
> nombre de poètes qui méritent à notre époque l'appellation
> de *nouveaux*; mais nous nous étions habitués à considérer la
> musique comme un art désuet et presque tombé dans le
> marasme. Tout y était ténébreux, vide, privé de vie, immobile et
> asservi à l'esthétique et à la beauté, abstractions pour lesquelles
> nous n'avons plus aucune sort de considération. (*CA*, p. 475)

> (We know of a few painters and a small number of poets who
> in our time deserve to be called new, but we had gradually
> become used to considering music as an outmoded, practically

---

[30] James R. Lawler, *The Language of French Symbolism* (Princeton: Princeton
University, 1969), p. 232.

stagnating art. Everything in it was dark, empty, lifeless, immo-
bile–it was a slave to aesthetics and beauty, two abstractions to
which we no longer attach any importance.) [31]

The irony of this statement has less to do with the persistent mu-
sicality of Apollinaire's verse than in his attribution, elsewhere, of
eternal, "aesthetic" qualities to the presumably more provisional,
more "contemporary" plastic arts. Nowhere is the idea of aesthetics
more apparent than in Apollinaire's impulse to promote the idea of
"geometry" as the *raison d'être* of the new painting: "The geometric
aspect that struck so many people upon seeing the first cubist paintings was due to the fact that those paintings rendered an essential
reality with great purity and that the accidental or anecdotal aspects
of the subject [had] been eliminated." [32] For the painter, geometry
was the intuitive structure coordinating the plastic investigation of
three-dimensional objects with two-dimensional form. (In Gómez
de la Serna's *Picasso*, the painter is quoted as saying: "If a painter
asked me what was the first step necessary for painting a table, I
should say measure it." [33]) As later critics have charged, this coordinating effort only subordinated the real object to the painting itself,
which had attained an independent, privileged reality. As Apollinaire put it in 1912: "Verisimilitude no longer has any importance,
for the artist sacrifices everything to the composition of his
picture." [34] In the final analysis, geometry was composition itself, the
formal structuration of the picture for which phenomenal reality
was sacrificed–to discover its noumenon, as it were, in the act of
composition. In this way the new art's relation to the old reiterates
the former hierarchy of music to literature, as Apollinaire makes explicit in his essay, "Sur la peinture" ("On Painting"): "An entirely
new art is thus being evolved, an art that will be to painting, as
painting has hitherto been envisaged, what music is to literature. It
will be pure painting, just as music is pure literature." (*AA*, p. 197) [35]

---

[31] Apollinaire, "New Music" in *AA*, p. 391.
[32] Apollinaire, "Cubism," in *AA*, p. 256.
[33] John Golding, *Cubism: A History and Analysis 1907-1914* (Boston: Boston
Book & Art Shop, 1968), p. 62.
[34] Apollinaire, "On the Subject in Modern Painting" in *AA*, p. 197.
[35] "Sur la peinture" can be found in Apollinaire's *Méditations esthétiques: Les
Peintres cubistes*, L. C. Breunig and J. C. Chevalier, eds. (Paris: Hermann, 1980),
but not in his *Chroniques d'art*. Parts of the essay, however, were taken from "Les
Trois Vertus plastiques," which is included in *Apollinaire on Art* as "On the Subject
in Modern Painting."

For the Cubists, however, this new plastic purity involved a shift in sensual allegiance from the visual to the tactile, which proved to be the most inimical feature of the new art to Apollinaire's abiding lyric sensibility. The first casualty of this shift was color itself, the very feature of painting the Symbolists believed had the strongest affinities with music as an abstract tonal system. For the Cubists, however, color was a residual feature of traditional illusionism against which the new art had launched a thorough critique. Far from an abstract tonal system, color was seen to be a sensual distraction that only reinforced illusionistic devices in painting. As a consequence Picasso and Braque began reducing the range of their palettes as early as 1907, retaining only brown, green, and yellow tones. This reduction allowed them to clarify their own conceptual negotiation between the older, illusionistic geometry of perspective and the newer, tactile geometry of painting as a plied, constructed surface. And although illusionistic sensations were never completely eliminated in works of Analytic Cubism, they were constantly jostled by certain "tactile" qualities [36] inherent to the materials employed: their flatness and texture, their spreading, oily quality exemplified in somber earth tones. As such, the new painting—unlike the older, voluptuously colored art of the Impressionists—had little sensual rapport with music.

What painting did share with the older conception of music was a new sense of autonomy from the world. If geometry continued to link painting with real objects through a structural analysis of them, it was to extract purely formal elements for the greater structural purity and unity of the work itself. At first Apollinaire saw this operation as a return to classicism, as when he described Braque's painting in 1908 as "more noble, more measured, more orderly" than Impressionist painting whose practitioners he described as "savages" in the vapid sway of visual sensation. [37] The poet would later reverse himself once he realized that Cubism was not a "noble and restrained art" [38] in retreat from the world, but that its very autonomy was premised upon a kind of intellectual revenge upon the world of things. After first describing Picasso as a kind of "plastic"

---

[36] Not to be confused with Bernhard Berenson's notion of "tactile values" elaborated in his chapter on the Florentine painters in *The Italian Painters of the Renaissance*, Revised Edition (Oxford: Clarendon Press, 1930), pp. 63-64.

[37] Apollinaire, "Georges Braque" in *AA*, pp. 50-51.

[38] Apollinaire, "The Cubists" in *AA*, p. 183.

surgeon dissecting reality, Apollinaire soon identified the Dionysiac implications of Cubism by quoting a Nietzschean aphorism:

"'O Dionysios divin, pourquoi me tires-tu les oreilles?' demande Ariane à son philosophique amant dans un de ces célèbres dialogues sur l'*Ile de Naxos*.

"'Je trouve quelque chose d'agréable, de plaisant à tes oreilles, Ariane. Pourquoi ne sont-elles pas plus longues encore?'"

Nietzsche, quand il rapporte cette anecdote, fait par la bouche de Dionysios le procès de l'art grec. [. . .] Voulant atteindre aux proportions de l'idéal, ne se bornant pas à l'humanité, les jeunes peintres nous offrent des oeuvres plus célèbres que sensuelles. Ils s'éloignent de plus en plus de l'ancien art des illusions d'optique et des proportions locales pour exprimer la grandeur des formes métaphysiques. C'est pourquoi l'art actuel, s'il n'est pas l'émanation directe de croyances religieuses déterminées, present cependant plusieurs caractères du grand art, c'est-à-dire de l'Art religieux. [39]

("'Oh divine Dionysus, why are you pulling my ears?' Ariadne asks her philosophical lover in one of the famous dialogues on the Isle of Naxos.

"'I find something very pleasant, very agreeable about your ears, Ariadne. Why aren't they even longer?'"

In this anecdote, Nietzsche put an indictment of Greek art into Dionysus's mouth. Wishing to attain the proportions of the ideal and not limiting themselves to humanity, the young painters offer us works that are more cerebral than sensual. They are moving further and further away from the old art of optical illusions and literal proportions, in order to express the grandeur of metaphysical forms. That is why today's art, although it does not emanate directly from specific religious beliefs, nevertheless possesses several of the characteristics of great art, that is to say of religious art.) [40]

Apollinaire goes on to identify religious art with Egyptian art, and in so doing adopts the Hegelian conception of art history which identifies Greek art with the balanced, sensuous embodiment of ideas and Egyptian or "Oriental" art with a disproportion-

---

[39] Apollinaire, "Sur la Peinture" in *Méditations esthétiques: Les Peintres cubistes*, pp. 62-63.

[40] Apollinaire, "The New Painting: Art Notes" in *AA*, p. 223.

ate, even monstrous, embodiment of ill-formed ideas. For Apollinaire, however, this disproportion is the evidence, as it were, for a more conceptual plasticity, of concepts being developed, organized through plasticity itself. Thus, it is the older art–not the Greek– which is more "cerebral" in nature because it comes to self-consciousness through material forms. Picasso himself intimated this reversal when he described African art's appeal to him for being more "logical" [41] than traditional Western art. The new art, then, was only religious in trying to extend plastic expression beyond its means because the ideas it sought to express were no longer deemed human (i.e., ill-formed by virtue of over-development). Hence, any adaptation of traditional or human proportions to those ideas could only result, like the pulling of Ariadne's ears, in distortion or fragmentation. Despite the fact that many of the Cubists were still able to exhibit under the banner of the "Section d'or" at this time (1912) and, like Juan Gris, actually employed the golden mean of classical aesthetics as a structuring device in their work, [42] Apollinaire seems to have concluded that the metaphysical impulse behind Cubism was non-classical and non-Euclidean–but not entirely alien either, involving a kind of otherness within classical metaphysics, just as Dionysus represented an "Oriental" member-deity of the Greek pantheon.

Thus, the "inhumanity" of the new art derives from a human impulse and suggests a diabolical over-extension of classical abstract thought itself. [43] The great technical feats of Apollinaire's day (the airplane, the wireless telegraph, the motion picture, electricity) were conspicuous expressions of advances being made in modern physics which seemed to relegate the imaginative accomplishments of poets and artists to a condition of cultural backwardness. Apollinaire believed that newness in painting involved the painter's intuitive identification of his plastic investigation with scientific investigation and its technological achievements. In the popular, studio

---

[41] Golding, p. 59.

[42] Mark Rosenthal, *Juan Gris* (New York: Abbeville, 1983), p. 29.

[43] Donald Kuspit has described the Expressionist aspects of Cubism in saying that "If Cubism is intellectualizing, it is so in the psychoanalytic sense, as an attempt to use abstract thought to prevent the emergence and acknowledgement of emotions, inner conflicts and fantasies–in effect to repress, even deny them." From "Cubist Hypochondria: On the Case of Picasso and Braque" in *Artforum*, Vol. 28 (September 1989), p. 113.

discourse on the new physics, the term "fourth dimension" emerged
as a useful, if somewhat faddish, notion of time in its general flow
through which everything is perceived in spatial simultaneism:

> Les nouveaux peintres, pas plus que leurs anciens ne se sont
> proposés d'être des géomètres. Mais on peut dire que la
> géométrie est aux arts plastiques ce que la grammaire est a l'art
> de l'écrivain. Or, aujourd'hui, les savants ne s'en tiennent plus
> aux trois dimensions de la géométrie euclidienne. Les peintres
> ont été amenés tout naturellement et, pour ainsi dire, par intui-
> tions, à se préoccuper de nouvelles mesures possibles de l'éten-
> due que dans le langage des ateliers modernes on désignait
> toutes ensemble et brièvement par le terme de *quatrième dimen-
> sion.*
>
> Telle qu'elle s'offre à l'esprit, du point de vue plastique, la
> quatrième dimension serait engendrée par les trois mesures con-
> nues: elle figure l'immensité de l'espace s'éternisant dans toutes
> les directions à un moment déterminé. Elle est l'espace même, la
> dimension de l'infini; c'est elle qui doue de plasticité les objets.
> Elle leur donne les proportions qu'ils méritent dans l'oeuvre,
> tandis que dans l'art grec par exemple, un rythme en quelque
> sorte mécanique détruit sans cesse les proportions.
>
> L'art grec avait de la beauté une conception purement hu-
> maine. Il prenait l'homme comme mesure de la perfection. L'art
> des peintres nouveaux prend l'univers infini comme idéal et c'est
> a cet idéal que l'on doit une nouvelle mesure de la perfection qui
> permet à l'artiste-peintre de donner à l'objet des proportions
> conformes au degré de plasticité où il souhaite l'amener. [44]

(The new painters do not intend to become geometricians,
any more than their predecessors did. But it may be said that
geometry is to the plastic arts what grammar is to the art of writing. Now today's scientists have gone beyond the three dimensions of Euclidean geometry. Painters have, therefore, very naturally been led to a preoccupation with those new dimensions of
space that are collectively designated, in the language of the
modern studios, by the term fourth dimension.

Without entering into mathematical explanations pertaining
to another field, and confining myself to plastic representation as
I see it, I would say that in the plastic arts the fourth dimension
is generated by the three known dimensions: it represents the

---

[44] Apollinaire, "Sur la Peinture," in *Méditations esthétiques*, pp. 61-62.

immensity of space eternalized in all directions at a given moment. It is space itself, or the dimension of infinity; it is what
gives objects plasticity. It gives them their just proportion in a
given work, whereas in Greek art, for example, a kind of mechanical rhythm is constantly destroying proportion.

Greek art had a purely human conception of beauty. It took
man as the measure of perfection. The art of the new painters
takes the infinite universe as its ideal, and it is to the fourth dimension alone that we owe this new measure of perfection that
allows the artist to give objects the proportions appropriate to
the degree of plasticity he wishes them to attain.) (*AA*, pp. 222-
223)

The new proportions are completely disproportionate in any illusionistic schema based on one-point perspective. The new painting entails a kind of all-points perspective to express space in its simultaneism. Cubist simultaneism, in its analytic phase, was (among
other things) the attempt to display the space within and around an
object all at once on the picture surface. This plastic feat required
the technical reconciliation of separate instances of perception. In
their book *Du Cubisme* of 1911, the painters Jean Metzinger and
Albert Gleizes provided a schematic explanation of what a Cubist
ideally did when he painted: "[Cubism means] moving around an
object to seize several successive appearances, which, fused in a single image, reconstitute it in time." [45] Such is the simultaneism of the
object; but only in being "reconstituted" on the canvas could simultaneism be reconciled to the human dimensions of the picture plane.

The attempt to resituate the fourth dimension in the second dimension wreaked havoc with illusionist principles to the point
where some believed pure abstraction was the intellectual *telos* of
Cubism. But pure abstraction was just one implication of the new
art. As art historian John Golding has indicated, a primary aspect of
Cubist simultaneism was the formal oscillation between the illusionist and abstract features of Cubist works. [46] It was this methodological oscillation that endowed Cubist works–despite the analytic
rigor of their original intentions–with an expressionist aura. [47]

---

[45] Jean Metzinger and Albert Gleizes, *Du Cubisme*, quoted by Christopher
Gray in *Cubist Aesthetic Theories* (Baltimore: Johns Hopkins, 1953), p. 86.

[46] Golding, p. 7.

[47] Kuspit, p. 113.

Futurism

At the same time, the intimacy of Cubism's fragmented icons–the bottles, tables, violins, playing cards, and other still-life props–reconfirm the human scale of cubist operations, cozily domesticated by the picture frame. Where the truly modernizing implications of Apollinaire's "inhuman" aesthetics are found are in the tracks of Futurist discourse that boldly inflect his intimations of an "esprit nouveau" with a monumentality and technological exhilaration that sometimes mimic the reifying rhetoric of commerce itself. Indeed, what Cubism gave to Futurist painting (the look of the new), Futurism gave back as a mode of discourse. This radical program, however, was quickly assimilated to French ideological prerogatives through the painters' pet abstraction of the "fourth dimension" and its mystic suggestiveness. Yet it needs to be stressed that the original impetus for simultaneism came from the Futurist manifestoes of Marinetti and Boccioni and were even quoted by Apollinaire in articles written for *L'Intransigeant* and other journals: "The simultaneousness of states of mind in the work of art, that is the intoxicating aim of our art." [48]

At the time, Apollinaire considered these simultaneous states of mind to be "dangerous," [49] a form of sensory overload that, like inebriation, left one astonished and critically bereft. It was the same criticism he had leveled against Impressionism in 1908 to justify the sober, monochrome paintings of Georges Braque. (*AA*, p. 50) But as we have seen, Apollinaire was not unsympathetic with expressions of Dionysian liberty. [50] If he considered the depiction of simultaneous states of mind to be dangerous, it was because he had not yet recognized those elements of his own aspirations in the Futurist agenda. His initial advocacy of Cubism's abstracting tendencies was based on the desire to find plastic corroboration of a pure aesthetic ideal that was anti-mimetic in the true spirit of Symbolism.

But Futurism revealed that the inhuman art of the future may

---

[48] Apollinaire quoting from "Les exposants au public" (exhibition catalogue to *Les Peintres futuristes italiens* at the Galerie Bernheim-Jeune, February 5-24, 1912) in "The Art World: The Italian Futurist Painters" in *AA*, p. 199.

[49] Apollinaire, "Art News: The Futurists" in *AA*, p. 203.

[50] As literary historian Leroy Breunig concludes in his own study, "Apollinaire et le Cubisme" in *Revue des Lettres Modernes*, Nos. 69-70 (printemps 1962), p. 23.

have actually resided in the elimination of pure aesthetic categories. Nor was this elimination without its own symbolist genealogy, as Futurism represented the megalomaniacal incarnation of synaesthetic discourse itself. This debt to Symbolism lingered on despite Futurist claims to the contrary: "We despise [Baudelaire, Mallarmé, and Verlaine] for having swum the river of time with their heads always turned back toward the far blue past, toward *le ciel antérieur où fleurit la beauté.*"[51] As with the Symbolists, the Futurists' intoxication with sensation allowed for a heightened synaesthetic confluence of experiences in which the living spectator was to be an active participant. In the plastic arts, Umberto Boccioni wanted his works to encompass the viewer himself through the plastic generation of "lines of force,"[52] suggesting both the movement of solid bodies as well as purely potential forces emanating from those bodies. Although today these "lines of force" suggest proto-Fascist rhetoric, it is no less true that Apollinaire construed such imagery as exaggerated symbolist analogues for pure light or inspiration. But unlike the aloof, contemplative readers of Symbolist poetry, the ideal futurist audience was a mob, and the pure light of inspiration was now incendiary oratory. The ideal Futurist work was highly theatrical, representing a cross-section of the arts in the hope of filiating work and spectator until everyone became the eager functionaries of a socio-aesthetic technology. Not surprisingly, for the Futurists, the ultimate synthesis of the arts was war itself. It is therefore revealing that Apollinaire's *Calligrammes*–which also combine elements from the different arts–often celebrated war as the context of their composition.

The flagrant impurity of futurist production both repelled and attracted Apollinaire. Yet he initially saw the futurist ambition for the arts to burst their traditional boundaries as an unwitting concession to retrograde mimetic aims–particularly when painting became the illustrative vehicle of literary intentions, and literature the vehicle of political propaganda. Apollinaire's politically innocuous, pre-war agitation for a pure plastic art caused him to see futurist ac-

---

[51] Filippo Marinetti, "Contra Venezia Passatista" in *Marinetti: Selected Writings*, ed. and trans. R. W. Flint and A. A. Coppotelli (New York: Farrar, Straus & Giroux, 1972), p. 66.

[52] Umberto Boccioni, et al., "The Exhibitors to the Public" in *Futurist Manifestos*, ed. Umbro Apollonio, trans. Robert Brain, R. W. Flint (New York: Viking, 1973), pp. 48-49.

tivism and theatricality as a divergence from plastic concerns and
an excuse for the reintroduction of the "subject" in art. But, as we
have also seen, the subject was not irreconcilable with the abstract
initiatives of Cubism. If Apollinaire sometimes pretended not to
notice cubist subjects or thought that their gradual disappearance
constituted their primary significance, it was because those subjects
seemed inconspicuous compared to futurist ones, which had a dynamic, fashionable sheen, covering a wide range of distinctly contemporary experiences–from dance halls to fast cars to armored
trains. By borrowing widely from the merely visual aspects of contemporary experience, futurist painting also produced, as Apollinaire saw it, a wide range of emotions that could only result in
"confusion." [53]

Despite his concerns, Apollinaire admitted to appreciating futurist titles in an article expressing his own hope that artists might
some day get beyond the cubist analysis of plastic problems and
create a more "synthetic" art: "In contrast to the deliberately analytic canvases of most of our young painters, these titles [*The City
Rises, Simultaneous Visions* (fig. 3), *Modern Idol, The Powers of a
Street, The Raid*, among others] contain some clues for a more synthetic kind of painting." (*AA*, p. 204) In light of Futurism's reintroduction of the subject and its promotion of aesthetic impurity (or
theatricality), Apollinaire's wish for a more synthetic art would
seem to be founded on precisely those things he disparaged in Futurism–particularly its "dangerous" (p. 203) idea of representing
the "simultaneousness of states of mind," which enabled the synthesis, in good Bergsonian fashion, of "what one remembers and
what one sees." [54] In short, he quickly identified Futurism's literary
potential, which he nevertheless castigated as plastic provincialism.
Apart from any antipathy for the Futurists' avowed nationalism,
Apollinaire's deeply ambivalent attitude toward their art sprang
from his own, still vague determination to "plasticize" the literary.
This task could not be achieved if true plastic aims were never fully
developed in their own sphere or if they too-quickly succumbed to
the temptations of the narrative "subject." On the other hand, Futurism's relaxation of aesthetic categories for the creation of a total
experience that would engulf whole societies had considerable ap-

---

[53] Apollinaire, "Futurism" in *AA*, pp. 255-256.
[54] Boccioni, p. 47.

peal for Apollinaire insofar as these developments hinted at the production of newer hybrid forms to be pioneered by poets themselves.

Robert Delaunay and simultaneous contrasts

The art of Robert Delaunay seemed to provide both a plastic and a theoretical antidote to Apollinaire's dilemma. In his large painting *City of Paris* of 1912, Delaunay had clearly achieved the monumental expression of simultaneist principles in a way that completely, if temporarily, satisfied Apollinaire, reducing the stature of the other movements in his eyes: "One must have the courage to say so: it is no longer a question of experimentation, or archaism, or of Cubism." [55] The painting, however, clearly evoked "literary" themes with its three graceful nudes occupying center stage; but now the poet eagerly accommodated such literary components in his writings on art. Why? Aside from the possibility that Delaunay was simply evoking classic literary themes that Apollinaire happened to like, the painter's new, "French" simultaneism "[epitomized], without any scientific paraphernalia, all the efforts of modern painting. Its composition [was] simple and noble. And no fault that anyone might find with it [could] detract from its truth." [56]

Apollinaire believed that Delaunay's work arrived at simultaneist principles through the pure and abstract principles of painterly creation and nothing else. He found confirmation of this not only in Delaunay's earlier, more "cubist" paintings of the Eiffel Tower, but in the painter's writings on color, in which it seemed that competing futurist and cubist simultaneisms of the literary "subject" and the plastic "object" had been theoretically transcended by a new concept. This concept was derived from Goethean theories of complementary colors (by way of Chevreul) and assumed the intriguing rubric of "simultaneous contrasts." By means of this definition, the notion of "simultaneism" as a form of modern experience that assumed multifarious representational modes was transferred to a realm of pure visual sensation, of which color, not abstract

[55] Apollinaire, "New Trends and Artistic Personalities" in *AA*, p. 219.
[56] Apollinaire, "The Salon des Indépendants" in *AA*, p. 212.

structure, was now the essence. Apollinaire explained Delaunay's ideas: "Delaunay believed that if a simple color really influences its complementary, it does so not by decomposing light, but by creating all the colors of the prism *at the same time.*" [57] "Every shade calls forth and is illuminated by all the other colors of the prism. This is simultaneity." [58] Thus, each color represented a certain inflection of all colors, all light. According to Delaunay, the eye alone of the sense receptors possessed true simultaneist capacities and, in this way, painting supplanted music as the preeminent creative medium:

> La simultanéité dans la lumière, c'est l'harmonie, le rhythme des couleurs qui crée la Vision des Hommes. La vision humaine est douée de la plus grande Réalité puisqu'elle nous vient directement de la contemplation de l'Univers. L'oeil est notre sens le plus élevé, celui qui communique le plus étroitement avec notre cerveau, la conscience [. . .] La perception auditive ne suffit pas pour notre connaissance de l'Univers. Elle n'a pas de profondeur. Son mouvement est successif, c'est une sorte de mécanisme, sa loi est le temps des horloges mécaniques qui, comme elle, n'a aucune relation avec notre perception du mouvement visuel dans l'Univers. [59]

> (Simultaneity in light, this is harmony, the rhythm of colors that creates the vision of mankind. Human vision is endowed with the greatest sense of reality since it comes to us directly from contemplation of the universe. The eye is our most elevated sense, the one that communicates most directly with our brains, our consciousness [. . .] Auditory perception is insufficient for our knowledge of the universe. It has no depth. Its movement is successive, it is a sort of mechanism, its law is the mechanical time of clocks, which, like the auditory, has no relationship at all with our perception of the visual movement of the universe.) [my translation]

Delaunay's presumption of spatial simultaneism over temporal succession derives from Leonardo da Vinci, though it also evokes a

---

[57] Apollinaire, "Modern Painting" in *AA*, p. 270.
[58] Apollinaire, "Through the Salon des Indépendants" in *AA*, p. 291.
[59] Robert Delaunay, "La Lumière" in *Du Cubisme à l'art abstrait* (Paris: S.E.V.P.E.N., 1957), pp. 146-147.

whole Romantic tradition of distinguishing the visual from the auditory on the basis of Kant's *a priori* categories of space and time. At the same time, one can also hear echoes of Baudelaire and Mallarmé, particularly in Delaunay's almost mystic yearning to encode the "idea of the universe" in a work of art. These citations were probably made under the influence of Apollinaire, as the term "Orphism" (the name of the art movement "invented" by Apollinaire and to which Delaunay alone belonged with full approbation) indicates, alluding as it does to Mallarmé's "Orphic explanation of the universe." Clearly, the assumptions of Orphist discourse originated in Symbolism, with one notable exception: the inversion of Symbolism's aesthetic hierarchy as it pertains to music and painting.

The color harmonies of Delaunay's cityscapes, windows, and Newtonian disks are the plastic recapitulation and refinement of nineteenth-century poetics. They could not, therefore, have revolutionized those poetics in turn. Hence, the theoretical similarities between Apollinaire's and Delaunay's "Fenêtres" are less indicative of avant-garde innovations in poetry than are their differences. As I will show later, Apollinaire's "Fenêtres" expresses a plastic sensibility mostly in spite of similarities to Delaunay's non-representational series of *Fenêtres*.

Virginia Spate, a historian of Orphist painting, has described the color harmonies of Delaunay's work as a "mobile structure" [60] that simulates not only the movement of the eye but visual perception itself before the conceptualization of objects in space ever takes place. This simulation is possible because color is light itself acting upon the eye, according to Delaunay. Yet it is also possible because of paint's tactile or physical manipulation of light through absorption and reflection. Paint, then, is the privileged medium of light in its prismatic divisions that constitute color. But paint's physicality as a medium, its qualities as a kind of object, is never critically examined and, therefore, retains an almost immediate relation to the visual and metaphysical truth of light in Delaunay's system. (One can only speculate, then, as to whether Delaunay would discard painting for the even purer, if pixelated, luminosity of the video screen today.)

---

[60] Virginia Spate, *Orphism: The Evolution of Non-figurative Painting in Paris 1910-1914* (Oxford: Clarendon Press, 1979), p. 78.

Synthetic Cubism and collage

The cubist invention of collage, however, undercuts Delaunay's vagueness about the materiality of paint. Whatever the original motivations behind collage and *papier collé*, one of the ways they rejuvenated the Cubists' own plastic inquiry was through the reintroduction of divers colors to its austere palette. Yet the return of color posed no sensuous distraction from Cubism's formal imperative to negotiate the conceptual relation between illusionistic and two-dimensional space, since the colors that were reintroduced often inhered in the pasted materials of the collage elements. In this way, the material conditions of color were laid bare rather than obscured through a traditional reliance on paint as the familiar, even "naturalized," [61] medium of color.

Braque once said that his early Cubist work demanded the elimination of color because "[he] sensed that color could produce sensations which would interfere a bit with space. . . ." [62] Space had been the primary object of Braque's investigations, which he conceived of as "a tactile space . . . a manual space. . . ." [63] that paint could only convey in monochrome tones. Drained of most color, paint became a physical substance that could define tactile, manual space. In order not to invalidate the success of these early initiatives through the frivolous reintroduction of color, Braque sought to articulate color as a substance, not an aura; as material, not light. Its return as paint would only de-materialize it in the manner of the Impressionists, the Fauves, or the Orphists. The only feasible solution was to mediate color through alternative plastic media.

Collage itself actually stemmed from earlier, more painterly experiments with gravel, sawdust, and other substances first used by Picasso and Braque to enhance textural/tactile values. As a result of those experiments Braque "saw to what extent color depended on matter." [64] As a material attachment, collaged color became–according to William Rubin–an "autonomous sign . . . now on, not illusionistically in, the picture." In this way, color was "liberated from

---

[61] The term is used in Norman Bryson's *Vision and Painting: The Logic of the Gaze* (New Haven: Yale University, 1997 [1983]).

[62] Golding, p. 111.

[63] *Ibid.*, p. 82.

[64] *Ibid.*, p. 121.

objects." [65] Yet the objects from which color was liberated were those of depicted reality. Color's new autonomy as sign exposed its old dependency in a new way. Like all signs, color depended on matter itself, the heterogeneity of which determined the possibility of color's own diversity. Different colored paints were simply different colored materials that shared an oil base. Collage showed how to move beyond paint without sacrificing plasticity.

The dependency of color and illusion on painterly materials showed to what extent a new formal materialism had subsumed the analytic concerns regarding depicted space or reality. Reality no longer seemed "depictable" in either illusionistic or abstract terms. Reality was always constructed; it relied on the cogency of coordinated material and social signs to insinuate its higher truth. If collage seemed to jeopardize reality as such in its older, aesthetico-metaphysical formulation, it vigorously asserted the importance of fabricated realities. The new art was important because it was a product of human ingenuity and interaction and thus was on a par with material production in general. This rather defensive rationale for art production showed how much the Cubists wanted to dissociate the art of painting from an aesthetics of *esprit*, or truthful ideas of nature, and resituate it as an aesthetics of production, or the semiotic manipulation of matter. It was precisely this emphasis on matter or "construction" that allowed painting to eschew symbolist idealism without succumbing entirely to a materialist ideology that demanded mimetic formulae. A certain heterogeneity, implicit in collage, characterized the new aesthetics of matter, whereby anything previously disallowed in art production could be employed. Through a *discordia concors* of contrasting materials and illusionistic fragments, a plastic rapprochement emerged that was critical to designating the work's "autonomy," to validating it as a constructed reality among others. Such was the irony of an art striving for a new synthesis of art and reality, that its claim to autonomy soon became the cornerstone of the pervasive, public-display ethos of "Do Not Touch." This tenacious philosophy concerning the status of the finished artwork was implicit in Apollinaire's descriptions of the new "synthetic" techniques:

[65] William Rubin, *Picasso and Braque: Pioneering Cubism* (New York: Museum of Modern Art, 1989), p. 40.

Picasso a parfois renoncé aux couleurs ordinaires pour composer des tableaux en relief, en carton ou des tableaux de papiers
collés; il suivait alors une inspiration plastique et ces matériaux
estranges bruts et disparates devenaient nobles parce que
l'artiste leur insufflait sa personnalité à la fois robuste et déli-
cate. (CA, p. 354)

Moi, je n'ai pas la crainte de l'Art et je n'ai aucun préjugé
touchant la matière des peintres. Les mosaïstes peignent avec des
marbres ou des bois de couleur. On a mentionné un peintre ita-
lien qui peignait avec des matières fécales; sous la Révolution
française, quelqu'un peignit avec du sang. On peut peindre avec
ce qu'on voudra, avec des pipes, des timbres-postes, des cartes
postales, ou à jouer, des candélabres, des morceaux de toile cirée,
des faux cols. Il me suffit, a moi, de voir le travail, il faut qu'on
voie le travail, c'est par la quantité de travail fournie par l'artiste
que l'on mesure la valeur d'une oeuvre d'art. (CA, p. 370)

(Picasso sometimes abandoned customary paints in order to
compose three dimensional pictures of cardboard or collages; in
these instances, he was obeying a plastic inspiration, and these
strange, rough, and disparate materials became ennobled because the artist endowed them with his own strong and sensitive
personality.) (AA, p. 269)

(I personally am not afraid of art, I harbor no prejudices about
the materials painters use. Mosaicists paint with pieces of marble
or colored wood. Mention has been made of an Italian painter
who painted with fecal matter; at the time of the French Revolution, someone who painted with blood. They can paint with
whatever they wish—postage stamps, postcards or playing cards,
candelabras, pieces of oilcloth, starched collars. For me it is
enough to see the work, one must be able to see the work. It
is the amount of work accomplished by the artist that determines
the value of a work of art.) [66]

Apollinaire's seeming desire to equate the value of a work with
the amount of labor put in to it is accompanied by an equal and opposite desire for the ennoblement of the work by virtue of the
artist's personality. The art is the man, as it were, in a modern reiteration of Buffon's dictum on style. But Apollinaire's man, it would

---

[66] Apollinaire, "Pablo Picasso" in AA, p. 281.

seem, was not only a genius but a day laborer too! The work itself recapitulated the artist's split persona: It was both art and plain work, ennobled and mundane. In widening the range of materials for use, the Cubists precipitated the conditions for a plastic–as opposed to a futuristically theatrical–synthesis of painting and non-painting. By the standards of the time, this innovation implied a more disturbing synthesis of art and non-art, form and non-form. Through the deliberate suspension of both mimetic and purist aesthetics, Picasso and Braque allowed alien elements to penetrate the structure of the traditional painting, as a result of which its status became undecidable at a certain level of discourse. By opening up art to non-art, to a kind of materialist short-circuiting of illusionistic devices via real ones (real postage stamps, real newspaper clippings), Cubism signaled both art's accelerated disappearance under the onslaught of reality and its limitless potential for expansion through the aestheticization of everything.

This strategy was different from that of the Futurists, whose multi-media extravaganzas sought to enmesh reality in a dizzying swirl of simultaneous acts of aesthetic aggression. Instead, the cubist work dissimulated a certain surface passivity, subjecting itself to formal spoliation by unconventional materials and media. If, according to Leo Steinberg, the depicted space of early cubist works visually oscillated between apparent depth and literal surface in a "reciprocity of directions" [67] that was more sexual than formal, synthetic Cubism displayed, through a total exposure of its technical apparatus, an obscene "solicitation" [68] for a new kind of defilement.

At the same time, an aesthetic cooptation was immanent in that defilement: what might initially be perceived as pollutants derived from gritty reality were shown up as a wide range of new formal systems or media at the disposal of the "autonomous" plastic surface. Collagist materials came from high and low sources, yet were all strangely equalized through the eclecticism of the aesthetic exchange. The relative two-dimensionality of these divers materials became the lowest common denominator of pictorial autonomy. But some of these media played dirty tricks (as they had been invited to do). Like the industrial oil cloth printed with chair-caning

---

[67] Leo Steinberg, "The Polemical Part" in *Art in America* (March/April 1979), p. 121.

[68] In Compagnon's sense, *La Seconde Main*, pp. 23-24.

that Picasso used in his *Still Life with Chair Caning* (1911) [fig. 4], they artificially introduced illusion to the picture once again as a surface device–something slapped on top. Printed letters suggested absolute flatness, yet the word fragments they sometimes formed suggested hidden or superimposed meanings. Trompe-l'oeil nails illusionistically in the picture symbolically threatened a kind of externality as objects piercing the picture plane. Surface itself was shown to be a debatable designation along with the frame, whose role in picture making was being complicated by the formal oscillation between real and illusionistic objects–as Apollinaire makes clear: "The object, either real or in trompe-l'oeil, will doubtless be called upon to play an increasingly important role. It constitutes the internal frame of the painting, marking the limits of its depth just as the frame marks its exterior limits." (*AA*, p. 279)

Thus each new element acquired a formal ambiguity that situated it both in and out of the picture. It was an art of consistent self-contradiction, as Ernst Gombrich has written, where each identity bled or slid into its non-identity by way of *passage*, a material or symbolic trespass of depicted or imagined boundaries. As Steinberg has written, most definitions of *passage*, beginning with William Rubin, "denote a kind of brushwork or hatching that 'passes' across suppressed contours to unite disparate elements." [69] The consequence of this passing of fluids, as it were, is that objects "locked in one spatial register [open] upon an apparent distance–without drain of materiality or detriment to [their] station." [70] In the case of collage, fragmented objects arbitrarily locked in categories of reality open on to categories of form and back again. Collage elements, like sandpaper or printed matter, only seemed unaesthetic (hence more real) because they were not commonly deployed as painterly materials. They represented the intrusion of one medium or sign-system onto another, since both paint and newspapers had claims upon the "habitus" (as Bryson calls certain societies) about what constituted the maximal indicative of reality. But in the clash of these systems, in the sheer effrontery of such mediumic juxtaposition and *passage*, the semiotic constructedness of reality obscenely exposed itself.

---

[69] Steinberg, p. 121.
[70] *Ibid.*, p. 122.

A similar clash of systems would be engineered by Apollinaire and others in poetry, where alien elements were also introduced (or seemed to be)–without "drain of materiality," as it were. In certain instances, new elements were truly alien in the original spirit of cubist collage and its clash of plasticities. Works with handwritten versus typeset words, pasted documents with graphic signs that were not linguistically based, foreign language components (Pound's ideograms) or simultaneously performed works with accompanying, extra-textual gestures, all announced the mostly non-linguistic sources of these collagist adjuncts. But for the most part, the alien quality of poetic collagist elements was mitigated by the more common practice of simply introducing non-literary, non-discursive elements in jarring, provocative, and fragmentary ways in order to evoke plastic collagism without completely abandoning language–and even, at times, accommodating discourse in some fashion. The distinction between true plastic collage and a kind of exaggerated or teratological practice of citation is therefore difficult to maintain with absoluteness.

In *Theory of the Avant-Garde* Peter Bürger interpreted the invention of collage as a definitive transition in modernist expression to the allegorical mode in Benjamin's sense. Collage works, then, represent a collection of fragments artificially joined together, hence, emptied of any definitive representational significance. They ceased representing an infiltration of "the real" and became hermeneutically dense or indecipherable signs. The "meaning" of such a work could only be posited or "allegorized" by the viewer or reader according to his or her own purposes within the community, i.e., in general conformity with the imperatives of a particular sociohistorical habitus. Yet, as we have seen, the collage fragment can achieve dual status as a non-signifying formal element and a partial mimetic referent. Its materiality always suggests–because of its fragmentation–a plurality of original contexts yoked together in some new metonymic formulation. Before examining the variable ways in which different plastic strategies inform Apollinaire's poetic production, some poems should be considered on the basis of collage technique alone, which is a vital component of all their plastic affinities. To appreciate the novelty of verbal collage in Apollinaire's poetry, it is important to recognize the extent to which the poet subjects language as much as possible to a "plastic" treatment without extricating it from the medium of language. Such a treatment leaves the circumstantiality of language intact without resorting to the anathema of "communication" and the organicism it implies. This new language also distinguishes itself from the literary heritage implicit in poetic language and frees itself from any necessity of streamlining into coherent discourse whatever literary referentiality persists. Language becomes a kind of material to be collected, shuffled, adjusted, and reorganized at the scene of writing. In this way, the heteroclite texture of lived circumstances can be presented as linguistic or semiotic items available for scrutiny without being "represented" as a natural order.

THREE POEMS: "LUNDI RUE CHRISTINE," "LES FENÊTRES," "LETTRE-OCÉAN"

The poem "Lundi Rue Christine" provides a starting point for the critical examination of Apollinaire's collage techniques in *Calligrammes* because the verbal fragments composing it can be plausibly identified with a generic setting–a Parisian brasserie–though this formal schema should not restrict the poem as some kind of "Universal Poetic Experience" (to parody Bryson's terminology) of Parisian brasseries. Much as the still-life does in Cubist paintings, the brasserie cunningly contextualizes the various bits of speech whose logical relations, however, remain unclear. Such a setting allows the fragments to be loosely configured as overheard or remembered utterances within a possible context; yet, that very context is an artificial designation, an imaginary matrix through which the fragments and snatches of speech are only provisionally interconnected while their referents occasionally lure the reader away into other social registers simultaneously inflecting the whole. However, it is precisely this luring away, this interpretive potential that releases the poem from any mimetic grounding, a grounding that, in itself, offers only the most rudimentary of readings. The arbitrariness of the collagist combinations allows the fragments to resonate as simultaneously contrasting signs of the *socius* that fluctuate between low-brow and high-brow, mundane and literary.

For instance, the opening lines suggest a criminal plot being discussed in hushed, sinister tones ("Si tu es un homme tu m'accompagneras ce soir" [If you're a man, you'll come with me tonight]), while subsequent lines suggest a more amicable rendez-vous in distant lands ("Quand tu viendras à Tunis je te ferai fumer du kief" [When you come to Tunis we'll smoke some hashish]). (C, pp. 52-53) The lines both contrast and converge in a way that conforms with Steinberg's characterization of *passage* between formal plastic elements. Further on, the phrase "Voici monsieur" could be something the waiter or bartender says; but it could also be the poet's direct comment to the (male) reader apropos of the preceding line: "C'est complètement impossible," which itself may be either an overheard exclamation or an ironic description of the reader's interpretive impasse. Each phrase oscillates between formal perception and social sign.

Clearly the idea of a café offers the reader a rationale for the range of verbal elements, the very triviality of which give the poem a certain mimetic aura. But their sequence, interaction, and contrasts thwart any sense of sustained narrative or mimetic intention. With the exception of several purely descriptive statements punctuating the poem ("Le chat noir traverse la brasserie," "La fontaine coule," "Le sol est semé de sciure" [The black cat crosses the restaurant, The fountain flows, The ground is covered with sawdust]), most of the lines have an air of the peripheral, the inconsequential, or the inscrutable because they carry traces of their *énonciation*, their original contexts as syntagmatic utterances in which they uniquely discursively cohere. In the poem, they ultimately do not. The episodic circumstances generating such a phrase as "Écoute Jacques c'est très sérieux ce que je vais te dire/ Compagnie de navigation mixte" (Listen Jacques, what I'm going to tell you is very serious/ Shipping company combine) is not narratively followed up. Is the second phrase what Jacques needs to know? Or is it simply the non sequitur produced by the juxtaposition of different collage elements? Would any collage element have produced the effect of a non sequitur, or is this particular one necessary as a suggestive link to some other theme in the poem—such as international trade and travel ("A Smyrne à Naples en Tunisie")—or as a suggestive polysyllabic contrast? If the order of the phrases is necessary for the poetic effects Apollinaire wants to produce, those effects may indeed be so subtle as to be indistinguishable from those produced by some other, purely chance arrangement he might have made. Indeed, it may be a chance arrangement that just happens to resonate poetically at certain moments for a certain reader. At certain points in the poem one wonders if the order of phrases could be altered without unduly altering the poetic effect. As Philippe Renaud has written, "Apollinaire crée une confusion entre le contingent et le nécessaire, l'extérieur et l'intérieur, le hazard et la fatalité: ou, si l'on préfère, . . . il jette un doute sur la valeur de ces oppositions" (Apollinaire creates a confusion between the contingent and the necessary, the external and the internal, chance and fate: or, if one prefers, . . . he casts doubt on the value of these oppositions). [71]

In this way, Apollinaire seems to share Mallarmé's ambition to create an impersonal poetry where authorial self-expression cedes the initiative to pure language, language as a kind of etymological resonance. But at the same time, the language of "Lundi Rue Christine" is fraught with the kind of demotic provisionality that Mallarmé disparaged as journalism. What the poem conveys is the circumstantiality, *per se*, of language in an actual (and quite common) setting where verbal elements freely collide in perception. The setting, then, is a physical arena of simultaneous verbal contrasts where spoken language (*parole*) relinquishes discursive continuity and citational accommodation, but retains a quality of phenomenal specificity when captured in writing. Although "detaching" (in Derrida's sense), [72] capturing, and reorganizing this public language would seem to give it the status of pure or systematic language (*langue*), its phenomenal residues are too much in evidence, their contrasts too jarring to be explained by the esotericism of symbolist poems. The notion of a mimetic frame of reference, then, is significant not for providing a narrative, but for pinning all the verbal signs into a demotic, hence anonymous register. Their citational quality is compromised by the provisionality of the setting. An arbitrariness is maintained, discursive motivations are ablated. People do not cite the banal, the commonplace, the cliché, they simply repeat them. Citation always exfoliates in an ecstasy of allusions, references, footnotes, and internal documentation: it is the *jouissance* of the postmodern scholar. Apollinaire's reorganization, then, could be described as a kind of *brocante*, a plastic operation that makes poetic use of a more provisional or "found" language without resorting to anecdote. The language admits of no canonical authority; only the reader can project such a meaning through allegorization. Yet the

---

[71] Renaud, p. 292.
[72] Jacques Derrida, "Restitutions" in *The Truth in Painting*, Geoff Bennington and Ian McLeod, trans. (Chicago: University of Chicago, 1987), p. 279.

words and broken phrases, commonplace though they were, still enacted a form of verbal "solicitation" of the writing/collaging subject (the poet), thus creating a vital tension with the very de-familiarizing techniques that remain operative in the finished poem. Through collage, Apollinaire has created a hybrid language that is neither functional nor pure but one of cultivated contingency by which the heterogeneity of *parole* in its spatial simultaneism acquires poetic being. (In other words, the synchrony of this language is not systematic, eternal, but diachronically–hence arbitrarily–determined.) If these verbal shards ambiguously interconnect at other formal levels it is to indicate a new complicity of chance and poetic necessity. Consequently, an element of provisionality enters into the process of interpretation, as Benjamin shows in his definition of allegory.

In this way the poem presents a collision of fortuitous utterances that are not, in a certain measure, the work of an author; that are not, at a certain historical moment, acceptable as a legitimate poetic endeavor. The textualization of such speech, stripped of any discursive justification, was an affront to textualization itself, where it was valued only for its rhetorical or narrative uses–not for any accidental formality it displayed. In "Lundi Rue Christine" narrative devices for framing the vernacular have been reduced to a minimum as evidenced by the three descriptive phrases mentioned above. Such devices linger as connective traces of narrative with its insinuations of perceptual continuity, just as f-holes linger in cubist paintings as evidence of deconstructed violins. But the newer, contaminating elements (the collage elements) seem strangely undefined or arbitrary in their placement, abutting or coalescing, contrasting or passing into each other in ways that defy simple communication and that signal a series of conflicting codes. For this reason, many critics see mostly provocation in verbal collage, a defacement of the poetic. Henri Behar, for instance, has theorized that verbal collage represents a "confrontation" between written and spoken language, the original and the cliché, through a material displacement. [73] Yet the displacement itself produces internal frames, which in turn suggest the fluidity or provisionality of all frames. Apropos of the different registers of language that concern Behar, this shifting of contours is as much an instance of confrontation as it is of blurring

---

[73] Henri Behar, "La Saveur du réel" in *Europe: Revue littéraire mensuelle. Cubisme et littérature*. Nos. 638-641 (juin-juillet 1982), p. 104.

distinctions, of *passage*, where subversion and cooptation are indistinguishable. An illustrative example in "Lundi Rue Christine" is
found in the first four lines:

> La mère de la concierge et la concierge laisseront tout passer
> Si tu es un homme tu m'accompagneras ce soir
> Il suffirait qu'un type maintînt la porte cochère
> Pendant que l'autre monterait

> (The concierge's mother and the concierge will let everyone through
> If you're a man you'll come with me tonight
> All we need is one guy to watch the main entrance
> While the other goes upstairs)

(C, pp. 52-53)

The verb "maintînt" is in the *passé simple*, which, according to Renaud, sounds absurdly literary in the context of the whole passage.
It represents a sort of collage within a collage, a subversion of a
subversion, sort of like the illusionistic chair-caning on the piece of
oilcloth in *Still Life with Chair Caning*. In short, collage not only
juxtaposes different realities, but insinuates (or even reveals) rapports between them through the ambiguity of *passage* and the im-
brication of literature and talk. This ambiguity is in the nature of
language as *matière*; it is language in its heterogeneity, contingency,
and marginality before any rhetorical or ideological framework can
be posited wherein the literary and the vulgar, the musical and the
functional, are rigorously segregated on the basis of their presumed
message.

The apparent symbiosis of verbal collage and demotic French
in "Lundi Rue Christine" is more difficult to establish in "Les
Fenêtres" where the traces of spoken language have the tenor of literary persiflage. Like "Lundi Rue Christine," "Les Fenêtres" was
partly composed in a Parisian bar. Yet the network of images goes
far beyond the confines of a particular setting or of particular literary claimants in order to encompass (or abandon itself to) the
whole world. At the same time, those elements that are traceable
(through documentation) to the original context reveal a conscientious effort on Apollinaire's part to conceive the poem as a collaborative exercise in which snippets of speech become directly identifiable with individual speakers and, in this way, lose their anonymity.
They become, at least in time, conventional citations, a colloquy of

texts, canonized voices, imbricated with more commonplace speech and fragmented in a way that reduces discourse to simple language components (in the sense of Benveniste's distinction between *langue* and *discours*).[74] In the opening lines of "Les Fenêtres" the collage technique assumes the character of a literary contest, revealing the formal malleability and ideological insouciance of the new technique, which isolates and combines, in the spirit of the game, verbal elements from both high and low social registers:

> Du rouge au vert tout le jaune se meurt
> Quand chantent les aras dans les forêts natale
> Abatis de pihis
> Il y a un poème a faire sur l'oiseau qui n'a qu'une aile
> Nous l'enverrons en message téléphonique
> Traumatisme géant
> Il fait couler les yeux
> Voilà une jolie jeune fille parmi les Turinaises
> Le pauvre jeune homme se mouchait dans sa cravate blanche

> (From red to green all the yellow dies
> When parakeets sing in their native forests
> Giblets of pihis
> There's a poem to be done on the bird with only one wing
> We'll send it by telephone
> Giant traumatism
> It makes your eyes run
> Do you see that pretty girl among the young women of Turin
> The poor young man blew his nose with his white tie)
>
> (*C*, pp. 26-27)

As André Billy attested[75] these lines were written at the Crucifix Bar, rue Daunou, where Apollinaire, Billy, and René Dalize were drinking vermouth "de Turin," the specialty of the house. On remembering he was late with a preface for an exhibition catalogue to Delaunay's *Fenêtres* series, then on display in Berlin, Apollinaire wrote down the first line of the poem and invited his companions to contribute lines of their own. The first clearly alludes to Delaunay's color theory. (*C*, p. 351) Yet at the time of its enunciation, the line suggested something else to Dalize who contributed the second

---

[74] Compagnon, p. 51.
[75] Renaud, p. 298.

line about colorful, new-world birds singing in tropical forests. Their singing and the repeated vowels of their name–"aras"–seem to persist (via "natale") in the syllabic assonance of the third line: "Abatis de pihis." At the same time, giblets of "pihis," the legendary Chinese birds who fly in pairs, sharing each other's wings, show Apollinaire continuing the bird imagery, if parodically rendering it as a meal–a reminder of the context in which the poem was being written, but also, metaphorically, the poem's contents. Furthermore, the reference to pihis alludes to Apollinaire's "Zone" in *Alcools* where the pihi is likened to Icarus (and his modern symbol, the airplane), whose presumption and fallibility seemed endemic to the new spirit of invention Apollinaire promoted in the arts.

Billy's contribution of line four, "Il y a un poème à faire sur l'oiseau qui n'a qu'une aile," deftly reveals the self-referential nature of the poem-in-process, which–like Icarus, the pihi, or Baudelaire's albatross–oscillates between dull circumstance and mythic flight, or "banal and lyric language." [76] The succeeding line, "Nous l'enverrons en message téléphonique" (We'll send it by telephone), refers to the "banal" necessity of sending the poem off to Berlin, but also to the lyric possibilities of what was then a new medium, faster than flight. The girl and the poor young man in the next lines may indeed recall people actually seen at the bar by chance, but the girl, at least, can be identified, once again, with the poem itself, budding as it does between glasses of vermouth (les Turinaises?). The girl as metaphor for the poem seems less farfetched in light of Apollinaire's later, fuller development of the theme in "La Jolie rousse" (The Pretty Red-head). The young man, however, is harder to reconcile with poetry as such. Is he like a poem in some way? The blowing of his nose seems gratuitous here and so indeed might the attempt to explain it as anything but a joke at traditional poetry's expense.

But suddenly everything in the poem changes, and the reader no longer recognizes the setting for the poetic "contest" that seemed to be the engine of the poem in its early stages (Billy only corroborates it for the first few lines). Thus the hermeneutic of the poem as a constellation of semiotic clues to a "real" setting nullifies itself. One sees that such "settings" have very little bearing on the

---

[76] S. I. Lockerbie, "'Les Fenêtres' et le poème créé" in *Revue des Lettres Modernes. Apollinaire 5*. Nos. 146-149 (1966), p. 17.

poem as a unified (or disunified?) construct. Now the poem unexpectedly, yet "familiarly," addresses an unknown person, "tu": "Tu soulèveras le rideau" (You will raise the curtain). Is it someone in Apollinaire's group? Some unnamed person of the poet's acquaintance or purview? Perhaps the projected reader? All of these options are available to the reader as ways of unifying different aspects of the poem. But external evidence suggests a completely different hermeneutic framework that shifts the poem from a game of literary creation to creativity in general, albeit with reference to painting, as the first line–like the *incipit* of an automatic text–affirms. Delaunay has claimed the image of the curtain as his own–literally–saying it refers to one in his studio where Apollinaire also worked on the poem and saw the painter's latest additions to the *Sun and Moon* series. [77] Several lines that follow substantiate this claim; yet it bears repeating that the proprietary claims of individuals to certain detachable elements are always suspect, just as the claim that poems themselves can be exclusively delineated by either perception or style, content or form, is itself a contestable assertion that Derridean theory potentially deconstructs:

> Tu soulèveras le rideau
> Et maintenant voilà que s'ouvre la fenêtre
> Araignées quand les mains tissaient la lumière
> Beauté paleur insondables violets
> Nous tenterons en vain de prendre du repos
> On commencera à minuit
> Quand on a le temps on a la liberté
>
> (You'll raise the curtain
> And now see the window opening
> Spiders when hands wove the light
> Beauty paleness fathomless violets
> Vainly we'll try to take some rest
> We'll begin at midnight
> When you have time you have liberty)
>   (C, pp. 26-27)

Curtains, windows, and light are all traditional images of the painter's art, so it makes traditional "sense" to think of the window

---

[77] Spate, p. 78, and Greet, p. 352.

here as a painting Delaunay has unveiled in which his familiar concentric disks of complementary or contrasting colors issue like sun-
light reflected by the structural web of the artist's brightly colored
composition. Those "spider" hands may have been the artist's
hands that wove the light (note also that the French word for spider
web, "toile d'araignée," contains a pun on the word for canvas,
"toile"). But they also suggest Apollinaire's hands that were editing
Delaunay's essay "La Lumière" for publication at the time. [78] Yet
again, these first three images may refer to the creation of the poem
itself in which each line suggests an unveiling of meaning, a web of
relations that mutually reflect and enhance each other. The beauty,
paleness, and unfathomable violets seem to operate on both poetic
and painterly levels as a statement of sublime enjoyment in creation
that, in the following line, offers no repose for the eye or the imagination which can read and reorganize all the signs in an infinite
regress of assimilations. (Delaunay's paintings have often been described as vibrant screens of fluctuating color that vigorously exercise the eye, [79] an observation that might be compared, in turn, to
the Peircean schematic of accumulating interpretands for any sign.)
Indeed, if one's creative life begins at midnight–as suggested by the
penultimate line–both dreaming and waking hours involve some
kind of creative endeavor. The last line confirms this hypothesis; it
seems to be a statement of life itself as perpetual creation and re-
creation.

The shifting, disparate sequence of images seems to mimic the
random, meandering, indeterminate qualities one sentimentally associates with "Life" and its creative power. Although the images
grouped above have a certain thematic resonance of self-conscious
text production, no logical sequence of events is narrated. The
shifts in verb tense corroborate the radical randomness of the images: The curtain will be raised, but the window is already being
opened when hands wove the light. Once again, the last line quoted
above modulates each action and isolates the question of verb tense
by introducing the subject of time. All time is appropriated in the
syntax of these lines–past, present, and future. Yet the temporal
athleticism of these lines is a feature of language itself, language as a
system of tense inflections. Such simultaneous knowledge brings

---

[78] Spate, p. 78.
[79] *Ibid.*, p. 32.

creative freedom and, thus, language itself (*langue*) analogizes the visionary power of simultaneism and the fourth dimension. Yet it would be a mistake to confuse these conflicting verb tenses with the discursive articulations needed to demonstrate a systematic comprehension of syntactic structures. Indeed, this mélange of conjugations seems more indicative of the sub-proficiency of the language of the street: *parole*–that category of language constituting everything that has ever been said as opposed to everything that can properly be said, a "simultaneism" of concrete utterances or the work of *énonciation*.

Such a mélange is very different from the dramatic articulations one finds in a poem like "Le Musicien de Saint-Merry" (also in *Calligrammes*) in which simultaneous impressions of urban life are announced by such marking phrases as "Puis ailleurs . . . A ce moment . . . En même temps . . . Dans un autre quartier." Such an elaboration parallels the more mimetic brand of simultaneism that informed Delaunay's figurative painting, *City of Paris*. But in "Les Fenêtres" simultaneism emerges through the clash of verb tenses–a clash that has the cogency of multiple and simultaneous utterances. This cacophony is achieved, not by systematic imitation, but by the rigorous, methodical appropriation of speech. In this way speech becomes not something one has but something one takes, like a material object. Poetry becomes an act of robbery, not imitation, and yet with this rough extortion, a kind of integrity is maintained wherein no cited source is "grafted" or streamlined in order to fuse seamlessly with other discourses in an illusory transparency of thought. Instead, their features coalesce or contrast as they will. Nor does the poet steal fire anymore, he steals liquid currency–the currency of an un-self-conscious, spoken language. As Mallarmé said, a language of coins.

Such appropriation is the plastic manipulation of speech. Collage, then, is the self-conscious manipulation of un-self-conscious language, the language of others (with its referential or commercial taint) who cannot predict to what uses their words will be put. But because they are the anonymous, dis-individuated members of a collectivity, they do not care. The theft is no crime, no act of plagiarism. It is random, accidental, and ubiquitous, the result of the poet's inhuman, hence "spontaneous interaction with the world." [80]

[80] Timothy Mathews, *Reading Apollinaire: Theories of Poetic Language* (Manchester: Manchester University, 1987), pp. 130-131.

Yet such acts of collagist appropriation become discreetly methodical, prompting some, like Michel Décaudin, to misconstrue the
process: "Le collage devient une forme d'écriture, l'auteur s'avance
masqué, s'appropriant les voix des autres" (Collage becomes a form
of writing, the author advances in disguise, appropriating the voices
of others). [81] What Décaudin fails to recognize is that collage does
not credit its sources, because unlike citation, it does not have to.
Nor does it streamline its sources to reinforce another individualized or authorial argument.

The poem's close association with the work of Delaunay has invited strong comparison with the painter's aesthetics of simultaneous contrasts, as if the poem were a kind of verbal color wheel or
pure linguistic structure without tincture of quotidian referentiality.
Claude Debon, for instance, writes that "Il s'agit . . . d'appliquer à
la langue la technique dont Delaunay se sert en peinture, de glisser
d'un terme à l'autre par association et complémentarité. . . . Les
mots s'arrachent à leur sémantisme pour composer la symphonie
du monde" (It is a question of applying to language the technique
used by Delaunay in painting, of gliding from one term to the other
by association and complementarity. . . . Words are uprooted from
denotation to compose the symphony of the world). [82] J. G. Clark,
on the other hand, focuses on the role of colors as "primordial et
déterminant," [83] identifying contrasting images with those colors in
the spectrum that are signalled by specific color-denoting or color-
connoting words such as "orange," "soleil," "diamant," or even
"oursin," through a web of symbolic associations. Rosanna Warren,
however, asserts that the syllable, not the color or image, constitutes
the abstract linguistic element most closely analogous to the facets,
wedges, or disks of color used in Delaunay's paintings. [84] Syllabic
difference can be both a semantic and a phonetic vehicle; yet, in
conveying semantic distinctions, syllables can simultaneously engender phonetic repetition or tonal *passage* (Warren uses art termi-

[81] Michel Décaudin, "Apollinaire et Picasso" in *Esprit*. No. 61 (janvier 1982),
p. 83.
    [82] Debon, pp. 56-59.
    [83] J. G. Clark, "Delaunay, Apollinaire, et 'Les Fenêtres'" in *La Revue des Lettres
Modernes. Apollinaire 7*. Nos. 183-188 (1968), p. 102.
    [84] Rosanna Warren, "Orpheus the Painter: Apollinaire and Robert Delaunay"
in *Conversant Essays: Contemporary Poets on Poetry* (Detroit: Wayne State University, 1990), p. 553.

nology here). I have already given the example–not used by Warren–of "aras," "natale," and "Abatis de pihis," which illustrates her
thesis that the syllabic syncopations of semes and phonemes abstractly reproduce the meaning of the very first line, "Du rouge au
vert tout le jaune se meurt," by suggesting a subtle phonetic glide
between semantic oppositions not unlike those between the complementary colors of red and green.

If all these arguments seem to take an almost Mallarméan distance from the objects enumerated or appropriated in the poem, it
can be attributed to a reconstituted symbolist yearning to affirm language's ideality through selectively emphasizing its affinities with
abstract systems of color or tone. It is precisely language's non-com-
mitment apropos of ideality that distinguishes Apollinaire's most
experimental poetry. As Timothy Mathews has written, the difference between *Alcools* and *Calligrammes* is the creative tendency in
the latter to open up the text "to every circumstance of the
present," [85] while also recognizing the impossibility of locating stable
signifieds within the play of textual signifiers. Any locus of meaning
at the scene of appropriation largely dissipates in reception–cedes to
Benjaminian allegory–unless to some extent the sign *is* the thing it
represents, a synecdoche of its actual utterance, or has an explicit
formal association with the name of the subject who utters it. This
latter case is that of the actual quotation, conscientiously documented in order to refer one back to a proprietary source and ensure a
kind of bibliographic canonization. Interestingly, the identification
between "Les Fenêtres" and Delaunay's brand of simultaneism frequently occurs in ignorance of the external evidence that gives such
a comparison discursive legitimacy. However, without documentation confirming that Apollinaire wrote or compiled elements of this
poem in Delaunay's studio, such comparisons, while seeming to be
purely analogizing, are most strongly indicative of a collagist sensibility that preserves the aura of an *énonciation*, but not the explicit
authorship of a particular discourse. Where such authors can be
identified, collage verges on citation itself; indeed, it actually *is* citation whenever the sources are conspicuously textual, discursively
premeditated through a conscientious grafting of elements to
achieve a sentential and syntactic consistency, the wholeness of a

---

[85] Mathews, p. 127.

body. [86] But collage only preserves the sensory or material circumstances of the *énonciation*, its feel or ambiance of circumstantiality without the proprietary stamp of the allusion or quotation. But when formal elements can be identified as originating in specific circumstances, they become collage elements. In this way collage encompasses both more and less than a formal process of citation by also encompassing what is extraneous, arbitrary, even irreconcilable with proposed structures of reading since its very gratuitousness may constitute its significance.

If one considers the concluding line of the passage quoted above as a purely spontaneous utterance deftly redacted in a series of other utterances, the comment regains some of its original whimsicality and humor. "Quand on a le temps on a la liberté": readers of old French newspapers will quickly recognize the titles of two prominent French journals here and see the intended joke. In so being, the sentence deviates in some measure from the neat interpretation I gave it above as a statement of creative freedom. Now it becomes a derogatory statement concerning the relative merits of two prominent daily newspapers: one is as good (or as bad) as the other. Furthermore, André Billy has claimed that these papers were, indeed, the two evening journals his party had purchased before reaching the Crucifix bar. [87] This information distinguishes the latter line (on purely external evidence) from those lines immediately preceding it that putatively refer to the Orphic creativity Apollinaire associated with Delaunay's work. The line then acquires a certain gratuitous autonomy on the basis of this evidence, an autonomy like that of line nine, where the young man blows his nose.

Despite the sound arguments for attaching this line, gleaned from different circumstances, to other lines produced in Delaunay's studio–i.e., to make symbolic reference to time and freedom or to explain shifting verb tenses–the very act of attaching it here has a formal significance divorced from such themes. It is the ambiguous rejoinder of collagist strategy to symbolist imperatives: the sentence accidentally, gratuitously, jibes with the Orphic tendency of these lines. Apollinaire's redaction of this line involves a calculated dis-

---

[86] Apropos of this question, Compagnon writes: "Elle [la citation] est un organe motile, mais elle serait déjà un corps propre, vivant et suffisant [...] et c'est pour alimenter cette représentation que la citation est exemplairement une phrase: la moindre unité de langage autonome et fermée sur elle-même." Compagnon, p. 31.

[87] Renaud, p. 298.

juncture of creative time through the intentional retrieval of an ordinary, albeit jocular, utterance that acquires significance only accidentally. That this redaction was formally meditated is evidenced by the very ordinariness of the objects named–*Le Temps* and *La Liberté*–not the abstract concepts these journals were named after. My reason for emphasizing the common referents of these terms and not the abstract concepts becomes clear when one recalls that newspapers were the choice collage elements utilized by Picasso, Braque, and Gris. Thus, Apollinaire seems to have been in earnest when he initially gave his collection of *Ondes* (the first section in the standard edition of *Calligrammes*) the title of "Moi aussi je suis peintre." Nor was he referring to the pictorial calligrams alone as most critics have assumed, but also to some of the *vers libre* in the collection.

At the same time, the reference to newspapers anticipates the globalizing simultaneism of the rest of the poem and thus invests cubo-synthetic procedure with a futuristic exhilaration. In his art criticism, Apollinaire wrote enthusiastically about the newspaper itself as a synthetic object that engulfs time and space in its juxtaposed, paste-up columns, imperially objectifying the whole world for mass consumption. In replicating certain features of both journalistic and editorial strategy in a rough yet condensed way, Apollinaire's poem can be seen as a lively and ironic retort to Mallarmé's own statements in "Crise de vers" against journalistic language and, more importantly, to the symbolist poet's bitter renunciation of the language of the street in his own version of "Les Fenêtres" where he describes in more graphic terms what has been referred to so far in this study as *parole*: "le vomissement impur de la Bêtise" (the reeking spew of Stupidity), [88] Apollinaire has clearly employed collagist strategy as an affront to these sentiments, as an aesthetics of impurity by which banal language has the formal effect of transgression–like snot blown on a chaste, white tie.

But more than "la Bêtise," this language of common parlance is the poetic language of the future and of world communications–a truly inhuman, technologically filtered language that makes no sense without reference to its conditions of production, just as the poem "makes no sense" without reference to its own conditions of

---

[88] Mallarmé, "Les Fenêtres," trans. Hubert Creekmore, in *Selected Poetry and Prose*, pp. 10-11.

production, without reference to the social formations that allow such production. The poem is less an instance of *écriture*, as Décaudin avers, than of redaction and print, the modern technology of writing, which is why collage is so well adapted to Apollinaire's synthetic aims. Subsequent lines in "Les Fenêtres" confirm the futuristic delirium of Apollinaire's new spirit at the same time as they evince the complicity of cubist and Orphist discourse in harnessing the explosive potentialities of banal, referential, yet atomized language.

Bigorneaux Lotte multiple Soleils et l'Oursin du couchant
Une vieille paire de chaussures jaune/devant la fenêtre
Tours
Les Tours ce sont les rues
Puits
Puits ce sont les places
Puits
Arbres creux qui abritent les Câpresses vagabondes
Les Chabins chantent des airs à mourir
Aux Chabines marronnes
Et l'oie oua-oua trompette au nord
Où les chasseurs de ratons
Raclent les pelleteries
Étincelant diamant
Vancouver
Où le train blanc de neige et de feux nocturnes fuit l'hiver
O Paris
Du rouge au vert tout le jaune se meurt
Paris Vancouver Hyères Maintenon New-York et les Antilles
La fenêtre s'ouvre comme une orange
Le beau fruit de la lumière

(Winkles Codfish multiple Suns and the Sea Urchin of sunset
An old pair of yellow boots in front of the window
Towers
Towers are the streets
Wells
Wells are the squares
Wells
Hollow trees sheltering vagabond mulattoes
The Chabins sing melancholy songs
To brown Chabines
And the wa-wa wild goose honks to the north

Where raccoon hunters
Scrape the fur skins
Glittering diamond
Vancouver
Where the train white with snow and lights flashing
through the dark runs away from winter
O Paris
From red to green all the yellow dies
Paris Vancouver Hyères Maintenon New York and the Antilles
The window opens like an orange
The lovely fruit of light)

(*C*, pp. 26-29)

The first line of this grouping has been the object of so much study that any further analysis would simply beg the question. Suffice it to say that a number of puns are at work which condense divers mollusk and fish imagery with those of heavenly bodies ("soleil" itself can mean starfish or, when combined with "levant," an East Asian mollusk–the opposite, presumably, of the quirky "Oursin du couchant," the sunset sea-urchin). [89] I would only add that the line is like a list of big and small items linking sea and sun–some deriving, perhaps, from Delaunay's solar imagery, some deriving from the *poissonerie* outside the literal window of his studio–which displays the nuclear potential of words. The old pair of yellow shoes before the window were also claimed by Delaunay. (*C*, p. 349) In so being, they, too, literalize his painted *Fenêtres* as real windows with a sill opening onto a real world. But this transformation places the reader in the same old shoes, as it were, as Mallarmé's "moribond sournois" (a wry, but moribund old man) in his symbolist precedent, who looks out of a hospital window to behold Infinity. In the new poem the viewer beholds the modern world in the fourth dimension–in other words, a scientific or "bad" infinity. But Derrida has taught us all the folly of attributing exclusive ownership to old footwear and that such shoes are always unlaced with every reading.

At the same time, subsequent lines connote this shift from vertical to horizontal planes by offering definitions of "towers" and "wells" that might well be taken as their opposites: "streets" and "squares." Most critics have noted the similarity of this planar

---

[89] Renaud, p. 352.

transposition to Analytic Cubism which sought to reconcile objects in illusionistic depth with their conceptual elaboration on a two-dimensional plane. But such an interpretation seems only partly correct; aside from choosing an object ("Tour" with a capital, read "Tour Eiffel") that alludes to a frequent motif in Delaunay's paintings (not Picasso's or Braque's), the tower's horizontalizing redefinition as a street places it in its urban context. As a play on another meaning of "tour," the juxtaposition also suggests movement through the city. With the wells and squares, Apollinaire creates a kind of contour map of the city, its overlaid networks of travel routes and commercial centers. When one considers the tower's function of transmitting and receiving radio messages, the tower itself heralds the vast simultaneism of international communications, of which it is the center, like the pivot of some great, lateralized ferris wheel. Its information network expands across the entire globe like a media "toile d'araignée." This lateralization of vertical objects seems to be an early evocation of what Leo Steinberg identified as the reorientation of the picture plane in the postmodern context from the "window" to the "flatbed" (a term suggestively derived from the print medium) as a precondition for a radical shift from natural vision to cultural production, [90] and, I would add, from idealism to modern materialism. As Steinberg states, even Picasso's cubist collages "hark back to implied acts of vision" [91] as opposed to this almost neuro-tactile lateralization and concentration of the worldspace in a way that suggests the conjunction of technology with the social formation.

The final (or bottom) word in the group under consideration is "Puits," which evokes an archaeological depth but also puns on "puis" ("then"), which marks a sudden transition to the strangely bucolic yet historically modern image of the "Arbre creux qui abritent les Câpresses vagabondes." Suddenly the spatial orientation of the preceding lines has made a trans-Atlantic leap to the Antilles (where Câpresses–French inhabitants–are found [92]), but also a miraculous leap back in time announced by the surreptitious "puis" of "Puits," reinforced by the "ant-" of the "Antilles" islands, and

---

[90] Leo Steinberg, "Other Criteria" in *Other Criteria: Confrontations with Twentieth-Century Art* (Oxford: Oxford University, 1972), pp. 82-84.
[91] *Ibid.*, p. 82.
[92] Renaud, p. 352.

subsumed in the allusive "Chabins" and "Chabines" that follow (offspring of interracial marriages [C, p. 353]). A new simultaneism of races, cultures, and histories is reflected in this leap, which Apollinaire reinforces with the pastoral "airs à mourir" of the Chabins (which may also refer, according to Philippe Renaud, to an Antillean sheep [93]). An elegiac nostalgia peeks out in these lines; Apollinaire's regret for the past occasionally issues, despite his best efforts, from between the collagist fissures of simultaneist exhilaration.

But the poet quickly interrupts this lament of Antillean lovers with the loud, apocalyptic blare of geese, trumpeting to the north. American fur trappers come to mind, diamonds, Canadian cities, railroads and snow, and finally back full circle to Paris and the opening line of the poem: "Du rouge au vert tout le jaune se meurt": From one extreme to the other, some subtle, fragile thing is dying. This unacknowledged sentiment reoccurs in the random naming of six cities in the second penultimate line: Paris Vancouver Hyères ("vent couvert hier") Maintenon ("maintenant") New-York et les Antilles: Present, Future, Past. Thus, the discourse of time catches up with the spatial randomness of place names. This totalizing experience of space and time offered by the poem (a kind of window) is then also given a name: "orange," the intimate, sensuous equivalent of light and enlightenment, a luscious microcosm of the world of imagination and "knowledge," tangy and lewd, appealing to all the senses at once: it is a word one hears, a color one sees, a smell and a taste one savors, an object one touches. But the symbol of the orange is not inevitable or decisive. Its spherical and sensuous concentration of the totalizing impulse of the poem (at least the second half) remains an allegory. One cannot discount the purely arbitrary conditions that also inform such a selection. One cannot forget that "le poème est . . . la création en train de se faire, la mise en oeuvre d'une technique très nouvelle dans laquelle le principe d'association se met comme spontanément au service d'une synthèse universelle . . ." (the poem is creation in the act of making itself, the application in a work of a very new technique in which the principle of association made itself available, as if spontaneously, to a universal synthesis). [94]

---

[93] *Ibid.*, p. 352.
[94] Debon, p. 59.

This synthesis depends for its success on a kind of failure, a plurality of elements whose synthesis is only, ultimately, a formal one, a provisional one, an artificial nexus of interpretive struggles for discursive linkage, *passage*. The uneasy truce in "Les Fenêtres" between Apollinaire's totalizing literary aesthetic (a kind of Orphic Futurism) and a certain tolerance of the gratuitous, plastic interjection–the collage fragment (the overheard statement that unexpectedly solicits, excites, or incites an otherwise inattentive listener)–also holds for some of his calligrams proper, particularly "Lettre-Océan" [figs. 5 & 6], which in many ways is a calligrammatic restatement of the structural implications of "Les Fenêtres." The web-like, concentric structures one must take some pains to discover in "Les Fenêtres" because of the poem's rugged, collagist texture, become immediately apparent in "Lettre-Océan" because of its spatio-visual elaboration of elements. This visual synthesis of verbal elements through a doubled concentric patterning reminiscent of two sun-like bodies is almost immediately identifiable in the poem. [95] Because of this "immediacy," these two conspicuous shapes would seem to corroborate the traditional distinction between visual and aural perception on the basis of the former's immediacy and the latter's temporality; this distinction has also insinuated itself into discussions of painting and poetry with the latter invariably linked to music as a temporal or performative art. Yet through the conspicuous visual patterning of "Lettre-Océan," Apollinaire emphasizes the graphic features of poetry as printed matter, and the immediate structural perception that allows.

Without this visual device it is by no means clear whether the verbal elements could ever convey any such notion of structure through a conventional, sequential reading. As Pénélope Sacks-Galey has written: "La lecture à haute voix est tout simplement condamnée par cette impossibilité de dire la figuration" (Reading out loud is simply condemned by the impossibility of being able to say the figuration). [96] Thus, any sure sense of the poem's structure becomes unobtainable without reference to its strictly visual manifes-

---

[95] This partly depends on the layout: the two halves of the poem were originally presented in *Les Soirées de Paris* on facing pages, but subsequently appeared on recto and verso pages, as they continue to do in later published editions. *C*, p. 380.

[96] Pénélope Sacks-Galey, *Calligramme ou Ecriture Figurée: Apollinaire inventeur de formes* (Paris: Lettres Modernes, Minard, 1988), p. 7.

tation. In this way the structure itself acquires a formal autonomy from the verbal and typographic elements composing it, its very transcendence suggests a certain allegorical disjuncture between the significance it lends to elements composing it and their intrinsic significance as discrete verbal statements. (Raymond Queneau has written: "L'espace oriente le texte qui se trouve alors fragmenté. L'image n'est plus tributaire du discours, elle s'émancipe" (Space orients the text, which then finds itself fragmented. The image is no longer dependent on [the] discourse, it emancipates itself). [97] Such disjuncture becomes obvious when one sets about reading the poem. Because the visual structure is given, the order of reading becomes entirely subjective. Any narrative, phonetic, or rhythmic links between statements that would be evident in a given sequence of expressions in an ordinary text become purely arbitrary here because the spatio-graphic orientation of "Lettre-Océan" affords the reader a certain liberty concerning how best to proceed. Discursive and even syntactic connections are severed in the same way that modern painting asseverates and jumbles the spatial relations that would yield illusionistic images.

Thus the (abstract) figuration of the poem introduces a component of chance, if not into its construction, at least into its reception (albeit within boundaries, like a game). The reading of the poem, the order in which its elements are consumed, is open-ended like the geometric figures themselves, whose lines emanate from two centers, shooting out either to their twin center on the recto or verso side of the page (establishing a visual dialogue), or out beyond the bounds of the book itself. At the same time, the figures–in conformity with the whole idea of geometry as a "plastic grammar"– tend to provide certain negotiable patterns of reading based on the visual appeal of specific elements, shapes, and zones. The large bold type and the non-verbal, graphic bits are the most conspicuous of these elements: Mayas, TSF, República Mexicana Tarjeta Postal, and the series of wavy lines here and there. These typographic markers solicit not the concentrated "gaze" of the decoding, perceiving viewer, but his undisciplined "glance," [98] the scopic feature most correspondent to the vagaries of desire. One also tends to zero-in on the circular forms and the words printed at their

---

[97] Quoted in Sacks-Galey, pp. 5-6.
[98] See Bryson, pp. 117-122.

centers, just as one's eye is quickly drawn to focal or vanishing points in graphic compositions. Another tendency, usually delayed in the process, is that of reading the concentric circular forms either clockwise or counterclockwise, centripetally or centrifugally.

In this regard, the glance becomes increasingly channeled into patterns that evoke conventional reading strategies, to which the poem also makes its appeal. Some lines do move from left to right, top to bottom, and one of the first sustained "chunks" of verse one assimilates is, naturally, near the top of the poem:

> J'étais au bord du Rhin quand tu partis pour le Mexique
> Ta voix me parvient malgré l'énorme distance
> Gens de mauvaise mine sur le quai à la Vera Cruz

> (I was on the banks of the Rhine when you left for Mexico
> Your voice reaches me in spite of the huge distance
> Seedy-looking people on the pier at Vera Cruz)
>
> (C, pp. 58-65)

These lines act as a narrative framing device for the collaged post-card putatively from Apollinaire's brother that follows, a message possibly quoted verbatim and thus continuing the theme of com-munication over long distances by post. One may or may not in-clude in the preceding "chunk" the little triangular figure introduc-ing it: "Je traverse la ville, nez en avant, et je la coupe en 2" (I cross the city, nose in the air, and I cut it in 2). Because of its smaller type, one sometimes neglects to read this almost marginal calligrammatic element in the order its position at the top of the page might sug-gest; yet, the figure is important to the overall structure of the poem by describing an event that is formally replicated there. Upon read-ing and relating it to some of the other, more visually conspicuous elements of the poem, one realizes that the given visual structure is not simply an abstract, solar disk in duplicate, but a kind of map of a city that the persona in the three line-fragments physically travers-es as the structural outlines schematically traverse it. One also real-izes that the city in question is Paris, not Vera Cruz (though Paris is the "true cross" or crossroads of global communications) when one reads the phrases in the centers of the circular patterns: "Sur la rive gauche devant le pont d'Iéna" (On the left bank in front of Iéna bridge) and "Haute de 300 mètres" (300 meters high). (C, pp. 58-

65) The first phrase geographically locates the Eiffel Tower; the second re-presents it in the spirit of the futurist "wireless imagination" (*imaginazione senze figli*), which used numerical figures to convey a more rapid and modern lyrical feeling not unlike the use of such abbreviated symbols in electronic messages today (this technique also explains Apollinaire's numerical "2" at the beginning of the poem and other typographic features). In this way, Apollinaire presents the reader with two versions of Paris, one personal, one technological, with the Eiffel Tower at its hub and the poet himself somewhere in the vicinity. The poet and the tower (both "nez [né] en avant") become extensions of and limitations on each other, both doubling and dividing the city between them as complementary yet competitive agents of perception, communication, and imagination.

When one remembers that the tower was originally used as a radio transmitter (the "wireless"), one begins to see how the visual schema of the poem can be related more precisely to the verbal fragments throughout. The series of wavy lines can now be understood not simply as ocean waves (*ondes*) but as radio waves; the bold TSF can now be deciphered as "Transmission Sans Fil" (wireless transmission). In concentric zones around the tower, one sees/hears the hum of simultaneous speech, whether from pedestrians below, voices on the airwaves, remembered messages or poetical musings, even automobiles. Although the visuals independently convey an abstract structure that superficially resembles the concentric disks of Delaunay's paintings, it is specific verbal components, visually "highlighted," that allow one to concretize that structure as a representation of Paris as a communications center with the Eiffel Tower at its core. Thus, although the visual autonomy of the structure persists, the visual and verbal are inextricably linked and mutually reinforcing here as a specific representation. In this way Apollinaire's calligram distinguishes itself from certain futurist poems to which it has been compared, poems whose verbographic inter-connections are only incidental. [99]

Like a cubo-futurist painting, "Lettre-Océan" presents two faces of the metropolis simultaneously: as a receptor of in-coming

---

[99] See Willard Bohn's study comparing "Lettre-Océan" with Futurist Carlo Carrà's collage-poem "Festa Patriottica," which uses a similar concentric design incorporating political slogans cut and pasted from newspapers. "Circular Poem-Paintings by Apollinaire and Carrà" in *Comparative Literature* 31:3 (Summer 1979).

information, a hub of global communications; and as a beacon of the future, a technological and cultural transmitter of the new. In the poem's grand design, Apollinaire seems to identify himself almost completely with modern technological (and political) hegemony. The conversation and collage components of the poem accommodate themselves quite well to the overall schema, which must be read as a semiotic product of the modern social formation. Even the facsimile collage of his brother's postcard from Mexico–although suggestive of a "bygone" mode of communication at a particular instance of the social formation–makes reference, like the wireless, to global distances being traversed by means of a vast communications network that represents a seemingly benign outgrowth of European and American expansion (note the two U.S. cents required for postage). In this respect, it is interesting that the various collage elements–the postage stamp and the postcard–are both "simulated." They are not actual postage stamps and postcards (which would make the poem, like Carrà's "Festa Patriottica," a unique plastic work intended primarily for exhibition, not reproduction), but calculated substitutions provided through the medium of print. [100] By avoiding de facto plasticity here, in refusing to adulterate the printed surface with any unique, physical collage component, the poet never actually crosses the line between poetry and painting and greatly facilitates the mediation of his seemingly "found" fragments to his overall, totalizing design. By virtue of this assumption of totality, even the most errant collage components, the most glaring verbal discontinuities, are visually and poetically recuperated to an enterprise of globalization through mechanical and electronic reproduction.

Nevertheless, these "simulations"–because of their ambiguous formal qualities–hint at deeper, subversive desires that the overall visual design would otherwise repress. This desire manifests itself in two ways: 1. in the personal, sometimes lyrical, asides that, under technological pressure, resign themselves to a status of ideological irrelevance and ineffectuality in contrast with the new; and 2. in the incidental allusions to political upheavals and popular attitudes that

---

[100] In a letter to André Billy, Apollinaire described this use of the print medium as follows: "Quant aux *Calligrammes*, ils sont une précision typographique à l'époque où la typographie termine brillamment sa carrière, à l'aurore des moyens nouveaux de reproduction que sont le cinéma et le phonographe." Quoted in Denis Bordat's *Apollinaire* (Paris: Hachette, 1983), p. 109.

connotatively exist, as it were, in the shadow of new denotations. In both of these categories, instances of compliance and non-compliance with the poem's otherwise totalizing vision can be detected. For example, in the line, "de vos jardins fleuris fermez les portes" (Shut the gates of your flowering gardens) (*C*, pp. 58-65), Apollinaire implies a resolute turning away from the past, yet with a symbolist flourish that betrays the real nostalgia undercutting such resolutions. "Tu ne connaîtras jamais bien les Mayas" (You will never really know the Mayas) similarly indicates an irrevocable distance between the past and present, yet the typographic enlargement of "Mayas" mysteriously links that culture with the poem's overall design and the modernity it implies.

While a network of global communications would seem to facilitate expressions of popular resistance to dominant ideologies, it also has a tendency–in the spirit of facilitation–to process such expressions for rapid, mass consumption–with a view toward manufacturing consensus. In those instances where the language evokes popular speech or alludes to civil disturbances, Apollinaire shies away from overt political commentary in favor of hackneyed slogans, slang, and sexual innuendo: "Vive le Roy," "Vive la République," "Evviva il Papa," "A bas la calotte" (Down with priests), "Hou le croquant" (Boo the peasant), "et comment j'ai brulé le dur avec ma gerce" (and how I rode hard with my sweet), "non si vous avez une moustache" (not if you have a mustache). (*C*, pp. 55-56 and 381) A more radical politics enters the circuit of ideologies in the poem only as a kind of threat, an even greater menace to the personal, it would seem, than the ubiquity of modern technology. Two lines, "Gens de mauvaise mine sur le quai à la Vera Cruz" (Seedy-looking people on the pier at Vera Cruz) and "Tout est calme ici et nous sommes dans l'attente des événements" (Everything is quiet here and we are awaiting events) (*C*, pp. 58-65), allude to the fact that Apollinaire's brother was in Mexico during a civil war. A threatening, criminal element lurks around the harbor of Vera Cruz where Albert seems to be located and his postcard, or Apollinaire's use of it, leaves one in total suspense. In light of these allusions, the "tremblement de terre" on the second page takes on political overtones that would seem to challenge the world order the poem otherwise celebrates.

Thus, at the same time that the accidental elements contribute and fortify a dominant structure that is visually concretized in the poem, they also assert a concomitant autonomy of their own in simultaneous contrast, as it were, to an otherwise closed system. The structure adds depth and significance to the merely fortuitous, as the fortuitous opens up the structure to its own provisionality. In achieving this balancing act between chance and necessity, Apollinaire carefully synthesizes a number of strategies drawn from experiments in the plastic arts. "Lettre-Océan" represents the culmination of his own ambitions for a poetry that would display plastic virtues yet–as the synthesis of poetry and art–also transcend the plastic itself to become a kind of multi-media *gesamkunstwerk* for the Twentieth Century. None of the calligrammatic experiments undertaken after "Lettre-Océan" were as ambitious or encompassing, confining themselves to specific strategies of a representational, diagrammatic, or collagist nature by turns, rather than synthesizing them in one, global statement. This falling away from the ideological challenges of plasticity becomes, in the course of the Twentieth Century, characteristic of a certain strain of avant-garde poetry whose representatives ultimately disallow themselves any total submersion in a plastic poetics (unlike, say, the Concrete Poets of the post-war period). Instead, experiments in the plastic arts are seen as a way of modulating, invigorating, and distinguishing their personal inflection of a more general, romantico-symbolist tradition with which they have an ironic relationship.

CHAPTER II

PIERRE REVERDY

W HEN André Breton incorporated Pierre Reverdy's now famous definition of the image into the first *Manifeste du surréalisme* (1924), he credited an insight to the older poet that actually had a long history. It is perhaps to Breton's own credit that he
deferred to another where so many had conveniently reiterated an
ancient idea about the creation of images as if it were an original insight. Certainly each restatement constituted a new version, but the
central concept remained very much the same as a formula for novelty. The creative juxtaposition of different elements is integral to
the production of poetic surprise, which had become a requirement
in the wake of Baudelairean and Apollinairean statements concerning its poetic necessity. Surprise, or what Walter Benjamin called
shock, set the stage for explicit theorizing about the mechanics of
shock-production in poetry, and it was in this context that Reverdian image theory distinguished itself as a modern articulation (influenced by Lautréamont's famous example [1]) of ideas propounded
somewhat differently, at different times, by Samuel Johnson [2] and
Edmund Burke. [3] Nor was Reverdy unique in his own time for mak-

---

[1] "Il est beau . . . comme la rencontre fortuite sur une table de dissection d'une
machine à coudre et d'un parapluie!" Comte de Lautréamont (Isidore Ducasse),
Oeuvres complètes: Les Chants de Maldoror, Lettres, Poésies I et II (Paris: Éditions
Gallimard, 1973), pp. 233-234.
[2] In describing the work of the English "metaphysical poets," Johnson wrote:
"the most heterogeneous ideas are yoked by violence together." Quoted in T. S.
Eliot, "The Metaphysical Poets" in *Selected Prose of T.S. Eliot*, ed. Frank Kermode
(New York: Harcourt, Brace, Jovanovich, 1975), p. 60.
[3] Describing the sublime poetic image in *Enquiry into the Sublime and the
Beautiful*, Burke writes: "w. in the infinite variety of natural combinations we must
expect to find the qualities of things the most remote imaginable from each other

ing succinct, repeated pronouncements on the subject. Indeed, Filippo Marinetti had issued similar statements about analogy just a decade before in his "Technical Manifesto of Futurist Literature." As he wrote: "analogy is nothing more than the deep love that assembles distant, seemingly diverse and hostile things." [4] It seems possible that recognition of this fact compelled Breton to attribute the definition to Reverdy alone as a way of dissociating his own ideas of automatism from any appearance of indebtedness to Italian Futurism, with its celebration of technology and war in ways that were inimical to surrealist aims.

AUTONOMY AND COMMUNICATION: REVERDIAN POETICS AND SYNTHETIC CUBISM

Whatever Reverdy's own indebtedness to Futurism, a striking divergence of *régime* impresses the reader of his essay "L'Image" (1917), where the poet writes: "L'image est une création pure de l'esprit. Elle ne peut naître d'une comparaison mais du rapprochement de deux réalités plus ou moin éloignées . . ." (The image is a pure creation of the mind. It springs not from a comparison but from the bringing together of two, more or less distant realities . . .). [5] No mention of a deep love that assembles hostile things, the joy of sowing discord. Reverdy's rhetoric is purified of futurist passion and provocation; instead, he speaks simply and calmly of rapprochement and intellect and he limits his variables to two. It is a postwar definition of analogy in which the violence of juxtaposition has subsided or become invisible, and the diversity of elements has simply disappeared. Marinetti's "love" was like an electrical jolt, the delirious simultaneism of excitable people in a crowd at a dance hall, in a theatre, in a riot. Naturally, it was in the sphere of performance, spectacle, and arguably, war, that the Futurists excelled. Reverdy's

---

united in the same object." Quoted in W. J. T. Mitchell, *Iconology: Image, Text, Ideology* (Chicago: University of Chicago, 1986), p. 128.

   [4] F. T. Marinetti, "Technical Manifesto of Futurist Literature" in *Marinetti: Selected Writings*, trans. R. W. Flint and Arthur A. Coppotelli (New York: Farrar, Straus & Giroux, 1972), p. 85.

   [5] Pierre Reverdy, "L'Image" in *Nord-Sud, Self Defence et Autres Écrits sur l'Art et la Poésie (1917-1926)* (Paris: Flammarion, 1975), p. 73. All parenthetical or indented translations of Reverdy's prose or poetry are my own, unless otherwise noted.

definition, on the contrary, was conceived in Paris during the war and post-war years of the late nineteen teens, when other effects of war could be seen. A general tone of austerity characterizes his writings just as an eerie stillness seems to pervade his poems, which could be analogized as the *natures mortes* of a de-populated world.

A similar distinction can be made between Reverdian and Apollinairean poetics. Apollinaire's flirtation with Futurism and totalizing vision of modernity caused him to formulate a poetics of technological diversification that was equally theatrical in its attempt to combine artistic and literary media, among others, and which culminated, as we have seen, in the invention of the calligram. Despite the anti-symbolist, pro-plastic nature of his most radical innovations, Apollinaire retained a persistently hierarchizing attitude toward the different arts–only, it was the painters, not the composers, that he saw as the poets' chief competitors in creating a universal, transcendent art. His intense desire to accede to some higher, yet inherently poeticizing art form could not be realized unless the poets assimilated and surpassed the discoveries of the painters. Ironically, it was through the use of combinatory procedures, the plastic mixing of media, that the miraculous production of an all-encompassing mode of expression would be forged under the "inhuman," truth-seeking flame of Apollinairean inspiration or *esprit nouveau*. [6] Yet this new expressiveness would circumvent the entire anecdotal apparatus of representation. The very expression of Apollinaire's new spirit in poetry would be plastically realized at the same time, a virtual thing-in-itself requiring, presumably, no explanatory mediation.

Reverdy, too, promoted the concept of a poem being its own justification, a thing in itself that rivaled, not represented reality. Yet this existential autonomy could not, in conformity with his attitude, be achieved through borrowing elements or attributes from another art. For Reverdy, a true poem was a pure creation of the

---

[6] This concept is described as a kind of "spirit of initiative" in the manner of modern scientists. Artists creating in the new spirit accept everything, especially "surprise," in their search for imaginative truth. Such a search involves experimentation and mixing media, and Apollinaire explicitly links the task of the poets with, among other things, an expanded awareness of typographical possibilities. See Apollinaire, "The New Spirit and the Poets" (1918) in *Selected Writings of Guillaume Apollinaire*, trans. Roger Shattuck (New York: New Directions, 1948), pp. 227-237.

mind, as was a true painting, and both pointed the way toward the
fundamentals of creativity; any reciprocity of means or flagrant imitation of another art could only provide "a facile and dangerous appearance of novelty." [7] Apollinaire's attempt to create a plastic poetry that both exploited and dissimulated visual space was strongly
disapproved of by Reverdy who saw the calligrams as regrettable
"mélanges impurs." [8]

The subtle paradox of Reverdy's attitude is the fact that despite
defining the poetic image as a "bringing together of distant realities," the actual mixing of media indulged in by Apollinaire in his
poèmes tableaux went beyond the bounds of what Reverdy considered sustainable poetic invention. Such high-risk experimentation
in the spirit of the antitradition futuriste could only result in accidents, impurity, and general confusion of the sort known as conventional communication, the randomness and multiplicity of everyday
languages that the Symbolists disesteemed. Thus, in the more traditional spirit of Baudelaire's correspondences, Reverdy's rapports between distant realities had certain innate limitations as a precondition of their rightness, appropriateness. The ambiguity of Reverdy's
definition of the image emerges when he states: "Plus les rapports
des deux réalités rapprochées seront lointains et justes, plus l'image
sera forte–plus elle aura de puissance émotive et de réalité poétique." (The more distant and sound the two reconciled realities
are, the stronger the image will be, the more emotive power and poetic reality it will have.) [9] A certain adequacy or proximity of elements is prescribed through the word juste against the possibility of
over-interpreting lointain. The distant elements must be indigenous
to the poetic means, thus assuring not only the linguistic base of the
poetic product, but the suitability of the elements for a new criteria
of selection or "style"–i.e., the way a poem produces a certain aesthetic emotion (or surprise). In a sense, then, the distant elements
were required to imply or refer to each other by virtue of an understood similitude or aesthetic adequacy. Thus, Reverdy tacitly observed the borders between expressive technologies established by
Baudelaire whom he revered as the creator of pure poetry by rid-

---

[7] Reverdy, "Sur le cubisme" in Nord-Sud, p. 16.
[8] Étienne-Alain Hubert, "Pierre Reverdy et la 'poésie plastique' de son temps"
in Europe: Revue littéraire mensuelle: Cubisme et littérature. Nos. 638-641 (June-
July 1982), p. 115.
[9] "L'Image," Nord-Sud, p. 73.

ding it of "didacticism, passion, morality, and truth" [10]–those more flagrant assertions of the anecdotal.

Yet one must distinguish Reverdian poetics from those of the Symbolists in general, whom he accused of a damaging tendency toward idealism (of emphasizing the abstract over the concrete, the extraordinary over the ordinary) in their works and of failing in their initiatives insofar as "ils n'extériorisèrent jamais qu'un sentiment momentané et nous voulons, avec la connaissance de tous les sentiments, comme éléments, créer une émotion neuve et purement poétique" (they only ever exteriorize momentous feelings, and we want, in using all sentiments as elements, to create a new and purely poetic emotion); he adds, however, that "ils ouvrirent cependant une ère nouvelle dont, chose curieuse, les peintres furent les premiers à profiter" (they opened up, however, a new era from which the painters, curiously, were the first to profit). [11]

Curious indeed that the road to pure poetry should first be traveled by painters who displayed a more democratic inclusiveness (apropos of the sentiments) than their literary predecessors whose own "momentous sentiments" were now to be excluded from the new democracy of feeling. We begin to see Reverdy's ambiguous relation to painting, which he refuses to imitate through any expansive appropriation of means, yet which he emulates for its own expanded applications of other means, or "elements"–which seem more conducive of producing the required poetic emotions of the new style. The irony of Reverdy's relation to painting is very much a paradigm of the irony already noted in his definition of the image: in both he reconciles elements of sufficient distance to create surprise, true novelty, but shuns radical appropriations of the futuristic stamp that tend to break down the categories he is enlarging and that affirm the random, *hazardous* adventure of aestheticizing life. Indeed, for Reverdy, some categories are irreconcilable: "Deux réalités contraires ne se rapprochent pas. Elles s'opposent" (Two contrary realities cannot be reconciled. They oppose each other); [12] they produce not an image but a fantasy, a chimera. Such experiments threaten the identity of the poetic object, and it is this objective in-

---

[10] Robert W. Greene, *The Poetic Theory of Pierre Reverdy* in *University of California Publications in Modern Philology*, Vol. 82 (Berkeley: University of California, 1967), pp. 1, 61, 63.

[11] Reverdy, "Essai d'esthétique littéraire," in *Nord-Sud*, p. 41.

[12] "L'Image" in *Nord-Sud*, p. 73.

tegrity that obsesses Reverdy and roots him firmly in late cubist aesthetics, and not in the surrealist tradition, the juxtapositional techniques of which seem motivated by a metaphorical impulse toward
the marvelous, the Bretonian "spark" of recognition that only fully
occurs in the unconscious.

According to Edward Fry, Reverdy sought a general principle of
art and found it first in painting: "L'auteur cherche à établir ici un
principe esthétique général qui, bien que fondé sur sa compréhen-
sion de la peinture cubiste, peut se rapporter également à la littérature" (The author tries to establish a general aesthetic principle
here that, although based on his understanding of cubist painting,
can be applied equally to literature). [13] But he later came to resent
being called a "cubist" poet, preferring that his work not be "sad-
dled with a label from another art" [14] as increasing numbers of
French scholars began doing before the advent of World War II.
Reverdy's pique, however, should not prevent one from recognizing
his debt to cubist theory and practice. As Mortimer Guiney has
written, cubist painting and so-called cubist poetry do not reflect
each other, but correspond via underlying laws and filiations. [15]
When works in the different arts participate in what Reverdy considered the fundamental principles of creation, they clearly emerge
as parallel, almost twin procedures for the poet.

On the face of it, there would seem to be an obvious affinity
here with the classical notion of *ut pictura poesis* in which the sister
arts of painting and poetry mutually invoke each other's alternative
realities as if by virtue of the physical proximity of their respective
organs of perception, but which remain operatively irreducible to
each other's media. Hence, the poem that is like a talking picture
continues, nevertheless, to be a poem and would never be confused
with a picture the way a calligram might be. Yet this mutual invocation of classical literature and painting consists both in making explicit comparisons between them and in maintaining the mimetic
impulse common to both arts, i.e., either as the descriptive representation of events or as the illusionistic reproduction of appearance. But these concerns are very far from the principles advocated

---

[13] Edward Fry quoted in *Cubisme et littérature* by Mortimer Guiney (Geneva:
Librairie de l'Université, Georg et Cie., S.A., 1972), p. 76.

[14] Michel Decaudin and Étienne-Alain Hubert, "Petite Histoire d'une appellation: 'Cubisme littéraire'" in *Europe*, p. 18.

[15] Guiney, p. 3.

by Reverdy. Both he and the Cubists share a fundamentally Platonic distrust of that mimetic impulse, whether as literary anecdotalism or visual illusionism. The correspondences among the various elements that make up a "true" work of art or poetry are by no means intended to fool the senses by conforming with the logic of phenomena-imitation, any more than they are intended to yoke together radically inconsistent elements to produce fantastical chimeras. Essentially, Reverdy and the Cubists believed that conventional reality as well as fantasy proceeded from the same mania for illusionism.[16]

Nevertheless, the illusionistic phenomena of so-called everyday reality still have a place in their aesthetic systems. Indeed in painting, the program depends on making those phenomena more intellectually consistent with the picture plane by reconciling illusions of volumetric depth with literal flatness. As E. H. Gombrich stated in *Art and Illusion*, the novelty of Cubism was in shaking up the consistency of illusionistic data through literalizing, on the surface of the picture plane, the unseen aspects of represented objects as a way of making up for the shortcomings of human vision.[17] Thus Cubism was realist in a literal way, but never literally realist in any naturalistic way. It was a realism premised not upon the workings of nature and its appearance, but on the workings of the human mind and its knowledge of nature (though Reverdy still assumes the noumenal reality of mental processes). From this standpoint, nature involved a continuing intellectual supplement that both compensated for and competed with (some might argue produced) natural appearances. Thus one can see how the critical work of anti-naturalism and anti-illusionism vied with and finally overwhelmed the idea of the natural through the production of competing human realities. As we shall see, Reverdy's poetry involved a parallel attempt at shaking up logical, narratological, and grammatical conventions in poetry by condensing and overlapping fundamental linguistic "elements" (or perspectives) in a new grammar of poetic construction.

In one of his earliest writings in *Nord-Sud*, the literary magazine he edited from 1917 to 1918, Reverdy elaborated a theory of cubist painting that would provide the foundation of his own poetics. "On

---

[16] As a painterly example of the latter, consider the fantastic, yet highly illusionistic art of Salvador Dalí.

[17] E. H. Gombrich, *Art and Illusion* (New York: Pantheon, 1961), pp. 281-282.

Cubism" immediately distinguishes between representational and presentational art, confirming in the process that cubist painting –though a plastic art–was indeed an art of presentation or "creation," according to his terms, and not of reproduction or interpretation. [18] Visual perspective is disparaged for being a technique of representing the visual appearances of objects; in dispensing with a unified perspective, Cubism employs objects exclusively as elements of an aesthetic construct: "Les objets n'entrant plus que comme élément, on comprendra qu'il ne s'agit pas d'en donner l'aspect, mais d'en dégager pour servir au tableau, ce qui est éternel et constant (par exemple la forme ronde d'un verre, etc.) et d'exclure le reste." (With objects entering only as elements, one understands that it is not a question of presenting their appearance, but of releasing from them–in order to serve the picture–what is eternal and constant (for example, the round form of a glass, etc.) and to exclude the rest.) [19] The conceptual and presumably "eternal" aspects of objects are translated into strictly aesthetic elements ("objects re-formed and conceived by the mind") [20] in visual and dimensional conformity with the flatness of the picture plane, which becomes the criterion of their existence for the artist:

> . . . l'on crée des oeuvres qui, en se détachant de la vie, y rentrent parce qu'elles ont une existence propre, en dehors de l'évocation ou de la reproduction des choses de la vie. Par là, l'Art d'aujourd'hui est un art de grande réalité. Mais il faut entendre réalité artistique et non réalisme (. . .); c'est le genre qui nous est le plus opposé.

> (One creates works that, in detaching themselves from life, return to it because they have their own existence outside of any evocation or reproduction of the things of life. In this way, the art of today is an art of great reality. But it must be understood as artistic reality and not realism [an art of imitation]; this is the style that is most opposed to ours.) [21]

Thus Cubism is opposed to realism and yet constitutes a discrete form of realism that exists alongside or in competition with it.

---

[18] "Sur le cubisme" in *Nord-Sud*, p. 17.
[19] *Ibid.*, p. 19.
[20] Reverdy, "Le Cubisme, poésie plastique" in *Nord-Sud*, p. 145.
[21] "Sur le cubisme" in *Nord-Sud*, p. 20.

In formulating a theory of Cubism, Reverdy brings two presumably distant realities together, aestheticism and realism, which, in the end, seem rather to be generic supplements of each other and not opposed at all, despite his claims to the contrary. What Cubism does is dissociate itself from the narrative or illusionistic dimension of art. It separates itself from the narrative or literary impurities of academic, realist, or impressionist painting in order to become more itself, to rely more exclusively on its basic plasticity, its ontogeny as an assemblage of painted elements, of poetic phrases. Reverdy credits Picasso with this insight:

> C'est que Picasso, depuis ses débuts jusqu'à sa toute dernière époque, . . . s'est toujours efforcé vers un art de conception réaliste–non pas . . . chargé de littérature et toujours d'une idéologie du dernier ordre–mais un art réellement plastique, soucieux de la réalité des objets jusqu'à leur *matière* [italics mine], en dehors de tous les charmes, de tous les pièges, de toutes les illusions et apparences trompeuses de l'atmosphère. Un art matérialiste, d'un temps où la science, en expliquant tant de mystères, en les alignant au degré de phénomènes, ne permettait plus à des artistes préoccupés d'un idéal solide et sain et non pas nébuleux, de se perdre dans les nuages tendres et dangereux qu'avait formé l'impressionisme.

> (It is because Picasso, since his appearance up to now, was always striving toward an art of a realist conception–not burdened by literature and an ideology of the lowest order–but a truly plastic art, anxious for the reality of objects with respect to their *materials*, outside of any charms or snares, any illusions or deceptive atmospheric appearances. A materialist art of an age when science, in explaining so many mysteries, in aligning them with ordinary phenomena, no longer permitted artists preoccupied with a solid and sound–not nebulous–ideal, to lose themselves in the fluffy, treacherous clouds formed by Impressionism.) [22]

Thus the conceptualism motivating the cubist revolution is hardly distinguishable, according to Reverdy's formulation, from the materialism of its plastic means. The new realism is a form of competitive material proliferation of man-made objects that exteri-

---

[22] Reverdy, "Pablo Picasso et son oeuvre" in *Nord-Sud*, p. 190.

orize an inner reality, an eternal reality of creation. Reverdy does not question the inner reality he proposes—perhaps not surprising for a convert to Catholicism who lived much of his later life at a monastery.

It was Juan Gris who first elaborated this new, materialist aestheticism, when he distinguished between analytic and synthetic Cubism, the early and late phases of a plastic investigation that began by distorting perceived objects to get at their essence and gradually arrived at the creation of "incomparable objects" that vied with reality.[23] Every reader of modern art history knows the story of how Gris took his paintings out of the studio and into the woods to see how they measured up to "reality." Having arrived somewhat late on the scene, he clearly saw his own work as the quintessence of the synthetic phase. Gris acknowledges the importance of Picasso and Braque in undertaking the "heroic" work of identifying and seizing upon the more stable properties of objects of representation and recognizing their compatibility with the compositional prerogatives of painting. As a consequence, Gris was in a position to codify this procedure as a strictly compositional method through which the painter began with an abstract, proportional system for organizing the picture plane and moved toward greater object-particularization in the process. If Picasso and Braque began with the object and modulated it in accordance with compositional requirements, Gris began with an idea of compositional proportions and gradually moved toward identifying its elements as items existing in everyday bourgeois reality. According to Gris, if reality is usually represented pictorially, "[his] method of work is exactly the opposite . . .":

> It is not picture X that manages to correspond with my subject, but subject X that manages to correspond with my picture.
>
> I call this method a deductive method because the pictorial relationships between the colored figures suggest to me certain private relationships between the elements of an imaginary reality. The mathematics of picture-making lead me to the physics of representation. The quality or the dimensions of a form or a color suggest to me the appellation or the adjective for an object. Hence, I never know in advance the appearance of the object represented. If I particularize pictorial relationships to the point

---

[23] John Golding, *Cubism: A History and Analysis (1907-1914)* (Boston: Boston Book and Art Shop, 1968), p. 114.

of representing objects, it is in order that the spectator shall not do so for himself, and in order to prevent the combination of colored forms suggesting to him a reality that I have not intended. [24]

Gris has called his method "classical," and it is no accident that his work was associated with the painters of the *Section d'or* (golden mean). Yet Gris' classicism is not of the Platonizing kind, moving out from appearances and illusion to the light of abstract truth; Gris' classicism, as we see, is more neoplatonic or gnosticizing, beginning with a hypostatized system and gradually descending through levels of intellectual mediation or compromise to a point of greater and greater definition, pulled as if by a love of the particular. As Gris himself has said in turning around a statement of Braque's: "J'aime l'émotion qui corrige la règle" (I like the emotion that corrects the rule). [25] In this way, pictures and picture-making become a mode of concretizing the absolute, humanizing the abstract, and externalizing the self to ensure a measure of communication. [26] What Gris' work communicates is a perfective doxology of painterly construction, integral works that perfectly fulfill the conceptual and compositional dilemmas that first gave rise to them in the same way that tools perfectly fulfill a particular function. Furthermore, it communicates as a "novel" artistic production that nevertheless objectifies time-honored, "classical," or institutional categories of art. There is limited critical communication between the categories of art and the world. There is an integral "juxtapositionism" taking place here where a protective force field or electromagnetic zone holds art and life together and apart at the same time. The futurist impulse to break down this zone has been abandoned, and a similar surrealist impulse is held in abeyance.

This effect is nowhere better demonstrated than in comparing Picasso's and Braque's revolutionary use of collage with Gris' own preference for *papier collé*. The breakdown of institutional categories of art and life that was threatened by the use of collage–i.e., because collage introduced heterogeneous, non-art matter to the

---

[24] Juan Gris, "Writings" in Daniel-Henry Kahnweiler, *Juan Gris: His Life and Work*, trans. Douglas Cooper (New York: Curt Valentin, 1947), p. 138.

[25] Georges Braque, quoted by Mortimer Guiney, *La Poésie de Pierre Reverdy* (Geneva: Librairie de l'Université, Georg & Cie., S.A., 1966), p. 70.

[26] Christopher Gray, *Cubist Aesthetic Theories* (Baltimore: Johns Hopkins, 1953), pp. 130-132.

field of the aesthetic and insinuated a non-exclusive material basis for all formal or semiotic constructs–was gradually arrested as these heterogeneous contaminants were modulated or refined to become mere technical innovations, pictorially adaptive procedures. Colored paper, cut and sized to fit the dimensions and shapes of a predetermined compositional arrangement, was a more aesthetically amenable operation than appending pieces of the daily newspaper in a spirit of graffitism. As William Rubin has noted, *papier collé* affirms the unity of the medium, but collage involves a category-threatening mélange of genres, a form of *passage* between entities. [27]

If one begins with his theoretical statements about poetry, Reverdy's own method could be construed as proceeding from general poetic principles to particular works, in basic conformity with Gris' own deductive method. Yet he has also written that aesthetic theory usually summarizes, retrospectively, a painstaking process of stylistic development for the poet; [28] therefore, a synergism of personal, historical, literary, and in this case, painterly influences and prototypes would need to be investigated. In either case, Reverdy's theoretical claims for his poetry are the same ones that Gris makes for his paintings: "Créer l'oeuvre d'art qui ait sa vie indépendante, sa réalité et qui soit son propre but, nous paraît plus élevé que n'importe quelle interprétation fantaisiste de la vie réelle." (To create the work of art that has its independent life, its reality, and that is its own aim, seems to us more elevated than no matter what fantastical interpretation of real life). [29] Furthermore, Reverdy also suggested that his actual writing process was not unlike Gris', insofar as the poems also began with an idea of structure–the purest, almost wordless verbal structure, as it were–and only gradually revealed more concrete, signifying aspects of itself by reference to ob-

---

[27] William Rubin, *Picasso and Braque: Pioneering Cubism* (New York: Museum of Modern Art, 1989), p. 36.
[28] Robert Greene has summarized Reverdy's position as it was first elaborated in "L'Esthétique et l'esprit" in *L'Esprit nouveau*, No. 6 (mars 1921), pp. 667-674: "[Reverdy] does not feel . . . that theory matters ultimately as much as works (p. 670). He makes a definite distinction between theory and aesthetic, theory clearly being prior to specific works of art [i.e., poetry and painting] (and thus remaining essentially extrinsic to art), and aesthetic being totally derived from works (pp. 671-672). His distinction is significant because it shows his basic disdain for the a priori theorizing of manifestoes . . . and, implicitly, his approval and even encouragement of a posteriori theorizing." In Greene, p. 39.
[29] "Essai d'esthétique littéraire" in *Nord-Sud*, p. 41.

jects in everyday reality, objects not unlike those suggested in paintings by Juan Gris: a table, a writing or drawing instrument, parts of the body, a bottle of some kind, a newspaper, an open window, the particularization to which both men gradually succumbed after beginning with an abstract premise of purity, mathematics, pure visual or verbal speculation. As Reverdy wrote in *Self-Defense*: "La logique d'une oeuvre d'art c'est sa structure" (The logic of a work of art is its structure).[30]

We have already seen how forms and colors suggested to Gris "the appellation or the adjective for an object," yet it is difficult to imagine a pure syntax without words, or words without a particular linguistic matrix–such as French–and at least the aura of correspondence to material things (without this correspondence, language becomes pure logic or mathematics). Yet Reverdy's poetics seems to hinge on such an idea of syntax, free of specific appellations, adjectives, or relative pronouns (although pronouns and prepositions seem crucial to it). One must try to imagine a poetic process that begins with an abstract system of verbal relations, as yet unspoken, that only gradually cedes to a convenient, second stage in which a vital compromise with communication has been made through articulating the coordinates of emergent images by ambiguous reference to objects and object-relations. Before taking this leap of faith, one may ask whether syntax, as a method of disposing words, wouldn't demand real words from the outset as the only viable way of elaborating the full range and complexity of the method it constitutes. From this point of view, it would seem that the purest syntax would also be the most cultivated and most encompassing deployment of words, figures, and images. But Reverdy rejects this complexity as proceeding from a verbal art of imitation, not of creation, which relies on a "fundamental syntax." It is a very simple, almost pre-linguistic syntax Reverdy wants to evoke through a paratactic procedure by which the meaning of words themselves is called into question, as if to allow them to function more abstractly–as shapes, forms, colors, and lines do:

> Si la syntaxe est l'art de disposer les mots, selon leur valeur et
> leur rôle, pour en faire des phrases–restant logique avec nous-
> mêmes–nous dirons qu'on n'imite pas plus la syntaxe de quel-

---

[30] Guiney, *La Poésie de Pierre Reverdy*, p. 37.

qu'un qu'on n'imite son art–à condition de s'entendre sur la signification de ce dernier mot et ne pas le vouloir faire synonyme
d'imitation. Aujourd'hui il semble que, pour nos habituels critiques, syntaxe doive supposer immanquablement complication
et alambiquage. Alors tout dépend des modèles qu'on a pris.
Nous conseillons ceux qui nous ont donné l'exemple de la sim-
plicité.

Pour un art nouveau, une syntaxe nouvelle était à prévoir;
elle devait fatalement venir mettre dans le nouvel ordre les mots
dont nous devions nous servir. *Les mots eux-mêmes devaient être
différents. . . .*

(If syntax is the art of disposing words, according to their value
and their role, in order to make sentences of them, we would say,
to be consistent, that one no more imitates the syntax of someone than one imitates his art–provided one understands the significance of this last word and does not read it as synonymous
with imitation. Today it seems that, for our usual critics, syntax
must inevitably assume complication and convolution. Then
everything depends on the models one has chosen. We recom-
mend those who have given us the example of simplicity.

For a new art, a new syntax was to be foreseen; it was fated
to come and put the words we use in new order. *Words themselves had to be different. . . .*) [my italics] [31]

It is through simplifying, condensing, and paring-down language that a fundamental, pre-communicative, pre-conscious syntax will display itself in the poetry of Reverdy. If indeed the poet
cannot evoke an idea of pure verbal structure without, finally, resorting to particular verbs, nouns and adjectives, it is still necessary
to simplify the language as much as possible in order for a purified
syntax to be recognized as the conceptual core of his works, as the
intellectual premise from which individual poems are "deduced."
Furthermore, to the extent that such simplified syntactic elements
(words, phrases, sentences) correspond to physical objects, everyday occurrences, or different human sentiments, those "elements"
themselves are quite ordinary items or "conditions" in a (usually)
urban context. Yet, extracted as they are from the full panoply of
verbal discourse, these ordinary elements acquire a semantic myste-
riousness, which must be investigated.

---

[31] Reverdy, "Syntaxe" in *Nord-Sud*, p. 80.

STILL-LIFE POEMS FROM *LA LUCARNE OVALE, AU SOLEIL DU PLAFOND, POÈMES EN PROSE,* AND *LES ARDOISES DU TOIT*

In his determination to keep the language simple, Reverdy is like a verbal scientist who wants to limit the number and complexity of variables in the working lab of poetry. For instance, the title of his collection *La Lucarne ovale* (1916) is a figure of urban austerity, as if the poet had retired to a little attic chamber in order both to observe the modern world from a remove and to block out the perceptual overload of the metropolitan experience–not to mention the verbal proliferation that conceals (rather than conveys) the conceptual purity of poetry. No sign here of Apollinaire's lyric globetrotting. Reverdy's poems are usually short, and the spaces evoked, quite small. Yet this compression, far from minimizing the poetic effects of his work, reveals an almost atomic potential, the semantic instability of his elements. Simple physical objects and the circumscribed space in between become the referential counterparts to Reverdy's syntactic experiments. In fact, Reverdy's pure syntax often seems to depend on the physical disposition of concrete words between the four borders of the page (this becomes particularly clear in *Les Ardoises du toit* [1918]). Within those borders, the poems virtually elaborate the magnetic aura of words and broken phrases. His study provides a controlled environment for examining the shock of imploded space.

But if the partial contours of objects, spaces, and various human sentiments are traced in the language of the poems, their exact relationships–like the exact syntactic relations among word groups making up the poems–are never discursively articulated in a completed poem of Reverdy. As in the paintings of Juan Gris, the elements of the work acquire a degree of particularization by way of their representative capacity. But this capacity is only partially utilized–at the level of component image terms and not at the level of imagery itself. Thus, also in conformity with Gris' work, no definitive perspective on the assembled elements of the work can be established. As Jean Shroeder–one of Reverdy's first critical biographers in America–explains:

> The terms of Reverdy's images often bear relationships which
> have no given existential meaning or, if they do, the contexts are

constantly changing. If the latter situation prevails, the images overlap with the result that the new context is continuously annulled by that which is about to follow. The perpetual replacement of context brings to mind [. . .] cubist painting in which several visual contexts are superimposed one upon the other by planes oriented in different directions. There is, essentially, no real context because as one experiential impression begins, it is superceded by another such impression resulting from a randomly intersecting plane.[32]

Images overlap, cancel, or double each other, yet, contrary to Shroeder's suggestion, there is nothing random about the process—either in Reverdy's or Gris's work. Furthermore, while entertaining variant syntactic readings, certain poems and paintings reveal degrees of representational particularization and even discursive coherence. This tension between a discursive potential and a calculated semantic density that impedes that potential for the sake of aesthetic purity is illustrated in the poem "Le Sang troublé" from *La Lucarne ovale*:

"Le Sang troublé"

Un trou noir où le vent se rue
Tout tourne en rond
La fenêtre s'éloigne de la glace du fond
–Le vin n'y est pour rien
C'est un paysage sans cadre

Les numéros qui sont dans ma tête commencent à
     Tourner
Et l'allée s'allonge
L'ombre du mur d'en face s'allonge
Jusqu'au plafond

On entend venir quelqu'un qui ne se montre pas
     On entend parler
     On entend rire et on entend pleurer
     Une ombre passé

Les mots qu'on dit derrière le volet sont une menace

---

[32] Jean Shroeder, *Pierre Reverdy* (Boston: Twayne, 1981), p. 62.

(A black hole where the wind flings itself
Everything turns in a circle
The window distances itself from the mirror at the back
–The wine has nothing to do with it
It's a landscape without a frame

The numbers in my head begin
    Turning around
And the lane stretches away
The shadow of the opposite wall stretches out
Up to the ceiling

One hears someone coming who does not appear
    One hears speak
    One hears laugh and one hears weep
    A shadow passes

The words one says behind the shutter are a threat) [33]

The absence of conventional punctuation immediately creates opportunities for syntactical overlap between lines. And although Reverdy limits this potential by varying the length of his lines so that their spatial disposition is more or less self-punctuating, the grammatical subjects of the different statements often coalesce, toning their predicates in a way that establishes interpretive corridors between them, regardless of their sequential relation. The reading of the poem, then, is as much an overall spatial operation as a temporal one.

Reverdy's avoidance of explanatory connectives ensures that we cannot say exactly what the black hole at the beginning of the poem signifies: a hole in a wall? in a bottle? the window mentioned later? The wind turning everything around suggests that the hole is a physical aperture into a room, yet the apparent non-sequitur about the wine not having anything to do with it suggests that, in a way, it does–that the "going in circles" caused by the wind is comparable

---

[33] Reverdy, "Le Sang troublé" from *La Lucarne ovale* in *Plupart du temps, I (1915-1922)* (Paris: Gallimard, 1969), p. 85. All subsequent quotations from the poetry of Pierre Reverdy (except for the text of the unnamed poem incorporated into Juan Gris' painting *Still Life with Poem*) will refer to this text by the abbreviation *PT*.

to drunkenness and that the opening through which the wind blows is a form of mental receptor. The frameless landscape of line five, however, creates an even greater surprise–tactically dissolving the window and the mirror (inexplicably drawing apart in line three) that might have once contained it. The enclosed physical space seems, ironically, to have burst open through a process of mental internalization. Reverdy's ambiguous syntagms establish phenomenological coordinates that are never fully integrated into a set of logical physical relations. The physical space seems at the mercy of an unexplained delirium–the troubled or bad blood (Rimbaldian "mauvais sang"?) of the title.

To the extent that he establishes iconic coordinates, Reverdy delimits a typical cubist space, complete with window, wine bottle, and mirror (Gris himself once used an actual mirror fragment as a collage element neatly fitted into an illusionistic mirror-frame). [34] Furthermore, the perspectives on those objects seem to shift and overlap, resulting in a kind of imaginative doubling or parody of the real. These iconic references continue in the next verse in which numbers–conventional symbols/tools of order and sequence–tumble around in the presumed speaker's mind. Such numbers can be found in many cubist paintings of the synthetic phase, insofar as numerical figures were seen as having a pure, unmediated flatness that required no illusionistic reconciliation with the picture plane, while at the symbolic level they squared easily with the cubist enthusiasm for mathematics. It is important to note that, despite references to numbers tumbling out of their conventional positions, no parallel typographic turbulence occurs in Reverdy's poems, unlike Apollinaire's calligrams where signs overtly do the things they say (thus exemplifying Nelson Goodman's notion of *exemplification*–in which a work becomes an instance, an expression, of what it represents). [35]

As if to emphasize the tohu-bohu of spatial relations, the next line presents a path (*allée*) and a wall (*mur*) that individually stretch out (*s'allonge*), revealing a dimensional and perspectival ambiguity of the verb *s'allonger*. Second and third dimensions, horizontal and vertical

---

[34] Described in Mark Rosenthal, *Juan Gris* (New York: Abbeville, 1983), p. 29. The painting is called *The Washstand* (1912).

[35] Nelson Goodman, *Languages of Art* (Indianapolis, Indiana: Hackett Publishing, 1988), pp. 51-52.

directions, inside and outside are all encompassed by the semantic applications of the verb, which is startlingly arrested by another surface, the ceiling (*plafond*). Thus, distant conceptual categories and faculties, once commodiously occupying an "ordinary" space, all seem to be getting farther and farther apart the more the poem makes use of their proximity. This paradox finally consumes the "speaker" himself. In the third verse, the personal voice that indirectly identified himself in line six (*ma tête*) dissolves into the French *on*, which can mean both a de-personalized "one" or a multiple "we." The voice has simultaneously assumed the plural first person and singular third person case. An additional third person (*quelqu'un*) is heard speaking, laughing, crying–contradictory actions that suggest his own multiplicity (albeit not in any gendered sense–yet he never appears, a fact that suggests his own insubstantiality. Furthermore, a shadow passes, which may or may not belong to the someone (*quelqu'un*) just mentioned. Yet the phrase itself involves a form of "shadowing" insofar as the noun *ombre* in this particular phrase masks, yet discreetly re-intimates, the more common use of the word *ange*. When one says "un ange passe" in French, it signifies an embarrassing pause in conversation. Such a silence is both reinforced and made ominous through Reverdy's substitution, which anticipates the final line by both masking and "shading" language.

Do these ambiguities "explain" the last line of the poem, that the words spoken behind a shutter are a threat? Does the shutter signify that we, as readers, are situated once again near the room or space we thought we occupied within the imaginative confines of the first verse? If so, we now seem to look in from the street, from the perspective of the someone (*quelqu'un*) who never appeared or the person whose shadow may have passed by. Perhaps we are the ones who caused the "shadow" of an embarrassed silence in the penultimate line. We realize as readers that we too occupy a perspective outside the space of the poem and may ourselves be the object of a threat. Book covers are not unlike the shutters from behind which the putatively menacing words are spoken. There is bad blood all around, and words become a kind of poison if we look for a specific answer. We cannot say where we stand in the poem or what the poem means. Could the title itself be a play on words, such as to say, *sens troublé*? Whatever the case, one must consider the play of elements: how their paratactic arrangement suspends meaning, yet not the meaningful analysis of that suspension.

Still Life with Poem

"Le Sang troublé" provides a useful point of comparison between Reverdy and the Cubists because the poem is not conspicuously motivated by any specific ekphrastic or collaborative endeavor. Yet such collaborations took place between Reverdy and Gris, who together produced an album entitled *Au Soleil du plafond* (1955). Although first published nearly thirty years after the painter's death (1927), the collection represents the belated fruit of a collaborative effort that began in 1915, when Gris used a Reverdy poem as a pseudo-collage element in his famous painting *Still Life with Poem.* [fig. 7] This work provided the inspiration for a projected series of twenty paired lithographs and poems to be called *Entre les 4 murs et sur la table* that Reverdy later changed to the title we have today. Gris completed only eleven of the twenty proposed lithographs before a disagreement resulted in the abandonment of the project. Later, in 1947, Reverdy revised the poems in conformity with his insistence on the autonomy of the separate arts. Only two of the original poems are known, including one ("Moulin à café") that was literally attached as a label to Gris' lithograph, *Coffee Grinder, Cup and Glass on a Table* (1915). The poem that appears in the painting *Still Life with Poem* is actually Gris' *trompe l'oeil* imitation of Reverdy's handwritten poem. The discovery in 1985 of the actual unpublished poem by Reverdy among Gris' papers proved that the artist's rendering was faithful,[36] thus confirming a suspicion on the part of scholars that the original texts were highly responsive to the paintings and not vice versa, as Reverdy's later editions might lead one to believe.[37] The text of the poem follows:

> Se tiendrait-elle mieux sous ton bras ou sur la table? Le goulot dépassait d'une poche et l'argent dans ta main, moins longue que la manche.
> On avait gonflé le tuyau de verre et aspiré l'air.

---

[36] René de Costa, "Juan Gris and Poetry: From Illustration to Creation" in *Art Bulletin*, 71:4 (December 1989), p. 679.

[37] Andrew Rothwell, "Cubism and the Avant-Garde Prose-Poem: Figural Space in Pierre Reverdy's *Au Soleil de plafond"* in *French Studies: A Quarterly Review*, 42:3 (July 1988), p. 302.

Quand celui qu'on attendait entra, les premiers assistants
s'attablèrent. . . . Et la flamme qui luit dans leurs yeux . . . –d'où
leur vient-elle? [38]

(Would it go better under your arm or on the table? The bottleneck sticks out from a pocket and the money in your hand,
less long than the sleeve.
We had inflated the glass stem and inhaled.
When the awaited one entered, the first assistants sat down
at the table.... And the light shining in their eyes . . . –where did
it come from?)

According to René de Costa, who first analyzed the newly discovered text, the poem compares Gris' *Still Life* with Cézanne's
The Card Players (1890-92), which had been exhibited for the first
time in 1911 at the Louvre. Like Cézanne's work, Gris' painting includes some playing cards–schematically rendered to accentuate
their flatness–and some other, more volumetric items that Gris
plays with visually to achieve the required reconciliation with the
picture plane. These objects include the table itself, a bottle, a glass,
and a pipe, all of which are mentioned or evoked in the poem. But
the basis for De Costa's interpretation of the poem as comparing
the two paintings is found in the last line, which concerns the "first
assistants" or "attendants" who seat themselves at the table. [39] De
Costa wrongly asserts that they are the ones for whom we, or someone else, waited, or, in her view, the ones for whom the painting
"waited." Yet the awaited one is singular (*celui*), the assistants, plural; in fact, the assistants, who may or may not be coextensive with
whomever was waiting, were waiting for someone or something besides themselves to enter before they sat down, i.e., before they
could enter the framework of iconic and other formal signs that
help make up Gris' own picture. Although it seems plausible that
the "premiers assistants" refers to Cézanne's card players and, in a
meta-painterly way, the forebears of Gris' own artistic methods
(Picasso and Braque immediately come to mind), the one that
they await in order to participate explicitly (*s'attabler*) in the aesthetic game of the painting (*tableau*), is the poem itself. (In the
aesthetic game of the poem, however, they could also be simply

---

[38] De Costa, p. 679.
[39] *Ibid.*

awaiting the reader before sitting down to complete the imaginary picture of the poem itself.) In a sense, then, the poem refers to the painting before the painting's completion–i.e., before Gris actually incorporated the finished poem itself into the structure of the as yet unfinished painting. It is known that Gris often left pre-determined areas or planes incomplete before adding certain colors or collage items, to complete the overall work and thus achieve a level of definition or particularization according to his representational intentions. [40] In this instance, Gris' particularizing impulse required a specific poem by Reverdy, which in turn was dependent upon the specific method Gris employed in this particular painting.

The close collaboration between the two men is also substantiated in the poem, which art historian Mark Rosenthal has compared to Gris' own structural organization of the painting. In *Still Life with Poem* many represented surfaces and planes that would normally appear to recede into depth from a particular perspective, actually pile up in the picture itself, seeming almost to project forward or spill out of the containing frame. The corner of the table itself illusionistically juts out of a red, frame-like ground. This "piling up of planes," [41] whereby the logic of appearances is thwarted through a visual parataxis of discrete surfaces (tables, cards, bottles, glasses, and pipes), parallels the syntactic piling up of verbal elements, which results in similar contradictions apropos of the physical relations between different referents of the poem–such as the "hand less long than the sleeve," or the glass stem that one "inflates" or "swells" while nevertheless breathing in the air.

But these are general similarities, whose criteria might be satisfied by almost any good cubist painting. More precise correspondences are less obvious, yet they do exist. For instance, although the pocket (*poche*) out of which the bottleneck is sticking in the poem is a coat pocket, the *poche* actually represented in the painting is simply a series of colored planes that conceal all but the cork and mouth of the bottle. (However, this "pocket" is also transparent insofar as Gris shows us the diagrammatic outline of the bottle behind–or against–the black and green facets of the plane.) But it is the tightly compressed middle line of the poem (like a connecting passage or "communicating vessel" between the other, larger parts)

---

[40] Rosenthal, p. 46.
[41] *Ibid.*, p. 77.

that reveals Reverdy's close collaboration in Gris' painting process, as opposed to a more basic, ekphrastic referencing. "On avait gonflé le tuyau de verre et aspiré l'air." To be *gonflé* is to be swollen up or inflated. In the second verse, someone (who?) has swollen or inflated the *tuyau de verre* and has breathed in the air. The literal translation of these words is "glass stem," yet a glass stem cannot be inflated or breathed through. If the idea of inflating or breathing through something is semantically adhered to, one would have to interpret *tuyau de verre* either as glass in the process of being made or "blown," or as a glass tube or pipe of some kind with special physical properties. Gris' painting prompts the latter reading (albeit as a possible allegory of the other), first, through its inclusion of a smoking pipe. One may object that the pipe is made of wood, but one can also say that it is transparent–like glass–insofar as the wooden table surface is seen underneath it, except at the tip of the pipe stem, where it sticks out just beyond the ledge of the table (much as the bottleneck sticks out from the so-called pocket) and is painted gray.

But there are other ways of reading these words with reference to the painting. One will also notice that the glass in the painting has some fluting represented on the cup portion. Interestingly, *tuyau* can also mean "fluting," as on a column or pleated skirt. The rather schematic fluting appears to enlarge the glass in perspective and thus swells its initial capacity. A shadow portion assuming the outlines of a glass has been added to the side; yet this shadow does not shade, but rather increases the size of the original shape, thereby suggesting an enlarged or "inflated" version of the glass. One also notices that the "stem" of the glass is much fatter than the initial size of the glass would require; and if one observes that the reflected light on the stem is inconsistent with one-point perspective, one can infer that these white lines are really the trace of something else, a kind of white shadow outlining the shape of an original stem in graceful conformity with the initial proportions of the glass. The process of enlarging these visible proportions in order to reconcile the glass to the synthetic requirements of Gris' painting is being meta-poetically played upon in Reverdy's poem through a correspondingly complex *jeu de mots*. Furthermore, he grafts the idea of the visually altered drinking glass to that of the pipe by using the two verbs *gonflé* and *aspiré*, to create a most paradoxical synaesthesia of smoking through glass, a glass tube or bottle, which hints again at the idea of glass blowing–the making of glass–which in turn provides an analogue for the making of the poetic and painterly tableau.

Taking this analogue further in terms of the making of the poem itself, one discovers yet another, more literary dimension to the above *jeu de mots* in which *tuyau de verre* can be heard as *tuyau de vers*. Hence, the language of the poem itself becomes a vital passageway through which one breathes after it has been properly expanded, i.e., after the semantic densities of this tightly compressed image have been opened up to create, 1. a connection between the first and last parts of the poem (the "still life" and the "genre scene," as it were), and 2. an aerated passageway into the poem that has been provided for (yet also created by) the reader, who, as a kind of "awaited one," understands the properties of poetic and painterly materials, which begin to "swell" with a kind of life or "come together" (*se rapprochent, s'attablèrent*) as a vibrant tableau whenever such a reader agrees to "ante-up" in the aesthetic game he or she has been invited to take part in. In essence, then, only the imagination can answer the last line of the poem: "Et la flamme qui luit dans leurs yeux ... –d'où leur vient-elle?"

The poem was revised by Reverdy as "Bouteille" (another *tuyau de verre*) in *Au Soleil du plafond* (1955). [42] The edited poem bears only minor resemblance to the original one, which demonstrates, as we have seen, a more open-ended dialogue with the silent discourse of painting (although there can be no doubt that it also stands as a

---

[42] The text of "Bouteille":

> La bouteille au centre de feu, à bout de bras ou sur la table. Dans la forme des mains, dans la source des poches–il y a de l'or et de l'argent–il y a de l'esprit dans la manche. Quand la couleur coule à pleins bords–quand l'air s'embrouille dans les branches. Le coeur va plus loin que les yeux, la flamme renaît de la cendre. Entre le fil qui coule et le trait lumineux les mots n'ont plus de sens.
> On n'a plus besoin des mots pour se comprendre.
>
> (The bottle at the center of fire, at arm's length or on the table. In the form of hands, in the well of pockets–there is gold and silver–there is spirit up the sleeve. When color runs to the very edges–when air gets tangled up in the branches. The heart goes further than the eyes, the flame is reborn in the ashes. Between the running thread and the luminous image, words no longer make sense.
> We no longer need words to be understood.)

In *Au Soleil du plafond et autres poèmes* (Paris: Flammarion, 1980), p. 25.

poem in its own right). In changing the poem, Reverdy seems to have been somewhat over-sensitive to scholarly assertions of being strongly influenced by another art–of being derivative or "imitative" in some sense. As a result, the poet more fully adheres to his theoretical parameters in "Bouteille" by making certain that it, along with the other poems in *Au Soleil du plafond,* simply parallel the concerns of the accompanying lithographs without referring directly to any specific compositional strategy undertaken in them. This attempt to reduce the appearance of indebtedness and to ensure the greater autonomy of his own work in juxtaposition with the work of the deceased Juan Gris (who, by the time of the publication of *Au Soleil du plafond,* was very famous, while his literary counterpart still lived in relative obscurity), seems partly motivated by a continuing sense of inter-artistic rivalry after the painter's death.

Nevertheless, such "parallel" concerns still manage to hold between the two media, as Andrew Rothwell reveals in his own study of *Au Soleil du plafond.* Rothwell convincingly establishes the idea that the surface and edges of a table, conventionally employed as the ground of still life paintings, provides the joint referential boundaries of the poems and lithographs in a way that highlights the formal properties of a work of art or literature. [43] The table provides a referential "framing device" in six of the poems that begin or end with the word "table" and that include other objects typically represented in cubist paintings, such as coffee grinders, pipes, guitars, violins, lamps, and bottles (all of them hollow, "containing" objects, hence, frame-like, passage-like). For Rothwell, the table constitutes "the 'normative' power of mimesis" from which both the poems and paintings attempt to escape through "contradicting" (in Gombrich's sense) either the illusionistic surface or discursive cohesion of presumably "normative" artistic or literary procedures. [44] Thus the contradictions among the signs' various referential functions represent, for Rothwell, the formal abandonment of the mimetic function *per se.* This seems overstated, however, given the obvious utility of referentiality and the semiotic recognitions it makes possible even in conditions of contradiction.

---

[43] In this respect it is worth noting that the original title for the project was "Entre les 4 murs et sur la table." Rothwell, p. 303.

[44] *Ibid.*, pp. 303-304.

More interesting is the fact that, in revising the poem that eventually became "Bouteille," Reverdy combined elements from another poem entitled, "Et maintenant," an approach that says a lot about Reverdy's own poetic techniques that seem to continue the plastic strategy of assemblage employed by Apollinaire in his most innovative works. Indeed, the idea that a poem is largely a calculated combination of prepared elements, increasingly allows Reverdy to treat syntactic components–or lines–as almost plastic resources (but not quite) that can be provisionally stored and recombined in new assemblages until they coalesce with that special aura of surprise that constitutes poetic emotion.

"Traits et figures" and "L'Esprit sort"

An early poem entitled "Traits et figures" from his first published collection *Poèmes en prose* (1915), suggests that such tactics of an almost physical storage, retrieval, and recombination of verbal elements indeed constituted Reverdy's writing technique:

> Une éclaircie avec du bleu dans le ciel; dans la forêt des clairières toutes vertes; mais dans la ville où le dessin nous emprisonne, l'arc de cercle du porche, les carrés des fenêtres, les losanges des toits.
> Des lignes, rien que des lignes, pour la commodité des bâtisses humaines.
> Dans ma tête des lignes, rien que des lignes; si je pouvais y mettre un peu d'ordre seulement.
>
> (A clear patch of blue in the sky; in the forest, clearings, all green; but in the city where design imprisons us, the circular arch of the portico, the right-angled frames of the windows, the ovoids of the roofs.
> Lines, nothing but lines, to accommodate human structures.
> In my head are lines, nothing but lines; if I could only put some order there.) (*PT*, p. 35)

In this little poem, Reverdy uses figures of drawing and architectural design to make a statement about his technique in a way that is ironically disparaging, as if he felt imprisoned by his own poetry. His poetry, he seems to say, is not the kind that is known for its color, clarity, or natural imagery. Reverdy's is an urban poetry–not of color and light, but of line and form. Lines proliferate in the city in all shapes and guises: circles, squares and ovals (reminding one of Cézanne's invocation of the circle, square, and cylinder as the foundations of art). But these forms and systems of human ingenuity have "conveniently" imprisoned humanity itself. In the last line, the human speaker internalizes the external restraints of urban organization. The lines multiply in his head. They have assumed a life all their own, proliferating with an almost natural fecundity. The language reveals the irony of their hold upon the imagination: they are, after all, "nothing but lines"; yet their proliferation creates confusion, chaos, the opposite of everything represented by the imagery of natural light in the first verse. By ending with the express wish of putting some order there in his head where the "lines" are multiplying, the poet punningly states his own objectives in poetry. Indeed, the poem is an example of putting "a little order" there where the lines of poetry beset him, being, as it is, one of the more straightforward among his oeuvre. We realize from the standpoint of poetics that the word "lines" represents a clever foil for Reverdy's notion of artistic elements, either in painting or poetry. They are the syntactic or compositional "units" of the creative process, and they seem to be everywhere. In both cases they have a material density for Reverdy that is peculiarly asphyxiating. Putting them in order is a way of letting in some air or light. On the other hand, there is also the suggestion of an obsessive fixation and reiteration of those lines as revealed by the repetition in "Traits et figures" itself of the line "rien que des lignes." Anyone who has read Reverdy at length will recognize his tendency to take lines from one poem and reuse them in others with no or only minor adjustments. Furthermore, the simplicity of Reverdy's vocabulary often makes the poems sound repetitive, "as if," according to Anthony Rizzuto, "the same poem were being written over and over again." Indeed, this phenomenon prompted Gaëtan Picon to remark that "Chaque poème est le même poème" (each poem is the same poem).[45]

In contrast to the sense of lines imprisoning someone or enclosing a space, holes and windows provide both a kind of ingress for sudden, unaccustomed feelings of drunkenness or hatred (as we

[45] Both quotations in *Style and Theme in Reverdy's "Les Ardoises du toit"* by Anthony Rizzuto (University, Alabama: University of Alabama Press, 1971), p. 131.

have seen in "Le Sang troublé"), as well as escape routes, secret or expedient passages to the exterior in order to evade the oppressive, material weight, it would seem, of modern, commodity culture. For instance, in "L'Esprit sort" (*Poèmes en prose*), Reverdy recreates the stifling ambiance of an overstuffed library and a sense of panic that compels the speaker to scratch a hole in the wall and climb out into the street for fresh air (only to discover more walls, more dust). The same might also be said of the sentimentalized *éclaircies* and *clairières* of "Traits et figures." Space itself is often the apparent goal of some private quest, yet it seems just as often to evade the disembodied voice of the poet/speaker throughout Reverdy's oeuvre, as it does in "L'Esprit sort." For Reverdy, space is materially dependent and acquires a kind of plastic solidity in the same way it does in cubist paintings, where any illusion of open vistas, yawning voids, or empty vessels is thwarted through its own material representation and through the operations of *passage*, as Gombrich has described it.[46]

Reverdy achieves this solidity through a compromise with visual media that comes perilously close to the very kind of *mélange impur* he disparaged in the work of Apollinaire. Only, instead of borrowing plastic strategies directly from the visual arts (such as collage or conspicuous varieties of type) and enjoying them in *flagrante delicto* (as Apollinaire does in his calligrams), Reverdy makes use of the plastic values inherent to print, exploiting free verse's monogamous adherence to the left margin through his own typographic adulterations. The blank spaces between words and phrases become a conspicuous, syntactic element of Reverdy's poetic medium. If words represent the hard data of poetic language, the spaces in between are the visual evidence of formal manipulation, a syntactic strategy of disposing words in new ways and breathing new life–a kind of hermeneutic uncertainty–into everyday communication. As Reverdy himself writes in "Syntaxe":

> ... si on ne veut pas comprendre qu'une disposition typographique nouvelle soit parallèle d'une syntaxe différente et que cette syntaxe soit en rapport avec l'oeuvre nouvelle, qu'on s'en tienne à la très digne incompréhension.

---

[46] Leo Steinberg, "The Polemical Part," in *Art in America* (March/April 1979), p. 121.

(If one does not care to understand that a new typographic disposition is parallel to a different syntax and that this syntax is
connected with the new work, then one is maintaining a most
dignified incomprehension). [47]

Thus, Reverdy resorts to simple word placement to create a typographic analogy for his notion of a primary, abstract poetic structure informing individual works. Yet it is a plastic strategy with
which his poetic medium–via print–has become consistent in modern times. The visual aspect of poetic structure is less a matter of
mixing media, than of being responsive to the visibility, the "naked-
ness" of print. In this way, Reverdy not only reinforces the idea of
structure informing the creation of verbal artifacts, but flaunts the
poem's typographic disposition, its basic plasticity in all its technological sheen (i.e., as type, not as handwriting per certain Apollinairean calligrams), as it both exhibits and engenders a distinctly
modern syntax.

"Façade"

The magnetic aura of Reverdy's words and phrases has been
mentioned, yet the analogy is worth restating here as one considers
how the poet deploys space in his more visually distinctive works,
such as those in Les Ardoises du toit. Clearly, the Mallarméan poetics of Un Coup de dés is partly operative in such poems where the
typographic disposition of the lines is experimentally manipulated.
Yet the space one finds in Un Coup de dés seems infinite, a cosmos
traversed by comet-like phrases with age-old memories; Reverdian
space is more confined, contemporary, a matter of availability within and around the ubiquitous body of print. Reverdian space is being condensed, pressed on all sides as verbal elements and their material referents succumb to an irresistible process of magnetic
attraction. Yet in condensing that space, it almost seems to acquire
mass. It becomes a syntactical substrate through which words and
phrases yield their semiotic gradations. Indeed, the spatial organization of word-groups and the timely distribution of blanks in certain
poems become a visual aid to reading. As Anthony Rizzuto writes

---

[47] "Syntaxe" in Nord-Sud, p. 82.

in his excellent linguistic study of *Les Ardoises du toit*, "The visual arrangement controls the reading process by way of speed, pause, grammatical structures (i.e., subordinate clauses, prepositional phrases, isolated words)." [48]

Rizzuto continues: "Visual verse helps to slow the reader down, to parcel out linguistic-syntactic components in a more deliberate fashion . . . [all of which] corresponds to an analytic vision of the world. . . . The reader is obliged to deal with reality in its details, as a series of brief and separate notations, and not as a grammatical and intellectual synthesis only." [49] To the extent that Reverdy's poetry is analytical, the object of that analysis is not only the world, but language itself, the very tool of that analysis, a maneuver that displays a degree of self-consciousness ironically characteristic of a more "synthetic" mode in Gris' sense of the word. Thus, analysis and synthesis are clearly the complementary features of a process whereby word-groups and the object-relations they evoke are assimilated to the manifest structure of the poem (just as one would have to acknowledge the analytic dimension of Gris' "synthetic" art). Yet those very elements are also subtly, visually alienated from the other elements with which they are poetically coordinated. Space acts as both a medium and barrier of language, as language in turn apportions and cancels space. Type alternates with blanks through a kind of orchestrated digital binarism of syntactic units to produce a cluster of images, tensely suspending themselves within the borders of the framing page. The juxtapositionism or parataxis that appears to be the operative basis of the Reverdian image is accompanied, then, by a strategy of visual disjunction, a subtle distancing of elements to ensure both the structural integrity and discursive indeterminacy of the whole work. Thus, Reverdy's visual poetics of intercalated verbal fragments is a sort of balancing act, whereby the two, component terms of Reverdian images are delicately positioned or staggered by a nearly invisible third component: the blank space, the pause, the missing connective or comma, the calculated enjambment. Space both suspends and reconnects verbal elements, is both manifest and concealed—as when it hides behind a string of words, condensing unaccustomed components in a single phrase, substituting one word where another should be.

---

[48] Rizzuto, pp. 13-14.
[49] *Ibid.*, p. 141.

Reverdian space is always self-consciously surreptitious. This helps prevent the surprising juxtapositions it promotes from ever becoming excessive, unconscious, or accidental, from ever overwhelming the balance of linguistic stresses that remind the reader he is still in the house of art. Thus, unlike the Surrealists, Reverdy engages in a form of limited, highly conscientious juxtapositionism that exploits the contradictory facets of an otherwise coherent milieu.

"FAÇADE"

Par la fenêtre
            La nouvelle
Entre
            Vous n'êtes pas pressé
Et la voix douce qui t'appelle
Indique où il faut regarder
            Rappelle-toi
                        Le jour se lève
            Les signes que faisait ta main
Derrière un rideau
                        Le matin
A fait une grimace brève
Le soleil crève sa prunelle
            Nous sommes deux sur le chemin

(By the window
            The news
Enters
            You are not in a hurry
And the soft voice that calls you
Indicates where to look
            Remember
                        The day breaks
            The signs that your hand made
Behind a curtain
                        The morning
Made a brief grimace
The sun bursts its pupil
            We are two upon the road)
                                    (PT, p. 164)

The visual organization of the lines helps to establish a vocal counterpoint of responding clauses and a visual harmonics of aligned clausal groups. These typographic syncopations are complemented by an irregular rhyme scheme that punctuates the poem (*fenêtre/entre; nouvelle/appelle/rappelle/prunelle; lève/brève/crève; ta main/matin/chemin*). The dynamism of the typographic shifts announces itself with the word *entre* (as a verb, "enters," as a preposition, "between"), which thrusts itself upon the left margin (or between the preceding and following lines) with surprising impact, facilitated by its partial echo of the word *fenêtre* in the first line, through which some vaguely important "news" arrives (or a "new woman/girl," modifying the encounter). The transition is ambiguous: as a verb, it seems forceful and quick, necessitated both by the brevity of the line and the visual isolation of *entre*; but as a preposition, it suspends meaning, causing one to hesitate with a sense of "in-betweenness."

But the next line, longer, seems to comment on this brusque movement by formally reminding the reader(s) or unknown protagonist(s) of the poem, "Vous n'êtes pas pressé" (You are not in a hurry). The poem's apparent self-commentary continues in the two regular lines that follow, as if the "soft voice" were the voice of the poem itself in a more traditional, familiar mode, a voice that now assumes an intimate tone by using the informal *tu*. The voice–which could also be a signified voice, the voice bringing the "news," perhaps, or the voice of the "new girl"–indicates "where one must look." It is a reassuring moment for the reader. The poem will guide one to its meaning; it will reveal the "news" or message mentioned in the second line (or, if interpreted as a girl, she herself becomes the focus of the poem's attentions). To learn this news is a matter of following the poem's instructions, of noting the interrelations between the words and their organization in and in front of space, both an imaginary space in the world of the poem and a literal, two-dimensional space on the page. It is a question of filling in the blanks, as it were.

But in a quick shift to the right, the command "Remember" follows. Its central placement beneath the preceding line and, indeed, at the center of the whole poem, gives this imperative a mysterious resonance. Remember what? What one has just read? That one is not in a hurry? That the voice will tell one where to look (hence, that poetry is predictable)? Yet as a spatially centered word-group, the line is unconventionally de-centered by virtue of being indented or visibly out-of-step with the left margin. Perhaps it is not reassuring at all; perhaps it is to remind us of what is unpredictable, of an element of surprise engendered by such sudden typographical shifts or, on the other hand, heralded by the dawn that arrives in the next line.

As if to confirm the suggestion that line seven is a warning, the next line seems to slide in from the side. Far to the right of any preceding line, the poet introduces the idea of the morning, which seems to rise in the distance—on the periphery of the poem itself. Clarity, consciousness, enlightenment, all potentially hovering on the margin, slowly insinuate their bright properties into our dreamlike uncertainty. The line now seems to answer what it was we were supposed to remember; it seems majestic, worthy of remembrance, and yet, the line break, the little skip it makes to the right, also holds the dawn at bay, makes it seem trivial, a pointless distraction from the succession of luminous questions we almost thought were developing a coherent pattern.

If the rising day really is only a distraction, the line that follows ("Les signes que faisait ta main") could also be interpreted as the grammatical object of "Rappelle-toi." The two lines are also in conspicuous alignment. And yet more lines follow, all of which seem to complete or introduce each other:

> Rappelle-toi
>   Le jour se lève
>   Les signes que faisait ta main
> Derrière un rideau
>   Le matin
>   A fait une grimace brève

One can easily group these lines in different ways to form variable readings, from: "Rappelle-toi, le jour se lève . . . le matin . . ." to "Rappelle-toi . . . les signes que faisait ta main derrière un rideau. Le matin a fait une grimace brève" to "Rappelle-toi . . . les signes que faisait ta main? Derrière un rideau le matin a fait une grimace brève." By virtue of Reverdy's visual poetics, all these readings are possible, as well as the contradictions they yield. The most perplexing of these involves the phrase "Behind a curtain," which conspicuously floats as the potential modifier of either the preceding or the following line by virtue of its placement between the two and flush left. The intriguing image of signs being made behind a curtain is partly canceled, partly reinforced by another, almost opposing image of the morning making a face behind a curtain. Both images are imposing, the first for being surprising, the second for seeming a cliché (just barely rescued by the morning's grimace). They also have opposite interpretations, since the morning is surely visible from behind a curtain, while the hand signals may not be. But this opposition is only apparent in the same way that the words *matin* and *ta main* in each image (conspicuously ending two lines and shadowing each other in terms of position) are near anagrams of each other—suggesting that their differences are only a matter of position, of simple sequential arrangement before the screen or window of interpretation. By the same token, gestures, curtains, and suns are all visual signs that both conceal and reveal meaning, that both illuminate and "blind," depending on a certain condition of reception.

If one integrates these hermeneutical potentialities with other aspects of the images' positional arrangement on the page, new meanings seem to slide out from under the very type. The phrases, "Les signes que faisait ta main/ Derrière un rideau," follow each other with a certain visual deliberation insofar as the shift of the second phrase—though drawn out to the left of the first—almost rolls alongside it, like a curtain sliding away, or across, the words just above (or behind) it. In this way, the line now seems to refer almost to itself, as if the "signs made by your hands" were those of the words themselves in all their hand-made physicality. Yet in relation to the second phrase, the words, "The morning," seem rather to leap out from what precedes them, as if flaunting themselves and their visual separation from the other lines. Hence, the typographic isolation of words is again contrasted with a typographic density of word groups to reinforce a notion of communicative simplicity versus density, of clarity versus obscurity, of communication versus mystery.

The penultimate line condenses these antipodes of revelation and blindness with a figure of the sun as an eye that bursts its pupil and thus, mysteriously, acquires absolute vision. The pupil—the black hole of reception, as it were—bursts its own boundaries as if to integrate absolute light and darkness. (This figure brings to mind Georges Bataille's idea of the pineal eye, a sort of Icarian or Oedipal organ of hubristic will [it emerges from the top of the brain] that achieves a horrifying absurdity in its operation, blinded as it is by an impulse to behold the sun.) The conceptual inconsistencies and typographic disjointedness of the overall poem seem to have condensed themselves in this impossible image. Distant realities have come together in this single line without necessarily reconciling their apparent contradictions. And yet, the typographic disjunctions have been annulled in this line, as suggested by its flush left position. The image in the last line, however, displays no such paradox in itself ("We are two upon the road") while its appearance, its practical banality, is almost miraculous given the logistical refusal of the rest of the lines to cohere in a way that would prompt its simple anecdotalism. The fact that "two" are on the road (two people? two eyes?) suggests that some separation or dissociation has been overcome, some discrepancy resulting from the logic of multiple signs (each of which have both a "façade" and a depth) has been resolved, neutralized. A message has been conveyed, and the two upon the road–in becoming "we" (*nous*)–have penetrated the deictic barriers of syntactic otherness. But the reader cannot say exactly how it happened. He or she could reconcile it with the details of the poem by inventing a story, perhaps, in which a message is delivered that prompts a morning walk or journey; yet the sequence of events never reveals itself, any more thàn the literal sequence of lines ever really confirms the various actions or events being potentially described. Some lines even group themselves non-sequentially across typographic patterns, making only the subtlest use of a syntactic or prosodic parallelism through which selected details resonate.

One cannot necessarily "see" where one is going in any poem by Reverdy, but one can use one's eyes to feel the way–typographically, as it were. An ambiance of mystery suffuses these poems, even though the details may seem all too common. The settings, objects, and sentiments, all have the lackluster appearance of life in a Parisian garret. But the structured integration of elements endows them with the same qualities of surprise one extracts from the simple objects one finds in cubist paintings. Like those paintings, the representational features of the poems are ordinary and repetitive; yet each work makes its appeal as a special kind of puzzle–always new, always astonishing.

On the other hand, there is a residue of mystery in the work of Reverdy that distinguishes his concerns from the Cubists' and aligns him with the Surrealists. This residue gives his poetry a certain emotional affinity with the paintings of Giorgio de Chirico. In many ways, Reverdy's structures are Chiricoesque in the way they apportion space, while space in turn distorts and distends them, altering their relations to the world, disturbing any normative perspective on the simplest phrases in a way that creates a shadowy, internal architecture fraught with a sense of hidden danger. Thus even the simplest elements take on a strange subjective resonance. However, the two men approach their work from very different theoretical starting points, with De Chirico emerging as more of an illusionist than Reverdy could be called an anecdotalist (albeit an illusionist whose distorted perspectives take issue with themselves much as Reverdy's multiple, broken perspectives do).

Reverdy distinguishes himself from the Surrealist poets insofar as his experiments with verbal fragments and visual space reveal a degree of conscious deliberation that official Surrealism eschews, opting instead (at least in theory) for the marvels of automatism—a sort of repressed Futurism of the unconscious. Reverdy never resorted to automatism, nor had any interest in the direct expression of human desire or emotion. Aesthetic emotion was all. For Reverdy, human desire had to be kept in abeyance, never made explicit because it all too easily insinuated itself even among the most ordinary objects. Violence and confusion were an unacceptable potentiality, so he reduced the risks by working in a highly controlled environment. It was a maneuver he seemed to replicate in his life by withdrawing from Paris to a monastery at Solesmes.

This control is evident in the symmetry and clarity of his poetics. Reverdy wanted to liberate poetry from any mimetic function in order to establish the autonomy of poetry from the things it represented, thus ensuring ontogenic parity between them. The autonomy of the literary object provided a kind of metaphysical insurance of the work's communicative potential, i.e., by encoding its own, distinctive message outside of any requirement to "make sense." The separate but equal status between poetry (i.e., art) and life in terms of mutual respect was the basis of several other theoretical positions taken by Reverdy, including the separation between the arts as a strategy of establishing a more effective mode of communication between them (especially where a fundamental understanding about the true nature of artistic creation had been reached, as with Cubism). This necessary separation between the arts, in turn, framed the whole Reverdian discourse on the juxtaposition of elements that defined the image. Thus, Reverdy's notions of competing autonomies was the key to the idea of the image, where the "surprise" of genuine communication between distant things superceded the conventional communication of a more anecdotal, traditional imagery in the same way that art's exclusivity made true communication between art and life possible.

Yet despite this remarkable theoretical consistency, Reverdy's poetry remains one of mystery whose emotional effects seem inconsistent with–or only accidentally derived from–his cubist methodologies. On this ironic basis, then, his example provided an emotional counterpart to the speed-writing and games of chance that were at the core of the surrealist revolution. As we shall see, Surrealism tentatively embraced Reverdy in the same way it underhandedly embraced certain strategies of conscious artistic control–despite its claims to total automatism, the direct expression of human desire, unmotivated by any aesthetic intention.

CHAPTER III

ANDRÉ BRETON

As a young man, André Breton was well acquainted with Reverdy and Apollinaire. Their influence is clear in his use of both Reverdy's definition of the image and Apollinaire's neologism (*surréalisme*) as the name of the movement he led. Yet these appropriations were adapted to Breton's program in ways that little resembled their original manifestations. Furthermore, Breton's critical adaptations paralleled his distinctive attitude toward the relationship among the formal arts. If there was agreement among the three poets concerning the status of music (which Breton himself called the "most confusing of all forms" [1]), their different positions vis-à-vis the relationship of poetry to painting went to the core of their respective ideals.

For Breton, this relationship was largely a technical issue that had been superceded by the more vital relationship between life and its unmotivated expression in any form, whether verbal or plastic. [2] In the end, formal categories of expression could be maintained or transgressed according to the surrealist efficacy of doing so. Yet there was a certain evolution of thought on this matter beginning with the premise, shared by Apollinaire and Reverdy, of the absolute necessity of overcoming anecdotal representation–the kind of retrograde illusionism or narrative verisimilitude that cretinized the imagination through explaining (and thus promoting) what was

---

[1] André Breton, "Surrealism and Painting," in *Surrealism and Painting*, trans. Simon Watson Taylor (New York: Harper & Row, 1972), p. 1. Subsequent citations in English from this essay will appear in the text as *SP* followed by the page number.

[2] Jennifer Mundy, "Surrealism and Painting: Describing the Imaginary," in *Art History*, 10:4 (December 1987), pp. 492-508.

all too familiar. (Breton made his point by attacking the realist novel in the first *Manifeste du surréalisme*.[3] Yet the general problem of
representation and the efficacy of different semiotic systems was far
from settled for any of them, and the variations of thought between
them had serious ramifications with respect to the situation of
painting in the Surrealist Movement.

SURREALIST ANTI-AESTHETICS: BRETON VERSUS REVERDY,
APOLLINAIRE

As we have seen, an idea of commensurable or competing autonomies informed Reverdy's attitude toward the relationship between the categories of art and life, literature and painting, and the
"distant" elements that combined to make up the poetic image.
Reverdy's was a discourse of separation between the categories, a
separation that paradoxically insured a stronger, more viable interaction between those categories or elements. But that distance had
to be gauged and the individual elements in a work of art or an image had to be chosen, according to Reverdy, with intellectual care,
just as the separate arts had to be cultivated through the conscientious development of style. Nothing was left to chance, which, for
Reverdy, was synonymous with the random, everyday processes of a
world unredeemed by art. Chance endangered art and true communication by encouraging conventional communication and the kind
of traditional mimesis he regarded (in conformity with the Symbolists) as a simple accident of custom. Furthermore, chance was the
operational principle, or lack of one, behind all sorts of *mélanges
impurs* that lacked the expressive autonomy of the separate arts.
Reverdy considered such hybrids as a further extension of the
mimetic principle–despite any appearance to the contrary–whereby
one art imitated another through the utilization of elements and
techniques proper to the other, resulting in the degradation of both.
   Although strongly influenced by "cubist" poetics in such early
poems as "Forêt Noire" and "André Derain," Breton became dis-
enchanted with Reverdy's aesthetic categories, which he believed

---

[3] Breton, *Manifestes du surréalisme* (Paris: Gallimard, 1987), p. 17. Subsequent
citations of this edition will appear in the text as *MS*.

were orchestrated at the expense of "life." And although he admired the Reverdian definition of the image for revealing how certain juxtaposed elements opened up the imagination to unknown worlds, Breton attributed the discovery and success of such juxtapositions to the workings of chance:

> Il est faux, selon moi, de prétendre que 'l'esprit a saisi les rapports' de deux réalités en présence. Il n'a, pour commencer, rien saisi consciemment. C'est du rapprochement en quelque sorte fortuit de deux termes qu'a jailli une lumière particulière, *lumière de l'image*, à laquelle nous nous montrons infiniment sensible.
>
> (It is wrong, as I see it, to claim that 'the mind has grasped the relation' between two contending realities. It has not, to begin with, seized anything consciously. In some way it is the fortuitous connection between two terms that have sparked a particular light, the light of the image, to which we have shown ourselves to be infinitely susceptible.) (*MS*, pp. 48-49) [4]

Unlike Reverdy, Breton saw chance neither as the substrate of conventional social reality, nor as the enemy of genuine creative expression. Instead, chance was the very basis of creativity and the liberator of expression, albeit one that remained adversely disposed toward the aesthetic. Breton believed that creative expression went beyond aesthetic distinctions between art and life and the generic conventions separating various modes of expression. Later, Breton would describe it as simple "lyricism": "At the time, I understood lyricism to be the spasmodic surpassing of controlled expression. I was convinced that this surpassing could result only from a considerable emotional rush, and that in return, only this surpassing could generate deep emotion." [5] Life and emotion and the fortuitousness that characterized them had eclipsed art in Breton's view—but not to the disadvantage of creative expression.

From this standpoint, the severance between art and life advocated by Reverdy, far from achieving a purer mode of communication, only isolated the aesthetic object from reality and placed it precisely within the strata of illusory forms of knowledge that Bre-

---

[4] All translations are my own unless otherwise indicated.
[5] Breton, with André Parinaud, *Conversations: The Autobiography of Surrealism*, trans. by Mark Polizzotti (New York: Paragon House, 1993), p. 31.

ton pejoratively labeled "rational thought." It was aesthetical prejudice and the cultivation of technique, not chance, that was integrally bound to the dominant ideology of social convention (as art historian Norman Bryson essentially confirms with his theories of
semiotic recognition and behavior patterns within the social formation). [6] It was genre, prescribed style, and convention that robbed
artistic and literary production of their untrammeled development.
An over-emphasis on the adequacy of technique–on the selection of
elements, on establishing boundaries between different media, genres, and styles and cultivating them solely within their established
domains–was simply a formal restraint or tool for the social and
ideological mitigation of expression. (To the extent that Reverdy
avoided these mitigations, Breton indicated that his poetic work
had escaped the controls imposed by his own theory.)

Thus, highly cultivated forms of aesthetic judgment had no validity in the universe of surrealist expression any more than polite
conversation did. The criteria became one of surrealist expression
tout court, hence the plethora of creators working in different media and styles, free of any requirement of technical mastery. Furthermore, the use of chance in surrealist production eliminated any
formal boundary between subject and object, medium and message,
such that the categories ideally became indistinguishable and reality
could now be recognized as alternative modes of self-projection
and idiolectic sign production.

Breton's emphasis on the role of chance as a way of freeing expression from controls and integrating it with reality aligns him
more closely with Apollinaire, who, along with the Dadaists, helped
pioneer the use of chance in poetry. But Apollinaire used chance in
two ways: as a mode of production and as a function of reception.
Not only did chance yield primary, expressive processes such as verbal collage, it also characterized the secondary, receptive processes
with respect to his calligrams in which the simultaneous appearance
of verbal and visual elements disrupted the linearity of normative
reading procedures. Breton himself greatly admired the works of
Apollinaire in which a technics of chance had been productively employed. He praised the poem "Lundi Rue Christine" for its "conta-

---

6 Norman Bryson, *Vision and Painting: The Logic of the Gaze* (New Haven: Yale
University, 1997 [1983]), pp. 39-41.

mination of poetry with the demotic."[7] He had even adopted certain collagist strategies in which poems were made from bits of advertising copy with conspicuous typefaces ("Le Corset Mystère," for instance). Apollinaire influenced these experiments—although this influence was largely subsumed by the stronger one of Dada, where cut-ups were typical.[8]

On the other hand, Breton had serious scruples about Apollinaire's cultivation of chance for purposes of reception, particularly as it pertained to the calligrams. Although chance played a part in their reception, the calligrams, like Mallarmé's "Un Coup de dés...," were rigorously structured compositions in which chance operations were replaced by a more formalized technique through which the simple appearance of arbitrariness was created. This illusion of chance was less of a problem for Breton than the formal calculation involved in producing it. Therefore, unlike Reverdy, Breton criticized the calligrams not for being too imitative, but for being too aesthetic! Nor was Breton concerned that such innovations produced *mélanges impurs* that would result in aesthetic confusions. Instead, he was troubled by the formal pleasures they provided by carefully integrating iconic and symbolic sign systems: i.e., an orchestration of graphic non-verbal signs that functioned on the basis of a unique, physical, and "effective" similarity to their objects, and linguistico-discursive signs that depended on arbitrary codes of substitution or an "assigned" contiguity to their objects.[9] The problem for Breton was not the combination of these signs in single works as much as the calculated coordination necessary to produce symbolic effects, rich significances—in other words, their tendency to "direct" the interpretant in ways that reinforce artistic conventions. Thus, in Breton's view, Apollinaire had ultimately succumbed to the sort of formal preoccupations that completely sub-

    [7] Anna Balakian, "Breton in Light of Apollinaire" in *About French Poetry from Dada to "Tel Quel": Text and Theory*, ed. by Mary Ann Caws (Detroit: Wayne State University Press, 1974), p. 51.

    [8] It is worth noting here that an early Dada periodical, *Le Cabaret Voltaire*, included Apollinaire's poem "Arbre" in the June 1916 issue. Hence, it seems fair to say that certain cubo-futurist devices employed by Apollinaire "contributed" to Dada techniques. See Leroy C. Breunig, "From Dada to Cubism: Apollinaire's 'Arbre'" in *About French Poetry*, pp. 26-39.

    [9] Antoine Compagnon, *La Seconde Main, ou le travail de la citation* (Paris: Éditions du Seuil, 1979), p. 80.

sumed the productive use of chance, despite his having originally pioneered it. [10]

The calligrams also betrayed Apollinaire's "progressist" aspirations in pitting poetry against painting for the wholesale, technological overhaul of expression. This overhaul represented, for Breton, a misguided and fatuous attempt to catch up with the wizardry of modern technology and the new social reality it created–materialist, capitalist, nationalist, and futurist–which Apollinaire, in Breton's view, had rather blithely accepted. Despite the fact that Apollinaire conceived his experiments as a way of overcoming language's "exchange" function in modern society, his attempt at restructuring poetry as a more encompassing, plastic medium had the opposite effect for Breton. The plastic invigoration of verbal expression would lead to its own commodification as an aesthetic object, a kind of exalted consumer item that fit in quite well with the commercial mechanisms driving social reality. Again, this irony was attributed to the formalizing tendency in art and literature, which found its complement in social alienation or reification. That Apollinaire should conceive his new poetics, or *esprit nouveau,* as a totalizing expressive endeavor in competition with technology simply drove the point home for Breton. [11]

AUTOMATIC EXPRESSION AND THE "INTERIOR MODEL"

If Apollinaire had totalizing ambitions for his work, they were not without Bretonian counterparts. Like Apollinaire, Breton aspired to an immanence of expression that would surpass all expression, that would revolutionize it to the point ceasing to represent life and instead *becoming* it, i.e., by allowing that life to freely dictate expression, hence, to obviate any technical premeditation involved in expression. In the meantime, certain techniques were necessary to reacquaint humanity with the more spontaneous life

---

[10] Breton, *Conversations*, pp. 16-17. See also, Marguerite Bonnet, *André Breton: Naissance de l'aventure surréaliste* (Paris: Librairie José Corti, 1975), pp. 128-129.

[11] Breton, "Caractères de l'évolution moderne et ce qui en participe" in *Les Pas perdus* (1924) in *Oeuvres Complètes I,* ed. Marguerite Bonnet, Philippe Bernier, Étienne-Alain Hubert, José Pierre (Paris: Gallimard, 1988), p. 293. Subsequent citations of any work included in the *Oeuvres Complètes* will appear in the text or notes with the title of the work, followed by *OC* and the page number.

experience Breton believed it had lost–thanks to the social reality of work and its "communicative" priorities. (*MS*, pp. 13-15) Yet· this life was not to be revealed in bridging formal aesthetic categories for the purpose of inventing newer and better ones. True life was discovered by ignoring these issues altogether and focusing instead on such marginal, aleatory phenomena as dreams, slips of the tongue, chance encounters and other situations that revealed unconscious desires. Works of art could be a part of this process, but less for their aesthetic facility than for their commensurability (often accidental) with such phenomena, phenomena that, in turn, helped establish a new criteria of the beautiful as a function of this revealed life. The reality Breton sought–a surreality–was still a material one. But instead of the opacities of the material world (for which only rational analysis was possible), surreality was transparently coextensive with the transcendent world as well. In a word, surreality was "marvelous" and the marvelous was "innate in the world." [12] Furthermore, for Breton, "il n'y a même que le merveilleux qui soit beau" (only the marvelous is beautiful); hence, it could fecundate artistic and literary works even of the lowest order. (*MS*, pp. 24-25)

The rudimentary techniques Breton employed to expose this other reality in no way corresponded with the rigors of artistic invention exemplified by Apollinaire's calligrams. The plasticization of the verbal sign was simply too delicate an operation for the discovery of a truth that was supposed to have universal validity. According to Breton, Apollinaire's idea that the literary could achieve immanence through the formal, self-conscious deployment of its own graphico-plastic qualities was an illusion based on the over-valuation of iconic signs (signs that functioned on the basis of effective similarity and which thus required a demanding technology of semiotic reproduction) and the under-valuation of uninhibited verbal expression (signs that functioned on the basis of an "assigned contiguity," the use of which could become automatic and thus

---

[12] J. H. Matthews, *André Breton* (New York: Columbia University, 1967) p. 11 and p. 21, on "opacity." See also Balakian's introduction to *André Breton Today*, ed. Anna Balakian and Rudolf E. Kuenzli (New York: Willis, Locker & Owens and *Dada/Surrealism*, 1989), p. 5, on Michel Maffesoli's concept of "transcendent immanence" in which Surrealism's emphasis on the precarious and the aleatory show it to be "a form of the real that is particularly concrete, which is involved to the highest point with everyday existence."

achieve a kind of effective contiguity or causal relation to the self and the unconscious). Indeed all modes of plastic expression had an air of academic training for Breton, who had deep misgivings about their general capacity to respond to the unconscious solicitations that fascinated him. Plastic expression was inherently formalizing because physical matter was stubborn, nonmalleable; thus the medium itself was complicit, as it were, in the formalist confidence game. [13] Furthermore, numerous initiatives in the plastic arts toward a more spontaneous expression left him strangely dubious. Despite his admiration for certain artists and their works, [14] he continued to have theoretical doubts about the viability of an uncontrolled, automatic mode of plastic expression (with the possible exception of photography, which Breton himself used to illustrate his best known books: *Nadja* and *L'Amour fou*. At the time of the first *Manifeste du surréalisme*, automatic writing, more than any other technique, seemed to have won his full confidence as a medium of the unconscious based on its rapid responsiveness to chance formations of thought.

In this way, thought—in its pre-conscious, pre-rational, "formless" state—was the reality for which the verbal and the plastic were both mediating, representational forms. Yet in some measure the verbal was more closely associated than the plastic with "expression," i.e., the representation of self in such manner as the work of art is "possessed by" [15] or emanates from the self. Media or mere representation could not have the same intimacy with this internal reality by virtue of their physical separation from the self. Painting's expressivity was a secondary aspect of its representational capacity and thus at a remove from the interior life Breton privileged. The verbal—whether as writing or speech—came closest to absolute fu-

---

[13] Françoise Py quotes Breton on the matter of "jongleries techniques" in her article "L'Oeil sauvage" in *Europe*. No. 743 (mars 1991), pp. 136-137; yet J. H. Matthews asserts that "Technique receives attention in Surrealism only so far as its utilization promotes the emergence of poetry [i.e., not "art"]" in his article "André Breton and Arshile Gorky" in *André Breton Today*, p. 42.

[14] Before writing the first *Manifeste du surréalisme*, Breton wrote many celebratory articles on artists whose use of chance operations had revealed precisely the way in which he believed the plastic arts could achieve immanence of expression. In fact, Breton's own ideas of verbal automatism, though derived primarily from Pierre Janet's *L'Automatisme psychique*, often found confirmation in the activities of artists, not poets. These articles appear in his early collection *Les Pas perdus* (1924).

[15] Nelson Goodman, *The Languages of Art* (Indianapolis, Indiana: Hackett Publishing Company, 1988), pp. 51-52.

sion with this reality through the acceleration of its technics. By means of acceleration, the formal, rational, and mimetic qualities of representation began to break down. Speed transformed representation itself into something else: an even purer expressivity, i.e, thought as a function of immediate desire. Speed writing was Breton's best approximation of the pure speed of thought. Automatism thus enabled Breton to disparage formal representation while fully incorporating it into his surrealist agenda, since automatic writing was admittedly the representation of the internal surrealist "voice." Indeed, Breton tacitly acknowledged that the immanence of any mode of expression was relative to its representational convenience, since even the most accelerated automatic texts involved the syntactical representation of thought, hence a degree of premeditation. [16] As a result, other, non-automatic modes of representation–despite the "impediments" of a necessary virtuosity–could be included in the surrealist program. The sheer variety of surrealist expression in both literature and the arts derives from this fundamental dichotomy: the aspiration toward immanence of expression and the simultaneous tolerance of formal and illusionistic substitutes as a kind of programmatic expedient. [17] Thus, the plastic arts found a place in the Surrealist Movement and gradually acquired a status all their own in Breton's imagination. [18] (Certain technologies such as film

---

[16] André Breton, "Artistic Genesis and Perspective of Surrealism," in *Surrealism and Painting*, p. 70. Subsequent citations in English from this essay will appear in the text as *SP* followed by the page number. Of course, to acknowledge a degree of premeditation in writing grammatically is not to say that mere syntax is a "discipline"–as Breton accused "certains sots" of believing in his "Introduction au discours sur le peu de réalité."

[17] Breton confirmed that he regarded illusionism as an expedient when he later conceded the "weakness" of such approaches as the illusionistic depiction of dreams (*SP*, p. 70).

[18] The American scholar J. H. Matthews has written of Breton's changing attitude toward the plastic arts: "We can be sure, of course, that, being in the beginning less confident of the suitability of painting than of poetry to Surrealism's aims, Breton was inclined at first to seek as many points of contact as possible between the two media, to bring them closer together by treating the former as he would the latter. But it is evident too that, as the years went by, Breton became convinced of his right to make the same demands upon the painter as upon the poet. By 1939, he could describe the work of Masson as 'plastic metaphor in its pure state,' and insist, 'I mean literally untranslatable.' In an essay on recent trends in surrealist painting, written the same year, he returned to the case of Yves Tanguy to describe the elements typical of his painting as 'the words of a language which we do not yet understand but which soon we shall read and speak, about which we are going to discover it is the language best suited to new exchanges.'" In Matthews, *André Breton*, p. 26.

and photography obviously precipitated this shift in attitude as well, since they eliminated the problem of technical mastery through their own automatism.)

For his part, Breton undertook certain theoretical maneuvers in order to accommodate the plastic arts in a surrealist capacity. But this shift only took place after conveying his initial qualms in the first *Manifeste du surréalisme* –primarily by means of omission. Not a single painter was asked to sign the manifesto and the few artists mentioned cannot necessarily be characterized as the surrealist type. [19] Breton did, however, leave the door open to a future surrealist art by offering up a paradigm of the automatic image as an instantaneous linguistico-eidetic experience. In the text, after rejecting the Reverdian idea of the controlled production of images, he describes an image that once came to him spontaneously as he was on the verge of falling asleep:

> . . . c'était quelque chose comme: "Il y a un homme coupé en deux par la fenêtre" mais elle ne pouvait souffrir d'équivoque, accompagnée qu'elle était de la faible représentation visuelle d'un homme marchant et tronçonné à mi-hauteur par une fenêtre perpendiculaire à l'axe de son corps.

> (. . . it was something like: "There is a man cut in half by the window" but there could be no equivocation, accompanied as it was by a faint visual representation of a walking man divided at mid-level by a perpendicular window at the axis of his body.) (*MS*, pp. 31-32)

The spontaneous production of images in the mind assumed a double aspect for Breton, who, in a footnote, admits

> Peintre, cette représentation visuelle eût sans doute pour moi primé l'autre [représentation verbale]. Ce sont assurément mes dispositions préalables qui en décidèrent. Depuis ce jour, il m'est arrivé de concentrer volontairement mon attention sur de semblables apparitions et je sais qu'elles ne le cèdent point en netteté aux phénomènes auditifs.

---

[19] Bonnet, *Naissance*, p. 380, and in "Le Premier rendez-vous de la peinture surréaliste" by Alain Jouffroy in *XXème siècle*. No. 38 (juin 1972), p. 17: "Breton ne parle pas de peinture dans ses premiers Manifestes . . . les seules peintres, désignés en tant que tels, sont Picasso et Braque pour leur papier collés [. . ."

(As a painter, this visual representation would doubtless, for me, have superceded the other [verbal representation]. Assuredly, it is my predisposition that determines the matter. Since then, I have taken to concentrating my attention voluntarily on similar apparitions and I know that they cede nothing in distinctness to auditory phenomena.) (*MS*, pp. 31-32)

What surprises the reader who imagines all surrealist juxtapositions to be random and strange is the obvious equivalency or logical correspondence between the auditory and optical components of the image (an equivalency contested in Magritte's *La Clé des songes* or *Ceci n'est pas une pipe* in which depicted objects either do not correspond to their verbal labels or are negated by them). Furthermore, Breton's literal statements indicate that neither mode takes any inherent precedence over the other; it is simply a question of perspective (i.e., the writer versus the painter). Yet by relegating his discussion of the visual properties of the automatic image to a footnote, Breton the writer reveals his own preference for the auditory. He can thus say one thing and clearly mean another, by way of a formal, *graphic* maneuver. Indeed, by cutting his text in half, he subtly reinforces the image of a "man cut in half" at mid-level; but he also undercuts the parity his literal statements would vouchsafe the two perceptual modes—the two halves of the man, as it were. It would seem, then, that the man cut in half by the window is Breton himself, auto-asseverated in the Rimbaldian spirit of "Je est un autre" with regard to the visual dimension of his own unconscious. It is a graphico-plastic strategy that unintentionally exposes his own hierarchizing tendencies apropos of verbo-visual dichotomies. Much of this distrust of visual signs seems to emanate from the fact of their "effective," hence rational, relation to externality, in contradistinction to verbal signs which have an "assigned" or arbitrary relation to their objects, but, paradoxically, an effective relation, as Breton assumes, to a hidden internal reality. Even in the instance of the eidetic image of the man cut in half by the window, the verbal description Breton provides becomes the adequate sign for his experience of it, while a visual rendering, no matter how similar, would only render it from without. It would be a representation, not an expression, in Nelson Goodman's sense of the distinction. In a sense, visual signs were too interdiscursive for Breton's purposes, too reliant upon a kind of rational intercourse and thus emblematic of the difference he saw between internal reality (a surreality) and external social convention—a sort of foreign object within the body of the self and the body of true self-expression.[20]

Breton's famous opening dictum of "Le surréalisme et la peinture" (1928) that "L'oeil existe à l'état sauvage" (The eye exists in a savage state)[21] acquires a certain ironic force in light of the above. This irony is not merely circumstantial, as the rest of the essay retains a subtly disparaging tone toward the visual despite the celebratory appeal of the opening statement. Such an attitude is surprising in view of Breton's rhetorical intention of raising the status of the plastic arts within the Surrealist Movement. We know this was the case, given fellow-Surrealist Pierre Naville's all-out polemical assault on the residual aestheticisms of Breton's theory.[22] Breton was now compelled to defend art in the face of Naville's bombastic iconoclasm. Thus, despite his own qualms about painting and art in general, it was clear that a great many plastic art works—perhaps even the idea of art itself—possessed a surrealist quotient he was not prepared to relinquish to theory.

The savage state of the eye was defined like this: "Seeing all, but not seeing, seeing what was not visible . . ." (*SP*, p. 1). Hence, an eye that looked inward. True sight for Breton—though "precise" and "distinct" according to Marcelin Pleynet[23]—involved a certain primitive non-discrimination like that of automatism: a kind of fundamental, uncritical syntax of internal images that refused to coincide with any verifiable organization of space and its contents. Instead, surrealist sight operated according to a deliberately "naive" systematics of fluid juxtapositions whereby perceived and imaginary object-elements could be hybridized in a way that opened up unforeseen object-relations. This "primitivism" was integral to both eidetic and verbal imagery as the surrealists imagined it to occur spontaneously in the brain (as in oneiric activity).

---

[20] Compagnon uses a similar analogy to describe the use of citations. Compagnon, p. 32.

[21] André Breton, "Le Surréalisme et la peinture" in *Le Surréalisme et la peinture* (Paris: Éditions Gallimard, 1965), p. 1.

[22] John Russell summarized Naville's position in the following way: ". . . 'neither pencil-marks made at random, nor recaptured dream-images, nor the imagination's fantasies' could be accepted as valid expressions of surrealism," in *Max Ernst: Life and Work* (New York: Harry N. Abrams, 1960), p. 82.

[23] Marcelin Pleynet, "Painting and *Surrealism and Painting*" in *Comparative Criticism*. Vol. 4 (1982), pp. 35-36.

But if automatic verbal phenomena could be represented in automatic writings free of any excess burden of rational modification, Breton continued to doubt that automatic eidetic experience could be plastically rendered with the same success. In Breton's assessment, formal aesthetics were still a liability for the plastic arts, even though he asserted that they were destined (unlike music) to "strengthen the idea of human greatness." (*SP*, p. 1) So how was Breton to improve their surrealist standing? He did it by saying that where such works were not "subordinated to a choice of [conventional or anecdotal] elements," and referred only to a "purely internal [eidetic] model" like the internal "voice" to which surrealist syntax referred, he was willing to envisage paintings as nothing "other than a window," through which one literally saw the other reality. (*SP*, p. 2) Unlike the internal voice, however, the paradigm of the "internal model" seems to have had a static quality that made it theoretically amenable to formal and illusionistic rendering. In other words, Breton was now prepared to suspend his disbelief and accept illusionism and its accompanying formalisms wherever they functioned solely to reveal the "not visible" or the "jamais vu" by projecting internal models onto the scopic field in the manner of a "primitive" imagination. (*SP*, p. 4) Surrealist painting had to bear an effective similarity to internal, eidetic images, not to external images whose spatial and iconographic syntax had rigidified after a long history of illusionistic rendering. It was overly dependent on conventional expectations of art–a series of visual *citations* of Old Masters and classical models, not of the *jamais vu*. The internal eye, on the other hand, was infinitely sensitive to chance configurations that the unconscious, at least, "recognized," in Bryson's sense, as figures of a surrealist semiosis of a new social formation. If Breton remained unconvinced that plastic sign production could achieve automatic immanence through an ecstatic, combinatory acceleration, the "windows" it *could* provide at least opened onto surrealist landscapes and thus had an instructive value. In short, Breton chose to partially suspend his critical attitude toward plastic representation in the same way he had for verbal representation, only now he openly declared it as a kind of theoretical allowance. The two, somewhat contradictory, poles of surrealist expression in both literature and the arts could now be abstracted as those cases that were automatic, serial, and similitudinous, versus those that referred to an interior model, were static, and functioned on the basis of eidetic resemblance.[24] At the same time, however, the model for the latter could not be fully known or defined–it simply generated clues to its unrepresented, unvoiced meaning: pure, inadmissible desire (like that of the *id* in Freudian terminology).

If Breton's concessions to plastic expression seem tentative, the matter is complicated further by the essay, "Le Message automatique" (1933) in which–relations among the other arts notwithstanding–the auditory now takes definite precedence over the visual as far as the latter pertains to verbal images.[25] As Marguerite Bonnet explains in her study of Breton and Surrealism's early years, the visual élan of the automatic verbal image became for Breton a sort of mental drift from the authentic verbal message. He saw the visual component as more of a by-product than an integral part of the image, writing: "Comment tolérer le passage si égarant de l'auditif au visuel?" (How does one tolerate the passage, so distracting, from the auditory to the visual?).[26] Nonetheless, in asserting that verbal images prompt internal eidetic phenomena as a sort of secondary response, Breton goes on to say that these secondary phenomena are more compelling than the primary visual phenomena prompted by actual iconic images. This paradox is explained by the fact that the visuality of verbal images is completely internalized, hence, not literally seen:

> . . . je tiens, et c'est l'essentiel, les inspirations verbales pour infiniment plus riches de sens visuel; pour infiniment plus résistantes à l'oeil, que les images proprement dites. De là la protesta-

---

[24] Michel Foucault has described the difference between resemblance and similitude: "Ressembler suppose une référence première qui prescrit et classe. Le similaire se développe en série qui n'ont ni commencement ni fin, qu'on peut parcourir dans un sens ou dans l'autre, qui n'obéissent à aucune hiérarchie, mais se propagent de petites différences. La ressemblance sert à la réprésentation, qui règne sur elle; la similitude sert à la répétition qui court à travers elle. La ressemblance s'ordonne en modèle qu'elle est chargée de reconduire et de faire reconnaître, la similitude fait circuler le simulacre comme rapport indéfini et réversible du similaire au similaire." *Ceci n'est pas un pipe* (Paris: Fata Morgana, 1973), p. 61.

[25] Robert Lebel, on the contrary, has tried to show that Breton was able to "reconnaître dans l'image visuelle l'indispensable complément, et peut-être même le véhicule privilégié de l'image poétique, contrairement à 'l'image auditive,' qualifiée par lui de 'confusionelle'" ("André Breton et la peinture," in *L'Oeil*, November 1966, No. 143, pp. 10-19). As we shall see, he has confused the musical auditory with the verbal auditory, the latter of which dictates the nature of the poetic visual image.

[26] Breton, "Le Message automatique" in *Point du jour*, quoted in Bonnet, p. 393.

tion que je n'ai jamais cessé d'élever contre le prétendu pouvoir 'visionnaire' du poète. Non, Lautréamont, Rimbaud n'ont pas vu, n'ont pas joui *a priori* de ce qu'ils décrivaient, ce qui équivaut à dire qu'ils ne le décrivaient pas, ils se bornaient dans les coulisses sombres de l'être à entendre parler indistinctement et, durant qu'ils écrivaient, sans mieux comprendre que nous la pre-mière fois que nous les lisons de certains travaux accomplis et ac-complissables. 'L'illumination' vient ensuite.

Toujours en poésie l'automatisme verbo-auditif m'a paru créateur à la lecture des images visuelles les plus exaltantes, ja-mais l'automatisme verbo-visuel ne m'a paru créateur à la lecture d'images visuelles qui puissent, de loin, leur être comparées. C'est aussi dire qu'aujourd'hui comme il y a dix ans, je suis en-tièrement acquis, je continue à croire aveuglément (aveugle . . . d'une cécité qui couvre à la fois toutes choses visibles) au triom-phe, par l'auditif, du visuel invérifiable.

(. . . I consider, and this is the main point, verbal inspirations to be infinitely richer in visual sense, infinitely more resistant to the eye, than images proper. Thus the protestation I have never ceased to raise against the supposed "visionary" power of the poet. No, Lautréamont, Rimbaud did not see, did not enjoy *a priori* what they described, which is the equivalent of saying that they did not describe it: they confined themselves to backstage shadows where they heard the beings indistinctly speaking, with-out, as they wrote, understanding any better than we do the first time we read certain accomplished and accomplishable works.

In poetry, verbo-auditory automatism has always seemed to me, on reading, to be productive of the most exalting visual im-ages; verbo-visual automatism, on reading, has never seemed to me productive of visual images that can be remotely compared with them. This is also to say that today, just as ten years ago, I am entirely acquitted; I continue to believe blindly (blind . . . the sort of blindness that covers all visible things at the same time) in the triumph, by the auditory, of the unverifiable visual.)[27]

One suspects that Breton, aside from a general distrust of the visual, shifted his position because of ideological doubts accruing to the plastic arts in the course of ejecting from the Surrealist Move-ment Salvador Dalí–whose sharp-edge illusionism gave Breton's in-

___
[27] *Ibid.*

ternal model an aggressive external vitality. (This "paranoïaque" phase of Surrealism will be discussed later.) Yet, if a sort of negative evolution can be traced with regard to these matters, it is a splintering, spiral movement fraught with reversals, ambiguities, and the mitigating circumstances of the Surrealist Movement as a whole, in which so many painters actively participated. The theoretical relationship between the verbal and the visual, between poetry and painting, was mediated and humanized by the broader context of what Donald Kuspit has called Breton's "elective affinities," [28] a simultaneism of surrealist action in both the arts and letters (and beyond) undertaken by various practitioners.

MUSEUM INTERIORS: *CLAIR DE TERRE*

Beyond participation in surrealist quarterlies, mutual correspondence, and other collective activities, Breton's elective affinities are demonstrated in the many dedications of his poems to poets and artists–particularly in *Clair de terre* (1923). Among those mentioned are De Chirico, Picasso, Max Ernst, Francis Picabia, Man Ray, and Marcel Duchamp, all of whom also figure in his collection of early writings *Les Pas perdus* (1924). At the same time, many of the poems in *Clair de terre* address the relation between automatic expression and its "slower" alternatives, exemplified, it would seem, by illusionistic painting itself when ever it made the surrealistically necessary reference to an "interior model." It should be added, however, that most of the poems are not themselves automatic texts and thus display a certain static quality as finished literary works. When Breton is not simply describing dreams in a narrative vein (as in the five texts dedicated to De Chirico), he juxtaposes "distant elements" more or less conscientiously in conformity with Reverdian technique (although the effects are very different, according to his temperament and choice of elements). [29]

---

[28] Donald Kuspit, "Dispensable Friends, Indispensable Ideologies," in *Artforum*. 22 (December 1983), pp. 56-63.

[29] This difference in temperament is driven home by the fact of Breton's great admiration for and Reverdy's intense dislike of the poetry of Lautréamont whose "Beautiful as ..." images brought together distant realities Reverdy considered inappropriate.

Nevertheless, if *Clair de terre*[30] never directly demonstrates the "uncontrolled expression" Breton sought, it at least thematizes such expression (i.e., utilizes it as an "interior model") at the expense of its thematic other: the finished work, usually symbolized in the text as a work of plastic art attended by all the literary metaphors of hardness, coolness, flatness, and color. The finished work, apart from being categorized as a product of human reason, conscious deliberation, is also characterized by decay, a sense of the traditional art object's cultural decline or increasing irrelevance in the modern age. This quality is made explicit in the poem "Plutôt la vie" (Choose Life):

> Plutôt la vie que ses prismes sans épaisseur même si
>   les couleurs sont plus pures
> Plutôt que cette heure toujours couverte que ces
>   terribles voitures de flammes froides
> Que ces pierres blettes
> Plutôt ce coeur à cran d'arrêt
> Que cette mare aux murmures
>
>   (*CT*, p. 72)

> (Choose life instead of those prisms with no depth even if
>   their colors are purer
> Instead of this hour always hidden instead of these
>   terrible vehicles of cold flame
> Instead of these overripe stones
> Choose this heart with its safety catch
> Instead of that murmuring pool)
>
>   (*EL*, p. 65)

Consequently, the thematic contrast between controlled and uncontrolled expression hinges upon a symbolic treatment of the relation between the visual and the verbal, the plastic and the textual. For instance, Breton's dream narratives dedicated to De Chirico ("Cinq rêves") are troubled by enigmatic scenes of artistic production and museums of the bizarre. In the first one, the dreamer (Breton) examines plaster casts of the larger-than-life mustaches of several fa-

---

[30] Subsequent citations of this text refer to the Gallimard edition published in Paris, 1966, which will appear as *CT*. The translations are taken from *Earthlight*, trans. Bill Zavatsky and Zack Rogow (Toronto: Coach House Press, 1993), which will appear in the text as *EL*.

mous writers before entering a room where he follows the example of two poets (one is Reverdy) and sits down to write verses. But upon starting he finds that he can only manage to write the words "La lumière ..." before tearing up the paper and starting over, an action he repeats again and again. In the fourth section, after trying to conjugate a new tense of the verb "être," Breton finds a book with a section entitled "Enigmatique." The meaning of the text, of course, escapes him; all he can remember are the illustrations of mythological or ecclesiastical characters in the middle of

> ... une salle cirée immense qui ressemblait à la galerie d'Apollon. Les murs et le parquet réfléchissaient mieux que des glaces puisque chacun de ces personnages se retrouvait plusieurs fois dans la pièce sous diverses attitudes .... (*CT*, p. 41)

> (. . . an immense, waxed room that looked like the Apollo Gallery [in the Louvre]. The walls and the parquet floor reflected better than mirrors since each of these characters could be found any number of times in the room in various positions . . . .)
> (*EL*, p. 40)

Later on, a dictionary similarly yields illustrated definitions of words and the dream ends with Breton and Louis Aragon carrying two empty picture frames up the Champs Élysées which they protect from rain by leaning them, at easel-height, under the upper moldings of the Arc de Triomphe. Thus, throughout the dream-narratives we encounter scenes of writing, or scenes with texts or known writers, in which a work of visual art is simultaneously presented, but in a commemorative or illustrative capacity, or, as in the last description, as a notable absence–an empty frame–through which another, more "vital" expression (in this case, of the open streets) flows.

   In addition to the frequent thematic association between verbal and visual forms, the verbal imagery of the narratives has a certain visual drift that reveals Breton's irresistible attraction to the plastic arts (and their metonymic scenes of presentation–e.g., the gallery, the book illustration) as a nostalgic concretion or "interior model" of his own ambition for automatic verbal expression. He cannot help dreaming of automatism as an archaeological tool for unearthing unconscious artifacts for display in a modern museum or in the open air. For instance, in the poem "Il n'y a pas à sortir de

là" (There's no way out of here), dedicated to Paul Éluard, Breton
describes the mental objects of automatic representation as if they
were layered geological sediments that had acquired the transparency of museum vitrines: "O vitres superposées de la pensée/ Dans la
terre de verre s'agitent les squelettes de verre" (O superimposed
windowpanes of thought/ In glass earth glass skeletons are stirring);
and later, bulky cultural icons like those enshrined in the Louvre
acquire surrealist buoyancy: "Tout le monde a entendu parler du
Radeau de la Méduse/ Et peut à la rigueur concevoir un équivalent
de ce radeau dans le ciel" (Everyone's heard of the Raft of the
Medusa/ And could if it came down to it conceive of an equivalent/
of that raft in the sky). (CT, pp. 64-65; EL, p. 58)

In "Mille et mille fois" (A thousand thousand times), dedicated
to Francis Picabia–an artist known for his iconoclastic use of language in his work–Breton explores the cabbalistic theme of assigning numerical values to letters, in this case the eleven letters of an
unuttered name (perhaps his own). But Breton combines this mystic idea with the Rimbaldian one of assigning colors to vowels: "Ils
sont de onze couleurs différentes et leurs dimensions respectives
vous feraient mourir de pitié" (They are eleven different colors and
their respective/ dimensions would make you die of pity). (CT, p.
80; EL, p. 71) Thus, abstract colors acquire graphic dimensions as
letters, becoming in the process a construction:

> Ma construction ma belle construction page à page
> Maison insensément vitrée à ciel ouvert à sol ouvert
> C'est une faille dans le roc suspendu par des anneaux à
>   la tringle du monde
> C'est un rideau métallique qui se baisse sur des
>   inscriptions divines
> Que vous ne savez pas lire

> (CT, p. 80)

> (My construction my beautiful construction page by page
> House insanely glazed in the wide open sky the wide open earth
> It's a fault in the rock suspended by rings from the
>   curtain rod of the world
> It's a metallic curtain that comes down on divine
>   inscriptions
> That you don't know how to read)

> (EL, p. 72)

Finally, "Silhouette de paille" (Silhouette of Straw), the poem dedicated to Max Ernst, offers a monologue evoking a whimsical, almost flirtatious entreaty from the "feminized" automatic voice to the more homogeneous art work or "interior model," from artistic process to artistic product, from uncontrolled expressiveness to controlled expressions, although a fair amount of dialectical cross-dressing is going on:

> Donnez-moi des bijoux de noyées
> Deux crèches
> Une prêle et une marotte de modiste
> Ensuite pardonnez-moi
> Je n'ai pas le temps de respirer
> Je suis un sort
> La construction solaire m'a retenu jusqu'ici
> Maintenant je n'ai plus qu'à laisser mourir
> Demander le barème
> Au trot le poing fermé au-dessus de ma tête qui sonne
> Un verre dans lequel s'ouvre un oeil jaune
> Le sentiment s'ouvre aussi
> Mais les princesses s'accrochent à l'air pur
> J'ai besoin d'orgueil
> Et de quelques gouttes plates
> Pour réchauffer la marmite de fleurs moisies
> Au pied de l'escalier
> Pensée divine au carreau étoilé de ciel bleu
> L'expression des baigneuses c'est la mort du loup
> Prenez-moi pour amie
> L'amie des feux et des furets
> Vous regarde à deux fois
> Lissez vos peines
> Ma rame de palissandre fait chercher vos cheveux
> Un son palpable dessert la plage
> Noire de la colère des seiches
> Et rouge du côté du panonceau
>
> (*CT*, pp. 74-75)

(Give me the jewels of drowned women
Two cribs
A scouring-rush and a tailor's dummy
Then forgive me
I don't have time to breathe

I'm a magic spell
Solar construction has detained me up to this point
Now I have nothing to do but let things die
Ask to see the schedule
And make it snappy the closed fist above my ringing head
A glass in which a yellow eye opens
Feelings too open
But princesses cling to pure air
I need pride
And some flat drops
To fertilize the pot of musty flowers
At the foot of the stairs
Divine thought in the starry pane of blue sky
The look on the women bathers is what kills the wolf
Let me be your girlfriend
The girlfriend of fires and ferrets
Thinks twice about you
Polish your sorrows
My Brazilian rosewood oar makes your hair sing
A sound that you can touch empties the beach
Black from the anger of the cuttlefish
And red towards the sign)

(*EL,* p. 67)

After listing the kind of incongruous elements that might appear in a Chirico painting (the tailor's dummy, for instance), the playful interlocutor begins making excuses for herself, her chattery yet "spellbinding" haste. However, *this* spell is up to pace with modern schedules ("au trot" [make it snappy]); it rings like an alarm, yet has a certain glass fragility ("ma tête qui sonne/ Un verre dans lequel s'ouvre un oeil jaune" [my ringing head/ A glass in which a yellow eye opens]), a jaundiced vision unaccustomed to the demands of controlled expression yet not without affinities with or affections for it. Hence, as feelings and personal interiors "open" in the automatic rush of language there remains in her speech some hesitation: "princesses" still cling to pure air, have pride, require some "gouttes plates/ pour réchauffer [leur] marmite de fleurs moisies" (flat drops/ to fertilize [their] musty flowers) as automatic texts often required a theme or "interior model" to prompt the rush of language. "Pensée divine au carreau étoilé de ciel bleu" (Divine thought in the starry pane of blue sky): a kind of transcendent observatory or astronomical map is also required, presumably something possessed by the object/person she addresses.

At this point in the poem the notion of the silent interlocutor as visual image develops an almost passive elegance that seems to tame the wildness of (verbal) speed. Sexual roles change for a moment as the visual assumes the Cézannesque allure of women bathers that tame the predatory wolf of the heart. But just as quickly, the speaking wolf calls itself a girl, girlfriend of ferrets and fires who "thinks twice" ("regarde à deux fois") before the sacred aura of the interior model and its plastic or visual extensions, advising it to polish its sorrows. Finally, a surprising image of the picture as water (reflecting pool? hence, portrait?) combed by the speaker's rosewood oar to make it sing (the comb of language? whereby the plastic is now, in its own way, tamed, trained to take on verbal conventions?). As the plastic learns to sing, sound, conversely, assumes the properties of touch. Yet there are risks involved, too, as the visual acquires an oceanic ominousness as residues of patriarchal anger blacken its plastic shores. All signs, visual and verbal, are red now.

As the preceding analysis reveals, the dichotomies of speed and hardness, fluidity and purity, female and male overlap and even metamorphose into each other at different stages, suggesting that the relations being considered are themselves unstable, with all the dynamics of a raucous love affair. The deliberate attack on the aesthetic had the peculiar effect of sustaining its unconscious vitality in the form of "interior models," and insofar as paintings remained sacred icons, not of external nature or social convention, but of the unconscious, Breton was far from abandoning the religion of art that sustained his reorganized adoration. As such, paintings were holy relics he could kiss with his unconscious, the encounter miraculously generating imaginary complexes in which the verbal and visual became intertwined. But it needs to be stressed that an underlying ambivalence about painting marks these acts of critical celebration with a fundamental irony. As a practitioner of automatic writing, Breton fundamentally worried that painting could never fully transcend its necessity of resemblance and, thus, of being always a form of citation or copy with obvious technical precedents. It is a doubt that nevertheless depended on his simultaneous and almost absolute faith that automatic writing represented a pure transcription of the unconscious and *not* merely a series of half-remembered citations. For Breton, the automatic method for which he was primarily responsible would always frustrate such acts of citation, which depend on logic, reason, and discursive deliberation–Breton's putative enemies.

BRETON AND FOUR SURREALIST PAINTERS: ERNST, MASSON, DALÍ, MIRÓ

As the poems of *Clair de terre* reveal, a residual "literary" technics is evident that seems to be the verbal equivalent of the painter's "interior model." Reverdian image-dynamics help to elaborate this model, thus revealing the persistence of Breton's literary memory. It was another allowance he had made for Surrealism and for himself; yet these "concessions" could be validated by their results–especially in painting, which had the sheen, if not the absolute rigor, of everything Breton seemed to expect from Surrealism. They conveyed the marvelous without any excessive technical display. The artist whose activities most closely paralleled, at this stage, Breton's various initiatives to achieve surrealist expression was, I believe, Max Ernst.

Max Ernst

Ernst's surrealist genius lay in his ability to serialize the juxtaposition of plastic elements in a way that spontaneously figured an "interior model" and thus ceded to its unexpected order. Although his famous early collages were only exhibited in 1921, Breton saw them first in 1920 and immediately recognized in them the possibility of a surrealist art.[31] [fig. 8] As he later declared, "It is no exaggeration to say that the first collages of Max Ernst, with their extraordinary power of suggestion, were received by us as a revelation."[32] In "Genèse et perspective artistiques du surréalisme" (Artistic Genesis and Perspective of Surrealism) he wrote: "In fact, Surrealism had immediately profited from his 1920 collages, which introduced an entirely original scheme of visual structure yet at the same time corresponded exactly to the intentions of Lautréamont and Rimbaud in poetry." (*SP*, p. 64) Ernst himself later credited

---

[31] Jouffroy, p. 16.
[32] Breton, *Conversations*, p. 54.

these poets in a way that clearly validated Breton's earlier enthusiasm by referring to his collages as the "chance meeting of two distant realities on an unfamiliar plane" and otherwise characterizing
his technique as "the alchemy of the (visual) image." [33] But what is
most important in Ernst's work is the process of serialization whereby plastic elements "automatically," as it were, yield the outlines of
an "interior model" through hallucinatory syntheses, or through
succumbing to a perceptual non-differentiation on the part of the
artist. [34]

   In his article "André Breton et la peinture," Robert Lebel main-
tains that Ernst's hallucinatory metamorphosis of plastic elements
was like automatism "en se bornant à enregistrer la juxtaposition ir-
rationnelle et chaotique des images perçues dans leur 'succession
hallucinante'" (in limiting itself to recording the irrational and
chaotic juxtaposition of images perceived in their "hallucinatory
succession"). [35] Yet a more illuminating comparison can be made
with Breton's various collagist poems, whose elements succeed each
other in accordance with the demands of an interior model. The
simplest example has already been mentioned, Breton's "Corset

---

[33] Max Ernst, *Beyond Painting* (New York: Wittenborn, Schultz Inc., 1948),
pp. 12-13.

[34] Ernst described the creation of his early collages, a description summarized
by John Russell: "'I was struck,' he wrote later, 'by the obsessional interest which I
was taking, in spite of myself, in the pages of an illustrated catalogue which lay to
hand.' The plates were educational in intent, and had to do with anthropology, psy-
chology, minerology, paleontology, and the use of the microscope. The figurative elements thus brought together were so remote from one another in their everyday
connotations that the catalogue as a whole became palpably absurd. But that very
absurdity provoked within him a sudden intensification of the visionary faculty. 'I
experienced a hallucinating succession of self-contradictory images–double images,
triple images, multiple images–laid one on top of another with the imperious rapidi-
ty which characterize our memories of a love-affair or the visions which come to us
when we are half asleep and half awake. These images demanded to be put on new
levels of experience. Their encounters had to take place in a new Unknown and in a
place from which the idea of "fitness" and "propriety" was excluded. All that I had
to do was to take a plate from the catalog and add to it. I painted or drew in docile
fashion, whatever presented itself to me. Adding a patch of color, pencilling in a detail or two, a landscape which had nothing to do with the objects already represented, a desert, a new sky, a geological cross section, a floor, a simple straight line to
represent a horizon, I secured for myself an exact and permanent image of my hal-
lucination. And what had been simply the most banal pages of advertisement became so many dramas, revelatory of my most secret desires.'" From *Max Ernst:
Oeuvres de 1919 à 1936, Cahiers d'art*, Paris, 1937, in *Max Ernst: Life and Work* by
John Russell (New York: Harry N. Abrams, 1960), p. 51.

[35] Lebel, p. 18.

mystère" in which the accumulated bits of advertising copy seem to reinforce the fundamental mystery of the corset and the mystery of the title itself, which was taken from a sign in a shop window that intrigued Breton. His reliance on external "bits" to compose the whole transferred the automatic process from an internalized linguistic system to the more dialectical one of finding elements that chanced to conform with some inexplicable need, desire, or interior model. Thus, in both Max Ernst's collages and Breton's collage poems, the "external object had broken with its normal environment and its component parts had, so to speak, emancipated themselves from it in such a way that they were now able to maintain entirely new relationships with other elements, escaping from the principle of reality but retaining all their importance on that plane" albeit primarily by virtue of the plastic dimension of those elements. (*SP*, pp. 64-66)

A more difficult, if surrealistically streamlined version of this activity is the collage poem, found in Breton's first *Manifeste du surréalisme*, whose title, "Poème" [fig. 9], less readily identifies an interior model, yet whose symmetrical, totemic organization of lines–all centered, one after the other–suggests that Breton had systematically pared down his collagist techniques to give them the repetitive, incantatory, yet visual appearance of a simplified automatic approach. This "symmetricalized" succession of elements also suggests–like "Corset mystère"–the figure of a woman to whom the poem seems to address itself in line 15 ("Madame") as the "artisan quotidien" or cosmetician of her beauty. But if these references suggest an eroticized interior model, the bulk of the poem works hard to obscure that figure and thereby frustrate any easy mental image from forming. The elements, despite their visual patterning and syntactical clarity, are uneasily associated, offering no familiar semantic transition. What do a burst of laughter, a pair of silk stockings, and iron bars have to do with the sudden "saut dans le vide" (leap into the void) and the "premier journal blanc/ du hasard" (first blank newspaper of chance) (*MS*, pp. 54-56) that jump off the page at different intervals?

A hint is given in the lines "s'aggrave/ l'agréable"–to aggravate the agreeable. A phonico-graphic agreement between elements yields a semantic oxymoron and we realize that with each transition between collage components the "poem" is negotiating the gap between an idea of a work's literary significance and the insignificant chatter of its parts extracted from the mundane world of advertising, cosmetics, journalism, and political sloganeering. It is an "irritating" definition of beauty arrived at by assimilating consumer signs of the beautiful, with their trivial surface appeal, to some unknown depth of interpretation, and vice versa. The technique yields a rough semantic surface, a complicated texture that militates against the cosmetic seductions of the individual collage elements' entreaties, such as: *éclat de rire, les plus belles pailles, l'agréable, l'artisan quotidien de votre beauté, bas de soie, tout pourrait s'arranger si bien, du beau temps, courte et bonne, au bal des ardents.* Each of these entreaties seem intensified by the variety of typefaces used, typefaces that give each *énoncé* the kind of visual sensuosity that advertising exploits so well.

By actually cutting out typographic bits and pasting them together according to an unconscious pattern of succession, Breton has produced not only a verbal collage but a verbal prototype of Ernst's *frottage* technique, described in *Au-delà de la peinture* (Beyond Painting) as "the intensification of the irritability of the mind's faculties by appropriate technical means, excluding all mental guidance." [36] The technical means involved pressing paper or canvas over particular surfaces (natural or artificial) and rubbing it with a crayon or brush to yield surprising graphic imagery. After multiple rubbings of this sort, their assembled parts–a kind of aggravated collage–transfigured themselves into an unexpected (or only half-expected) figure of some bizarre persona, animal, plant, or landscape as exemplified in Ernst's *Histoire naturelle.* [fig. 10] Breton's verbal frottage involved a more frustrated caressing of typographic elements, of message-fragments drawn from the world of advertising that never quite collect themselves into a whole. It is the pervert's obsessive attention to body parts at the expense of the whole individual providing them for his delectation. Indeed, "Poème" is a kind of plastic premonition or technical "precapitulation" of Breton's later "L'Union libre," the famous catalogue of his wife Jacqueline Lamba's intriguing body parts.

It is easy to allegorize these works as "unconscious" paeans to unspecified women, persons, or bodies. But all paeans are conscious and the real importance of Breton's and Ernst's technique is the extent to which its products lose any aura of "mental guidance"

---

[36] Ernst, p. 8.

or involuntary citation. The processes they employ are less humanizing than Breton would have one believe (as when he says of automatism that "les mots font l'amour" [words make love]). [37] The
serializing, speeded-up modes by which the putative body or
beloved is enjoyed suggests–beyond love or admiration–a desire for
the dismemberment and re-organization the body as a new chimera
of the mind, free of any obvious mythological coordinates. The
boundaries of these internal models are fluctuating and the process
of iterating them involves the random, directionless consumption of
partial objects–those bodiless, free-floating orifices or nodules (or
mechanistic substitutes)–for symbolic gratification in the bliss of
expression, the "flow" of language. This restless, serial fixation on
parts metamorphoses the whole into a kind of exploded landscape
in which the poet/consumer roams at increasing speeds through an
open space. But the automatist enjoys that space only in glimpses,
scopic fragments forever luring him or her on to adjacent zones beyond their immediate purview–in contrast to the more totalizing
concepts of the self-contained, individual body, or the Renaissance
landscape, receding by stages into depth.

In these collage works Ernst and Breton juxtapose plastic elements in a way that collapses the boundaries between body and
space. Juxtaposition condenses elements, subjects them to a kind of
"plastic speed" by which normal distances between features and
landmarks are traversed. But this plastic speed, like chance in Apollinaire's calligrams, is more formal than performative. The speed in-
heres in the effect, not the production of the work, which remains
time-consuming. For Breton, pure automatism ensures a new consistency between performance and form, production and product,
insofar as speed reduces the risk of premeditation to which collage
is vulnerable. Collage is ultimately too close to quotation or citation
for Breton (history and tradition constitute two nightmares from
which he is all too eager to awake). Speed increases the potentiality
of chance, accident, surprise sought by the collagist by making
them inhere in the operation itself. Although elements are presum-

---

[37] Breton, "Les Mots sans rides" (1922) in *Les Pas perdus* (1924) in *Oeuvres
Complètes I*, p. 286. As the Futurists did with "les mots en liberté," Breton wants to
disabuse his reader of any idea that language "means," or represents *a priori* meanings (and those imperfectly, as traditional *jeux de mots* humorously suggest in exposing linguistic dysfunction), but rather creates meaning, or operates according to
a "generative principle," as J. H. Matthews calls it in *André Breton*, pp. 38-41.

ably juxtaposed by chance in the collage process, the act of physically cutting and pasting introduces all the characteristics of deliberate structuration whereby the hoped-for interior models surreptitiously succumb to external ones or even conventional prototypes. Speeding up the means of expression provided what seemed a failsafe solution for the poet or artist attempting to reduce to a minimum the controls over expression.

On the other hand, automatism was devoid of the ambiguities of medium and semiosis inherent to collage, in which the plastic qualities of language (as print) could be exaggerated (and vice versa) in order to expand the technical range of both language and plastic media. In forsaking this ambition, Breton's strategy veered away from both cubist and futurist practice, but seemed also to leave behind the unconscious potential of semiotically ambiguous or undefined matter. But Breton considered the fusion of different media merely a technical simultaneism, not a liberation of expressive means (as he considered automatism to be). Breton was after a different kind of simultaneism that involved exaggerating the conditions of production in a specific medium–in his own case, writing. Instead of treating the arts as extensions of each other, Breton saw speed as a way of metamorphosing the verbal arts without unduly over-reaching in the technical sphere. Thus, while futurist speed was about absorbing or homogenizing different media in order to extend their hegemony over life and thus transform it into theater, now, with automatism, certain adaptable media could metamorphose their own symbolic systems into vehicles of unconscious desire. Indeed, for Breton, the homogenization of different media was possible and desirable in the unconscious alone.

If the main purpose of automatic writing was to break down rational discourse, its subtler virtue, for Breton, was an almost scientific precision as a recorder of "marvelous" discourse, a sort of *discours jamais entendu*, disencumbered of the weight of tradition, the necessity of literary accommodation. But to do this, certain linguistic (as opposed to discursive) controls had to be maintained–ironically, to engender expressive freedoms of another sort. Despite the high speeds automatic writing was supposed to attain, Breton's writings are almost always consistent with the rules of French syntax. Rarely do they dissolve into ungrammaticality [38] and it would

---

[38] A notable exception can be found in Breton's and Philippe Soupault's

seem that, rather than exploiting the discontinuities of speech (as much Dada poetry does), the high-speed syntactic vehicles of automatic writing were well greased. Syntactic integrity required considerable concentration yet had to be maintained in order to expand the semantic range of those variables (words) occupying its structures (sentences). Thus, syntax–the swift, unmotivated, and formal logic of language (as opposed to the deliberate, motivated ones of rhetoric and discourse)–became a sort of contour line around which new images, new objects, new creatures, and new worlds were half-traced as normal semantics opened up to its delirious entreaty.

André Masson

Because of his contempt for what he called "technical matters," Breton left few clues concerning what might constitute a graphic automatism. However, in the same footnote to the first *Manifeste du surréalisme* in which the visual drift of verbal automatism is discussed, he does briefly hypothesize how a painter might capture unconscious solicitations:

> Muni d'un crayon et d'une feuille blanche, il me serait facile d'en suivre les contours. C'est que là encore il ne s'agit pas de dessiner, *il ne s'agit que de calquer*. Je figurerais bien ainsi un arbre, une vague, un instrument de musique, toutes choses dont je suis incapable de fournir en ce moment l'aperçu le plus schématique. Je m'enfoncerais, avec la certitude de me retrouver, dans un dédale de lignes qui ne me paraissent concourir, d'abord, à rien. Et j'en éprouverais, en ouvrant les yeux, une très forte impression de "jamais vu."

> (With a pencil and a blank sheet of paper, it would be easy for me to follow its contours. There again, it is not a matter of drawing, *it's a matter of tracing*. I would well represent a tree, a wave, a musical instrument, all things of which I am incapable of furnishing the most schematic outline at this moment. I would

---

"Eclipse," a section in *Les Champs magnétiques* (1919). Written at higher speeds than any of the other sections, the syntax of the writing breaks down as Bonnet confirms. *Naissance*, p. 180.

plunge, with the certainty of finding myself again, into a maze of lines that at first do not seem to me to lead to anything. And I would experience, upon opening my eyes, a very strong impression of "jamais vu.") (*MS*, p. 32)

In this way, the artist must simply trace his "unseen" impressions, open his eyes, and discover the surreal. It is a form of copying that, upon verifying the results with open eyes, shows itself to have no verifiable phenomenal object. We do not examine it with our senses but with the dream-sense of our senses.

A striking comparison can be made between this description and a similar one by André Masson apropos of his own experiments with automatic drawing, which began in late 1923 before his first meeting with André Breton the following year. Although Masson, like Breton, entered an almost dream-like state when he composed his automatic drawings, his dreamscapes were not inhabited by the sort of ready-made objects described above, but a kind of chaos, or "maze of lines" from which surprising, visual motifs emerged. Describing the process, Masson said: "(a) The first condition was to make a clean slate. The mind freed from all apparent ties. Entry into a state bordering on trance. (b) Surrender to the interior tumult. (c) Speed of writing." [39] The last condition seems more of a retrospective gesture to Breton, almost anticlimactic, than a vital component of the process his own drawings initiate. Masson's graphic lines definitely move faster than those of syntax, breaking off less frequently than written script, which must, in the end, accommodate its automatism to the serial binarism of discrete, allographic, linguistic units. Masson's drawings foretell the automatism of pure line, an unbroken, autographic continuity, restlessly fluctuating across what becomes the magnetic surface of the paper, a surface liberated from linguistic stops.

An early, untitled drawing [fig. 11] reveals Massonian automatism at its highest speeds, wherein both the continuities and discontinuities of the line argue the rapid motor-responsiveness of the artist's hand to unconscious impulses and disturbances–a kind of seismograph of the brain. Circles, ovals, and spirals of lines swirl around a collapsed center, according to what Masson calls "the

---

[39] William Rubin and Carolyn Lanchner, *André Masson* (New York: Museum of Modern Art, 1976), p. 107.

rhythm of the line" whereby "an unbroken ring abolishes space–spirit of heaviness." [40] Thus, the line, though still construed as a "recording device," seems freed of certain representational functions involved in classic automatism. Its speed and rhythm give it an absolute lightness of being by which the plastic is abolished and replaced with a kind of bodiless movement that is nevertheless graphic. It is like syntax without recognizable parts of speech, a graphic glossalalia. It is interesting that the automatic graphic line dissolves visual representation in the way that glossalalia–as in the work of Antonin Artaud–dissolves verbal representation. This similarity would suggest, then, that Artaud's activities were more integrally "automatic" than Breton's, which, as indicated earlier, evidenced a sort of secondary visual drift in terms of both the mental event and the expression itself.

But neither Masson nor Artaud saw automatism as the vehicle of a new, abstract purism. As his automatic works reveal, Masson's linear maelstrom is strangely regulated, or punctuated, by conspicuous little dots and hooks, stops and starts. It echoes visually with clusters of lines that wriggle into illusionistic fingers, cupped hands, breasts and nipples. Other lines follow human contours, often terminating in the V-shape of the female groin or in an anus. These limbs and contours overlap each other such that–as Masson wrote–"Une forme ne sera qu'un passage à une autre forme" (One form will only be the passage to another form). [41] Thus the line remains a contour of eroticized zones and the human body is transmogrified into a libidinal galaxy of partial objects, loosely orbiting each other in a web of graphic "strokes." Absolute speed of lines is, in the final analysis, too abstract for the early practitioners of graphic automatism. What at first seems a process of dissipating the external object results, in the end, as the distillation and sacralization of its parts as centers of erotic concentration. Other formalizing frameworks are subtly introduced to ensure their aesthetic sacralization. As Masson himself has written:

> Ce qui caractérise en grande partie les dessins automatiques–et cela plaisait beaucoup à Breton–c'est le fait qu'ils ont un haut et

---

[40] *Ibid.*, p. 109.
[41] Florence de Méredieu, *André Masson: Les Dessins automatiques* (Paris: Blusson Éditeur, 1988), p. 37.

un bas. Quoique très souvent on les expose et on les reproduit à l'envers! Au départ, il n'y avait presque jamais ni haut ni bas, mais inconsciemment, je m'arrêtais quand je voyais que je ne pouvais pas aller plus loin, cela sans aucune idée compositionelle.

(What characterizes the automatic drawings to a great extent –and this greatly pleased Breton–is the fact that they have a top and a bottom. Although very often they are displayed and reproduced upside down! At the beginning [of the process], there was almost never a top or bottom, but unconsciously, I stopped myself when I realized I couldn't go any further without an idea of composition.)[42]

If Breton conceded that automatic texts and drawings were subject to a degree of premeditation, he also insisted that this premeditation was not at odds with the constituent of spontaneity at work in the process. Breton, like Masson, invoked the idea of a "rhythmic unity for both eye and ear" and that this "correspond[ed] to a non-differentiation between sympathetic and formal qualities, non-differentiation between sensory and intellectual functions." (*SP*, pp. 68-70) The idea, then, of the "rhythmic unity of the line" provided a particular formal strategy with automatic viability, i.e., a sort of companionable premeditation at the core of spontaneity. Using this idea as a way of comparing graphic and literary automatism, one discovers a striking parallelism between Masson's drawings and Breton's writings, if only at those moments when Breton himself delves deeper than usual into the darker regions of his unconscious. If the automatic productions of individual artists and poets are simply inflections of a collective automatism by which everyone participates in "the dream" (as Breton once wrote),[43] Breton comes clos-

---

[42] *Ibid.*, p. 20.
[43] Two statements substantiate this claim: In the *Manifeste du surréalisme* Breton writes: "Seule la mémoire s'arroge le droit d'y faire des coupures, de ne pas tenir compte des transitions et de nous représenter plutôt une série de rêves que le rêve" (Memory alone arrogates to itself the right to make cuts, not to keep transitions, and to represent to us, rather, a series of dreams instead of the dream) (*MS*, p. 21). In "Le Message automatique": "Le propre du surréalisme est d'avoir proclamé l'égalité totale de tous les êtres humains normaux devant le message subliminal, d'avoir constamment soutenu que ce message constitue un patrimoine commun . . ." (The distinctive quality of surrealism is to have proclaimed the equality of all normal human beings before the subliminal message, to have constantly maintained that this message constitutes a common heritage . . .). In Breton's *Point du jour* (Paris: Gallimard, 1970), p. 191.

est to participating in Masson's dream in text No. 9 of *Poisson solu-ble* (dedicated, ironically, to Artaud, Masson's true kindred spirit):

> Sale nuit, nuit de fleurs, nuit de râles, nuit capiteuse, nuit sourde dont la main est un cerf-volant abject retenu par des fils de tous côtés, des fils noirs, des fils honteux! Campagne d'os blancs et rouges, qu'as-tu fait de tes arbres immondes, de ta candeur ar-borescentes, de ta fidélité qui était une bourse aux perles serrées, avec des fleurs, des inscriptions comme ci comme ça, des significations à tout prendre? Et toi, bandit, ah tu me tues, bandit de l'eau qui effeuilles tes couteaux dans mes yeux, tu n'as donc pitié de rien, eau rayonnante, eau lustrale que je chéris! Mes imprécations vous poursuivront longtemps comme une enfant jolie à faire peur qui agite dans votre direction son balai de genêt. Au bout de chaque branche il y a une étoile et ce n'est pas assez, non, chicorée de la Vierge. Je ne veux plus vous voir, je veux cribler de petits plombs vos oiseaux qui ne sont même plus des feuilles, je veux vous chasser de ma porte, coeurs à pépins, cervelles d'amour. Assez de crocodiles là-bas, assez de dents de crocodile sur les cuirasses de guerriers samouraïs, assez de jets d'encre enfin, et des renégats partout, des renégats à manchettes pourpres, des renégats à oeil de cassis, à cheveux de poule! C'est fini, je ne cacherai plus ma honte, je ne serai plus calmé par rien, par moins que rien. Et si les volants sont grands comme des maisons, comment voulez-vous que nous jouions, que nous en-tretenions notre vermine, que nous placions nos mains sur les lèvres des coquilles qui parlent sans cesse (ces coquilles, qui les fera taire, enfin?). Plus de souffles, plus de sang, plus d'âme mais des mains pour pétrir l'air, pour dorer un seule fois le pain de l'air, pour faire claquer la grande gomme des drapeaux qui dor-ment, des mains solaires, enfin, des mains gelées! (*OC*, pp. 361-362)

> (Night of filth, night of flowers, night of groans, giddy night, muffled night whose hand is an abject kite held back by strings on all sides, black strings, shameful strings! Countryside of white and red bones, what have you done with your horrendous trees, your arborescent candor, your fidelity that was once a purse of serried pearls, flowers and inscriptions scattered here and there, meanings, taking one thing with another? And you, bandit, ban-dit, oh! you slay me, water bandit defoliating your knives in my eyes, don't you take pity on anything, radiant water, lustral water that I cherish! My imprecations will hound you for ages like a

frighteningly pretty child brandishing after you its flowering
broom. At the tip of each branch, there is a star and that is not
all, no, succory of the Virgin. I want to see you never again, to
riddle with buckshot your birds that aren't even leaves any
longer, to chase you from my door, hearts with pips, brains of
love. Enough crocodiles over there, enough crocodile teeth on
the breastplates of samurai warriors, enough ink spurts, and
renegades everywhere, renegades with purple cuffs, with black-
currant eyes, with chicken hair! That's done with, I'll hide my
shame no more, nothing will calm me, less than nothing. And if
the shutters are as high as houses, how do you expect us to play,
or maintain our vermin, or lay our hands on the lips of ever-babbling shells (these shells, who will silence them at last?) No more
breath, no more blood, no more soul, but hands to knead the air,
to make the bread of air golden only once, to flap the great gum
of sleeping flags, solar hands, in short, frozen hands!) [44]

The "sale nuit" of the first line functions as a kind of magnetic
pole for the peregrinations of Breton's automatic thought which
both strains against and gravitates toward it through a sustained
rhetoric of imprecation. But the "night of filth" is, all at once, a
time, a place, and a persona, erratically metamorphosing, yet consistently assuming the deictics of second-person singular: "you," the
object of "my" hostility, with the presumed speaker providing the
rhetorical counterpart in a dialectical framework not unlike Masson's compositional "top and bottom." Thus Breton's automatic
syntax generates a relatively stable discursive movement that parallels the formal consistencies of Masson's automatic drawing. As
Masson's graphic line successively redefines the surrounding space
of the page as overlapping vestiges of the human figure, Breton's
syntactic line similarly establishes recognizable rhetorical contours
across otherwise shifting semantico-symbolic registers. As we shall
see, elements of discourse overlap and contradict each other as successive waves of automatic thought shift the denotative coordinates
of an obsessive, denunciatory rhetoric. As a result, even the deictic
regularity of "I" and "you"—subject and object—begin to coalesce in
surprising ways. It is, in embryo, the surrealist notion of non-differentiation between expression/representation, spontaneity/formality,
interiority/exteriority as it occurs in automatic works.

---

[44] Breton, "Night of filth, night of flowers . . ." in *Poems of André Breton*, trans.
Jean-Pierre Cauvin, Mary Ann Caws (Austin: University of Texas Press, 1982), p. 45.

How does this happen? From the outset of the poem, the reader identifies an almost abstract entity being conceptually mutilated through the sustained verbal animosity of an unknown speaker. The very adjective of "sale nuit" is more projective than descriptive and any innocence or neutrality night may actually have is impugned with each adjective or genitive. Night's salacious attributes quickly accumulate in the first sentence (although, curiously, not all of the attributes are derogatory in themselves—only in the contemptuous tone with which they are delivered) and gradually assume a physical, human aspect through the synecdoche of night's human hand. This hand, in turn, is metamorphosed into a kite constrained by innumerable strings (or, in a pun on *fils*, shameful, black "sons"—bringing to mind Rimbaud's "Saison en enfer"). It seems strange—irrational—that one kite should require so many strings. In fact, Breton has literalized the meaning of *cerf-volant* (kite) by imagistically rendering it as a bounding (yet abject) stag that strains against the ropes of unknown hunters or all-too-well-known (if racially "illegitimate") sons. In this way the conventional, metaphorical meaning of *cerf-volant* gives way to an unconventional, literal meaning upon which successive images elaborate "unconsciously." This maneuver recurs at important moments in the poem through the "accidental" misinterpretation of the phonic entities making up certain words. (Sound, then, is one key to the poem's semantic incongruities.)

With the "campagne d'os blancs et rouges" (countryside of white and red bones), Breton's "sale nuit" assumes the guise of a landscape—one that has somehow been pruned of a former, innocent vitality ("candeur arborescente"), or fullness of meaning ("significations à tout prendre"). Yet those former meanings are also described as filth ("tes arbres immondes"), indicating that fecundity (trees) and decay (bones) are somehow aligned. Ironically, the voice now seems to curse the landscape for shedding the very filth that prompted its contemptuous label of "sale nuit" in the first place. Thus the voice simultaneously curses the landscape's acquired morbidity. The idea of filth, then, straddles the antinomies of fecundity and decay, life and death, in a way that suggests their interchangeability. The night of filth becomes a mysterious locus where opposites can stand in for or coalesce with each other, as in dreams (a poetic phenomenon consistent with Freudian ideas of "displacement" and "condensation" as described in *The Interpretation of Dreams*).

Another, more surprising reversal occurs in the next sentence: "Et toi, bandit, ah tu me tues, bandit de l'eau qui effeuilles tes couteaux dans mes yeux, tu n'as donc pitié de rien, eau rayonnante, eau lustrale que je chéris!" (And you, bandit, bandit, oh! you slay me, water bandit defoliating your knives in my eyes, don't you take pity on anything, radiant water, lustral water that I cherish!) The voice's anger now turns upon a kind of thief of night (as opposed to night itself), a thief who assumes the contradictory qualities of life-giving water and murderous/castrating pruning shears (is he like the water, or merely stealing it? is the pitilessness an attribute of the thief himself or the cherished water?). Yet it is the blinding knives themselves that are defoliated by the watery bandit. If the thief comes as an apocalyptic judge, it is one who, in enucleating the speaker, seems also to be disabling himself, shearing his own locks, as it were. The image, once again, is the paradoxical elaboration of a phonico-semantic overlap whereby killing another becomes a form of self-destruction through a kind of Sadean identification: "ah tu me tues," such that you not only kill me–you *you* me. In this way, non-differentiation is ironically thematized in the context of rendering judgment, of making critical distinctions. Hence, any judgment, criticism, condemnation or curse, here, seems to redound to whatever judge or critic pronounces it. It is Oedipean self-punishment.

In light of the above, the automatic text seems "unconsciously" (as Masson might say) to introduce non-automatic, formal qualities with all the earmarks of self-conscious literary production. Through a continuous, unbroken, yet rhythmic line of iteration a whole thematics of self-criticism and self-conscious creation emerges in the poem. If automatic expression is supposed to reveal the uninhibited "whole" self that rational expression represses, that self seems to bifurcate instantaneously in the act of enunciation, no matter how automatic. Uninhibited self-expression seems simultaneously to induce psychological self-mutilation, with the text serving as the record of how the unconscious becomes self-aware. Thus automatism itself initiates the return of the various non-automatic procedures that *it* would, theoretically, repress. In this way, elements of the poem acquire a new significance: the "sale nuit" would seem to be the idea of the unconscious; its hand, the automatic expression of the unconscious; and the "fils noires," the actual traces (or son-like products) of automatic writing that, in expressing the uncon-

scious, also capture and kill it. Automatic writing, then, is the subject of this poem: it is the unconscious that it consciously betrays,
that it "prunes" of all abundance via automatic selection.

"Assez de jets d'encres enfin, et des rénegats partout . . . C'est
fini, je ne cacherai plus ma honte . . ." (. . . enough ink spurts, and
renegades everywhere . . . That's done with, I'll hide my shame no
more . . .). This confession of shame seems to call for an end to
writing, and yet earlier, shame itself was identified with the very
scrawl of the written line, the constraining binds of (or bonds with)
the "fils honteux." Therefore, the only way for the voice "not to
hide" its shame is to keep on writing, keep on "reproducing."

> Et si les volants sont grands comme des maisons, comment
> voulez-vous que nous jouions, que nous entretenions notre ver-
> mine, que nous placions nos mains sur les lèvres des coquilles
> qui parlent sans cesse (ces coquilles, qui les fera taire, enfin?).

> (And if the shutters are as high as houses, how do you expect us
> to play, or maintain our vermin, or lay our hands on the lips of
> ever-babbling shells (these shells, who will silence them at last?).)

Of course, "volants" rhythmically echoes "cerf-volant" such that
the beast/kite of the unconscious has metamorphosed into the shutters of "une grande maison"–a veritable museum, like that of "Cinq
Rêves." The voice seems to inquire, "How can one create if one's
own creations tend to metamorphose into oppressive forms and in-
stitutions that stifle creation itself. Yet in asking who will silence the
"ever-babbling shells at last," the voice seems to acknowledge its
own complicity in building those oppressive structures, in attempting to capture (to silence) that babbling shoal (and yet that babbling and those "vermin" also suggest a brood of children, children
who might live in "une grande maison"). This sentiment also implies that the creative task of silencing creative spontaneity is unful-
fillable. The voice will not silence the "lèvres de coquilles" (lips of
shells) that go on and on, because the source of their babble's enchantment is its inartistic otherness, its indeterminacy, its unpre-
dictability, hence, a kind of accidental and surprising beauty both at
odds and supporting the ponderous legacies weighing down on it.

Significantly, the French word for "shell" (*coquille*) also means
"misprint" (again the idea of an accidental offspring). It is not for

sake of high art, after all, that Breton's unconscious agitates–a sentiment conveyed in the last line of the poem: "Plus de souffles, plus
de sang, plus d'âme, mais des *mains* pour pétrir l'air . . . des mains
solaires, enfin, des mains gelées" (No more breath, no more blood,
no more soul, but hands to knead the air . . . solar hands, in short,
frozen hands!). Automatism thus shows itself to be a kind of manual art or motor artistry, the very elegance of which is achieved by accident, by the automatic misreading, mis-hearing, or misprinting of
signs which nevertheless reveal a tendency toward solidification
(*mains gelées*). Breton seems to acknowledge this tendency in a description of Masson's equally *manual* art that could well apply to his
own experiments with automatism: "Metamorphosis, germination,
and blossoming are captured at the moment when the leaf and the
wing are only just beginning to unfold and are shimmering with the
most disturbing, evanescent, and magical glow. Masson's painting
fixes the moment when the living being achieves consciousness, except for a dialectical fixing of the moment when the same being loses consciousness."[45]

Salvador Dalí

Inasmuch as Breton was willing to concede the conscious, formalizing dimension of a process that was supposed to be *un*conscious and *non*formalizing, one can see the emergence of other surrealist procedures that seemed, at first, to contradict the basis of
automatism. With the arrival of Salvador Dalí and his elaboration,
in 1930, of the paranoiac-critical method, Surrealism obtained a
new procedural allowance that its former postulates had complicated. Dalí's strategy originated–but was not limited to–the plastic arts
and made exuberant use of what Breton had disparaged as retrograde, academic illusionism. The painter described his method in
the following way:

> Toute mon ambition sur le plan pictural consiste à matérialiser
> avec la plus impérialiste rage de précision les images de l'irra-
> tionalité concrète. Que le monde imaginatif et de l'irrationalité
> concrète soit de la même évidence objective, de la même consis-

---

[45] "André Masson" in *SP*, p. 154.

tance, de la même dureté, de la même épaisseur persuasive, cognoscitive, et communicable, que celle du monde extérieur de la réalité phénoménique.

(My whole ambition concerning pictures consists in materializing, with the most imperialist rage for precision, the images of concrete irrationality. Thus may the world of imagination and of concrete irrationality have the same objective evidence, the same consistency, the same severity, the same persuasive, cognitive, and communicative solidity as that of the external world of phenomenal reality.) [46]

And further on:

L'académisme le plus analytiquement narratif et discrédité peuvent devenir des hiérarchies sublimes de la pensée à l'approche des nouvelles exactitudes de l'irrationalité concrète.

(The most analytically narrative and discredited academicism can become sublime hierarchies of thought with the arrival of concrete irrationality's new exactitude.) [47]

Dalí methodically cultivated paranoia in a way that was consistent with two distinct diagnostic categories: confusional and critical paranoia. ("The Dali 'Case,'" *SP*, p. 130) The first manifested itself as a delirium in which obsessive images spontaneously erupted in different lived or "concrete" circumstances; the second involved the integration of the image or idea with the most diverse elements of phenomenal reality through a sustained and rigorous mode of interpretation that organized such experience into a unified system, sometimes causing a contagion of the delirium by virtue of its apparent persuasiveness. [fig. 12] Thus, logic, reason, and other formal modes of thought could be harnessed to "systématiser la confusion et de contribuer au discrédit total du monde de la réalité" (systematize the confusion and to contribute to the total discrediting of the world of reality). [48]

---

[46] Salvador Dali, "Autour de la méthode paranoïaque-critique: La Conquête de l'irrationnel," in *Oui* (Paris: Éditions Denoël), p. 16.

[47] *Ibid.*

[48] Salvador Dali, "L'Ane pourri," quoted in "Délire paranoïaque et poésie" by Ruth Amossy in *Europe*, No. 743 (mars 1991), p. 42.

Dalí's method seemed to offer strategic advantages for the realization of Surrealism's goals in the area of social reality, i.e., to convince everyone of the reality of its practitioners' ideals. In emphasizing the systematic and socially contagious exteriorization of personal delirium, Dalí's method elevated mere "technical matters"–implicit in critical systematization–to a higher level of theoretical importance. This secondary enhancement of the technical, in turn, helped remove the veil of literary obfuscation regarding automatism's assumed "passivity." Once considered an absolute requirement for ensuring automatic writing's "documentary value of revealing 'mental facts,'" as Louis Aragon wrote in *Traité du style*,[49] surrealist passivity was not so much replaced by "active interpretation," as deconstructed by it. Indeed, from another perspective, automatic writings themselves could be seen as simply a high-speed verbal mode of systematization. Dalí himself later commented on the connection between the two strategies, remarking that their apparent contradiction concealed "a vital communication between the two experimental principles,"[50] much as Breton's "communicating vessels" operated by way of an unnoticed "capillary tissue." This was because all delirious ideas–according to Dalí and certain psychiatrists (Jacques Lacan, Émile Kraepelin)–have paranoiac potential, are always already systematized, and because "only the idealistic evasions of poets prevent them from recognizing the consubstantial systematizing potential of automatism itself."[51]

As Laurent Jenny concluded in his own study of the relation between automatism and the paranoiac-critical method: "'Active' automatism emerges, therefore, from solipsism, recognizing itself as symbolic manipulation, engaging collective values and hence it can lay claim much more convincingly than 'passive' automatism to effects of social confusion."[52] Jenny provides an instance of pure automatism's reduced stature in the surrealist agenda when he quotes Breton: "... the theory of automatism must be distinguished from its practice. Everything about the theory suggests a visual navigation,

---

[49] Louis Aragon, *Traité du style* quoted in Laurent Jenny's "From Breton to Dali: The Adventures of Automatism," trans. Thomas Trezise, in *October*, Vol. 51 (Winter 1989), p. 109.
[50] Salvador Dali, "Nouvelles considérations générales sur le mécanisme du phénomène paranoïaque du point de vue surréaliste," in *Oui*, p. 29.
[51] *Ibid.*, p. 37.
[52] Jenny, p. 110.

inspired by circumstances. It is subject to the most flagrant contradictions and changes of direction. Automatic practice, however, is
infinitely more synthetic. It makes use of all outside contributions:
spiritist, Freudian, or paranoiac-critical." [53]

Perhaps the earliest "sanctioned" literary evidence of a broader
definition of automatic practice was *L'Immaculée conception*, the
collaboration between Breton, Paul Éluard, and, in certain respects,
Dalí. The work itself was conceived as the synthesis of precisely the
techniques mentioned above, and, in it, the authors demonstrate an
awareness of the sort of "availability of means" author Peter Bürger
later attributed to the Avant-Garde in his *Theory of the Avant-Garde*.
Nonetheless, an ordering principle–both satiric and academic in nature–is employed as a way of monumentalizing the various practices
available to the Surrealists at this time. The overall framework was
conceived as a kind of literary polyptych with three main sections
that, beyond the Christian trinity, suggested a broader Hegelian
synthesis of individual (un)consciousness and absolute or historical
consciousness. Indeed, the framing titles (or related working titles)
preceded the actual writings, which were done, as Breton and
Éluard wrote in their introduction, "in fifteen days, and in that time
we consecrated to it only our hours of real leisure." [54] Thus, in a
sense, speed continued to be a component of the work's production,
and yet, one that now accommodated itself less to accident and
chance than to the deliberate portrayal of different mental states.

The most interesting aspect of the work, and the focus of considerable critical attention, is the first half of the middle section entitled *Les Possessions,* in which the authors, responding to the challenge of Dalí's method, undertook the "active mimesis of certain
psychotic deliriums" [55] through simulating the verbal manifestations
of mental disorders–i.e., the modern, secular versions of demonic
"possessions." In these so-called "essays of simulation" Breton and
Éluard attempted to blur the boundaries between reason and madness by demonstrating the delirious capacities of perfectly sane, rational individuals, who, for poetic purposes, had temporarily assumed the expressive characteristics of specific mental diseases. In

[53] *Ibid*, p. 114.
[54] Jacqueline Chénieux-Gendron, "Toward a New Definition of Automatism:
L'Immaculée conception," in *André Breton Today*, p. 75.
[55] *Ibid.*, p. 81.

an introduction to the "essays" they attested to the authenticity of correspondence between the work and the primary verbal features of the given diseases (mental debility, acute mania, general paralysis, dementia praecox, and delirium of interpretation) and denied the writings were mere pastiches of documented examples. Instead, they insisted that mental disease, the manifest "possession" of the mind by certain otherwise unconscious potentialities, was somehow *available* to normal thought as an expressive resource. [56]

A complete discussion of *The Possessions* and their formal and thematic relations to the overall work is not possible here. [57] However, a brief consideration of the "Essai de simulation du délire d'interprétation" offers a convenient transition to other Bretonian practices that are derived, in part, from Dalinian method and bear more directly upon Breton's interest in the plastic arts. As mentioned earlier, delirium of interpretation of the paranoiac kind involved the use of a primary obsessional image as the unifying symbol for various observable concrete phenomena. In the essay under consideration, the image is that of a bird, into which all things metamorphose by virtue of interpreting certain recognizable features of those things–such things as the Pont au Change, a bridge in Paris, whose name and stated proximity to a bird market becomes evidence for the speaker of the general metamorphosis of the human world into a kind of cosmic aviary. A narrative ensues in which a variety of concrete phenomena and expressions employing bird motifs are offered up as proof of the reality of the speaker's delusions.

From the standpoint of method, the above "simulation" would seem to share many of the same technical properties as the poem "L'Union libre," in which Breton's wife's body provides the lyrical nexus for a range of unrelated phenomena adjoined to its parts. But an important difference distinguishes the two works: "L'Union li-

---

[56] In a study, published in 1970 for the Faculty of Medicine at the University of Paris, Dr. Alain Rauzy, a psychiatrist, concluded that the essays of simulation in *L'Immaculée conception* were completely convincing except for the famous one of interpretive delirium, the bird imagery of which he found "too exceptional." See Antony Melville's introduction to *The Immaculate Conception*, trans. Jon Graham (London: Atlas Press, 1990), p. 13.

[57] For a more thorough discussion, see Melville's introduction to the English translation, *ibid.*; the study by Chénieux-Gendron, *op. cit.*; and Bonnet's notice in *Oeuvres Complètes I*, pp. 1629-1672.

bre" almost mechanically juxtaposes the elements without attempting to justify or explain the procedure. The simulation, on the other hand, seeks to persuade the reader–in delirious fashion–of the coherence and validity of an insane idea.

In this way one can see how interpretation itself becomes a privileged component of surrealist poetic endeavor at this stage. And while poetry can accommodate such explanation within its own artifacts, in the plastic arts, interpretation remains a kind of critical excess that nevertheless completes the work in an interdisciplinary, dialectical capacity ideally suited to the Hegelian concerns Breton had at the time.[58] Combined with the "paranoiac" imperative of externalizing the unconscious, the plastic arts suddenly acquired a new integrity as the concrete starting point for interpretive, yet nonliterary, activities Breton himself was now to pursue. Inspired by Dalí's "symbolically-functioning objects," Breton began producing similar objects of his own that reveal–perhaps even more than the "simulations"–the true complexity of certain paranoiac obsessions. Dalí's own description of one of Breton's "objects" [fig. 13] illustrates this point:

> Le plus complexe et difficile à analyser. Sur une petite selle de bicyclette est placé un réceptacle en terre cuite rempli de tabac, à la surface duquel reposent deux longues dragées de couleur rose. Une sphère de bois poli, susceptible de tourner dans l'axe de la selle, fait entrer en contact au cours de ce mouvement la pointe de celle-ci avec deux antennes de celluloïd orangé. Cette sphère est reliée par deux bras de même substance à un sablier disposé horizontalement (de manière à empêcher l'écoulement du sable) et à un timbre de bicyclette qui est supposé entrer en action quand est projetée dans l'axe une dragée verte au moyen d'un lance-pierres placé derrière la selle. Le tout est monté sur une planche recouverte de végétations sylvestres laissant apparaître de place en place un pavage d'amorces et dont un des angles, plus touffu que les autres, est occupé par un petit livre sculpté en albâtre dont le plat est décoré d'une photographie sous verre de la tour de Pise, près de laquelle on découvre, en ecartant le feuillage une amorce, la seule éclatée, sous un pied de biche.

---

[58] Breton was reading the Vera translation of Hegel in 1930 while writing the "Second Manifesto of Surrealism." He later attended lectures by Alexandre Kojève that strongly influenced *L'Immaculée conception*. Melville, *op. cit.*, p. 9.

(The most complex and difficult to analyze. On the little saddle of a bicycle is placed a terracotta receptacle filled with tobacco on top of which lie two long, rose-colored dragées. A polished wooden sphere that can turn in the axle of the saddle puts, in the course of its movement, the tip of the saddle in contact with two antennae made of orange celluloid. This sphere is connected by two arms of the same substance to an hourglass resting horizontally (so as to prevent the sand from pouring) and to the bell of the bicycle which is supposed to ring when a green dragée is shot into the axle by means of a slingshot placed behind the saddle. The whole thing is mounted on a board covered with forest vegetation that here and there shows a series of baited traps underneath, and, occupying one of the corners, more bushy than the others, is a little book sculpted in alabaster, the front of which is illustrated with a photograph, under glass, of the tower of Pisa, near which one discovers, on brushing aside the foliage, another trap, the only one sprung, under a doe's hoof.) [59]

The components of the preceding object/sculpture have no obvious function or meaning and yet one is immediately impressed by its assiduousness of construction and its aura of hidden significance. As Dalí himself recognizes, this significance is not easily discoverable and thus he concludes more generally, "Ces objets, qui se prêtent à un minimum de fonctionnement mécanique, sont basés sur les phantasmes et représentations susceptibles d'être provoqués par la réalisation d'actes inconscients" (These objects, which lend themselves to a minimum of mechanical functioning, are based on the fantasms and representations susceptible of being provoked by the realization of unconscious acts). (JVJ, p. 13) Yet, more than the concretization of dream acts and unconscious desires, these objects were to be the source of "convulsive beauty," the phenomenon of almost erotic surprise that occurred when a particular object or event marvelously corresponded to some inner necessity. More typically, this notion is referred to as "objective chance," i.e., when a certain "form" makes "manifest the exterior necessity which traces its path in the human unconscious." [60] But it is important to see

---

[59] Salvador Dalí, "Communication relative au hasard objectif" (1934) in *André Breton, Je vois, J'imagine: Poèmes-objets* (Paris: Gallimard, 1991), p. 13. Subsequent citations from this edition will appear in the text as *JVJ*.

[60] André Breton, *Mad Love*, trans. Mary Ann Caws (Lincoln: University of Nebraska, 1987), p. 23.

here that this particular idea, profoundly identified with surrealist activity, was in many ways derived from Dali, who had described paranoiac-critical activity from the outset as "an organizing and productive force of objective chance." ("The Dali 'Case,'" *SP*, p. 130) The difference between the two concepts is precisely the organizational and productive dimension of Dalinian method. In short, the symbolically-functioning objects were deliberate constructions, a way of organizing diverse elements to correspond with an obsessing idea–an idea that was often only discoverable by way of this very act of symbolically hierarchizing random elements.

Breton went on to develop his own variation on the symbolically-functioning object in the form of poem-objects. "Le poème-objet est une composition qui tend à combiner les ressources de la poésie et de la plastique et à spéculer sur leur pouvoir d'exaltation réciproque" (The poem-object is a composition that tends to combine the resources of poetry and art and to speculate on their reciprocal power of exaltation). ("Du Poème-objet," *JVJ*, p. 8) This Bretonian version of the symbolically-functioning object introduces verbal commentary and the cryptic labeling of parts to enhance the work's convulsive beauty and, at other times, simply to orient one's interpretation. One of the earliest poem-objects is entitled *1713*, a date that mysteriously attracted Breton by virtue of the graphic resemblance of the numbers to his own initials. The object itself is a series of slots or niches on a textured surface. The niches contain items or captions relating to various events in French history that took place in 1713 and which Breton ingeniously assimilates to a private schema. Yet without the poet's own commentary on the work, it seems unlikely that any innocent observer could ever interpret the poem-object satisfactorily.

More easily deciphered is an untitled one [fig. 14] in which a long caption, scrawled above the plastic elements that make up the object, describes the actual experience yielding those elements and exemplifying for Breton the workings of objective chance. The various linen napkins, folded in different ways and mounted on wood, are not of any aesthetic interest in themselves. Yet the viewer is irresistibly, "convulsively" drawn to a particular one that is rolled up and plunked, erect, into a squat wineglass. Its phallic appearance is unmistakable, especially when one notices the rather dainty folds of cloth at the tip, suggesting circumcision. On the other side stands another wineglass; but this one has a deep, jagged gash made by a knife, which still rests, blade down, in the glass. The narrative on the back mount explains the events relating to these items: after a meal at a restaurant, Breton and some friends were discussing various ways of folding up dinner napkins after eating and what personal significance it had for them individually. The poet Benjamin Peret's idiosyncratic method was particularly remarked. Everyone was astonished later when, by a pure coincidence, the waitress clearing the dishes from the table accidentally dropped a cutting knife into Peret's glass and broke it, severing the napkin from its perch. The "slip" immediately brought to mind the obvious castration complex.

Aside from the obvious black humor of the piece, this particular poem-object is indicative of Breton's gradual shift in emphasis from Dalí's paranoiac-critical method to the less charged idea of objective chance, which essentially allows the poet to be *disponible* or "available" to chance encounters without aggressively commandeering them (or seeming to) for one's own paranoiac purposes. In short, objective chance allowed Breton to continue indulging in symbolic manipulations of the Dalinian stamp, but under the aegis of another name. Symbolically-functioning objects and their residue of artistic construction could be replaced by "found objects," eccentric items that simply welled up by chance from modern society at large, but which defied the "depreciation of the aesthetic value of objects via mass production . . . [through] unleashing the powers of invention." [61] It was a return, of a sort, to a more passive mode of automatism, and one that seemed, in light of Breton's later break with "Avida Dollars," to have a more surrealistically benign genealogy–via Marcel Duchamp, Man Ray, Giacometti, and Max Ernst. As in his preference for the Reverdian over the futurist definition of the image, Breton wanted to avoid any appearance of filiation with movements or individuals perceived as politically reactionary. This retreat was clearly indicated when he later described Dalí as "moins l'inventeur que le généralisateur [d'une méthode qui prend en fait] naissance dans la leçon de Vinci et les frottages d'Ernst" (less the inventor than the popularizer [of a method that in fact originated] in the lesson of Da Vinci and the *frottages* of Ernst). [62]

---

[61] André Breton, "The Crisis of the Object" (1936) in *Surrealism and Painting*, p. 277.

[62] Amossy, p. 40.

Joan Miró

If, as Donald Kuspit has written, Breton "depended on the criticism of his enemies for the expansion of his conception of surrealism [by regularly turning] friends out of the surrealist court," [63] his "uncritical" allies provided a form of sanction for Breton's occasional retreat to less troublesome theoretical postures. It comes as no surprise, then, that long after Breton's ultimate expansion and coordination of the resources of poetry and art in the poem-object, one should later find him toward the end of his career indulging in something very close to ekphrastic exercises, with all their residue of "imitation." If Breton had once prejudicially demoted painting in relation to poetry by consigning it to an imitative or representational category reliant upon iconic signs rather than to an expressive category reliant upon symbolic ones, he eventually succumbed to the imitative potential of poetry itself, a potential that inevitably gains momentum due to the effective contiguity (i.e., indexical relation) of poetry's intended or unintended discursive elements to the poet's internal mental objects. These latter, ekphrastic activities were less a way of expanding surrealist horizons than of taking stock of surrealist achievements. Breton's last "poetic" engagement with the problem of the plastic arts assumes the properties of a monumental, retrospective work in which the idea of the "series" has profoundly recomposed itself from one of random, automatic movement to sweeping, panoramic progression:

> L'ensemble des vingt-deux planches réunies sous le titre *Constel-*
> *lations* et qui, dans l'oeuvre de Miró, s'échelonnent entre les
> dates du 21 janvier 1940 et du 12 septembre 1941, constitue une
> série au sens le plus privilégié du terme. Il s'agit, en effet, d'une
> succession délibérée d'oeuvres de même format, empruntant les
> mêmes moyens matériels d'exécution. Elles participent et dif-
> fèrent l'une de l'autre à la façon des corps de la série aromatique
> ou cyclique de la chimie; considérées à la fois dans leur progres-
> sion et leur totalité, chacune d'elles y prend aussi la nécessité et
> la valeur de chaque composante de la série mathématique; enfin
> le sentiment d'une réussite ininterrompue, exemplaire, qu'elles

---

[63] Kuspit, p. 56.

nous procurent, garde ici, au mot série, l'acception qu'il prend dans les jeux d'adresse et de hasard.

(The ensemble of twenty-two plates united under the title *Constellations* and which, in the oeuvre of Miró, are spread out between January 21, 1940, and September 12, 1941, constitute a series in the most privileged sense of the term. It is a matter, in effect, of a deliberate succession of works using the same format and borrowing the same material means of execution. They resemble and differ from one another in the same way as the elements of the aromatic or cyclical series in chemistry; considered both in terms of their progression and their totality, each of them assumes the necessity and value of each component of the mathematical series; finally the feeling of an uninterrupted, exemplary success they procure for us retains here the same meaning in relation to the word "series" that it has in relation to games of skill and chance.) [64]

Constellations (1959) thus constitutes an impressive homage to a great painter, yet a painter Breton was wont to criticize in the past for "infantilism" and certain "intellectual limits" to his work. ("Genesis," *SP*, p. 70) It is interesting that for all its formal grandeur, the work contains no commentary at all on formal issues concerning the plastic arts in general, and few real references to Miró's gouaches in particular. Thus, in the final analysis, Breton's ekphrastic poems are slyly disappointing for the comparatist. Their primary ekphrastic property is the strict adherence to Miró's own titles for the original (yet accompanying) gouaches. The poems do, however, make liberal use of the iconography of birds, women, acrobats, night skies, bodies of water, suns, moons, numbers, rebuses, and stars, yet these too are derived primarily from the titles. The overall title of *Constellations* itself is important for Breton insofar as it situates the poem less in relation to Miró's work than the Mallarméan universe of "Un Coup de dés ...," judging by the last sentence in the above statement.

Where Breton comes closest, it seems, to verbally suggesting or describing the visual effect of one of Miró's gouaches is in the penultimate poem in the series, *Le Bel oiseau déchiffrant l'inconnu*

---

[64] André Breton, *Signe ascendant* (Paris: Gallimard, 1968), p. 127. Subsequent citations of this edition will appear in the text as *SA*.

au couple d'amoureux (The Beautiful Bird Revealing the Unknown to a Pair of Lovers). [fig. 15] It is also the only one of the poems that goes beyond expressing an intensely private, poetic response to Miró's work and actually makes general claims about the nature of plastic art from the perspective of Surrealism:

> Les bancs des boulevards extérieurs s'infléchissent avec le temps sous l'étreinte des lianes qui s'étoilent tout bas de beaux yeux et de lèvres. Alors qu'ils nous paraissent libres continuent autour d'eux à voleter et fondre les unes sur les autres ces fleurs ardentes. Elles sont pour nous traduire en termes concrets l'adage des mythographes qui veut que l'attraction universelle soit une qualité de l'espace et l'attraction charnelle la fille de cette qualité mais oublie par trop de spécifier que c'est ici à la fille, pour le bal, de parer la mère. Il suffit d'un souffle pour libérer ces myriades d'aigrettes porteuses d'akènes. Entre leur essor et leur retombée selon la courbe sans fin du désir s'inscrivent en harmonie tous les signes qu'englobe la partition céleste. (*SA*, p. 167)

> (The benches of the outer boulevards bend down in time under the embrace of vines that light up softly in a spangle of beautiful eyes and lips. While they appear vacant to us, around them those ardent flowers continue to flutter and infuse each other. They are to translate in concrete terms the adage of mythographers according to which the gravitational pull of heavenly bodies is allegedly a characteristic of space and carnal desire the daughter of that characteristic but which altogether forgets to specify that it is up to the daughter, for the ball, to adorn the mother. A single breath is sufficient to set free those myriads of egrets bearing achenes. Between their upward and their downward flight along the endless curve of desire all the signs encompassed by the celestial score are set down in harmony.) [65]

The gravitational pull of heavenly bodies seems to refer both to the galaxy of icons within Miró's painting (and the cosmos it suggests), as well as to the attractive powers of art works, found objects, or bodies in general, symbolized in the poem by the infusing "fleurs ardentes." This power is the result of the combined affect of their extension in space and the viewer's desire to traverse that space, a desire that is fundamentally carnal or "convulsive." The

---

[65] Cauvin and Caws, p. 225.

mythographer's adage, then, is that gravity and desire are "related" aspects of a universal attraction, but that the daughter of gravity (sexual appeal) adorns its many plastic forms—whether as planets, painterly icons of planets, or a host of mediating objects. Thus, a certain erotic appeal is a vital aspect of, perhaps even the key to, universal harmony. (Miró makes this eroticism explicit through the schematic rendering of vulvae throughout his series.) If there is one thing that generally characterizes surrealist art, it is its overt adornment of spatial and formal properties with the accoutrements of the spectacle, its eroticized elaboration of what were once aesthetic values. The conflation of art with heterosexual (usually male) desire is a primary lesson of official Surrealism. Thus, it is Breton, in the end, who is suggested by the mythographers and by the bird of the title, the bird who teaches the meaning of surrealist symbols to modern-day seekers of a special kind of carnal knowledge. The most explicit, "graphic" version of that knowledge assumes a plastic form, i.e., is translated in concrete terms ("traduire en termes concrets"). Perhaps that is why Breton's last long series of poems was conceived as a prose parallel to this alternative venue of surrealist knowledge—as if to ensure its continuing viability and vitality as an open mode of discourse with the concrete.

As the leader of one of the most influential and enduring avant-garde movements of this century, Breton gradually shifted his position vis-à-vis the surrealistic value of the plastic arts. Breton's early assessments tended to relegate the plastic arts to the level of an instructive expedient because they were considered the products of a formalizing, "citational" spirit rather than of the immediatist, "suigeneris" one Breton espoused. Whether in an illusionist vein or a more modernist vein (where principles of aesthetic construction predominate—as in Cubism), the creation of plastic art works involved, for Breton, the most deliberate cultivation of technique through semiotic imitation, reproduction, effective similarity, hence did not represent an optimally expressive vehicle for dismantling reason in the domains of either expression or action. Only with the formula of an "interior model" did Breton officially advocate a surrealist art *per se*. Once artistic "technique" was made theoretically permissible, it soon became indispensable as Breton's discourse acknowledged the desirability of systematically cultivating unconscious states—as suggested by Dalinian method in the late 1920s. As a consequence, Breton expanded the technical prerogative of automatism itself from a passive to an active mode. He also elaborated a surrealist variation on "objective chance" (both in his writings and in plastic forms) to explain "the way the subject's unconscious thought will operate upon reality, recutting it to the measure of their desires" and also to explain the "return of this new refashioned world in the form of a revelation. . . ." [66] Hence, not only the found object, but also the poem-object–the deliberate construction of that sense of "revelation"–helped to consolidate the position of the arts in both Bretonian rhetoric and practice. As we have seen, this practice combined the resources of poetry and art in a way that suggested their "non-differentiation" in the unconscious, even if the expression of that non-differentiation required their deliberate combination. Although one is tempted to accuse him of doing precisely what Apollinaire did in his calligrams, Breton's procedure more rigorously incorporates chance as a way of opening the breach between the two media to ensure their assimilation exclusively in the unconscious as opposed to one on the level of a new aesthetic. Hence, the poem-object does not transcend its combined media, but erodes them for the sake of the "confusions" that yield unconscious reality. That Breton should conclude his poetic career by writing a sort of lyric commentary on Miró's *Constellations* not only reveals his acceptance of graphic art as a medium that fully manifests surrealist aspirations, but as one that provides his own lyric expression with a vital complement–much as the waking state is complemented by the dream, and automatic writing by the internal voice. The psychological perspective on the relation between the arts has shifted since Apollinaire and Reverdy–from one of hierarchical dependency or competitive autonomy, respectively, to one of disinterested complementarity.

---

[66] Rosalind Krauss, *The Optical Unconscious* (Cambridge: MIT Press, 1993), p. 172.

CHAPTER IV

FRANK O'HARA

I N his apologetic letter of rejection to Frank O'Hara for the 1955
Yale Younger Poets prize (awarded to John Ashbery) W. H. Auden wrote: "I think you (and John, too, for that matter) must watch
what is always the great danger with any 'surrealistic' style, namely
of confusing authentic non-logical relations which arouse wonder
with accidental ones which arouse mere surprise and in the end fa-
tigue." [1] In a letter to Kenneth Koch, O'Hara responded to Auden's
comment, saying: "I don't care what Wystan says, I'd rather be
dead than not have France around me like a rhinestone dog-
collar." [2] In this way he confirms Auden's characterization, but only
after broadening the definition of "surrealistic style" to encompass
modern French poetry as a whole, and thus betraying the ambivalence the New York poets felt about having such a label.

Koch makes this attitude clear in an interview with Richard
Kostelanetz in 1991:

> No, it was not founded on Surrealism or Dada. Frank read the
> French poets and knew them, but his poetry was not surrealistic.
> It seems to me the surrealist attitude–trusting the unconscious
> more than the conscious, doing automatic writing, saying what-
> ever comes into your head, using accident in your poems, bring-
> ing in material from dreams–all those things that were program-
> matic for the Surrealists . . . these characteristics have by now
> become a natural and almost instinctive part of the work of
> many poets writing in English. You can find them in poets who

---

[1] W. H. Auden quoted by Brad Gooch, *City Poet: The Life and Times of Frank O'Hara* (Alfred A. Knopf, 1993), p. 261.
[2] Gooch, p. 261.

are not of the New York School. But whereas a good deal of surrealist poetry tends to stay in this world of dreams and the unconscious and magic, Frank's poetry very clearly comes back to
what would be considered ordinary reality. It always ends up
back on the streets, back with the taxicabs, and most of all back
with the emotional attachments in this life. [3]

Ashbery is more affirmative, however, explicitly enumerating French
avant-garde influences he sees as framing and modulating O'Hara's
work: "It is part of a modern tradition which is anti-literary and
anti-artistic, and which goes back to Apollinaire and the Dadaists,
to the collages of Picasso and Braque with their perishable newspaper clippings, to Satie's *musique d'ameublement* which was not
meant to be listened to." [4] Other, more academic writers have situated O'Hara's work not so much in a marginalized "other tradition" (as Ashbery calls it), [5] as in an American offshoot of a symbolist tradition subtly inscribed at the core of twentieth-century
avant-garde experiments. Thomas Meyer summarizes this tendency,
discovering in O'Hara's poems a "notion of surface . . . inherited
from Mallarmé via Apollinaire, coming as it did through Dada and
Surrealism on the way." [6]

The contrasts and conflations of these assessments arise from
Surrealism's being the repository of poetic experiments since the
Symbolists, yet a distinct entity within the Avant-Garde with its
own agenda and method. A general principle, however, separates
the dada/surrealist attitude from the symbolist/cubist one and pertains to the relative importance of the creative process for the first
group over that of the finished work for the latter. Consequently,
two modes of avant-garde discourse emerge that are closely connected yet vibrantly antagonistic. But O'Hara's generation felt little
obligation to maintain them in any doctrinaire way in the postwar

---

[3] Richard Kostelanetz, "Frank O'Hara and His Poetry" in *American Writing
Today* (Whitston Publishing, 1991), p. 205.
[4] John Ashbery, introduction to *The Collected Poems of Frank O'Hara*, ed. Donald Allen (University of California Press, 1995), p. vii. Subsequent citations of this
edition will appear in the text as *CP*, followed by the page number.
[5] Ashbery, "The Other Tradition" in *Selected Poems* (New York: Penguin,
1986), p. 208.
[6] Thomas Meyer, "Glistening Torsos, Sandwiches, and Coca-Cola" in *Frank
O'Hara: To Be True to a City*, ed. Jim Elledge (University of Michigan Press, 1990),
p. 94.

American context. Thus the Americans enjoyed a strategic flexibili-
ty that masked an underlying ambiguity about their assumed role as
the cultural heirs of the European Avant-Garde.

O'Hara had another reason to avoid taking sides: his interest in
the Avant-Garde paralleled that of the Abstract Expressionists who
were combining aestheticist and anti-aestheticist concerns in a new
way. At the time, Abstract Expressionism was seen as an accultura-
tive outgrowth of surrealist aspirations as they were adapted to
American conditions after World War II.[7] The linchpin of this association was psychic automatism boldly transferred to the medium
of paint.[8] Yet as "Action Painting,"[9] psychic automatism acquired
a new, aesthetic viability in shedding the surrealist orthodoxies that
had constrained it. In works by Jackson Pollock, Willem de Kooning, Franz Kline and others, the painted canvas became the plastic
correlative of unconscious processes, the spontaneous, non-verbal
expression of raw, psychic energy. Its status as art, however, was un-
abashedly proclaimed (not denied as the Surrealists tended to do),
thereby fusing cubist attitudes apropos of the finished work with
surrealist ones regarding action, process, immediacy. In this way the
new American painters re-enacted and resolved the drama of those
earlier aesthetico-ideological divisions among Symbolists, Cubists,
and Dada-Surrealists. Their action seemed exemplary, even heroic,
for O'Hara, in whose work the same divisions overlap and trans-
pose themselves in forms so ideologically attenuated as to yield an
eclectic outlook one might retrospectively term postmodern.[10]

---

[7] John Ashbery, "Yves Tanguy" in *Reported Sightings: Art Chronicles 1957-
1987* (Alfred A. Knopf, 1989), p. 26 and John Bernard Myers, *The Poets of the New
York School* (University of Pennsylvania, 1969), p. 9.

[8] Though there were distinct Surrealist prototypes by Max Ernst and André
Masson, they remained experiments, never sufficiently sustained to engender a
complete new style.

[9] Harold Rosenberg, "The American Action Painters" in *The Tradition of the
New* (Horizon Press, 1959), p. 23.

[10] O'Hara understood the connection between the French Avant-Garde and the
Abstract-Expressionists; but more importantly, he saw his own association with
the New York painters as a continuation of an avant-garde tradition inherited from the
French poets. In an interview with O'Hara in 1965, art historian and critic Edward
Lucie-Smith asked him about "this link between poetry and painting": "Well, it's
partly, I suppose, because of the French influence, in a way, on American painting.
You know [. . .] Apollinaire, Cubism, and all that sort of thing. [. . .] When we all
arrived in New York or emerged as poets in the mid 50s or late 50s, painters were
the only ones who were interested in any kind of experimental poetry, and the general literary scene was not. Oh, we were published in certain magazines and so on,

But certain comments of O'Hara's discourage making easy comparisons between his work and that of the Abstract Expressionists, not only because he responded to other painters as well (most importantly, Larry Rivers), but because of a persistent Reverdian assumption about the separation of the arts. In a statement for the Paterson Society (1961), O'Hara remarked:

> . . . you can't have a statement saying "My poetry is the Sistine Chapel of verse," or "My poetry is just like Pollock, de Kooning, and Guston rolled into one great verb," or "My poetry is like a windy day on a hill overlooking the stormy ocean"–first of all it isn't so far as I can tell, and secondly even if it were something like all of these that wouldn't be because I managed to make it that way. I couldn't, it must have been an accident, and I would probably not recognize it myself. Further, what would poetry like that be? It would have to be the Sistine Chapel itself, the paintings themselves, the day and time specifically. Impossible. (*CP*, 510)

Yet, as with Reverdy, O'Hara's categorical distinction between the two arts actually confirms the subtlety of his search for residues of communication, symptoms of filiation, among all of them. In an essay on the composer Morton Feldman, O'Hara opined: "the very extremity of the differences between the arts has thrown their analogies into sharp relief." (*SS*, 115) Thus a specific aesthetical sympathy with Reverdy may indeed underlie O'Hara's concluding line in "A Step Away From Them": "My heart is in my/ pocket, it is Poems by Pierre Reverdy." (*CP*, 258)

This theoretical sympathy is affirmed–if somewhat distended–through another path of poetic transmission: the American modernists–especially William Carlos Williams, who, like Reverdy, was highly responsive to cubist aesthetics. In "Frank O'Hara and the Aesthetics of Attention" Marjorie Perloff describes "how the French influence was gradually adapted to an American idiom [and] how O'Hara came to fuse the 'charming artifice' of Apollinaire and Reverdy with the vernacular toughness he admired in the

---

but nobody was really very enthusiastic except the painters." See Frank O'Hara, "Edward Lucie-Smith: An Interview with Frank O'Hara" in *Standing Still and Walking in New York*, ed. Donald Allen (Grey Fox Press, 1983), p. 3. Subsequent citations from any essay by O'Hara in this edition will appear in the text as *SS*.

poetry of Williams, Pound, and Auden." [11] Perloff further claims that Williams was O'Hara's favorite American poet, adding that the older poet's famous dictum of "No ideas but in things" (Paterson: Book I, 1946) was certainly "a cornerstone of O'Hara's aesthetic" [12] (even if O'Hara inverted the statement to read "No things but in ideas" in his poem "To A Poet" where he rhetorically counters Williamsian objectivity or "plainness" with his own "rococo/ self").

Williams's example offers a strong counterpart to French discourse and technique vis-à-vis the relation between poetry and art. It is Williams's approach to this relation that ultimately qualifies the formative influence he had on O'Hara. Thus the latter's poetics can only be fully understood by recognizing the French quotient in Williams's own poetics of the "thing" or object, particularly as they pertain to such early works as *Kora in Hell* (1916) and *Spring and All* (1923), which have been closely linked with Cubism and Surrealism by such scholars as Perloff, Bram Dijkstra, Henry Sayre, and, in some respects, J. Hillis Miller. The precedent Williams sets warrants further analysis here.

AMERICAN MODERNIST PRECURSOR: WILLIAM CARLOS WILLIAMS

In a letter to Williams about *Kora in Hell*, Wallace Stevens complains of the "casual character" of Williams's improvisations, saying that he himself has a "distaste for miscellany." [13] The criticism cuts to the core of Williams's project in that early work. Like Apollinaire, Reverdy, and Pound, Williams worked to overcome the moral and narrative strictures on the poetry of his day by focusing his imagination on "those things which lie under the direct scrutiny of the senses":

> The imagination goes from one thing to another. Given many things of nearly totally divergent natures but possessing one-thousandth part of a quality in common, provided that be new,

---

[11] Marjorie Perloff, "Frank O'Hara and the Aesthetics of Attention," in Elledge, p. 164.

[12] Perloff, "From 'Poetry Chronicle: 1970-71,'" in Elledge, p. 61.

[13] Wallace Stevens' letter to William Carlos Williams, April 9, 1918, in "Prologue to *Kora in Hell*," in *Selected Essays of William Carlos Williams* (New York: Random House, 1954), p. 12.

distinguished, these things belong in an imaginative category and not in a gross natural array. To me this is the gist of the whole matter. It is easy to fall under the spell of a certain mode, especially if it be remote of origin, leaving thus certain of its members essential to a reconstruction of its significance permanently lost in an impenetrable mist of time. But the thing that stands eternally in the way of really good writing is always one: the virtual impossibility of lifting to the imagination those things which lie under the direct scrutiny of the senses, close to the nose. It is this difficulty that sets a value upon all works of art and makes them a necessity. [14]

In the same prologue Williams cites the example of Marcel Duchamp's *Fountain* (1913) as a relevant instance of "lifting [things] to the imagination" through a process of selection divorced from any didactic or anecdotal motivation. [15] Yet in citing this example, Williams perhaps strikes a false note insofar as his own idea of artistic selection implies an almost redemptive function, while Duchamp's is more iconoclastic, mocking the notion of an artwork's inherent superiority to ordinary objects by suggesting that it is only the institutional framework surrounding art that makes it appear so. Williams's work is more affirmatively synthetic, insisting upon the imaginative "power which discovers in things those inimitable particles of dissimilarity to all other things which are the peculiar perfections of the thing in question." [16] Not to be confused with the "coining of similes," which depends "upon a nearly vegetable coincidence," [17] the construction of poems is a way of discovering properties of almost atomic power lurking in the elements of language that the poet can harness to achieve a new imagistic valency–unstable, ambiguous, and poetically explosive:

> The instability of these improvisations would seem such that they must crumble under the attention and become particles of a wind that falters. It would appear to the unready that the fiber of the thing is a thin jelly. [. . . Yet] the virtue of strength lies not in the grossness of the fiber but in the fiber itself. Thus a poem is tough by no quality it borrows from a logical recital of events nor

---

[14] William Carlos Williams, "Prologue to *Kora in Hell*," *op. cit.*, p. 11.
[15] *Ibid.*, p. 6.
[16] *Ibid.*, p. 16.
[17] *Ibid.*

from the events themselves but solely from that attenuated power which draws perhaps many broken things into a dance giving
them thus a full being. [18]

Although Williams's improvisations have been labeled "surrealist" by virtue of the attenuated power of bringing together dissimilar things, they are much more closely aligned with Reverdy and
Cubism. [19] Their elements are loosely yet deliberately assembled
and thus insist upon their own objecthood or "full being," an autonomy not derived from any "logical recital of events." Ironically,
Williams associates this logicality–endemic to the coining of similes–with chance, circumstance, or the "vegetable coincidence" of
things as they appear to the unimaginative. Chance is thus construed in symbolist terms, not surrealist, and Williams implies that
despite a loosening of the attention to yield the miscellany that
Stevens spoke of, his process of selection is self-conscious, a series
of startling juxtapositions intended to impress upon the reader a
sense of the "attenuated power" that discovers that "thousandth
part" of commonality, a sort of shared atomic particle of significance, between divers objects.

The contrast between the rudimentary quality of Williams's elements and the rigor he ascribes to the selection process is summarized in an essay on Gertrude Stein in which he allies their aesthetic
concerns:

> To be democratic, local (in the sense of being attached with in-
> tegrity to actual experience), Stein, or any other artist, must for
> subtlety ascend to a plane of almost abstract design to keep alive.
> To writing, then, as an art itself. Yet what actually impinges on

---

[18] *Ibid.*, p. 14.

[19] It is interesting to note, however, that Williams, in *I Wanted to Write a Poem*,
would retrospectively refer to his improvisations as "automatic writing," having by
then thoroughly familiarized himself with Surrealist techniques after translating
Philippe Soupault's *Last Nights of Paris* in 1929 and even being asked to co-edit
(with Breton) the Surrealist publication *VVV* in 1941. (See Henry Sayre's *The Visual Text of William Carlos Williams* (Chicago: University of Illinois, 1983), p. 24.)
Furthermore, Williams described poetry as "the driving forward of desire to a complex end." ("Introduction to *The Wedge*" (1944) in *Poetics of the New American Poetry*, ed. Donald Allen, Warren Tallman (New York: Grove Press, 1973)); nevertheless, this end always retained a conscious, formal character that he was inclined to
celebrate–not undercut through accident (in practice), or ideological opposition (in
theory).

the senses must be rendered as it appears, by use of which, only, and under which, untouched, the significance has to be disclosed. It is one of the major problems of the artist. [20]

The attenuated power combining dissimilar, if ordinary, things in Williams's improvisations is precisely this sense of abstract design in incipient form.

This syntax of infinitesimal similitude among diverse, sensuous elements shows a remarkable consistency with Reverdian poetics given the lack of references in Williams's oeuvre to the French poet's theories. A certain compatibility of technique becomes even more pronounced in the 1920s as Williams begins to treat language more and more "as physical material," giving it "a new relationship to its space" [21] and thus concretizing abstract design as the visual arrangement of that material. The earliest, simplest, and best-known example of this development in Williams's poetic is "The Red Wheelbarrow" from *Spring and All*:

> so much depends
> upon
>
> a red wheel
> barrow
>
> glazed with rain
> water
>
> beside the white
> chickens [22]

Bram Dijkstra correctly describes the poem as a picture not unlike photographs and paintings by the Stieglitz group (including Charles Demuth, a close friend of Williams), noting how it particularizes objects in an instance of time:

---

[20] Williams, "The Work of Gertrude Stein" in *Selected Essays of William Carlos Williams*, pp. 118-119.

[21] Henry M. Sayre, *The Visual Text of William Carlos Williams* (Chicago: University of Illinois, 1983), p. 7.

[22] Williams, "The Red Wheelbarrow," from *Spring and All*, in *The William Carlos Williams Reader*, ed. M. L. Rosenthal (New York: New Directions, 1962), p. 21.

[. . .] it is a moment, caught at the point of its highest visual significance, in perfectly straightforward, 'realistic,' but highly selective detail; each word has its intrinsic evocative function, focusing the object and its essential structural relationship to its
immediate surroundings in concrete terms. The words are facts,
the direct linguistic equivalents to the visual object under scrutiny. The object, moreover, retains complete autonomy; it is in no
way to be construed as a metaphor; rather, the very fact of its actual existence within the objective world, exactly according to
the terms in which it is described, constitutes a statement about
the objective world. [23]

Dijkstra goes on to show how Williams, in stripping the object
of "inessential detail" and providing a verbal equivalent of a picture
frame in the first phrase of the poem, "[raises] the place we inhabit
to such an imaginative level that it shall have currency in the world
of the mind." [24] Yet the picture-making capacity of language is
strictly linked here with language's representational function. Dijkstra fails to mention how Williams's arrangement of words concretizes the abstract as visual design. The lines of the poem follow
an almost classic mathematical formula, with three words to one in
each stanza. The pattern is visibly present, showing what appears to
be a fortuitous consonance with the represented elements. Has the
pattern been superimposed on the description, or does it arise organically from it? Insofar as each stanza conforms to a distinct descriptive component of the poem, the relation between pattern and
meaning appears natural. At the same time, however, the splitting
of two compound words in the middle lines–wheelbarrow and rain-
water (note that the former is correctly printed in the title)–suggests
the violence of superimposition, of forcing "natural" elements to
conform to an artificial pattern. To the extent that abstract design
and raw materials continue to seem harmoniously united, the brevity of the poem itself becomes an issue, hinting that any further elaboration of elements according to the given word ratios would expose the real discontinuity that is momentarily disguised.

Although he does not analyze the poem as I have done here,
Henry Sayre, in *The Visual Text of William Carlos Williams* (1983),

---

[23] Bram Dijkstra, *Cubism, Stieglitz, and the Early Poetry of William Carlos
Williams* (Princeton: Princeton University, 1969), p. 168.
[24] Dijkstra quoting Williams, *op. cit.*, pp. 168-169.

accurately links Williams's early poetic with the theories of Juan Gris, who was also a strong influence on Reverdy, as shown in Chapter II. [25] Interestingly enough, what for Gris was a deductive process by which abstract design gradually yielded concrete representational elements in its final form, was, in applying the method to poetry, just the reverse for Williams–as it was for Reverdy. Sayre describes this reversal:

> Despite the fact that Williams felt capable of a kind of abstraction–in *Kora in Hell,* for instance–which would require the kind of return to objective reality which Gris describes, the problem that tormented him most as a writer was quite the opposite of Gris's. We approach the painter's and the writer's media differently. If Gris could draw a design–a curved line, for example–which we accept as free of denotation, Williams could hardly write a word which would be similarly free. Before he would need to bother to retrieve for language its connection to objective reality, which is, after all, taken for granted, he had to establish some consistent sense of language's abstract side. Williams thus championed any art which contributed to his understanding of abstraction–from Stein's to Pollock's. [. . .] His work is the record of a constant effort to discover a place for abstraction in his poetry–an effort complicated, however, by his honesty: his realization that the order discovered in most modern work is one independent of objective reality, rather than one integrally related to it in any organic sense. Thus his poetry is torn by two seemingly contradictory allegiances: he believes in the necessity of order, the design of abstraction, but he will not deny the multiplicity and chaos of experience to merely satisfy this necessity. [26]

---

[25] Gris's influence on the poet is acknowledged in a letter Williams wrote in 1932 in which he asks: "Why do we not read more of Juan Gris? He knew these things (notions of abstract design) and wrote well of them" (quoted in Sayre, p. 8). Further discussions of Juan Gris appear in Williams's "Conversation as design" and in *Spring and All* where he describes Gris's work *The Open Window* (1921): "Here is a shutter, a bunch of grapes, a sheet of music, a picture of sea and mountains (particularly fine) which the onlooker is not for a moment permitted to witness as an 'illusion.' One thing laps over on the other, the cloud laps over on the shutter, the bunch of grapes is part of the handle of the guitar, the mountain and sea are obviously not 'the mountain and sea,' but a picture of the mountain and the sea. All drawn with admirable simplicity and excellent design–all a unity [...]" (quoted in Sayre, pp. 31-33).
[26] Sayre, p. 29.

The seemingly contradictory allegiances referred to here lay at the heart of Williams's earlier "synthesizing" ambition. The synthetic art of Juan Gris provided an aesthetic model for solving Williams's problem, a problem Williams himself appeared to solve in "The Red Wheelbarrow," but which he outgrew, in a sense, upon realizing that instead of synthesizing the categories of "abstraction" and "reality," it was more poetically interesting "to measure their inter-relations . . . to record how each effects the other." [27] Consequently, Gris's theories became less important as Williams's poetic structures burst the boundaries of his earlier work when he undertook such broad collagist poems as *Paterson* in the 1940s, with its mythic themes of male and female forces, the city and the country, the poet and America. Consistent with the goal of measuring these interrelations is the heady experimentation with meter throughout *Paterson*–which at times even dispenses with meter altogether when incorporating broad prosaic chunks (historical and epistolary texts) as both expansions and interruptions of the overall work. This experimentation led, according to Sayre, to the realization of a completely artificial relation of form and meter to the poem's contents in Book V. Not only did Williams cease to create any illusion of his meter emerging "organically" (rhythmically, syntactically) from the contents of his verse, but he began exposing the purely visual basis of its utilization. In modifying his notion of the *variable foot* used throughout *Paterson*–a modification he perfected in *Pictures from Breughel*–Williams began consistently enjambing his lines in ways that violated their "syntactic integrity" [28] and, thus, the sense that the visible design of the poetry was organically consonant with the natural syntax (or "breath" as Charles Olson called it) of the poetic utterance in the American idiom.

   In his meticulous biography of Frank O'Hara, Brad Gooch mentions that O'Hara's early readings of Williams included *Kora in Hell* and *Paterson* and that these continued to be his favorites throughout his life. [29] His interest in the latter, in which the visible design of the poem becomes all the more conspicuous by virtue of the patterns of enjambment, is hardly surprising given the near ubiquity of the strategy in O'Hara's own work. But O'Hara seems to insist on the arbitrariness of such maneuvers in a way that

---

[27] *Ibid.*, p. 9.
[28] *Ibid.*, p. 127.
[29] Gooch, pp. 172-173.

Williams, who rather imposes it to affirm the deliberate nature of his patterning, does not. O'Hara's designs are erratic, shifting, provisional, collapsible–like many of the experiences they describe. Indeed, while gaining in arbitrariness, while happily subjecting his lines to the sort of graphic manipulations by which form and content tend to diverge according to Williams's poetic, O'Hara actually comes a little closer to uniting them. Form and content become one because the form is freer, in keeping with the hectic pace of O'Hara's own experience. This extreme artifice, when it occurs, acquires all the characteristics of anti-formalism, indeed, a new, chaotic "naturalism"–not through preserving the syntactic integrity of the lines but by dissolving the idea of the line as an integral unit that is somehow resistant to any natural process of fragmentation and dispersal. In this way the poems, too, seem barely to hang together.

At the same time, O'Hara is unwilling to be the champion of pure "formlessness" in poetry. In an unfinished essay entitled "Design, etc.," [30] he asserts the formal integrity of works that seem to have none precisely because of their formal novelty. He does this by distinguishing poetic form from poetic design, claiming that design is "exterior, apparent," while form is "interior, mysterious"; thus design functions at the surface "[striking] the eye and ear" (SS, p. 33) and provides the technical locus of the most radical innovations in contemporary poetry. He adds, however, that "many contemporary poets emphasize the visual rather than the spoken organization of the poem" (SS, p. 33) to indicate the visual nature of the most important experiments. These involve a loosening of traditional design, which is often construed as a weakening of poetic form. But they actually enhance the form, according to O'Hara: "Where design is weak . . . the form is usually strong and may even be the reason the design is weak." (SS, p. 34) Thus, visibly "weak" design becomes the subtle indicator of a certain experimental vigor or formal complexity.

In his own work, "weak design" has to do primarily with the visible breaking up of the poetic line, the liberal use of surprising enjambments, and a new hyper-sensitivity to the physical space of poetic language in the print medium (in a way that coincides with the poet's hyper-sensitivity to his own body and the surrounding urban environment). Just as he flouts traditional expectations concerning the visual organization of poems, so he dispels similar no-

---

[30] O'Hara, "Design, etc." in SS.

O'Hara
as a particular,
practical,
his theoretical

tions about the oral or phonic dimension.[31] Form, then, is free of
the prosodic apparatus typically associated with it; it goes beyond
diction, design, or technique, thus allowing O'Hara to play fast and
loose with the elements of writing, indeed, to seem to give up all
technique, all artifice, to satisfy the otherwise inscrutable requirements of a new, inherent form. It is O'Hara's rejoinder to certain
American poets who, he thought, "[made] too much . . . because of
the New Criticism . . . about what is the comportment in diction
that you adapt."[32]

If O'Hara found important precedents for his so-called "weak
designs" in the poetry of Williams and Reverdy,[33] he did not share
their tendency to theorize about the formal integrity of their poetry.
Williams, for example, wrote that poems were "machine[s] made of
words":[34]

> When a man makes a poem [. . .] he takes words as he finds
> them [. . .] and composes them–without distortion which would
> mar their exact significances–[. . .] that they may constitute a
> revelation in the speech that he uses. It isn't what he *says* that
> counts as a work of art, it's what he makes, with such intensity of
> perception that it lives with an intrinsic movement of its own to
> verify its authenticity. Your attention is called now and then to
> some beautiful line or sonnet-sequence because of what is said
> there. So be it. To me all sonnets say the same thing of no impor-
> tance. What does it matter what the line "says"? [. . .] There is
> no poetry of distinction without formal invention....[35]

---

[31] An example of O'Hara's attitude is found in "Personism" where he ridicules
the more conventionally "musical" attributes of poetry: "Now, come on. I don't believe in god, so I don't have to make elaborately sounded structures. I hate Vachel
Lindsay, always have; I don't even like rhythm, assonance, all that stuff. You just go
on your nerve. If someone's chasing you down the street with a knife you just run,
you don't turn around and shout, 'Give it up! I was a track star for Mineola Prep.'"
(*CP*, p. 498)
[32] "Edward Lucie-Smith: Interview with Frank O'Hara" in *SS*, p. 12.
[33] O'Hara acknowledges his literary debt to Reverdy in Lucie-Smith's interview
(*SS*, p. 12) and in "A Step Away From Them"; and to Williams in "Personism: A
Manifesto" (*CP*, p. 498), "To a Poet" and "Poem Read at Joan Mitchell's," among
others.
[34] William Carlos Williams, "Introduction to *The Wedge*" (1944) in *Poetics of
the New American Poetry*, eds. Donald Allen and Warren Tallman (New York:
Grove Press, 1973), p. 138.
[35] *Ibid.*, p. 139.

Instead of plotting a formal procedure, O'Hara suggests that there is a mysterious, extra-poetic basis for form, which develops as if by accident as the writing poet interacts with the world (*SS*, p. 33). Yet the products of this interaction still require a certain formal strategy–albeit of cultivated carelessness, sophisticated sincerity, rigorous haphazardness. O'Hara stakes his poetic on the invisibility of such strategies, paradoxically utilized in an anti-formalist milieu. His position mirrors that of the Abstract Expressionists vis-à-vis the Cubists. In the spirit of surrealist anti-formalism, the Abstract Expressionists emphasize the dynamic aspect of their work, its violent, instinctual performance, rhetorically eschewing any hint of deliberate construction so dear to the Cubists. Yet Art remains sacred to them, hence form now resides mysteriously in the process, and in the work, only as the evidence of that process. Like the Abstract Expressionists, O'Hara retains an idea of form even though he intends to make full use of chance, speed, and the kind of innate creative energy the Surrealists believed exceeded the bounds of controlled expression.

O'HARA AND THE FATHERS OF DADA: "MEMORIAL DAY 1950"

In a way this ironic fusion of creative impulses was nothing new, considering the often destructive, anti-illusionist impulse of the Cubists themselves in their analytic mode, which, just as paradoxically, contributed to their reputation as the most subtle of formalists in their synthetic mode. In a remarkable early poem O'Hara pays tribute to the French Avant-Garde of the nineteen-teens and twenties. It also addresses the Williamsian conception of poems as made things or machines. Art, as the following poem says, "is no dictionary," (*CP*, p. 17) is not about meaning–yet meaning issues from the joints of this verbal construction like blood from a corpse in the presence of its undiscovered assassin. Thus, the expressionist, anti-formalist accent O'Hara gives both Williams's and the French's achievement is unmistakable (though its presence is only discoverable through the intervention of successive interpretants):

"Memorial Day 1950"

Picasso made me tough and quick, and the world;
just as in a minute plane trees are knocked down
outside my window by a crew of creators.
Once he got his axe going everyone was upset
enough to fight for the last ditch and heap
of rubbish.
          Through all that surgery I thought
I had a lot to say, and named several last things
Gertrude Stein hadn't had time for; but then
the war was over, those things had survived
and even when you're scared art is no dictionary.
Max Ernst told us that.
          How many trees and frying pans
I loved and lost! Guernica hollered look out!
but we were all busy hoping our eyes were talking
to Paul Klee. My mother and father asked me and
I told him from my tight blue pants we should
love only the stones, the sea, and heroic figures.
Wasted child! I'll club you in the shins! I
wasn't surprised when the older people entered
my cheap hotel room and broke my guitar and my can
of blue paint.
          At that time all of us began to think
with our bare hands and even with blood all over
them, we knew vertical from horizontal, we never
smeared anything except to find out how it lived.
Fathers of Dada! You carried shining erector sets
in your rough bony pockets, you were generous
and they were lovely as chewing gum or flowers!
Thank you!
          And those of us who thought poetry
was crap were throttled by Auden or Rimbaud
when, sent by some compulsive Juno, we tried
to play with collages or sprechstimme in their bed.
Poetry didn't tell me not to play with toys
but alone I could never have figured out that dolls
meant death.
          Our responsibilities did not begin
in dreams, though they began in bed. Love is first of all
a lesson in utility. I hear the sewage singing
underneath my bright white toilet seat and know

that somewhere sometime it will reach the sea:
gulls and swordfishes will find it richer than a river.
And airplanes are perfect mobiles, independent
of the breeze; crashing in flames they show us how
to be prodigal. O Boris Pasternak, it may be silly
to call to you, so tall in the Urals, but your voice
cleans our world, clearer to us than the hospital:
you sound above the factory's ambitious gargle.
Poetry is as useful as a machine!
                                        Look at my room.
Guitar strings hold up pictures. I don't need
a piano to sing, and naming things is only the intention
to make things. A locomotive is more melodious
than a cello. I dress in oil cloth and read music
by Guillaume Apollinaire's clay candelabra. Now
my father is dead and has found out you must look things
in the belly, not in the eye. If only he had listened
to the men who made us, hollering like stuck pigs!

                                        (*CP*, p. 17)

Not just a machine made of words, but a whole sewage treatment plant of history! Given O'Hara's admiration for Reverdy and
Williams, it is surprising to see him upending their poetics in a parodic elegy–written in part to them. Similarly, the eulogizing of Picasso is significant because his work is invoked primarily for its analytic, as opposed to synthetic, procedures: i.e., as a form of invasive
surgery or land-clearing, rather than benign construction. Thus
O'Hara wants to get at the heart, root, or foundation of aesthetic
syntheses. Indeed, the social and political analogues he links with
Picasso's toughness reveal the painter's genius in an almost menacing, futuristic light, a revelation that seems fitting in an occasional
poem intended,- prima facie, to commemorate the war dead, but
which is really about what America can learn from the European
Avant-Garde considered as a cultural war machine. As elegy it fore-
tells a miraculous politics of utility and excess, responsibility and
indulgence, through the agency of a new poetic candor.
    Though focusing on literary and art movements, the poem
demonstrates that creation and destruction are interdependent and
endemic to modern developments as a whole. As armies slaughter
each other for country and honor (the retrospective rubbish of
World War I), avant-gardists scramble to place selected detria on

the endangered fossils list of the collective imagination. With feigned ingenuousness, O'Hara characterizes such recuperative efforts as naming things: re-defining them in a sort of modernist Eden or Book of Life (qua dictionary). But just as such artists miraculously affirm or give meaning to the autonomy and dignity of objects, so they reveal the hegemonic potential of such acts when salvation metamorphoses into dominion, and creation slouches toward eschatology. Picasso, again, is the agent of this discovery: "Guernica hollered look out!" Like the balloon-headed figure billowing out of Guernica's window, the painting is a reminder about looking out, about opening art onto realities thought to have been unmasked by the Avant-Garde as mere illusion or convention, but now re-surging as political realities that threaten all life on the margins. But it is also about looking out for what is sinister in one's own creative impulse–especially as a late modernist enthralled by the achievements of early modernist mentors. This caveat is suggested by the ironic position of O'Hara's persona in the poem. Mesmerized by art and "busy hoping our eyes were talking/ to Paul Klee," his ephebic persona defiantly proclaims–like an unwitting Hitler youth–that "we should/ love only the stones, the sea, and heroic figures." But he is speaking in the context of America where such cultural, European sentiments seem misplaced. The enmity of the world swoops in on him in the form of caricaturally disciplining American parents, who break his guitar and can of blue paint (another Picassoid topos now sonorously reminiscent of Wallace Stevens' own use of it). World War II and its aftermath seem to break out in the poem when "all of us began to think/ with our bare hands." Thinking is a form of fighting and thus a new, more passionate process of analysis begins closer to home.

Yet even with its mayhem, the war proves intellectually fun: a certain pragmatism or technical facility (i.e., knowing "vertical from horizontal") keeps the horror within the political and imaginative category of a constructive undertaking. Under the mantle of American power, art retains its intellectual aloofness, its character of megalomaniacal play or masturbation; but it is also now a gift, one of modern Europe's many legacies to America, proffered through the subtle agencies of Surrealism, and thus metamorphosing itself in American hands: "Fathers of Dada! You carried shining erector sets/ in your rough and bony pockets, you were generous/ and they were lovely as chewing gum or flowers!/ Thank you!" Thus, even while acquiring the campiness of holiday greeting cards, avant-garde influences retain a certain elegance of construction, a certain deceptive quality of play that is habit-forming and deadly. The fathers of Dada, then, are like all fathers: their generosity is both beautiful and dangerous. A further corrective is required ("alone I could never have figured out that dolls/ meant death") and this corrective is love.

Love, then, is O'Hara's idea, the nervous, attentive, slightly sentimental gauge of poetic value by which he distinguishes himself from Williams, who, having "no ideas but in things," treats poetry as a form of cubo-dadaist construction with the building blocks of language. In surrealist fashion–but without the demands of surrealist theory–O'Hara insists on the responsibility of the artist or poet by making his own work an act of love: "Our responsibilities did not/ begin in dreams, though they began in bed." He dispenses with the Freudian obsessions and ideological watchwords that burden adult heterosexuals like André Breton and Delmore Schwartz, but gratefully accepts a lesson in love from the adolescent homosexual Rimbaud. Love teaches that poetry is not "crap"–the symbolic currency of childhood empires–poetry is serious, worldly, personal, didactic. But, in Rimbaldian fashion, it also teaches that crap isn't crap either: with pantheistic ardor, responsible love covertly assimilates to poetry the very elements it officially banishes–elements of infantile, fecal play. A new, more global, more ecological mode of play is set in motion in keeping with a new sexual freedom, with post-war abundance, and with America's popular self-conception as a power that "exists purely to inspire love." [36] In what has become a post-scarcity society, sewage [37] is shown to be "richer than a river," airplanes become toys, [38] and death, a new lease on life. Where something can always be made, apparently, from nothing, waste disposal and laying waste become productive functions; aesthetic excess and technological progress overlap as post-war wars (more ic-

[36] O'Hara, *Art Chronicles: 1954-1966* (New York: George Braziller, 1975), p. 41. Subsequent citations of any essay or interview by O'Hara from this edition will appear in the text as *AC* followed by the page number.

[37] Sewage that, like Whitman's America, is singing–as David Lehman observes in his chapter on O'Hara in *The Last Avant-Garde: The Making of the New York School of Poets* (New York: Doubleday, 1998), p. 183.

[38] At least, as Americans, we always thought so–as long as they were wreaking destruction somewhere else.

ing on the cake) offer lessons in both American prodigality and utility–or obversely, Soviet utility and prodigality. Yet the poet, idealis-
tically youthful still, somehow imagines his appreciation of Pasternak will keep his poetry "above the factory's ambitious gargle" in
either instance. Such is the magic of symbolic hegemony in 1950. In
a world where the concept of responsibility is already obsolete, the
empty word is triumphantly touted by the powers and poets that
be, each using it to attack its own other with the best of intentions.
O'Hara's persona falls into the same rhetorical trap by presuming
once again to teach the world a lesson, especially to the fathers: in
America the self-styled adult-child becomes father to the man, and
so this neo-Wordsworthian concludes with some thoughts on his
own biological father, a victim of the ever self-renewing new realism: "Now/ my father is dead and has found out you must look
things/ in the belly, not in the eye. If only he had listened/ to the
men who made us, hollering like stuck pigs!" Inasmuch as the final
clause dangles, both the creators and the created alternately have a
share as victims and victimizers in a process of revitalization. The
poem is a kind of proto-manifesto against the postmodern empty
sign, even as it actively empties its own signs in the process. And yet
there remains a persistent faith in an idea of responsibility, or that
the poet's integrity somehow pertains to poetry's real relation to the
world.

PARODIC EXPRESSIONISM: O'HARA, POLLOCK, AND RIVERS

O'Hara tries to assimilate formalist and expressionist strains of
the Avant-Garde into a more encompassing worldview where oppositions of form versus content, aesthetics versus politics are synthesized with a kind of useless American pragmatism. Such pragmatism, however, depends on the creators assuming a modern,
internationalist outlook without subjecting that outlook to any rigorous dialectical hashing. According to O'Hara, the Americans now
had to act out the fantasy of being extreme (*AC*, pp. 69-70), had to
determine what their emotional stake was in the globalizing thrust
of late modernism itself. Along with this paradoxically responsible
self-absorption came the injunction to remake the world in a new
and original act of creativity. It was not enough to imitate the Europeans; they had to venture out on their own–albeit in a way that the

Europeans had already done. Although both literary and artistic precedents had been set (Surrealism, Social Realism, the Mexican School), the work of the Abstract Expressionists best fulfilled this cultural necessity in O'Hara's view. In a late description of their achievement (1962), he describes the existential conditions that make their works possible:

> Underlying, and indeed burgeoning within, every great work of the Abstract Expressionists, whether subjectively lyrical as in Gorky, publicly explosive as in De Kooning, or hieratical as in Newman, exists the traumatic consciousness of emergency and crisis experienced as personal event, the artist assuming responsibility for being, however accidentally, alive here and now. Their gift was for a somber and joyful art: somber because it does not merely reflect but sees what is about it, and joyful because it is able to exist. It is just as possible for art to look out at the world as it is for the world to look at art. But the Abstract Expressionists were frequently the first violators of their own gifts; to this we often owe the marvelously demonic, sullen, or mysterious quality of their work, as they moved from the pictorial image to the hidden subject. (*AC*, p. 67)

The responsibility O'Hara describes had little to do with earnestly assuming the kind of moral and political positions advocated by someone like André Breton or Diego Rivera. It had more to do with the glamorous responsibility of taking the creative initiative at the moment when a historic opportunity presented itself. With the nation's new sense of pre-eminence and infallibility in the post-war world, certain American-based artists quickly accustomed themselves to the mantle of avant-garde extremism. Consequently, creative spontaneity became something of an accomplished style: what for the Surrealists was an arduous struggle to discover what pure spontaneity might be, was cultivated with an acquired self-assurance (if little fervor in the area of oppositional politics) by the New York painters. Unlike the Surrealists, the Abstract Expressionists were not ideologically opposed to their personal emotions or cultural ambitions. The American artists were intent on being not merely revolutionary or liberating, but great: if the new painting seemed to come naturally, seemed invested with personal sincerity, the painter's natural inclinations were nevertheless gilded with a sense of aesthetic accomplishment.

Symptomatic of this belief in a natural virtuosity was an insistence on the importance of content in works too often accused of having none (of being "decorative" in the case of the Abstract Expressionists, [39] trivial in the case of O'Hara). This insecurity about content seems to have motivated O'Hara's 1954 essay "Nature and New Painting," where he writes that "great art . . . is seldom about art, though frequently its insights are so compelling and so pervasive they can be applied to art as well as to their subject. . . ." (SS, p. 41) Though careful not to dismiss what is self-reflexive and self-defining in great art, O'Hara realigns such formalist concerns to support the expressionist thrust of his own argument: "From the Impressionists through the Cubists to the present, art has been involved with nature." (SS, p. 41) Hence, the subject of the new painting is not art itself, but the immediate experience of the artist in response to the present and to the world–an experience that is inherently expressive, naturally artistic. Nor is it about the representation of nature but the perception of nature as a creative impulse in humanity: "In past times there was nature and there was human nature; because of the ferocity of modern life, man and nature have become one" (SS, p. 42). To the extent that natural human expression is calculated, the calculation involved is appropriated to the cause of nature, to the "innermost will of the artist" (SS, p. 43), a will that verges on instinct. Thus, despite the many ways in which O'Hara's poetic disposition marks a prolepsis of the postmodern, much of his supportive theory is firmly rooted in modern Existentialist assumptions about universal human nature.

   In his monograph *Jackson Pollock* (1959) O'Hara writes that his subject was one of the few who entirely "gave himself over to cultural necessities which, in turn, freed him from the external encumbrances which surround art as an occasion of extreme cultural concern." (AC, p. 13) Thus culture itself is paradoxically liberating and cumbersome, and it is only the genius, only the one whose action spontaneously conforms to cultural necessity, who can overcome the external encumbrances that otherwise mediate his or her relation to culture. These encumbrances are primarily those of academic tradition, which sinisterly assimilate the artistic will, a will that can only be redeemed at the right historical moment through "dras-

---

[39] Rosalind Krauss, "Reading Jackson Pollock, Abstractly" in *The Originality of the Avant-Garde and Other Modernist Myths* (Cambridge: MIT Press, 1989), p. 226.

tic self-knowledge" (*AC*, p. 13) of the kind O'Hara attributes to
Pollock: "This is not automatism or self-expression, but insight."
(*AC*, p. 13) Thus, even though O'Hara emphasizes the mythological
themes of Pollock's work in his study, he is not simply stressing
contents over style, but offering a concrete analogy for how tradition must be assimilated to the new artistic will: the mythological
contents of Pollock's earlier works are not erased, but sedimented
and transfigured in his later non-objective works where he achieves
a state of what O'Hara calls "spiritual clarity" (*AC*, p. 25), the state
of knowing how to discriminate between cultural necessities and
their external encumbrances (incidental, academic precedents).
Thus it is a state of mind in which "the spirit can act freely and with
unpremeditated knowledge. . . . Only the artist who has reached
this state should be indicated by Harold Rosenberg's well-known
designation Action Painter, for only when he is in this state is the
artist's 'action' significant purely and simply of itself." (*AC*, p. 26)

  In this way, pure spontaneity or action moves beyond the technical facility of appropriated styles or procedures; but also, it
achieves a kind of poise or calm usually associated with formal virtuosity. O'Hara dissociates action from its surrealist precedents of
automatism (*AC*, p. 13), uncontrolled emotion (*AC*, p. 30), and accident. (*AC*, p. 39) Instead, the intensity of Pollock's action involves, "in its complete identification of the artist with his work, a
denial of accident" (*AC*, p. 39), hence, at least a partial denial of
Surrealism's influence on the Americans. In this way creative spontaneity, formerly associated with chance, now mysteriously enters
the realm of cultural necessity despite the instinctual, chancy nature
of its physical performance. O'Hara exempts Pollock from the vagaries of fortune and chance and mere history and places the artist
astride the juggernaut of existential forces that ultimately determine
history. Thus Pollock becomes an unimpeachable cultural icon
O'Hara can unequivocally admire, if not exactly accompany.

  Naturally O'Hara draws important lessons from Pollock's
method, particularly his use of line and a certain shift in painterly
scale. In each case he discovers and celebrates a sense of free bodily
movement, exhilaration, even violence. And although this movement implies a kind of macho vigor apropos of Pollock's work,
O'Hara's bouncing prose conveys the more nervous, sprightly energy of his own verbal restlessness. For instance, his description of
the artist's draftsmanship: "that amazing ability to quicken a line by

thinning it, to slow it by flooding, to elaborate that simplest of elements, the line–to change, to reinvigorate, to extend, to build up an embarrassment of riches in the mass by drawing alone." (*AC*, p. 32) Here the draftsman's line takes on all the metamorphic vitality of poetic lines, even straying into what may be a direct description of O'Hara's poetry. On the other hand, where Pollock's line betrays an "open nostalgia for brutality" (*AC*, p. 33) the description seems apt in both contexts (if for opposing reasons).

As for scale, it has less to do with the large size of many of the works than with their emotional impact, and thus has implications, once again, for O'Hara's own poetic procedures, which involve a similar sense of scale:

> The scale of the painting became that of the painter's body, not the image of a body, and the setting for the scale, which would include all referents, would be the canvas surface itself. Upon this field the physical energies of the artist operate in actual detail, in full scale; the action of inspiration traces its marks of Apelles with no reference to exterior image or environment. It is scale and no-scale. It is the physical reality of the artist and his activity of expressing it, united to the spiritual reality of the artist in a oneness which has no need for the mediation of metaphor or symbol. It is Action Painting. (*AC*, pp. 34-35)

As we shall see, O'Hara's poetry also assumes the scale of the poet's body in ways that both repeat and parody those above. The difference is that O'Hara's poetry, in assuming the scale of the body, requires a whole scene of writing as its canvas, a whole semantic arsenal as its ink. Yet, like the action painter, the poet's exertions are often temporally circumscribed by the immediate situation of the writing with as little premeditation or correction as possible. It is telling, then, that so much of O'Hara's poetry was concretely occasional, written on the spot–at lunch, at parties, in the office–where the referents of his physical situation were directly on hand, perceivable and usable depending on the exact vectors of the poem's dynamic.

But when O'Hara writes of Pollock's inspiration tracing "its marks of Apelles with no reference to exterior image or environment" (*AC*, pp. 34-35), clarification is needed. In O'Hara's poetry, things on hand are not specifically employed as a way of imaging

the writing body or of establishing the scene of writing as a narrative setting. Yet insofar as language (unlike graphic marks) is inherently referential, exterior objects and events do indeed enter the poetic canvas as a kind of "smorgasbord of the recognizable" (as the
painter Larry Rivers once called it) (*AC*, p. 118). To this extent, the
poetry can be said to fail to achieve the non-referentiality of Pollock's marks. Nevertheless, O'Hara's language often acquires a degree of semantic opacity that makes it strangely comparable to non-
representational marks and so verges on non-objectivity. What
finally links the two procedures, however, is the stress each places
on the artist's or poet's bodily presence in the work (Pollock once
described himself as being literally *in* his painting [*AC*, p. 39]), i.e.,
an idea of the creator and the work being physically and temporally
coextensive during the act of creation and that every stage of this
activity, every surge of energy, is fully evident in the final product.

In view of these procedural similarities, some comments are
called for concerning the short poem "Digression on Number 1,
1948" [fig. 16], which O'Hara audaciously incorporated into his
Pollock monograph. The poem describes an almost random catalogue of paintings on exhibition culminating in Pollock's monumental *No. 1*. Its movement suggests a restless looping–figure-
8-like–around a magnetic center (*No. 1* itself) and an increasing
concentration in the moment that is undoubtedly Pollockian.
O'Hara also allows for a certain randomness, incorporating whatever physically comes along (such as the European paintings in the
first half), yet with a kind of instinctual control in finding just
the right quotient of immediacy to avoid both sloppiness and over-
conscientiousness. But does this make it an abstract-expressionist
poem? Despite O'Hara's casualness, the poem still has a structure
that seems premeditated. Despite his refusal to be merely descriptive or symbolic, a residue of those things divorces his work, finally,
from the abstract quality of Pollock's automatism. Furthermore,
while the poem seems comparable to Pollock's *No. 1* in O'Hara's
terms of scale (i.e., emotional impact), one cannot dismiss the more
basic difference in terms of size. Indeed by including in his monograph a short poem about a big painting and calling it a digression,
O'Hara seems to be making fun of his own aspiration to be compared with Pollock. He even hints that the "sense of genius" (*CP*, p.
512) he obviously feels for Pollock is a kind of infatuation verging
on desire (as in the overly-sensuous phrase "his perfect hand" [*AC*,

p. 30]). Such sentiments reveal both the poet's attraction to and alienation from what is supposed to be his creative ideal. In the end, O'Hara's attitude is one of difference yet a certain covetousness apropos of Pollock's macho, heterosexual image, an image the poet can only assume with ludic irony in the McCarthyite, homophobic Fifties. [40]

The artistic influence, I think, that best explains this divergence of sensibility between O'Hara and his artistic idol is Larry Rivers. In contrast to the high seriousness of Action Painting, Rivers' art expresses a zany iconoclasm: "I didn't give a crap about what was going on at the time in New York painting, which was obviously interested in chopping down other forests. In fact, I was energetic and egomaniacal and what is even more: important, cocky, and angry enough to do something no one in the New York art world could doubt was disgusting, dead, and absurd." (AC, pp. 111-112) Although Rivers was discussing his painting George Washington Crossing the Delaware (1953), his remark could be applied to his entire oeuvre and his own stubborn adherence to representing the human figure and ordinary objects in his work, or what can be termed "content"–just what the Action Painters were accused of lacking. [41] Rivers' art proceeds from an appreciation of recognizability as the starting point for a free association that takes place. His "smorgasbord of the recognizable" (AC, p. 118), then, results from the freedom he feels in making personal, diaristic associations in his paintings. But he also associates objects on a more formal basis at times, effecting a kind of lateral slide into un-recognizability or abstraction, much as Pollock's earlier mythological themes disappeared in a web of fluid reverberations. Thus O'Hara could say of his friend (and, for a while, lover [42]) that he was "engaged in an esthetic [sic] athleticism which sharpens the eye, hand, and arm in order to beat the bugaboos of banality and boredom, deliberately invited into the painting and then triumphed over." (CP, p. 515)

---

[40] At least once Pollock called O'Hara a "fag" to his face and "was enough of a menace that O'Hara fled the Cedar [Bar] one night when he heard that Pollock was on a drunken rampage." (Gooch, p. 204) One might also compare O'Hara's attitude toward Pollock with that toward a more archetypal American hero in his poem "On Seeing Larry Rivers' Washington Crossing the Delaware at the Museum of Modern Art." (CP, p. 233)

[41] Krauss, p. 221.

[42] Gooch, pp. 227-240.

O'Hara even allows for an element of the accidental in Rivers' paintings that he could not in Pollock's because he saw the acciden-tal as un-heroic–a quality not without virtues in the context of his own or his friends' work, but subtly inappropriate for that of his heterosexual idol. Chance and accident occurred at the margins where O'Hara seems to have relegated himself both out of modesty and protest.

AUTOMATISM OF THE RECOGNIZABLE: FROM "EASTER" TO
"BIOTHERM"

In Donald Allen's anthology *The New American Poetry* (1959), O'Hara made one of his most explicit statements about his poetic:

> What is happening to me, allowing for lies and exaggerations which I try to avoid, goes into my poems. I don't think my expe-riences are clarified or made beautiful for myself or anyone else; they are just there in whatever form I can find them. [. . .] It may be that poetry makes life's nebulous events tangible to me and restores their detail; or conversely, that poetry brings forth the intangible quality of incidents which are all too concrete and cir-cumstantial. [43]

O'Hara's oscillation between the concrete and the intangible, the circumstantial and the abstract-essential, seems to take place within the same parameters of Rivers' oscillations between the recogniz-able and the unrecognizable and the different formal categories in between. In both cases it is a question of forms that are fully com-patible with a new commitment to content–the concrete, the cir-cumstantial, the recognizable–but not to any traditional syntax of space or human action. Recognizable objects and their signs are giv-en new metonymies through a highly personalized, idiolectic, and provisional system of assignment, classification. Such provisionality allows the poet or painter to exploit formal options while flouting formal régimes: "As for measure and other technical apparatus, that's just common sense: if you're going to buy a pair of pants you want them to be tight enough so everyone will want to go to bed

---

[43] O'Hara statement in *The New American Poetry 1945-1960*, ed. Donald Allen (Grove Press, 1960), p. 419.

with you." (*CP*, p. 498) Personal desire and the sense of immediate circumstances thus provide their own more discreet modes of seduction that constitute technique in O'Hara's action poems. For O'Hara, formal techniques arise as a kind of accidental consequence of his total commitment to the immediacy of personal experience and the desiring body of the moment, as presented in his pseudo-manifesto, "Personism." This commitment nevertheless preserves his poetry from the insincerities of the personal pose or reflective attitude in literature. O'Hara uses his immediate situation to shatter the edifice of the self-absorbed literary persona or self-portrait. In this way he avoids the trap of confessionalism–even in conditions of total self-indulgence. The personal achieves a kind of de-familiarization, even abstraction, through over-familiarity:

> Personism, a movement which I recently founded and which nobody knows about, interests me a great deal, being so totally opposed to this kind of abstract removal that it is verging on a true abstraction for the first time, really, in the history of poetry. Personism is to Wallace Stevens what *la poésie pure* was to Béranger. Personism has nothing to do with philosophy, it's all art. It does not have to do with personality or intimacy, far from it! But to give you a vague idea, one of its minimal aspects is to address itself to one person (other than the poet himself), thus evoking overtones of love without destroying love's life-giving vulgarity, and sustaining the poet's feelings towards the poem while preventing love from distracting him into feeling about the person. (*CP*, pp. 498-499)

Thus O'Hara asserts a capacity for abstraction, even formality, through a complete adherence to the personal. If this sounds contradictory, it is because O'Hara's criteria for abstraction is founded on his idea of painting, a criteria having nothing to do with the abstraction of certain literary movements, according to O'Hara: "Abstraction (in poetry, not in painting) involves personal removal by the poet." (*CP*, p. 498) Thus, even in the "Personism" manifesto, he indirectly links his poetic with the most advanced movements in painting.

"Easter" and "Second Avenue"

This linkage, and its abstracting effects on poetry, is achieved through attention to immediate personal space, thoughts, and affects, an attention sharpened by an emphasis on compositional speed. Speed is the calculus of O'Hara's poetry, yet its parallels with Pollock's method reconfirm its primary filiations with surrealist automatism–particularly in O'Hara's early poems "Easter" and "Second Avenue." The surrealism of these two long poems is nearly programmatic, conveyed through the clash of mythology and modernity in a swell of creativity that also characterizes Pollock's early art. [44] "But," as critic Anthony Libby writes in his essay "O'Hara on the Silver Range," "nowhere does early O'Hara come closer to early Pollock than in 'Easter,' O'Hara's wildly uneven high-velocity meditation on sex, death, sperm, shit, and the stars, which Kenneth Koch described as mainly 'a procession of various bodily parts and other objects across a vast landscape.'" [45] Libby compares this poem to Pollock's *Easter and the Totem*, painted in 1953, a year after the poem was written. But it is the more general tendency in Pollock's oeuvre toward dissolving mythological themes into furiously-spun webs of paint that invites comparison with O'Hara's poem. At the core of the poem is the title itself, seemingly unrelated to the contents, but gradually, as it were, glimpsed through and in the rush of images of life-generating, sexual forces feeding on the untimely decline of other such forces. One even reads of a black princess suggestively sacrificed as a kind of Dionysus/Persephone figure.

But most pertinent to the comparison with Pollock's art is the imagistic blur itself. O'Hara's lines–though conveying little of the personal attentiveness to immediate surroundings that one finds in the later poems–metaphorically thicken and thin in an effort to liquify, spread out, or defer meaning in long, unarrested, ejaculatory flows not unlike Pollock's or De Kooning's painterly dissolutions of figures and landscapes:

---

[44] Anthony Libby, "O'Hara on the Silver Range" in Elledge, pp. 131-155.
[45] Libby, p. 140.

When the world strips down and rouges up
Like a mattress's teeth brushed by love's bristling sun
a marvelous heart tiresomely got up in brisk bold stares
when those trappings fart at the feet of the stars
a self-coral serpent wrapped round an arm with no jujubes
without swish
without camp
floods of crocodile piss and pleasures of driving
shadows of prairie pricks dancing
of the roses of Pennsylvania looking in
     eyes noses and ears
those windows at the head of science.[46]

What here begins as a satiric indictment of the world of appearances (as a fabulous, chimerical drag queen), runs-on headlong, or
even sideways, into an inconclusive image of observational science.

"Second Avenue" is equally evasive; but where "Easter" is ultimately structured around an identifiable mythos, "Second Avenue"
merely tantalizes the reader before shifting, delicately or violently
by turns, into totally different registers of experience. For instance,
the poem's opening lines suggest a continuation of the earlier surrealistic strategy, a kind of verbal excess around an inexplicit idea.
O'Hara even explains the opening image of his poem as pertaining
to "a feeling that the philosophical reduction of reality to a deal-
able-with system so distorts life that one's 'reward' for this endeavor
(a minor one, at that) is illness both from inside and outside." (CP,
p. 495) But the poem does not maintain any such didacticism, and
the reader's tenuous awareness of different themes gradually cedes
to a sense of the poem's stupendous impenetrability, both overall
and in specific parts. The effect is consistent with O'Hara's attempt
at a kind of painterly abstraction by attending to verbal materials;
in fact, in his notes to the poem he specifically describes its language in terms of painting: "the verbal elements . . . are intended
consciously to keep the surface of the poem high and dry, not wet,
reflective, and self-conscious. Perhaps the obscurity comes in here,
in the relationship between the surface and the meaning, but I like
it that way since the one is the other (you have to use words) and I

---

[46] O'Hara, "Easter" in *The Selected Poems of Frank O'Hara*, ed. Donald Allen
(New York: Vintage Books, 1974), p. 41. Subsequent citations from this edition will
be identified in the text by *SP* followed by the page number.

hope the poem to be the subject, not just about it." (*CP,* p. 497) As in "Easter" one finds fluid, yet sticky, passages that draw the reader in different directions without apparent destination. Then, as if to tantalize the reader with the prospect of comprehension, O'Hara's narrator asks, "Is your throat dry with the deviousness of following?" and answers his own question with Bretonian mystification: "I lead you to a stream which will lick you like a wasp . . . ." (*SP,* p. 61) Such promises only persist in keeping the reader "high and dry."

Other clues in the poem are equally slippery, but they do seem to indicate a procedural shift that distinguishes "Second Avenue" and signals a future direction to O'Hara's poetry: "My heart will break through to casualness and appear in windows on Main Street." (*SP,* p. 60) Casual, yes, but instead of Main Street, one gets Second Avenue and scattered glimpses of New York, complete with "square carts with hotdogs/ and onions of red syrup blended . . ./ of Majestic Camera Stores and Schuster's." (*SP,* p. 66) Indeed, as O'Hara has written, "everything in [the poem] either happened to me or I felt happening (saw, imagined) on Second Avenue." (*CP,* p. 497) One first recognizes these elements in Part 5, when, inexplicably, the "I" of the poem meets "Joe, his hair pale as the eyes of fields of maize/ in August, at the gallery, he says you're the first Creon/ of 1953, congrats." (*SP,* p. 62) Increasingly, direct conscious experiences, casual perceptions pertaining to the poet's immediate physical or social environment, impose themselves like collaged bits of reality, not unlike those in the poetry of Apollinaire or, as O'Hara himself indicates, the Russian Futurist Vladimir Mayakovsky. The effect is very different from the hyperbolic metamorphoses engendered through classic automatism, yet it is just as surprising, even mysterious, because the seemingly trivial episodes have all been uprooted from whatever series generated them. Thus even O'Hara's friends, whose names are scattered through the poem, acquire a poetic glamour. Some of these are proper names, such as "John Ashbery" and "Mlle. Anne R. Lang" (or Bunny Lang, who was mentioned in a Haitian news article quoted verbatim by O'Hara); but others are ambiguously informal, including Joe (LeSueur), Kenneth (Koch), Larry (Rivers), Grace (Hartigan) and Bill (De Kooning), all of whom are identified in the notes. But names and situations familiar to O'Hara assume an abstract quality in the poem for anyone who is not familiar with them and for whom the notes become essential.

In the same notes O'Hara also describes "Second Avenue" as being similar to De Kooning's painting *Excavation* (1950), a description that prompts Anthony Libby, once again, to make specific comparisons between the works. [47] Unfortunately, while aspects of the two works are comparable (insofar as neither allows a recognizable figure or setting to assert itself fully), the painting seems controlled by an overall visual pattern and harmony of color, while the poem seems structurally conflicted by incompatible parts, procedures, concerns. Unlike "Easter," which demonstrates a thematic and procedural consistency that lends credence to the notion of such a one-to-one comparison, the bigger, structural discontinuities of "Second Avenue" indicate a sort of dysfunctional eclecticism with respect to O'Hara's plastic inspiration. The poem invites comparisons with the work of several artists all at once, including De Kooning, Rivers, and Hartigan, who become representatives of a broader, if never explicit, creative ideal for O'Hara. The most evocative description of painting comes toward the end of the poem in Part 10:

> Grace destroys
> the whirling faces in their dissonant gaiety where it's anxious,
> lifted nasally to the heavens which is a carrousel grinning
> and spasmodically obliterated with loaves of greasy white paint
> and this becomes like love to her, is what I desire
> and what you, to be able to throw something away without yawning
> 'Oh Leaves of Grass! o Sylvette! oh Basket Weavers' Conference!'
> and thus make good our promise to destroy something but not us.
>
> (*SP*, p. 70)

Through sheer creative grace or love—beyond that of Hartigan herself—faces, figures, personalities, and objects are aesthetically "destroyed" without boredom in an act of spiritual survival. Such aesthetic faith seems to lie at the heart of valid creation and touches upon the work of many of O'Hara's friends and heroes. But another instance suggests a more imitative, classical, and amorously sensual approach:

> Your feet are more beautiful than your father's, I think,
> does that upset you? admire, I admire youth above age, yes,

---

[47] Libby, p. 136.

in the infancy of the race when we were very upset we wrote,
'O toe!' and it took months to 'get' those feet. Render. Rent.
Now more features of our days have become popular, the nose
broken, the head bald, the body beautiful. Marilyn Monroe.
Can one's lips be 'more' or 'less' sensual?

(*SP*, p. 68)

O'Hara claims that this conversation took place with Larry
Rivers apropos of the latter's sculpture–although the emphasis appears to be on the body of the model/lover, even if they ironically
bring to mind classical fragments (O'Hara's "nose/ broken" and
"head bald"). The pastoral overtones and the references to both
writing and sculpting (rendering), reveal an early instance of "Personism" in which the poem becomes a dialogue between artists/
lovers about the(ir respective) sister arts. [48]

Finally, O'Hara identifies the following passage not with De
Kooning's *Excavation* but with one of his famous *Women* [fig. 17]
that he saw in the artist's studio:

You remained for me a green Buick of sighs, o Gladstone!
and your wife Trina, how like a yellow pillow on a sill
in the many-windowed dusk where the air is compartmented!
her red lips of Hollywood, soft as a Titian and as tender
her grey face which refrains from thrusting aside the mane
of your languorous black smells, the hand crushed by her chin,
and that slumberland of dark cutaneous lines which reels
under the burden of her many-darkly-hued corpulence of linen
and satin bushes, is like a lone rose with the sky behind it.

(*SP*, p. 67)

Even De Koonings can evoke Titians in O'Hara's universe of art;
yet interestingly, O'Hara also admits that the woman he described
was someone he actually saw "leaning out a window on Second Avenue with her arms on a pillow." (*CP*, p. 497) Equally important,
then, to the vertiginous slide of the description and its abstracting
effect (or what Marjorie Perloff, using Viktor Shklovsky, calls de-fa-

---

[48] It was in this spirit of inter-artistic dialogue, of course, that the two eventually
collaborated on *Stones* (1957), a series of lithographs in which the improvised and
intimate give-and-take of collaborative production between an artist and a poet
was, and may well remain, unmatched in the history of art and poetry.

miliarization [49]) seems to be the image's origins with a real human figure actually witnessed by chance. Simple, trivial, and random encounters with the simple, trivial, and random products of nature and society become endless resources for poetic de-familiarization, distortion, or elaboration.

Remarkably, the pursuit of the accidental and the ordinary resulted in some surprising correspondences between O'Hara's and Rivers' individual works. O'Hara's description of the real woman and his effort to metamorphose her into a De Kooning closely parallels the kind of painterly metamorphoses Rivers would later describe for O'Hara when asked about his painting *Second Avenue with THE* [fig. 18]. (*AC*, p. 118) Such correspondences reveal that in many ways, beneath the heroic inspiration of De Kooning and Pollock, another more intimate influence was daily at work on O'Hara, who strove just as hard to incorporate the immediacy of personal experience in his poetry as to expose the poetic process of incorporation in the final work.

A short poem that would seem to demonstrate these two aspirations very clearly and simply is the well-known "Why I am not a Painter." But rather than answer the question posed in the title, the poem tells a story that suggests that O'Hara *is* a "painter" because the poetic process he uses is so similar to the painterly one. The poem, however, is more emblematic than demonstrative of this process because of its clear, narrative development: both the poet and painter (in this case, O'Hara and Mike Goldberg) begin their respective works with some simple, recognizable idea; time passes and the process goes on, subsuming the original idea in a series of poetic and painterly decisions that disguise its relation to the finished product, except for the fact that the titles identify it (respectively, as "oranges" and "sardines"). The poem shrewdly describes what the earlier poem "Easter" actually does, and furthermore, what Pollock's oeuvre does in relation to figurative subject matter. But the poem differs from that earlier poetic experiment in more than narrative terms because it cleverly affects a more casual attitude toward daily, conscious experience. [50] It is precisely this at-

---

[49] Perloff in Elledge, p. 160.
[50] But as David Lehman reminds us in *The Last Avant-Garde*, pp. 344-345, the events described in the poem could never have happened and that "What looks spontaneous may really be the product of calculation, a fabrication . . . ."

titude that becomes the signature of what is most original in O'Hara's best work. Where O'Hara abandons storytelling and fully attends to immediate experience is in his famous I-do-this-I-do-that poems that combine Pollockian dynamism and Riversian intimacy. They are, in a sense, Action Poems, yet they are completely personal and new–a leap into the unknown, not an imitation.

I do this, I do that

One of the earliest I-do-this-I-do-that poems actually preceded "Second Avenue" and thus serves as a reminder that even within an individual's oeuvre the evolution of a poetic is never merely continuous, but fraught with discontinuity and simultaneity, with consolidation attended by regression and digression:

"Walking to Work"

It's going to be the sunny side
from now
      on. Get out, all of you.

This is my traffic over the night
and how
      should I range my pride

each oceanic morning like a cutter
if I
    confuse the dark world is round
round who
      in my eyes at morning saves

nothing from nobody? I'm becoming
the street.
      Who are you in love with?
me?
    Straight against the light I cross.
                  (*SP,* p. 57)

Though fully indicative of O'Hara's later voice, this poem readily exposes, through its visual design, a clear genealogy to the poetry of Reverdy and Williams. The voice and its "pride" cuts through the graphic space of the poem like a smart craft navigating choppy seas, or a darting arrow, turning unseen corners and traversing invisible crosswalks between enjambed lines. Like Williams, the voice is idiomatically American and deictically self-contained; but like Reverdy, it seems flushed and troubled by ineffable passions. It is intent upon treating the blank spaces of the page as unruly obstacles to its own fulfillments. Interestingly, the visual elements of this poem–its loose, lattice-like structure–can be seen in O'Hara's later work, appearing with sustained vigor in his longer poems, particularly the "F.Y.I." poems and "Biotherm." But the classic, short, I-do-this-I-do-that poems are usually more solid-looking (though equally riddled with enjambments). Most important, however, is how they concentrate a sense of the poet's immediate situation as both a statement and a technique.

One cannot doubt (although one sometimes does) that "A Step Away From Them," "Lana Turner Has Collapsed," "The Day Lady Died," "Rhapsody," "Personal Poem," or "Music" were all written on-the-go, as it were, in transit or at lunch. The ephemera of the moment is all too rapidly taken in and shot back like a series of quick glances, without being over-burdened by a sense of discrimination, of having to make anything but the most tenuous connections. Yet, as if acutely aware of the strict working limits of re-creative time (the lunch hour), the writing itself seems ironically regulated by reflexes–of the body, mind, and articulate tongue–as they occur, with an air of total candor, in a public space. O'Hara abandons classic, hermetic automatism (against its historical backdrop of sexual repression) for a kind of unembarrassed, workaday automatism–to be more in the work for its allotted duration. In writing this way, he could well say along with Pollock: ". . . the [work] has a life of its own. I try to let it come through. It is only when I lose contact with the [work] that the result is a mess. Otherwise there is pure harmony, an easy give and take, and the [work] comes out well." (AC, p. 39) Knowing the end of his lunch hour, commute, or walk is always only minutes away, O'Hara must work quickly to avoid losing contact with the poem which seems to grow out of both personal and cultural necessity. But because of the requirement of speed, a certain efficient sincerity is assured–along with a regular exit strategy: the idea of a stop-time. It is always there in the short poems, ready to put an end to all that racing ephemera (whether sought or chanced upon), yet ensuring a kind of tonal consistency across juxtapositional clashes. It is a game that works well for O'Hara, who plays by the rules he has set. As he told Edward Lucie-Smith: "I don't believe in reworking too much. And what really makes me happy is when something just falls into place as if it were a conversation or something. . . . Marvelous painting [is like that.] It looks like it took about three seconds." (*SS*, pp. 21-22)

But, as Andrew Ross has written, there is an ambiguous relation to the circumstantial in these poems that is like the Action Painter's obsession with surface: "this technical obsession [with surface] was underpinned by a whole ideology of depth—angst, alienation, autonomy—which marked the tradition of moral seriousness that was their heritage as artist-intellectuals." [51] It is perhaps easiest to recognize this depth in "A Step Away From Them" or "The Day Lady Died," in which the technical stop-time of the writing is complemented by the theme of personal death (whether of Pollock, Bunny Lang, or "Lady Day" [Billie Holiday]). O'Hara's attitude toward death becomes harder to decipher, however, when it is removed from the sphere of the personal to become "the enormous bliss of American death" in the poem "Rhapsody" (*CP*, p. 325), named after the 1954 film starring Liz Taylor. There is no way to determine whether this death is a big or a little one, let alone whether the poet belongs to it any more than "Tibet [is] historically a part of China." In the poem, O'Hara seems afflicted with a desire to have it both ways: to join a "myth of ascending" (suggested by a Madison Avenue address described as a portal to heaven) with that of descending (the urban jungle of 8,000,000 whose "Negroes" seem conspicuously representative); to reach a "summit where all aims are clear," and yet to move in a "smog of desire" through tunnels, in taxicabs, or "lying in a hammock on St. Mark's Place"; to be another proponent of dominant history, or to slip away into the relative immediacy of personal desire. Death and bliss, and by extension moral seriousness and verbal play, become reversible categories as the poem slides across images that refuse to take a stand concerning what may or may not constitute the soul of America: the alienating glamour of skyscrapers or the "challenge of racial attractions."

---

[51] Andrew Ross, "The Death of Lady Day" in Elledge, p. 381.

"Ode on Causality"

The poetics of speed in these poems is fraught, then, with a poetics of dead stopping or mortality. It is the technics of the former that necessitates those of the latter. But O'Hara's technique is not limited to that of speed and surprise, and in certain longer, commemorative works this poetics of mortality is thematized in association with the great painters O'Hara admired. If the relationship between O'Hara and Pollock in any way reflects the strategic dichotomy between desire and death in the I-do-this-I-do-that poems, the "Ode at the Grave of Jackson Pollock" (or "Ode on Causality" [*CP*, note, p. 542]) develops the subtle linkage of death and monumentality found in "Rhapsody."

> There is the sense of neurotic coherence
> you think maybe poetry is too important and you like that
> suddenly everyone's supposed to be veined, like marble
> it isn't that simple but it's simple enough
> the rock is least living of the forms man has fucked
> and it isn't pathetic and it's lasting, one towering tree
> in the vast smile of bronze and vertiginous grasses
>
> (*CP*, p. 302)

Although the "you" in this poem often refers directly to Pollock, it is not clear in these opening lines. Here, the lines probe the issue of commemoration itself and what forms are valid. In some ways the poet seems to address Pollock himself about the appropriateness of using a boulder to mark his grave, but he also seems to be asking himself about the requirements of his own elegiac stance. In both cases a "neurotic coherence" validates the choices made for being simple, lasting, and not "pathetic," i.e., not "wet, reflective, and self-conscious" (*CP*, p. 497). And yet both choices are historically resonant, even if they flout certain aspects of traditional commemoration, the sculpted marble or the strophic ode.

In the second "stanza" a visit to Pollock's grave with the child of a neighbor is described. The child Maude, who says, "'he isn't under there, he's out in the woods' beyond,'" is also, anomalously, identified with the rock. The comparison is both clarified and complicated later when, addressing Pollock as a sort of muse, O'Hara intones:

and like that child at your grave make me be distant and imaginative
make my lines thin as ice, then swell like pythons
the color of Aurora when she first brought fire to the Arctic in a sled
a sexual bliss inscribe upon the page of whatever energy I burn for art
and do not watch over my life, but read and read through copper earth

The child and the rock are both distant and imaginative. Given what one knows already of O'Hara's attitude toward poetic distance or "abstract removal" (*CP*, pp. 498-499), the relation between distance and imagination, like that between boulder and child, would seem to be more contradictory than metonymic. As such, the poem itself is conflicted–both distant, elegiac *and* imaginative, experimental. O'Hara implies that the elegiac ode is in transition, ready to assume new, anomalous forms. The matter of commemorative standards seems to disappear, like Pollock's ghost, in the woods of O'Hara's analogizing. He does not ask for moral guidance but creative energy and imaginative innocence–to write, in short, as Pollock painted, as if through a process of intellectual ebullience, ecstasy, ejaculation. Through this process apparently anything–all genres, all forms–can provide fuel for the living crematorium of art. And yet this crematorium preserves and immortalizes even the least admired of elements:

> and there's the ugliness we seek in vain
> through life and long for like a mortuarian Baudelaire working for Skouras
> inhabiting neighborhoods of Lear! Lear! Lear!
>   tenement of a single heart

O'Hara then offers the reader some gently parodic accounts of how great men were sung in times past, whether by French medieval *romanzers* or the shrewdly occasional Andrew Marvell, who celebrated Cromwell with cautious irony. Yet mention of the latter brings to mind other odes he wrote in "sweet scripts to obfuscate the tender subjects of their future lays." With this insinuating allusion to little T.C. and the pun on *lay* ("to be layed at all! romanticized, elaborated, fucked, sung, put to 'rest'") the connections between death and bliss are reinforced. There is the sense of exploitation in writing such odes, a kind of criminal, sodomite ecstasy at another's expense that can either be merely embarrassing: "worse than the mild apprehension of a Buddhist type caught halfway up/ the tea-rose trellis with his sickle banging on the Monk's lead window"; or more embittering: "unless the tea exude a little gas and poisonous fact/ to reach the spleen and give it a dreamless twinge that love's love's near/ the bang of alertness, loneliness, position that prehends experience." More than an opportunity for seductive verbal play on some important occasion or theme (such as causality), O'Hara's ode, in attempting not to apprehend, but to prehend experience in its language (i.e., as if to become experience instead of illustrate it), tempers its own verbal pleasures with the physical pain of frustrated apprehension, a sense of the permanent divide between experience and text, life and death. An avant-garde scandal of the historical elegy, O'Hara's ode imposes a state of loss upon the reader, or, what Roland Barthes calls "bliss": a crisis in the reader's relation to language. [52]

In the line quoted above about prehending experience, the lines of the poem itself, formerly swollen like tumescent pythons, freeze again into shards of ice–quick, pert propositions. O'Hara subliminally communicates the principle of his poem: to turn the long, self-reflective tones of commemoration into the sharp *staccato* of blissful self-abandonment. In doing so, multiple dialectical relations seem to achieve synthesis for O'Hara with "each in asserting beginning to be more of the opposite." Marvelously, this condensation of the elegiac ode into an almost ecstatic experience of self-loss, their blissful synthesis, is construed as causality–the movement from personal death to public commemoration, experience to art, and back again: "what goes up must come/ down, what dooms must do, standing still and walking in New York." Pollock's death, then, becomes a link in that dialectico-causal chain that will burn more energy for art. Hence, Pollock lives, is re-incarnated:

let us walk in that nearby forest, staring into the growling trees
in which an era of pompous frivolity or two is dangling its knobby knees
and reaching for an audience
                    over the pillar of our deaths a cloud
heaves
        pushed, steaming and blasted
                love-propelled and tangled glitteringly
        has earned himself the title *Bird in Flight*

---

[52] Roland Barthes, *The Pleasure of the Text,* trans. Richard Miller (Farrar, Straus & Giroux, 1975), p. 14.

A more synthetic attitude from that of Barthesian bliss finds hortatory expression in the lines above, lines that swing the pendulum of O'Hara's concerns back to that of the ode proper (albeit in new verse form), a hymn of praise expressing the hope of finding eternal celebrity in some sort of heaven. And yet the only celebrity available is that created by the living, by those like O'Hara who will see *Bird in Flight* as a title Pollock has earned. In this way the poem fluctuates between the commemorative demands of the conventional ode (by which Pollock is imaged among the heroes of traditional histories, the upholders of causality as it were) and the experimental needs of the personal ode (the poet responding to immediate circumstances in all their simultaneity). Thus "Ode on Causality" assumes a technique similar to that of Rivers' *George Washington Crossing the Delaware* as a parodic adaptation of a traditional genre, the recognizable elements of which both appear and disappear (as the outlines of a narrative structure) in the courses of creative play. Pollock the man provides the subject matter that becomes the starting point for a "Riversian" strategy of transformation–a movement toward verbal abstraction that leaves the reader breathless but still able to catch the reassuring glimpses of recognizable situations and forms. Where Pollock's "abstracting" method actually influences O'Hara's technique in a sustained and monumentalizing way can be seen in the late poem "Biotherm."

"Biotherm"

In his essay "Frank O'Hara: The Speech of Poetry," Mutlu Konuk Blasing describes "Biotherm" as a non-referential "poem of immanence" in which O'Hara "relinquishes as much as possible syntactic orders, subordinations, hierarchies . . . in order to sound a language intimate and intense, purified of 'rhetoric.'" [53] As the culmination of a conception of poetry that began as a species of Surrealism, "Biotherm," according to Blasing, also finds an analogue in Pollock's art insofar as the latter assumes "the scale of the painter's body." But instead of a language in scale with the body and, thus, with the singularity of immediate conditions of production (as in

---

[53] Mutlu Konuk Blasing, "Frank O'Hara: The Speech of the Poet" in Elledge, pp. 307-308.

the "I do this, I do that" poems), "the 'scale' of 'Biotherm' is the
poet's tongue, beyond a language that is the image of the tongue's
activity." [54] In this way the language of the poem assumes all of the
functions of the tongue (as speech organ, erotogenic organ, and di-
gestive organ) much as Pollock's drip-painting unconsciously assumes "body" functions (primarily eroto-excretory) beyond those
of artistic representation to become a form of graffitism or desecra-
tion. In other words, both languages in their respective media acquire basic functions in addition to those of signification, becoming
in the process temporally and physically contingent, hence, indiscriminate, infantile, heterogeneous, *informe.* [55]

Examples of this transformation occur in those parts of the
poem where language seems to develop the quality of masticated
food or even, at the end of the process, excrement (i.e., in the form
of nonsense, clichés, excessive alliteration or assonance, as in: "no
flesh to taste no flash to tusk/ no flood to flee no fleed to dlown
flom the iceth loot" (*SP*, p. 203) or "'if I thought you were queer I'd
kill you'/ you'd be right to, DAD, daddio, addled annie pad-lark
(Brit. 19th C.)" (*SP*, p. 207)). More than a surrogate for reality in
which time is staggered between signifier and signified, the language of "Biotherm," according to Blasing, assumes physical reality
for itself, thereby re-establishing the wholeness or oneness of time.
Ironically, the more completely language becomes its own reality or
object, the greater its psychotic potential. Indeed, reading "Biotherm" can be an almost maddening experience.

Blasing goes on to identify O'Hara's project with the work of
Antonin Artaud, whom O'Hara claims to have outdone in finishing
literature off: "For a time people thought that Artaud was going to
accomplish this, but actually, for all their magnificence, his polemical writings are not more outside literature than Bear Mountain is
outside New York State." (*CP*, p. 499) Yet Blasing decides that despite both men's efforts, neither can claim not to have written literature, because, as O'Hara himself said, "you have to use words," and
because of what Jacques Derrida identified (in "La Parole souf-
flée") as "the 'fatal complicity' of the destructive discourse, which
must inhabit the structures it would destroy." [56] Interestingly, Blas-

---

[54] *Ibid.*, p. 308.
[55] See Krauss's discussion of the destructive impulse in art and George Bataille's
term *informe* in "No More Play," *Originality*, pp. 53-54.
[56] Blasing in Elledge, p. 312.

224   SAVAGE SIGHT/CONSTRUCTED NOISE

ing does not seem to notice that O'Hara refers only to Artaud's polemical writings, where nothing if not "rhetoric" is employed. Yet, in at least one instance, Artaud can indeed be said to go further than O'Hara in using a completely non-referential language: the glossalalic writings in which he stretches the limits of the literary to become a kind of pure verbal rhythmics. In Artaud's glossalalia language truly operates on the "scale of the tongue," achieving subliminal otherness. "Biotherm" does not do this, its language retaining throughout a certain residuum of designation and significance, much as Pollock's paintings, for all their obsessive fixation on the physicality of the creative act and the flatness of the picture surface, retain qualities of illusionism. Blasing's "glossalalic" criteria seems out of scale with the poem's actual processes. He defends his position by referring to Gilles Deleuze's essay "The Schizophrenic Language" and saying that any such residual significance is experienced as "empty," "indifferent," "false." [57] If this emptiness seems no less applicable to some of Blasing's own more exaggerated claims, claims that are incompatible with other aspects of the poem, one must at least credit him for accurately identifying the most radical experimental features of the poem's language.

What finally prevents "Biotherm" from totally lapsing into non-referentiality, or even madness, is the same thing that prevents Pollock's work from being merely a paint-strewn surface in psychotic emulation of the anally expressive infant. Both works are ultimately neurotic, incorporating only temporary (if extreme) lapses of signification in conformity with a desire for openness of form [58] without precipitating its total eradication. Both still believe in the viability, the expandability of art, a cultural necessity predicated on a certain transgression or overflowing of its own perceived borders. If the concept of art is academically predicated on significance, modern artistic creation seems predicated on dissolving the borders between significance and non-significance (a combination of the insignificant and the unknown). Indeed, even Artaud's glossalalia is transgressively non-referential, not simply meaningless. As Pollock's non-objective works liquify the illusory borders of represented objects by making paint and process the sole objects of representation, O'Hara liquifies the borders between verbal collage

---

[57] *Ibid.*, pp. 315-316.

[58] O'Hara wrote of it: "I seem to have been able to keep it 'open' and so there are lots of possibilities, air and such." From *CP*, p. 554.

components and traditional citations (i.e., real language uttered in specific circumstances, or conscious parodies of literary prototypes) by insisting that the unconscious dimensions of such *enunciations*, revealed through verbal play, provide their own glue, their own mode of *passage* across the temporal ruptures of sense that separate them.

Yet in either case it is not enough that paint or language be the heterogeneous goo at issue, it must transmit at least an aura of significance across those fissures of sense–even if it be laughable, as it often is in "Biotherm." Laughter itself is inherent to the process, not madness; parody and infantile regression, not irreversible dementia. And although the overall design of the poem may be an elaborate joke about all-over painting, O'Hara's laughter is also specific, inhering in the details of the work and thus consistent with his own definition of scale: [59]

"vass hass der mensch geplooped
that there is sunk in the battlefield a stately grunt
and the idle fluice still playing on the hill
because of this this this this slunt"

> it's a secret told by
> a madman in a parlor car
> signifying chuckles
> *Richard Widmark*
> *Gene Tierney*
> *Googie Withers*
>
> (*SP*, p. 205)

Or,

> the dulcet waves are
> sweeping along in their purplish

---

[59] Larry Rivers also had some interesting things to say about painterly detail in his interview with O'Hara: "In the past you could walk right up to a painting if you were attracted, and the nearer you got the more intimate you felt with the work. There was something to examine close up. Today it doesn't make any difference *how* close you get, you're still just as far away as you were. There's nothing to learn from detail. Paintings are done close up. But today their impact is at a distance–the kind of painting that looks the same thirty feet away as it does at five feet. They're practically made to be in buildings. But I think there *should* be an appreciable difference in being near, in detail." In O'Hara's interview with Rivers, *AC*, p. 120.

way and a little girl is
beginning to cry and I know
her but I can't help because
she has just found her first brick
what can you do what

(*SP*, p. 203)

Though laughter is not immediately associable with Pollock's work, there is a sense in which O'Hara's method brings Pollock's to mind. As with that method, O'Hara's process is undertaken to head off madness, or at least unbearable sadness. There is a sense of personal crisis or emotional emergency behind the inside jokes and glamorous chatter, and it is this tension that the language of the poem keeps rubbing in, like the French lotion from which the poem takes its name. At the center of this emergency is a specific individual, mentioned in the full title of the poem: "Biotherm (for Bill Berkson)."

In addressing the poem to a close friend, O'Hara continues his poetics of "Personism," abstracting language for the reader by making the poet's real familiarity with someone the context of its production. He has moved beyond the framework of the lunch hour and entered the broader framework of a sustained personal relationship. Speed, then, ceases to be central to the overall technique, although it persists by virtue of serialized juxtapositions as well as within the collage components or fragmented scenarios themselves–as in the opening lines:

Its the best thing in the world   but I better be quick about   it
better be gone tomorrow

                              better be gone last night and
                    next Thursday better be gone
better be

                    always   or what's the use the sky
         the endless clouds trailing we leading them by the bandanna, red

(*SP*, p. 201)

Unlike the I-do-this-I-do-that poems, "Biotherm" reveals that a number of different personal experiences have been grafted onto it and that the poem has correspondingly expanded to suggest a course of several days, a series of encounters. The juxtaposed episodes follow, interrupt, and sometimes commingle with each other in a broader serial progression that O'Hara adroitly but ironically identifies toward the end of the poem with his personal experience–by citing another's: "mes poèmes lyriques, à partir de 1897, peuvent se lire comme un journal intime" (my lyric poems, after 1897, can be read as an intimate journal). (*SP*, p. 216) In this way, he seems to anticipate Derrida's contention that detached signs, whether in writing or any other semiotic system, can only be claimed in the most provisional way (unless by virtue of modern copyrights–i.e., *force* of law). Nonetheless, O'Hara makes exactly this provision through the very intimacy of his language. But instead of a series of lyric poems, he presents a series of fractured, modified episodes yoked together in one long poem. As the poem progresses, one begins to see Berkson's real importance to the almost diaristic form the episodes assume (even dates are given– primarily in August, September, and October). The episodes suggest encounters and conversations with Berkson that the poet has assembled and reworked according to his needs. Scattered comments throughout the poem provide suggestive clues about the nature of this relationship, both tender and tense, brilliant and brittle:

> I know you are interested in the incongruities of my behavior, John/ just as Bill you are interested in the blue paint JA Oscar Maxine Khnute/ perhaps you'd better be particularly interested POOF (*SP*, p. 202)

besides, the snow was snowing, our fault for calling the ticket
                                perhaps at the end of a very strange game
               you won   ? (?) ! (?)
      and that is important (yeah) to win (yeah)

                                            (*SP*, p. 202)

I don't think I want to win anything I want to die unadorned
                          (*SP*, p. 203)

but we will begin again, won't we
                         well I will anyway . . .
                          (*SP*, p. 204)

I would never leave you
if I didn't have to
                    you will have to too
                    Soviet society taught us that
                    is the necessity to be "realistic" love is
                              a football
                                        I only hear the pianos
            when possession turns into frustration [. . .]
            we are alone no one is talking it feels good
        we have our usual contest about claustrophobia
        it doesn't matter much
        doing without each other is much more insane

                                                    (*SP*, p. 206)

September 15 (supine, unshaven, hungover, passive, softspoken) I was very
                                                    [happy [...]

        why are you melancholy
                if I make you angry you are no longer doubtful
            if I make you happy you are no longer doubtful
                                        what's wrong with doubt

    it is mostly that your face
    is like the sky behind the Sherry Netherland
    blue instead of air, touching instead of remote, warm instead
                                                    of racing
    you are as intimate as a "cup" of vodka
                and when yesterday arrives and troubles us you
                            always say NO
                I don't believe you at first but you say no no no no
                and pretty soon I am smiling and doing just what I   want again
                            that's very important
                            you put the shit back in the drain
                            and then you actually find the stopper

    take back September 15 to Aug something
    I think you are wonderful on your birthday
                                        I think you are wonderful
        on all your substitute birthdays
                            I am rather irritated at your being born
                                        at all
                        where did you put that stopper

you are the biggest fool I ever laid eyes on
that's what they thought about the Magi, I believe

(SP, pp. 208-209)

the celestial drapery salutes an ordinary occurrence
the moon is rising I am always thinking of the moon rising
                      I am always thinking of you
                      your morality your carved lips
      on the beach we stood on our heads
      I held your legs it was summer and hot
      the Bloody Marys were spilling on our trunks
      but the crocodiles didn't pull them
      it was a charmed life full of
      innuendos and desirable hostilities
      I wish we were back there among the
      irritating grasses and the helmet crabs

(SP, p. 210)

The desirable hostilities between the gay O'Hara and his "available" but disinclined friend establish the structure and language of the poem as a whole. The subject matter proposed here, then, dictates the technique by which the reader is both irritated by and attracted to the work. As in "Easter," the image that summarizes the poem's concerns and links the intermittent subject matter with the overall technique is provided in the title. As O'Hara has written, biotherm is a sunburn lotion advertised as having attar of roses, lanolin, and plankton in it, "practically the most health-giving substance ever rubbed into one's skin"; but it also "hurts terribly when gotten into one's eyes." (<i>CP</i>, p. 554) At the same time, the word's etymology suggests "life heat" or "body heat"–desire, energy, nerves. As a mix of nutrient and sunscreen, desire and defense mechanism, biotherm is a fluid figure of both the language of the poem and the tense nature of the relationship it describes. Like biotherm, the language offers a lubricitous, protective medium, but one that suspends anyone "using" it (creating or reading it) in a state of frustrated possession like that of the poet in relation to Berkson. But such is language, for O'Hara, when it achieves the condition of poetry: "I only hear the pianos/ when possession leads to frustration." Like body heat, the language of the poem–both erotic and aggressive–is the energy O'Hara burns for art, an energy that yields in turn the same language in a different, processed form as poetry: a kind of alimentary secretion or ejaculatory surrogate (or waste product for some). Once again, as in Pollock's paintings, the process and product, energy and outcome, are so inextricably related that one cannot be understood without the other, a danger minimized by the fact of the product's disarming candor, as it were, about its own technique. Just as Pollock's paintings offer the exact record of the painter's artistic struggle in an objectified form that is metaphysically poised between solidity and fluidity, so "Biotherm" provides a record of another kind of struggle (for love, for friendship, for togetherness) in a way that both solidifies experience as a collagist accumulation of verbal episodes and then saturates them with the sense of the poet's living heat, his "fluid" desire for love *and* art. Thus minimal vestiges of the recognizable persist in this poem which obliquely commemorate a personal relationship that was in the un-making–a process that also seems to be going on between language and denotation in the poem. It is as if O'Hara wanted to erase, once and for all, the burden of semantic correspondences but could not avoid leaving some trace, some imprint of the merely personal or conventional in the sticky stuff of language (like verbal *biotherm*, as it were). Thus, even in his most conspicuously experimental works, the poet surreptitiously re-enacts what is still partially thematized in "Ode on Causality" as the commemorative impulse "to obfuscate the tender subjects of . . . future lays" (*CP*, p. 302).

CHAPTER V

JOHN ASHBERY

A LTHOUGH John Ashbery carefully enumerated French avant-
garde influences on Frank O'Hara in his introduction to *The
Collected Poems of Frank O'Hara,* he has consistently denied the
primacy of any such influence in his own work. Yet certain facts
about his career undercut this denial–including a ten-year expatria-
tion in Paris where he worked as an art critic for the *Herald Tribune*
until 1965–as do the terms of the denial itself, which exclude the
likes of Pierre Reverdy, Raymond Roussel, and Giorgio de Chirico,
participants in the Avant-Garde to whom he is clearly indebted.
What, then, is the avant-garde tradition–in Ashbery's words, the
"other tradition"–Ashbery would sidestep even as he acknowledges
certain of its by-ways (an "other" other tradition)? Surprisingly,
Ashbery himself provides a map of its influence through his writings on avant-garde painters, particularly the French. In this way
his own art criticism, like that of so many others, becomes a form of
a proto-poetics, while the theoretical relation between painting and
poetry repeatedly inserts itself into Ashbery's poetical ruminations
on novelty.

ALTERNATIVE AVANT-GARDES PAST AND PRESENT

Ashbery's evasiveness about his own avant-garde genealogy
seems to have been a reaction to W. H. Auden's and Harold Bloom's
disparaging associations of his "excesses" with Surrealism. [1] By the

---

[1] See W. H. Auden's foreword to Ashbery's first collection of poems, *Some Trees*
(New Haven: Yale University, 1956) and Harold Bloom's "The Charity of the Hard

1960s official Surrealism was old hat among serious avant-garde practitioners, from the French Situationists to American Pop Artists. Yet, in his own writings on the subject, Ashbery seems determined to retain its unofficial nature as a source of novelty by resuscitating marginal figures and forgotten precursors of the movement—less out of critical premeditation than simple appreciation. At the same time, he upholds the general framework of an anti-literary, anti-artistic attitude inherited from Surrealism by concurring with the poet/painter Henri Michaux (whom he interviewed in 1961) that it provided "*la grande permission*" and was thus to be valued "less for what [its members] wrote than for the permission they gave everybody to write whatever comes into their heads." [2]

Ashbery, then, seems interested in a broader, "acculturated" Surrealism that crosses the perceived limits of its Bretonian program and assimilates itself to new realities: "What has in fact happened is that Surrealism has become a part of our daily lives: its effects can be seen everywhere, in the work of artists and writers who have no connection with the movement, in movies, interior decoration and popular speech. A degradation? Perhaps. But it is difficult to impose limitations on the unconscious, which has a habit of turning up in unlikely places." [3]

Writing at different times in the 1960s, Ashbery discriminates among Surrealism's procedures and practitioners in a way that subtly illuminates his own poetic debts. Indeed, his critical evaluations help to differentiate his own procedures from those most closely identified with the official Surrealism of the 1920s:

> *Liberté totale* in Paris in the 1920s turned out to be something less than total, and if it was not total, then it was something very much like the everyday liberty that pre-Surrealist generations had to cope with. In literature it meant automatic writing, but what is so free about that? Real freedom would be to use this method where it could be of service and to correct it with the conscious mind where indicated. And in fact the finest writing of the Surrealists is the product of the conscious and the uncon-

Moments" in *John Ashbery*, ed. Harold Bloom (New York: Chelsea House, 1985), pp. 49-79. Ashbery's own reassessments of his artistic genealogy appear in various sections of his *Reported Sightings: Art Chronicles 1957-1989* (New York: Alfred A. Knopf, 1989). Subsequent citations of this edition will appear in the text and notes as *RS*.

   [2] John Ashbery, "An Interview with Henri Michaux" (1961) in *RS*, p. 398.
   [3] Ashbery, "In the Surrealist Tradition" (1964) in *RS*, p. 4.

scious working hand in hand, as they have been wont to do in all ages. But if automatic writing is the prescribed ideal for literature, what about art? Dalí's meticulous handling of infinitesimal brushes excludes any kind of automatism as far as the execution of his paintings goes, and perhaps even their conception was influenced by a desire to show off his dazzling technique to its best advantage. Breton called Miró the most surreal of the Surrealists, yet the deliberate wit and technical mastery of his work scarcely seem like tools to plumb the unconscious. [4]

According to Ashbery, the automatist inadequacies of surrealist painting were rectified only with the advent of the New American Painting, since "automatism was not a viable possibility in art until much later, in the hands of artists like Jackson Pollock." [5] Yet in seeing Abstract Expressionism as the first complete realization of plastic automatism, Ashbery is actually demoting its personal status for him as a poet. One cannot help wondering if this critical maneuver is not in part a way of distinguishing his own avant-garde poetics from the kind of empirical automatism one finds in O'Hara's poetry, particularly in its early, more derivative manifestations in such poems as "Easter" and "Second Avenue," the latter of which Ashbery once described as "a difficult pleasure." [6] Ashbery elaborates his critical view of automatism–albeit primarily as a form of writing–in an essay on Pierre Reverdy in which he claims that "Reverdy's poetry avoids the extremes of Surrealist poetry, and is the richer for it." In the same essay he implies that automatism remained an unachieved ideal for the Surrealists, who adhered to rules that necessarily conflicted with it:

> Though all rules were seemingly abolished, the poets were careful to observe the rules of grammar and syntax: "Take care," wrote Breton. "I know the meaning of each of my words and I observe syntax *naturally*: syntax is not a discipline, as certain oafs believe." But does one always observe these rules when one is writing automatically? And what, in fact, is automatic writing? Isn't all writing automatic? If one corrects a poem after writing it, doesn't one happen automatically on the correction? The dis-

[4] Ashbery, "The Heritage of Dada and Surrealism" (1968) in *RS*, p. 6.
[5] Ashbery, "Yves Tanguy" (1974) in *RS*, p. 26.
[6] Quoted in Alan Feldman, *Frank O'Hara* (Boston: G. K. Hall, 1979), p. 69.

cipline as it was practiced by the Surrealists seems arbitrary and sterile.[7]

By questioning the validity and usefulness of Breton's concept of automatic writing, Ashbery is really arguing for an expanded notion of the Avant-Garde and avant-garde procedures that no longer need conform (if they ever did) to the letter of the law of radical spontaneity in all its heroic pomposity. For many of the Surrealists, spontaneity of expression seemed to involve a constellation of de-personalizing techniques that, in different hands, had the potential of realizing exquisite forms in both plastic and literary media. Even the most anti-literary, anti-artistic practitioners ended up, according to Ashbery, reaffirming a certain artistry: "Picabia, Arp and Schwitters are the most notable Dada artists after Duchamp, and, as with him, one finds it difficult to imagine how their work could ever have been construed as anything but a high form of art." (RS, p. 7) Short of true automatism (a kind of total expression of individual consciousness), the governing principle Ashbery sees behind many surrealist works is a form of "self-abnegation in the interests of a superior realism, one which will reflect the realities both of the spirit (rather than the individual consciousness) and of the world as perceived by it: the state in which Je est un autre, in Rimbaud's phrase." (RS, p. 26) In the plastic arts, Ashbery detects these self-abnegating techniques in the work of Max Ernst, André Masson, Wolfgang Paalen, and Yves Tanguy in the form of collage, frottage, fumage ("smudges from a candle flame held close to the canvas"), sand painting, and painting upside down (p. 26). He finds literary analogues to such techniques in the writings of Raymond Roussel, elements of which he compared to the meticulous, interlocking shapes found in Tanguy's mysterious landscapes:

> They remind one of the fantastically complicated "*machines céli-bataires*" described in the novels of Raymond Roussel, one of the writers the Surrealists most admired (though he was not a member of their group). The title of one of Tanguy's early canvases, "*Les Vues*" (1929), may be an allusion to Roussel's long poem "*La Vue*," whose laborious cataloguing of minutiae prefigures

---

[7] Ashbery, "A Note on Pierre Reverdy," an unpublished essay (c. 1957-1958) quoted in John Shoptaw, On the Outside Looking Out: John Ashbery's Poetry (Cambridge: Harvard University Press, 1994), pp. 49-50.

Tanguy's spirit. Roussel's *"demoiselle"* in his novel *Locus Solus*–a kind of aerial pile driver capable of constructing a finely detailed mosaic of teeth–has the same almost insolent awareness of its own improbable being as the central colossus in Tanguy's "My Life, White and Black [fig. 19]." (p. 24)

For Ashbery, understanding the distinction between such techniques and presumably "pure" automatism is a prerequisite for understanding his own relation to the French and American Avant-Gardes, a relation that seems to turn on making a critical reappraisal of automatism. On the one hand, he sees automatism as a convenient myth–both for Surrealism's critics and its proponents: a myth no work can fully embody, yet one that points inexorably to a solipsistic austerity or abstraction in art and literature. On the other hand, he does not want to be irrevocably dissociated from that myth; therefore, he makes only the subtlest choice against Bretonian automatism for Rousselian paranomasia, Reverdian polyptoton, and the kind of attenuated phrasing of De Chirico's novel *Hebdomeros*. In the plastic arts, he does not disparage the achievements of the Abstract Expressionists and related avant-garde movements, but suggests their slight impoverishment in comparison to those of such artists as Yves Tanguy and Joseph Cornell, who, unlike the newcomers, " . . . keep all the stories that art seems to want to cut us off from without giving up the inspiring asceticism of abstraction." [8] In short, Ashbery likes the Surrealists as much for what is regressive about their technique as for what is presumably progressive, as much for what contributes to the technical "self-definition" of art [9] as for what detracts from it and thus abolishes formalistic definitions. To be avant-garde in the wake of the radical Avant-Garde is to have a kind of perverse recourse to tradition, illusionism, and obsolete form inasmuch as the moral or ideological implications of those things are now deemed to have been neutralized. "Self-abnegating" techniques move in this direction; yet Ashbery is prepared to go even further, finding avant-garde potentialities even within the most traditional means–by virtue of a kind of non-discrimination between the tradition and

[8] Ashbery, "Joseph Cornell" (1967) in *RS*, p. 17.
[9] I am referring to the work of Clement Greenberg who saw "flatness" as a definitive or primary quality of modern painting. See his essay "The Crisis of the Easel Picture" in *Art & Culture* (Boston: Beacon Press, 1965), pp. 154-157.

the other tradition, the figurative and the abstract, the narrative and the presentational, the speculative and the spontaneous. His description of the relation between the art of Tanguy and Pollock illustrates this tendency:

> . . . the arbitrary distinction between abstract and figurative painting did not exist for Tanguy, who painted real if nonexistent objects, so that his work is in a sense a fusion of the two, always in the interests of a more integral realism. The automatic gestural painting of Pollock, Kline, and their contemporaries looks very different from the patient, minute, old-master technique of Tanguy, yet he was perhaps the Poussin of the same inner landscape of which Pollock was the Turner. (*RS*, p. 27)

In a lecture at the Yale Art School published in *Artnews*, 1968, Ashbery offered his most comprehensive statement regarding his relationship to the Avant-Garde by tracing the outlines of an "invisible avant-garde" that presumably included himself. For Ashbery, the true Avant-Garde only properly exists in a condition of cultural tenuousness: unconsolidated and largely unrecognized, disestablished less out of a social hostility against it than uncertainty about it, its quality of *yet becoming*. It was this uncertainty and the risk involved in experimentation that attracted Ashbery to the Avant-Garde as a young poet. But in the late 1960s it became clear to him that the Avant-Garde had established its own tradition, distinct from a presumably established one, yet also very much like it in its enjoyment of growing popularity. As an increasingly celebrated socio-economic phenomenon (exemplified by the career of Andy Warhol), the Avant-Garde had come to resemble a very different –and much larger–military unit than its nineteenth-century label had originally suggested:

> What has happened since Pollock? The usual explanation is that "media" have multiplied to such an extent that it is no longer possible for secrets to remain secret for very long, and that this has had the effect of turning the avant-garde from a small contingent of foolhardy warriors into a vast and well-equipped regiment. In fact the avant-garde has absorbed most of the army, or vice versa–in any case the result is that the avant-garde can now barely exist because of the immense amounts of attention and money that are focused on it, and that the only artists who have

any privacy are a handful of decrepit stragglers behind the big
booming avant-garde juggernaut.[10]

Between the armed camps of the tradition and the other tradition,
only deserters, defectors and spies can maneuver, Ashbery argues,
for creative autonomy in a culture of oppositional conformities.
Putting a new spin on Eliot's theme in the essay "Tradition and the
Individual Talent," [11] Ashbery identifies "acceptance" as a primary
menace to the "individual talent," who risks absorption by one or
the other of these "traditions." At the same time, certain historic
acts of defiance in the face of acceptance are acknowledged to have
completely backfired, resulting in bad art–as the case of De Chirico
shows, whose late pastiches of Renaissance painting were the objects of Breton's withering scorn. But this latter example might be
viewed as an almost proleptic defense against the overwhelming acceptance Ashbery himself would receive after publishing *Self-Portrait in a Convex Mirror* (1972), which earned him the Pulitzer
Prize, the National Book Award, and the National Book Critics Circle Award. Recognizing both the danger and potential of wide-
spread acceptance, Ashbery has cultivated a skeptical insouciance
with regard to the competing "traditions"–in his own words, "a
kind of fence sitting/ Raised to the level of an esthetic ideal" as he
puts it in the poem "Soonest Mended" in *The Double Dream of
Spring.* [12]

Ashbery's apparent commitment to "fence sitting" makes it unclear whether the "other tradition" to which he so often refers actually represents the historic Avant-Garde or simply designates the
poet's eccentric middle way, a "new" negative capability that skews
the terms of "tradition" and "avant-garde." In the process, the
terms become reversible as Ashbery assumes a nomadic tangency in
relation to these two discursive poles of poetic production–one,
established/decaying, the other, emergent/proliferating. As these
poles increasingly come to resemble each other in a postmodern or
millennial culture of ubiquitous consumption that subsumes all

    [10] Ashbery, "The Invisible Avant-Garde" (1968) in *RS*, p. 392.
    [11] T. S. Eliot, "Tradition and the Individual Talent" in *Selected Prose of
T. S. Eliot*, ed. Frank Kermode (New York: Harcourt, Brace, Jovanovich, 1975), pp.
37-44.
    [12] Ashbery, "Soonest Mended" in *The Double Dream of Spring* (New York:
Ecco Press, 1976), p. 18.

SAVAGE SIGHT/CONSTRUCTED NOISE

traces of unassimilated space and its cultural ecosystems, Ashbery's
mannered idealism becomes a private holdout against the forces of
cultural homogenization.

    Several poems from *Houseboat Days* (1975), Ashbery's first col-
lection after *Self-Portrait*, evoke the human cost exacted by a van-
guard poetics that succumbs to its own institutionalization. "The
Other Tradition" allegorizes the popularization of the Avant-Garde
as a kind of public demonstration that overruns a solitary pine
grove: "They all came, some wore sentiments/ Emblazoned on T-
shirts, proclaiming the lateness/ Of the hour[.]" [13] The addressee
of the poem, whose appearance is significantly delayed by Ashbery
but who seems to have been present all along, remains poignantly
oblivious to a public acclaim that simultaneously renders him curiously obsolete: "Only then did you glance up from your book,/ Un-
able to comprehend what had been taking place, or/ Say what you
had been reading." This reading can only be at variance with the
subject's unexpected celebrity conferred by the crowd of the avant-
guard juggernaut calling meetings to order and leaving him "ex-
president of the event." Yet the new participants could never be

                    so deceived as to hanker
        After that cool non-being of just a few minutes before
        Now that the idea of a forest had clamped itself
        Over the minutiae of the scene.

Undisconcerted, the fellow poet-addressee finds all this pseudo-at-
tention merely "Charming, but [turns his] face fully toward the
night,/ Speaking into it like a megaphone, not hearing or caring."
Furthermore, in the last lines it is the celebrated poet's "forgetful-
ness" (unlike the attentive "remembering" of his fans) that alone
keeps the crowded avant-garde vessel afloat. It is not that the poet
actually forgets either tradition; rather, he deliberately ignores the
ideological motivations imputed to their differences. Nor is it a
form of Bloomian *misprision* whereby the tradition is reaffirmed
through reinterpretation, but what David Lehman has called a kind
of larceny: the free-handed utilization of "so much raw material, no

---

    [13] Ashbery, "The Other Tradition" in *Houseboat Days* (New York: Viking, 1977),
pp. 2-3.

strings attached, [with] nothing to acknowledge or be faithful to," [14] nor, above all, the didactic residues of Eliotic allusiveness. The key virtue of a true avant-garde poet, then, is disinterestedness rather than antagonism.

Noting the poem's allusion to Dante's description of Brunetto Latini as one who "Had run his race and won"–albeit across burning sands in the *Inferno*–John Shoptaw, in his extensive study of Ashbery's poetry, has suggested that "The Other Tradition" ultimately refers to the reception of Frank O'Hara's poetry. [15] Yet it could as easily be Ashbery himself, given the parallels between the two poets' literary destinies. If O'Hara did not live to "hear" all this appropriative flattery, Ashbery, who did, tries his best not to "care" about it, cultivating a sort of impertinent obsolescence that reflects his ambivalence about being avant-garde in the wake of the Avant-Garde.

But there is another form of obsolescence Ashbery unequivocally avoids, as revealed in the poem "And *Ut Pictura Poesis* Is Her Name" in the same collection. It is the obsolescence of assuming a strictly nostalgic, as opposed to critically open-minded, relation to the competing traditions that frame a poet's innovations. "You can't say it that way any more," the first line of the poem tells us. [16] Although what "it" is is not specified, the pronoun seems to refer to some timeless message that requires a certain formal refashioning. What is new, and what makes "it" new, is the manner in which it is said. [17] Insofar as the first line seems to comment on the title of the poem itself, the title's own novelty is called into question, as if to say that the only true avant-garde stance is that in which the last thing said is always already outdated. Or does the first line refer only to a part of the title, which fobs off a famous Horatian dictum as a woman's proper name: *Ut Pictura Poesis* (poetry is like painting). Significantly, this dictum also presents the relation between poetry and painting as one of harmonious parallelism or mutual attraction. It is as if the poem were saying that in order to make "it" (poetry, beauty, whatever) new, the avant-garde poet must constantly rethink, restate, resituate his or her poetry in relation to painting,

---

[14] David Lehman, "The Shield of a Greeting" in *Beyond Amazement* (Ithaca: Cornell University, 1980), p. 113.
[15] Shoptaw, p. 149.
[16] Ashbery, "And Ut Pictura Poesis Is Her Name" in *Houseboat Days*, pp. 45-46.
[17] Shoptaw, p. 193.

as if painting were poetry's own lover and thus in need of "courting." Furthermore, this lover is, in the modern spirit, independent, anomalous, alienated, as opposed to accommodating, constant, domesticated, in the classical spirit. Because classical symmetries or harmonies cannot be vouchsafed in the modern context, the ways in which poems continue to be like pictures are a measure of poetic vitality.

At the same time, if this relation can no longer be elaborated in terms of traditional comparison, neither can it be satisfactorily demonstrated in the form of yet another modernist "poem-painting" with its stark juxtapositioning or cubist cantilevering of verbal elements to create a "presentational" poetry that tries to *be* a kind of painting without referring to it. Thus, although classical aesthetics are out of the question, a residue of classicism's amorous attraction to mere beauty compels the poet to rethink modernist tactics as well–in favor, it would seem, of a somewhat more accommodating, if conditional, communicative strategy. As the poem says: "Bothered about beauty you have to/ Come out into the open, into a clearing,/ And rest." Instead of a strict poem-painting–i.e., the surrealistic portraiture of the title–Ashbery's poem offers instructions on how to write a new kind of poem-painting, instructions that double as friendly advice on how to "get a girl" (or guy), thus a kind of *ars poetica* as *ars amatoria*. Yet this advice is jolted at different moments in ways that recall the same modernist juxtapositional strategies the poem's discourse would partially circumvent. In short, the poem is a new chimera of Ovidian didacticism and Bretonian juxtapositionism:

> Now,
> About what to put in your poem-painting:
> Flowers are always nice, particularly delphinium.
> Names of boys you once knew and their sleds,
> Skyrockets are good–do they still exist?
> There are a lot of other things of the same quality
> As those I've mentioned. Now one must
> Find a few important words, and a lot of low-keyed,
> Dull-sounding ones. *She approached me*
> *About buying her desk. Suddenly the street was*
> *Bananas and the clangor of Japanese instruments.*
> *Humdrum testaments were scattered around. His head*
> *Locked into mine. We were a seesaw.* [my italics]

The word "seesaw" concretizes the overall strategy of the poem in an oscillating image that also resolves the instructive aspect of the poem with the promise of copulation. As both temporal movement *and* concrete object, the seesaw suggests both Time–here associated with the discursive, narrative, or lyric movement characteristic of literature–and Space–associated with the frozen or "timeless" appearance of the plastic art object. Moreover, the word also suggests an unexpected "rapport" between these two "sister" arts by juxtaposing the past and present tenses of "to see" in a compound noun that implies the temporality of "seeing" itself. In this way Ashbery contorts the modernist assumption that the plastic arts have an instantaneous appeal to the sense of sight, which experiences the relations among a work's visual elements simultaneously, enabling an immediate or accelerated apperception of its plastic properties, unlike the sense of sound, which experiences a work through time. [18] As a primary characteristic of the modern sensibility, this "simultaneism" was the literary Avant-Garde's rationale for the creation of a more "painterly," "objectivist," or "presentational" poetics in the first place. But for Ashbery, seeing ultimately takes just as long as hearing; thus, a certain temporalizing "discursivity" not only accompanies aesthetic judgments about the visual, but helps produce it. Furthermore, the relation between painting and poetry here is analogous to that between "modern" and "traditional" poetics (as the corresponding tenses "see" and "saw" indicate), and it is a quirky synthesis of the two that Ashbery sustains in the interest of a new realism. Ironically, the chief precedent for bridging these constellated categories of time/space, poetry/painting, discursivity/concreteness is surrealist automatism itself in accelerating the creative process and encouraging accidents (sudden, shocking juxtapositions that correspond to Breton's idea of "savage sight" in the sense of an instantaneous, indiscriminate inclusiveness [19]). Ashbery acknowledges this precedent by concluding the poem with an image that echoes surrealist interests, but with a proviso about fostering "understanding" and "communication" in ways that seem less self-consciously marvelous than those the Surrealists envisioned:

---

[18] This assumption can be traced to Lessing's Laocoön, the modernist implications of which are discussed in W. J. T. Mitchell's *Iconology: Image, Text, Ideology* (Chicago: University of Chicago Press, 1986).

[19] André Breton, *Surrealism and Painting*, trans. Simon Watson Taylor (New York: Harper & Row, 1972), p. 1.

> Something
> Ought to be written about how this affects
> You when you write poetry:
> The extreme austerity of an almost empty mind
> Colliding with the lush, Rousseau-like foliage of its
>   desire to communicate
> Something between breaths, if only for the sake
> Of others and their desire to understand you and desert you
> For other centers of communication, so that understanding
> May begin, and in doing so be undone.

Austere emptiness (the given? being?) and lush communication (the negative? the ideal?) are both components of the final product that seems to have been occasioned by some startling revelation–as if before a painting or beautiful person. The final image almost heuristically displays the elements of surrealist technique with its "empty mind" and excessive desire (described as a Rousseau–one of Breton's favorite painters). Thus, even at this later stage in Ashbery's career, after already re-evaluating his relation both to the Avant-Garde and to the "tradition," one can see the tenacious persistence of the poet's surrealist memory.

POETIC GENEALOGIES: TWO VIEWS OF ASHBERY

I have described Ashbery's tangential relationship with the other tradition as a post-avant-garde stance that nonetheless asserts its avant-garde credentials. Yet from another perspective, this itinerant, "self-reliant" strategy, has a long, Emersonian genealogy deeply ingrained in American letters. In "The Charity of the Hard Moments" Bloom wrests Ashbery's poetics from anything resembling a deflected avant-gardism (or "French silence" in Harold Rosenberg's phrase) and resituates it as a species of American sublime, grandly associated with Walt Whitman and Wallace Stevens, if in a somewhat reduced form. The reduction, however, causes certain headaches for Bloom, who takes considerable pains to formulate the concept of a "counter-sublime" arising from the unavoidable discrepancies of style and impulse between Ashbery and Stevens. The crux of the matter is Ashbery's critical distance (especially in some of his early works) from the coherent and controlling Stevensian persona, who, in privileged moments of poetic invention discovers intelligible and exhilarating orders in the world. [20] Ashbery's counter-sublime involves the dissipation of the poetic persona through different discursive registers that sneakily (and sometimes randomly) enter the fabric of the poem and corrode its habitual identification with an authorial persona. Oddly enough, Bloom sees this corrosion of the self/poem as a form of purification:

> For Ashbery, the privileged moment, like their images, are on the dump, and he wants to purify them by clearly placing them there. Say of what you see in the dark, Stevens urges, that it is this or that it is that, but do not use the rotted names. Use the rotted names, Ashbery urges, but cleanse them by seeing that you cannot be apart from them, and are partly redeemed by consciously suffering with them. [21]

The rottedness of Ashbery's language, however, is more rotted than Bloom thinks, deriving as it does from a French symbolist tradition, an idea he dismisses as nonsense. [22] But it is not nonsense and runs deeper than he admits, pertaining also to his American Orpheus, Stevens. The problem is that the "rottedness" Bloom identifies in Ashbery's poetry is less a matter of high and low speech than of language's own impediments to pure communication, to sheer transparency–a transparency Bloom likes to think of as the hallmark of the American sublime. Rather than seeing the fetidity of words –their way of spoiling even in the process of communicating–as something to be suffered for redemptive purposes, French poets writing in the symbolist tradition saw the virtue of allowing language to "stink" a bit, to call attention to itself as a medium, to distract the reader from the domineering assumption of "meaning." (Ironically, Symbolists such as Mallarmé also considered this aspect of language an indication of its purity.) It is a putrefaction lodged at the core of all subsequent avant-garde elaborations, from the cubist one of treating language as an almost physical medium, to the surrealist one of professing a kind of child-like faith in the accidents of language (another form of rot or "de-composition") and therein positing a new, "marvelous" transparency to the medium when

---

[20] Bloom, "The Charity of the Hard Moments," p. 51.
[21] *Ibid.*, p. 65.
[22] *Ibid.*, p. 60.

used "automatically." Thus, the "putrefaction" of language seems
to imply different things: a language voided of certain denotation
(i.e., semiotic de-familiarization), or a language overburdened with
hermeneutic potentiality by virtue of an almost crystalline encrusta-
tion of previous uses, all reflecting, resonating, reinforcing, but also
contradicting or canceling each other.

It is precisely this aspect of avant-gardism that some critics see
as a distinguishing feature of Stevens' own poetry. In his essay "The
Brushstroke's Integrity," Leslie Wolf not only recalls Ashbery to an
avant-garde tradition of painterly poetics, but in so doing, resituates
his assumed forebear Stevens in that tradition's pre-condition of
emphasizing the linguistic medium *as medium*. Wolf writes:

> The history of this attitude in poetry, from Baudelaire to Rim-
> baud through Mallarmé and Valéry and the moderns, has includ-
> ed a growing recognition that in order to create an instrument
> that works in the imagination, the poet must divert his
> material–the words of his language–from their habitual usage.
> And if the Symbolism of Mallarmé and Valéry never produced
> an art equal to the majesty of its theories, it nevertheless delineat-
> ed clearly the orientation that Pound, Eliot, Crane and Stevens
> brought to the task of writing poems during the first half of the
> century. [23]

Wolf goes on to show that this task was facilitated by the example of
modern painting, in which the idea of a medium as a desirable impediment to its otherwise presumed function of transparent communication found a conspicuously physical demonstration, particularly
in the work of the Cubists. Such work imparted the sense of a medium's materiality, its quality of physical contingency. In short, emphasizing the medium over the message in any art was conceived as a
painterly strategy *tout court* (even in music), while emphasizing referentiality–the illusionism of communication–remained literary, discursive, rhetorical or "linguistic" (in Stevens' usage). For Stevens,
this "painterly" emphasis on the medium (and as such, the *énonciation*) over a "linguistic" one on the message (the *énoncé*) constituted

---

[23] Leslie Wolf, "The Brushstroke's Integrity: The Poetry of John Ashbery and
the Art of Painting" in *Beyond Amazement*, pp. 232-233.

"abstraction" in poetry–the transporting of reality (habitual meanings) to the imagination by way of material deviations. [24]
    Like Bloom, Wolf sees Ashbery as descending from Stevens, al-
though not as American heir-apparent, but as the poet who took
Stevens' "French lessons" to an even higher level, upping the ante
in a kind of poker game of poetic experimentation. Furthermore,
Wolf sees Ashbery's descendant relation to Stevens in parallel with
that of the Abstract Expressionists to the Cubists, a parallel relation
grounded on the assumption that the late moderns–both painters
and poets–essentially accelerate a process of *mediumification* [25] undertaken by their predecessors: "From this point of view, Stevens
–Ashbery's favorite poet–is a kind of poetic 'cubist' out of whom
has sprung Ashbery's De Kooning: Stevens contradicts the object
but retains it as 'motif' in much the way Picasso did; but Ashbery,
like De Kooning, 'dares to remove the object further before recon-

---

[24] Wolf likens the process of "material deviation" in Hart Crane and Wallace
Stevens to Gombrich's notion of contradictory evidence in painting: ". . . the aim is
to fight the 'transforming influence' of 'illusion'; for illusion is what allows us to be
unconscious of the medium through which we are apprehending reality. Poets like
Crane and Stevens–and Ashbery–will not allow us this unconsciousness. One need
only consider Crane's arresting adjective-noun combinations–'improved infancy,'
'immaculate venom,' 'petalled word'–or his use of negating prefixes and suffixes–
'and your head unrocking to a pulse'–to see one form the poem's 'resistance' may
assume. Stevens' strategy is outwardly quieter, if no less insistent. One thinks of the
subtle sliding weights moving beneath his strategic repetition of words, transforming them into semantic merry-go-rounds, or the bold contradiction of some of his
gestures ('If all the green of spring is blue, and it is'–'Connoisseur of Chaos'). En-
tangled in a medium whose primary burden in ordinary usage is to refer to external
reality, the poet must arrange the 'brushstrokes' of his tableau in such a way that
they yield contradictory clues. To do this the poet must, as Stevens directed, approach language abstractly–that is, transport reality into his imagination. That way
he can 'use' reality without committing himself to any particular reality. The language must inevitably employ some species of 'deviation'–syntactic dislocation, dis-
sonant diction, variations within repetition–if the poet is to wrest his words from an
easy, habitual assimilation." (Wolf, pp. 234-235) I would only add that, in a general
way, the Latinate glamour of Stevens' poetic vocabulary oscillates between these abstractly "deviating" and realistically "communicating" alternatives by flaunting its
qualities as an elevated style while simultaneously conjuring a sense of its denotative
specificity.
    [25] In using this rather cumbersome term, I nevertheless want to point out its
analogous function with art historian Norman Bryson's notion of "style" in painting
as an impediment–fostered by historical circumstance–to the copying function
painting conventionally assumes in order to capture the supposed "universal visual
experience" of the viewer or artist. See Norman Bryson, *Vision and Painting: The
Logic of the Gaze* (New Haven: Yale University, 1997 [1983]).

structing it.'" [26] Thus it is that Wolf, while acknowledging Stevens' influence on Ashbery, modulates that influence as a function of the avant-garde impulse toward "the painterly," which he defines in Greenbergian terms:

> loose, rapid handling, or the look of it; masses that blot and fuse, instead of shapes that stay distinct; large, conspicuous rhythms, broken color; uneven saturations or densities of paint; exhibited brush, knife, finger or rag marks–in short, a constellation of physical features like those defined by Wölfflin when he extracted his notion of the *Malerische* from Baroque art. [27]

Ironically, the Greenbergian definition Wolf uses reveals that while in painting such *mediumification* contributes to the "self-criticism" or "self-definition" of art, in literature it involves a kind of corrosive re-definition in terms of another art: i.e., to think of language as language (semantically destabilized by virtue of tonal, syntactic, or typographic elements) and not as transparent communication is really to think of language in terms of another art, whether as paint or as music. [28]

If the derivation of painterly poetics from a French tradition seems sound, the association of Ashbery's own painterliness with Abstract Expressionism is more problematic. The ways in which De Kooning's art and Ashbery's poetry "abstract" their respective media from the objects they represent to create an "all-over" surface in specific works seems plausible according to the terms Wolf uses. But this consonance is the effect of formal analogizing and lacks a certain documentary grounding that might otherwise reveal a deeper critical sympathy between Ashbery and the New York School. Where this formal parallel starts to break down is precisely where Wolf attempts to move beyond the formal, Greenbergian notion of

---

[26] Wolf, p. 241 (quoting Wylie Sypher's *Rococo to Cubism in Art and Literature*).

[27] *Ibid.*, pp. 224-225 (quoting Greenberg's "After Abstract Expressionism" in *New York Painting and Sculpture*).

[28] Ashbery reveals certain symbolist ambitions for his poetry apropos of its relation to music in a statement quoted by Bloom: "I feel I could express myself best in music. What I like about music is its feeling of being convincing, of carrying an argument through to the finish, though the terms of this argument remain unknown quantities. What remains is the structure, the architecture of the argument, scene, or story. I would like to do this in poetry." (Quoted in Bloom's introduction to *John Ashbery*, p. 28).

the painterly and to associate Ashbery with De Kooning on the basis of a Rosenbergian principle of creative "action"–a personal, if unconscious, creative struggle external to the art object and its integral, mediumic necessity, the value of this object, therefore, deriving symbolically from that struggle or process and not from itself. Rosenberg writes:

> What gives the canvas its meaning is . . . the way the artist organizes his emotional and intellectual energy as if he were in a living situation. . . . Since the painter has become an actor, the spectator has to think in a vocabulary of action: its inception, duration, direction–psychic state, concentration and relaxation of the will, passivity, alert waiting. He must become a connoisseur of the gradations among the automatic, the spontaneous, the evoked. [29]

From this standpoint art is important as a record or sign of a certain heroic content with "the artist in attendance pumping it in." [30] Certainly both men's work offers a record of its own production, an abstracting process in which objects and images dissolve, merge, reform or disappear altogether. Furthermore, these records have the same non-hierarchical, all-over effects in their respective media (particularly in Ashbery's *The Tennis Court Oath* [1962], which Bloom angrily rejected as a work of "calculated incoherence" [31]). To this extent an idea of "process" remains compatible with that of the "painterly." But the spirit of heroic self-absorption is absent in Ashbery. It is an American inflation of an idea of automatism to which Ashbery self-consciously responds with self-abnegating strategies derived from pre- and peri-surrealist experiments. Furthermore, Wolf, who writes persuasively about the formal consonance of Ashbery's and De Kooning's art, seems at a loss to explain why such poems as "The Tennis Court Oath," "Leaving the Atocha Station," "The New Realism," and the monumental "Europe" all, in his view, "fail to sustain *energy*" (my italics). [32] The answer is simple: the

---

[29] Harold Rosenberg, "The American Action Painters," quoted by Wolf in *Beyond Amazement*, p. 239. Wolf's ellipses.

[30] Leo Steinberg's phrase, "Jasper Johns: The First Seven Years of His Art" in *Other Criteria* (New York: Oxford University Press, 1972), p. 54.

[31] Bloom, "Charity" in *John Ashbery*, p. 53.

[32] Wolf, p. 243.

works are based on poetic principles ultimately incompatible with his critical premises. Indeed, the work seems premised on the exhaustion or exhaustive repetition of avant-garde strategies. Yet Wolf deflects this criticism by denying the significance of the one conspicuous strategy of the poems (collage) that might justify this apparent energy drain. As a belated Dadaist, Ashbery resorts to a kind of ritual, deadpan collagism that highlights the self-abnegating character of his poetry as against the self-assertiveness of Abstract Expressionist art in its insistence on personal immediacy, energy, action. The poet David Shapiro has identified collage as the source of this deviation of sensibility:

> One of the curious effects of this transformation of "The Tennis Court Oath" into complete and seamless *collage* is the curtailing of the "I" as having much lyric or dramatic nuance. The "I" may now merely be the "I" *not of a persona* but of a piece of *newspaperese* or newspaper, or part of a story pasted, as it were, upon the poem. There is no more of Ashbery to this "I" than the "I" of an alien bit of prose from another source shockingly "fallen into" the poem. The "I" is, indeed, often necessarily linked to the continuous "ego" or "*je*" of the poem, but a radical deflation of its resonance or dignity has occurred. As a matter of fact, Ashbery in this period employs the various kinds of "I" much in the way more conventional masks are employed by Yeats or Eliot, but in Ashbery's extreme case there is only the bitter sense of the two-dimensionality of the collaged "I." This is schizo-analysis.[33]

In a sense, segments of the "I" as an entire, coherent identity are lost inasmuch as the poet's language not only cedes to the words, utterances, or meanings of others (exuberant citation), but to a random agglomeration, an almost mechanical process that transforms those human utterances into ineffable, alien materials. Thus the reverberations of accommodating human voices one recognizes in any modern intertextual procedure become a numbing crush of verbal shards, semi-dead zones of disconnected neuro-linguistic synapses (the postmodern detritus of modern literary imagination). Oblivious to the *énoncés* of "cited" sources, the radical text of Ashbery's "Europe" mostly empties the verbal blocks of any discursive, and

---

[33] David Shapiro, *John Ashbery: An Introduction to the Poetry* (New York: Columbia University, 1979), pp. 55-56.

sometimes even linguistic, significance. What might, in certain other cases, be an affirmation of authorial identity (his or her mastery of sources) not only cedes here to a radical interdiscursivity that deconstructs the authorial self, but one that refuses even the integrity of its components, their capacity for any logical, linguistic, or symbolic sequencing. The effect is that of a simultaneism of speech that fully encroaches on serialization itself, a serial progress that cannot be construed as discursively purposive, but only as plastic accumulation with its effects of verbal cacography. Cacography represents not just a confusion of texts or authors, but a verbal melée or glossalalia, an *écriture affolante* renouncing any principle of contradiction. [34]

By contrast, modern (and mostly scholarly) principles of discursive organization are at pains to preserve a modicum of meaning within the citation, a modicum of the *énoncé* within its appropriated *énonciation*, to yield up a whole identity. The assembled parts narcissistically mirror the self-aggrandizing author, even if the method itself, ironically, recalls that of Echo, who vainly employs the speech of others to requite a nugatory love that is all her own. The interdiscursivity of modern intertextuality/citation is ultimately, then, directed toward exalting the human subject–or, in this case, the author–and thus sustains the notion of the modern discursive entity as a whole, an individual. He is an Apollonian figure with a story to tell–a beginning, middle and end. He has a history, a destiny, and a moral to convey–all of it reinforced through his stupendous command of a plethora of external discursive entities (modern citations) that might otherwise subversively consume him, pull him apart in a sparagmos of contra-dictions (*sic*). In such conditions, who would not say, along with Montaigne, "que sais-je?" (as if he could really be credited for the originality for *that* statement).

But a cacography represents a first literary instance–no matter how ephemeral–of the theoretical death of the author and of the insight that certain constellations of words are no longer the emblems of any single human subject but a kind of universal, human issue that is consumed and excreted like any physical matter, but that just happens to be symbolic. As Salvador Dalí might put it: the only difference between mind and matter is that mind isn't matter. Such

---

[34] Antoine Compagnon, *La Seconde Main, ou le travail de la citation* (Paris: Éditions du Seuil, 1979), pp. 381-382.

word-matter becomes *detached* from human identity, like Van Gogh's shoes from their Van Gogh-ness. As verbal plastic, detached from the self, language empties itself of meaning but also opens itself to other, if arbitrary, hermeneutic potentialities. The latter case may simply involve the arbitrary intervention of a third party–as in Benjaminian allegory–to impose a bit of order on the mess (as Reverdy might say). But the former case must remain indecipherable, a schizoid situation in which linguistic particles just leak away (what Deleuze and Guattari call *la fuite*), [35] utterly de-territorializing themselves and reminding the reader of the quotient of madness in any reading of any text in contemporary capitalist society.

ASHBERY'S "EUROPE": POETRY IS GARBAGE

Ashbery's most notorious collage poem is the rambling, 111-section "Europe," which could almost be said, in keeping with the "bitter impression of absence" [36] engendered by Ashbery's self-abnegating techniques, not to have been *written* by the poet at all. The poem is mostly a "cut-up" of author William Le Queux's *Beryl of the Bi-Planes*, a World War I-era girl's book Ashbery "picked up by accident on one of the quais of Paris." [37] Thus, it is less a work of original writing than an extended, plastic adaptation based on a mass-produced object (hence, an "adaptation" that is more original than the work it utilizes as a "source") and thus should be analyzed less as literature than as an object. The appropriateness of the source work clearly has less to do with its literary merit than its lack of it–its low genre and accidental discovery. As literature, Le Queux's novel is about as impertinent a choice as that of a urinal as a work of sculpture; indeed, in a post-Duchamp era, the urinal has acquired a kind of iconic status.

But the poem is, ultimately, much more than a ready-made, and its relationship to Duchamp's sensibility and technique is more

---

[35] Gilles Deleuze and Félix Guattari, "Capitalism: A Very Special Delirium" (trans. David L. Sweet) in *Chaosophy*, ed. Sylvère Lotringer (New York: Semiotext[e], 1995), pp. 72-73.

[36] Ashbery, "The Skaters" in *Rivers and Mountains* (New York: Ecco Press, 1977), p. 39.

[37] Shapiro, p. 19. Although this fact is now well known, Shapiro seems to be the first critical expositor of Ashbery's work to have mentioned it.

complex than that of a simple reiteration. In a technical sense, the poem is closer to being an elaborately "assisted" found object with neo-Dadaist additions, subtractions, and verbal riddles (a sort of "cryptography"[38]) in the spirit of Raymond Roussel or even Duchamp's *Large Glass*. On the other hand, underneath these collagist manipulations and insertions, Le Queux's banal text remains, in many ways, the physical substrate of the poem—a cheap story reduced to even baser material, its residues of plot, dialogue, and description all interfering with each other and producing verbal noise, shredded print, semantic junk, on to which a literary meaning can be projected in the spirit of allegory, but never quite extracted except as popular genre material. Beneath this artificial heterogeneity a former cohesion, the sense of a lost un-original, can be faintly detected. Thus the plot of Le Queux's story acquires a certain structuring function[39] like that of the personal encounters between Bill Berkson and Frank O'Hara that punctuate the latter's long poem "Biotherm." But unlike the encounters there, the vague narrative glimpsed in "Europe" is totally unimportant, has no aura of personal expression, memory, or even interest. Any semblance of the personal is mortified in "Europe," being completely replaced with the pre-fab personae and sentiments of cheap fiction. If the self appears at all, it is in the interstices and accumulations of the poem, in the material collagist adjustments that themselves may only offer further occasions for self-concealment. It is the replacement of the self's *énoncé*, for the body's *énonciation*, but one that may be indistinguishable from those of all other bodies.

To the extent that "Europe" retains an aura of Duchampian iconoclasm, it does so in the more contemporary spirit of 1960s neo-Dada or "New Realism," the term for art that pitted itself against Abstract Expressionist values of heroic composition for the pre-fabricated compositions of everyday, manufactured objects. Emerging simultaneously and independently in Europe and the United States, the New Realists informally included such artists as

---

[38] Shoptaw, p. 6. This is Shoptaw's word for the process in which "crypt words" or "crypt phrases" are displaced by misrepresentative marker words or phrases, but are thereby still recoverable in the final poetic text.

[39] It should be noted, however, that only about a third of the entire poem can be directly traced to the book, and its plot elements are sparsely deployed. Imre Salusinsky, "The Genesis of Ashbery's 'Europe'" in *NMAL: Notes on Modern American Literature,* Vol. 7, no. 2 (Fall 1983), item #12.

Yves Klein, Jean Tinguely, Robert Rauschenberg, Jasper Johns, and even Andy Warhol. [40] The new realism it expressed—even as it re-utilized certain dadaist forms—was that of industrial, consumer reality as an inescapable fact of human identity, depriving it of any unique or transcendent meaning beyond that of parody or ritual mimicry. As Ashbery himself wrote in an exhibition catalogue of the New Realists for the Sidney Janis Gallery in 1962, the work represented the "continuing effort to come to grips with the emptiness of modern life." But he also wrote: "The most successful way of doing this seems to be to accord it its due. That is, to recognize that the phenomena evoked by the artists in this show are not [just] phenomena, but part of our experience, our lives—created by us and creating us." [41] Unlike their dadaist predecessors, these artists no longer upheld the products of industrial civilization as a provocation to aesthetic values but as confirmation of what those values were becoming. There was little trace in these works of Dada's giddy hysteria in confronting modernity—rather a casual aplomb, a cool facility with its vocabulary of accumulation and consumption. The *otherness* of modernity had infused these works without provoking the usual sense of outrage at a proportional loss of presumed self-expression in a work of art. Such self-expression was now recognized as just another form among many that modern reality provided, ready-made, for the artist to utilize, either in aggregate (Rauschenberg's junk sculptures and photo-silkscreens), in series (Warhol's Campbell's Soup cans), or in simple isolation (Johns's targets and flags). In his review, Ashbery goes on to clarify the appeal of manufactured objects and signs for these artists:

> But why the object? Why are objects any more or less important than anything else? The answer is that they are not, and that, I think, is the secret of their popularity with these artists. They are a common ground, a neutral language understood by everybody, and therefore the ideal material with which to create experiences which transcend the objects. . . . As the French critic Françoise Choay points out, speaking of Duchamp: "On one side the product of industry is denounced in its anonymity, its banality, its essential poverty which deprives it of human and poetic qualifica-

---

[40] Pierre Restany, *Art in America*, Vol. 51 (February 1963), pp. 102-104.

[41] Ashbery, "The New Realists" (1962) in *Reported Sightings: Art Chronicles 1957-1987* (New York: Alfred A. Knopf, 1989), pp. 81-82.

tions. On the other hand it still remains an object which a simple decision on the part of the spectator can tear out from its context to give it mystery and opacity. . . . The ready-made is satire, but at the same time it is also a proposition of asceticism and conversion." [42]

One can be shocked or intrigued: the decision is one's own. The meaning one gives it can no longer rely on any organic determination, but is arbitrarily posited–in conformity with Walter Benjamin's concept of allegory. [43] Such is the new realism.

The notion that art was less a natural entity to be heroically discovered in the interest of originality, progress, and other teleological values than an arbitrary selection based on given information opened a huge gap in the American Avant-Garde between the New Realists (and their late, alternative incarnation as Pop Artists) and the Abstract Expressionists. Yet elements of continuity can be identified in their works, albeit primarily in the neo-Dadaists' satirical use of the "painterly" techniques of their predecessors. The two most enlightening examples, apropos of Ashbery, are Johns and Rauschenberg, a number of whose works parallel or anticipate both the poet's attitude toward the recent past and his techniques of literary production in "Europe." [44] As critic Leo Steinberg has written of Johns, his "pictures showed essentially Abstract Expressionist brushwork and surface, differing from those earlier pictures only in the variable of the subject matter, [and thus] seemed to accuse the strokes and drips of the De Kooning school of being after all only a subject matter of a different kind; which threatened the whole foundation of Abstract Expressionist theory." [45] The painting *Liar* [fig. 20] seems to make this accusation explicit inasmuch as the

---

[42] *Ibid.*, p. 82.

[43] Peter Burger, *Theory of the Avant-Garde*, trans. Michael Shaw (Minneapolis: University of Minnesota, 1984), p. 69.

[44] In an interview with Fred Moramarco, Ashbery says: "When I came back to New York for two years (1964-65), I first began writing about art and one of the first things I wrote about was a show of Rauschenberg's, and Jasper Johns also had his first exhibition. At that time it seemed as though this was the next logical way in which daring in art could express itself. Somehow the kind of epic grandeur of someone like Pollock already needed to be looked at more closely. I can see now how those junk collages by Rauschenberg influenced me at that point." In Moramarco's essay, "John Ashbery and Frank O'Hara: The Painterly Poets" in *Journal of Modern Literature*, Vol. 5, no. 3 (September 1976), pp. 436-462.

[45] Leo Steinberg, "Jasper Johns ..." in *Other Criteria*, p. 22.

painting consists of an accumulation of grey, painterly "strokes and drips" evenly spread across the surface in an all-over manner, but with the imprint of the word "LIAR" along the top, made (presumably) by the "real" block letters illusionistically attached to the canvas by a hinge. In this case, the natural subject of art (in Steinberg's view, art as "analogue of a visual [or subjective] experience of nature" as in Abstract-Expressionist works [46]) is spoofed by the "artificial subject" of Johns's art (the printed word "LIAR"). The device, however, is not without irony, given that the lie also redounds to the block letters themselves, which in order to print the word "LIAR" have to be designed and arranged as mirror opposites of the letters they print. In other works, the painting confesses to its own illusionism, its recourse to conventional forms. It is the paradox of calling oneself a liar.

Another relevant example by Johns is his map paintings of the United States. [fig. 21] As in De Kooning's *Women,* the scale of the paintings is monumental and their brushwork conveys a self-consciously gestural, "personal" quality of execution. Yet the subject matter is conspicuously schematic, with the familiar outlines of the forty-eight states and surrounding territories providing a standard template, as it were, for the composition. Furthermore, the postal abbreviations for the states have been systematically, if beautifully, stenciled into their geographically designated spaces. If this recourse to technique were not enough, Johns's "loose, rapid handling" of paint succumbs to another systematics: that of using only primary colors, a criteria derived–with bitter Dada irony–from Abstract Expressionism's near theoretical opposite, Neoplasticism. In each of these ways, then, one discovers an Abstract Expressionist quality of the "painterly" being perversely combined with competing systems of information by which specific contents impose a form and a mode of composition.

Relevant examples by Rauschenberg include junk constructions and "combine" paintings that make use of both painting and ordinary three-dimensional objects and thus promote Steinberg's postmodern idea of painting as a "flat-bed picture plane" [47] (a horizontal and purely cultural "matrix of information," [48] as against the

[46] Steinberg, "Other Criteria" in *Other Criteria*, p. 84.
[47] *Ibid.*, p. 90.
[48] *Ibid.*, p. 84.

idea of painting as a vertical analogue of natural vision and against "the mystical qualities of medium made available [to that vision] . . . as compensation for loss of illusionism"). [49] The most famous of these "combines," and perhaps the one that directly inspired Steinberg's formulation, is Rauschenberg's *Monogram* [fig. 22] with its goat and tire mounted on a horizontal painted surface. Here Rauschenberg has shifted the whole orientation of the painted surface in order to accommodate an otherwise unassimilable found object, a stuffed Angora goat. Other assemblages utilize less conspicuous objects, but nevertheless use them in novel ways, as in *Winter Pool* [fig. 23], where a ladder, instead of combining upper and lower regions, forms a bridge between two painted side panels.

The relevance of such works to Ashbery's poem is their *disorienting* quality of constructed multiplicity—of combining disparate, junk elements and almost casually coordinating them to establish what Rauschenberg has called a "random order." [50] This quality can also be found in the artist's solvent-transfer drawings (the *Inferno* series) and silk-screen paintings, in which numerous images from popular culture are transferred to paper or canvas and, with modifications, combined to form complex, textured wholes—yet with many of their "transferred" elements retaining a kind of floating, mutually-interfering visual autonomy within those wholes. But perhaps the most immediately pertinent example by Rauschenberg is his notorious *Erased De Kooning* (1953). On the face of it, this work would seem an even greater provocation than Johns's by virtue of its actual defacement, even destruction, of a De Kooning drawing. Yet, as in Johns's *Liar*, latent ironies come to the surface of this radical gesture, since Rauschenberg's erasure acquires aesthetic significance by reference to what it eliminates (an irony not lost on De Kooning, who gave his permission [51]).

How do these works relate to Ashbery's "Europe"? As Ashbery has written of Johns's procedure, one should try to "build away from the edge of the canvas" [52] of Ashbery's poem by beginning

---

[49] Charles Altieri, "John Ashbery and the Challenge of Postmodernism in the Visual Arts" in *Critical Inquiry*, Vol. 14, no. 4 (Summer 1988), p. 815.

[50] Robert Rauschenberg quoted by Lawrence Alloway, "Rauschenberg's Development" in *Robert Rauschenberg* (Washington, D.C.: National Collection of Fine Arts, Smithsonian Institution, 1976), p. 7.

[51] Calvin Thompkins, *The Bride and the Bachelors: Five Masters of the Avant-Garde* (New York: Penguin, 1976), pp. 210-211.

[52] Ashbery, "Four American Exhibits of 1968" in *RS*, p. 253.

with certain framing or organizational devices at the boundaries, as it were, of the poem and relating them to the various compositional "givens" of Johns's work. In both men's work, it is precisely such given systems of organization that do the most to undermine the self-monumentalizing aspects of the last wave. The primary casualty of Ashbery's systematic mortification of the recent literary past is Eliot's "Waste Land" (although Williams's more sanguine *Paterson* runs a close second). [53] Eliot's masterpiece is evoked, however, only through the most deflationary or superficial of monumentalizing signs, whereby length replaces grandiosity and simple labels replace suggestive titles. Ashbery, then, has precariously premised the literariness of "Europe" on an almost arbitrary, involuntary memory rather than on any method of conscientious evocation. The very notion of influence has been flattened out here by labeling a long series of dubious "verses" with a bogus Eliotic subject. "Europe," like "The Waste Land," may indeed refer to a whole history of European culture, but it is the culture of one-dimensional man that is found in the poem (as the chauvinistic prose of Le Queux's novel and other journalistic sources reveals). Given such contents, the title seems just as likely to refer to a map of Europe or the Paris metro stop of the same name. Ashbery's title, then, is schizophrenically evocative *and* flat: like the state-names in Johns's *Map*, it is suggestively applied yet blandly ready-made; like the word "liar" in Johns's painting, "Europe" both emulates and mocks its historical predecessor (if more tonelessly here). Yet, in the final analysis, Ashbery's strategy has a sharp dadaist edge. To the extent that the title brings Eliot's poem to mind, it is less for the purpose of enriching Ashbery's own subject than for deflating "The Waste Land" itself. It is as though Ashbery had made the title of Eliot's poem–as opposed to the poem itself–the justification and technique of his own work by taking it quite literally and remaking Europe as if it were an actual garbage heap, real "trash" (in the sense of "literature," too). References to waste and garbage abound in "Europe," but they have little emotional resonance in a poetic landscape plagiaristically fashioned out of snippets of magazine articles and a patently jingoistic novel for English school girls. They simply label contents.

The next organizational feature of the poem that recalls Johns's work is its quantified scale, perfunctorily inflated by the sheer num-

---

[53] Shapiro, pp. 60-61.

ber of sections. If the 100-plus divisions give the work certain Dantesque proportions, Ashbery manneristically attenuates that number to remind us that these divisions correspond to no perfect,
classicizing order–simply a distended, entropic series. One may
therefore ask whether the accumulated sections really suggest a cosmic, Dantesque vision (in the spirit of Eliot), or if repetition and
number have been over-determined. (As the whole of section 2.
reads: "A wave of nausea–/ numerals[.]" [54]) Symbolic or not, the
series is tediously consistent, predictable–as one also finds in
Johns's work, which regularly adheres to complete, ordered systems,
whether of state-names, digits (0-9), or letters (A-Z). Ashbery ultimately levels the mannered monumentality of his poem by ending it
on a number whose very digits suggest mind-numbing repetition:
one . . . one . . . one . . .

Consistent with the numbering of the sections is the way the
lines of "Europe" mostly adhere to the left margin, a sort of base-
line to which the poet repeatedly and automatically resorts with
each return, as it were, of the typewriter carriage. Automatism here
is no longer passionately instinctual but merely mechanical, convenient, all of which helps contribute to the same "impression of absence" that one finds in Johns's paintings (which Steinberg himself
described as being "about human absence" [55]). At the same time,
however, there are deviations from this course that become all the
more conspicuous as a consequence. Certain sections defy the left
margin, assuming a kind of all-overness in miniature. Other lines,
from section 57, fall into seven couplets to form an eccentric son-
net. Another section has double columns (section 107), while yet
another offers a minimalist calligram (section 104). In their eccentric deviation from the general "rule" of the poem, these parodies
of poetic forms indicate other preoccupations of the poem that relate less to Johns's schematicism than to a more Rauschenbergian
impulse toward assemblage and erasure, collage and disjuncture
and their mutual interference (although this impulse is also evident
in Johns's work). Evidence of what may be the literal erasure of a
text occurs in these "deviations" mentioned above that assume the

---

[54] Ashbery, "Europe" in *The Tennis Court Oath* (Middletown, Connecticut:
Wesleyan University Press, 1962), pp. 64-85. Subsequent citations in the text will
refer to this edition.

[55] Steinberg, *Other Criteria*, p. 52.

appearance of certain cubist poems by Reverdy. But unlike those
poems, in which an architectonic organization is revealed, Ashbery's sections present something closer to random gaps in what
may once have been a coherent, descriptive line or passage:

28.

wishing you were a
the bottle really   before the washed
    handed over to her:
            hundreds
light over her
    hanging her
you can remember

85.

    ghost of stone–massive
        hangs halfway
polishing
        whose winding
Strong, sad half-city
    gardens
                        from the bridge of
        stair
                broom
    recent past symbolized
hair banana
does not evoke a concrete image
the splendid

The difficulties of comprehension here are less the result of in-
stilling new insights (say, of form, per Reverdy) than of simply withholding information. Yet the incompleteness produces an almost
accidental sense of poetic mystery (as well as funny juxtapositions)
not unlike that in Reverdy's poems. Thus, resupplying the missing
information would offer a great deal less than withholding it, since
such a disclosure would only reduce the poem to the tawdry truth
of its sources (in Section 28, a scene of laundering?; Section 85, a
travelogue?). In this way the simple technique of erasure imbues
the source text with an aura of the poetic it probably does not de-
serve. Simple in the extreme, erasure reveals the banality inherent
to all poetic techniques, the *raison d'être* of which is to provide a

shortcut to a desired effect. Yet Ashbery is prepared to go even further with his strategy, obliterating any such effect of aura by completely obliterating linguistic sense itself. Sections under almost total erasure represent nothing less than a radical demonstration of
the effects of the "plastic" attitude in poetry. Such sections are completely deficient as functional linguistic elements, deconstructing
any sense of unity or self-containment otherwise attributable to a
poem's parts. Both syntax and semantics are lost to the minimal linguistic fragments suspended in the allotted "spaces" of the sections.
As such, they almost fuse with adjacent sections, as if to erase their
own numbered headings.

But the compositional strategies are not confined to those of erasure or disjuncture and the poem frequently incorporates narrative
passages and popular clichés in all their prosaic integrity.[56] More importantly, the poem establishes subtle, self-reflective connections between these narrative chunks and the brittle detrita of the "erased"
passages through poeticizing themes of aviation, espionage, and war
as found in *Beryl of the Bi-Planes*. In this way the long poem seems
less a random collection of verbal junk than a kind of verbal junk
sculpture, an assemblage that makes creative use of randomness (an
idea corroborated in section 16: "when canvas the must spread/ to
new junk"). In keeping with statements Ashbery has made about his
poetry in general, the poem represents the attempt to keep "meaningfulness up to the pace of randomness. . . ."[57] Meaningfulness
seems most able to do this by disguising itself as meaningless clichés
(section 15 reads: "He is probably one of the gang") or impertinent
blocks of mundane narrative, the absurd clarity of which mock
one's incomprehension of the more disjunctive sections. Yet sometimes these clichés and blocks provide a commentary on the poem's
procedures through Ashbery's adroit thematization of elements
within them.

Such self-commentary occurs early in the poem in section 8—a
conspicuously un-versified paragraph (like those found in *Paterson*)
that establishes a narrative reference point for other, shorter collage
elements derived from the same or similar sources. The passage
from *Beryl* describes a scene of "engine trouble" on England's
Great North Road, engine trouble that, like the prose block itself,

---

[56] Shapiro, p. 75.
[57] Helen Vendler, "Understanding Ashbery" in *John Ashbery*, p. 185.

impedes all progress and corrects itself only with the final phrase: "All was now ready for the continuance of the journey," at which point the more regular technique of accelerated, atomistic collagism resumes. The idea here is that the engine of the poem is precisely the randomness and disjunctiveness that this passage of clear and simple prose disrupts with bland coherence (offering a sort of break for the reader not unlike the lunch break enjoyed by the two characters mentioned in the passage). Meaning, then, is what troubles this poem and it is no accident that the literal meanings it sometimes offers are so insipid, drawn from the jingoistic adventure story, the paranoid spy thriller, and the vapid romance. Even at full throttle, as it were, such "meaningful prose" is literarily stunted, even old-fashioned, inasmuch as the source book was written in the context of a war already superseded in historical memory by several others. Thus, as in many of Rauschenberg's early junk sculptures, Ashbery's choice of materials reflects a deliberate anachronism evidenced in the proliferation of bi-planes, telegraphs, Zeppelins, and balloons in this poem of the 1960s.

A culture and technology of national defense provides the substrate of Ashbery's own collagist technology of assemblage and erasure. His technique, then, pits him against the chauvinistic prerogatives of his sources and *he* becomes what Le Queux's characters identify as the "absolute, unthinking/ menace to our way of life" (section 7). This way of life is revealed in sections devoted to the honeyed collaboration of the ace pilots Beryl and Ronnie, whose mission is to prevent something called "the silencer" (phallus? fasces?) from falling into the wrong hands. A base narrative of sorts is provided from certain fictional passages the poet leaves relatively intact (many of them ironically versified), allowing the reader to make speculative connections to other, less integral blocks that have been cropped, asseverated, juxtaposed, or shrewdly distorted to reveal the more sinister aspects of such literature. As if in response to Le Queux's themes of espionage and secret messages, Ashbery yields a poetic alternative whereby the secret of banal prose (its *unconscious*, as it were) could only be deciphered through a process of re-scrambling. Some examples of this poetically adulterated, insinuating prose follow:

    13.   before the truth can be explained
          Nothing can exist.

15.   Absolve me from the hatred I never
        she–all are wounded against
        Zeppelin–wounded carrying dying
        three colors over land

16.   before I started
        I was forced to
        flying
        she said

30.   forget, encouraging your vital organs.
        Telegraph. The rifle–a page folded over.

        More upset, wholly meaningless, the willing sheath
        glide into fall .. mercury to passing
        the war you said won–milling around the picket
                fence, and
                noise of the engine from the sky
        and flowers–here is a bunch
        the war won out of cameos
        And somehow the perfect warrior fallen.

34.   you can't understand their terror
        means more to these people   waste
        the runt crying in the pile of colored
        snapshots offal in the wind
        that's the way we do it terror

75.   Like the public,
        reaction
        from Crystal Palace

80.   multitude headquarters shout there
        Because there are no
        because the majority is toxic

A whole culture of terror emerges from these fragments, poetically and plastically assisted to yield what seem their truer, totalitarian impulses. A sort of absolute, unthinking menace to other ways of life thus emanates from the Crystal Palace, as it were, of technological progress–particularly as it is pursued in the national interest. Backward or counter-technologies indicative of such "other ways" become tell-tale signs of sinister plots against the warriors of progress. Among those implicated among the "toxic majority" are the poet and the artist, classical distorters of truth:

> 107. The steel bolts
>   having been replaced
>   by *a painting of*
>   one of wood!
>   Ronnie, thoughtfully,
>
>   of the silencer
>
>   plot to kill us both, dear.
>
>   pet
>   oh
>
>   it that she was there

But perhaps their paranoia is justified! Nothing so meager as a plot to kill Le Queux's flying deuces, Ashbery's aim is to kill coherence itself and the vision of progress, unity, security such coherence promotes. Yet his purpose has a coherence all its own, an alternative coherence that springs from the need to create an order not out of chaos, but *of* chaos. As a consequence, its effects range across the whole poem, but are only occasionally referred to directly. These references themselves occur at random intervals, although they are never accidental when they do occur. By no means a consistent justification of the work's development, the references are merely pragmatic, a way of joining parts that may or may not go together. Like glue, they are often transparent (in the sense of invisible or disguised), but they also become cloudy and seep out at the joints they hold. It is this seeping out, this calculated self-exposure (like the earlier redundancy of a *painting* of a wooden replacement of a steel bolt) by which the poem admits to its own terroristic impulse toward an alternative order–albeit an order with a certain tolerance for the disorderly. Section 62 suggests the universality of this collagist predicament: "All of us fear the secret/ guarded too carefully/ An assortment[.]"

Such moments of self-commentary (moments when collagist cacography ascends to a level of virtual citation, implying Ashbery's

partial retention of the modern, authorial "I") are subtlest when
they occur in the form of un-assisted quotation as in the opening
line of section 38: "The roar of the engine, of course,/ rendered
speech impossible[.]" The engine of Ashbery's collagism does
much the same thing, even as it affirms that the "impossible"
speech of the poem that results actually conveys the true nature and
meaning (or secret) of speech. Other examples are embedded in
erased or jerry-rigged sections such as 107: "I don't understand
wreckage"; 90: "powerless creating images"; 85: "does not evoke a
concrete image"; or 73–which looks like leftover words at the margin of a damaged page, yet assisted (perhaps) with an inserted portion (italicized below):

> A least
> four days
> A surprise
> mothers
> suppose
> *Is not a "images"*
> *to "arrange"*
> [. . .]

Still other sections seem to comment directly on the "traditional" use of newspapers in collage. Section 57 includes the line: "The
newspaper is ruining your eyes[,]" while section 39 seems to allegorize the process in a narrative scene: "The newspaper being read/
Beside the great gas turbine/ The judge calls his assistant over/
And together they try to piece the secret message/ contained in today's paper." Of course, the best known example of such self-commentary is probably not collage at all but a direct statement of Ashbery's (section 10): "He had mistaken his book for garbage[.]"
Although it may be another tongue-in-cheek reference to "The
Waste Land," this sentence suggests that a methodological confusion between books and garbage has helped to keep meaningfulness up to pace with randomness, and modern poetry up to pace
with junk art.

As a totality, the poem can only be apprehended as a collection
of related verbal collage techniques intersecting and interrupting
each other in order to thwart the engines of verbal and ideological
coherence. The coherence it does offer–a kind of plastic coher-

ence–derives from an appreciation of these variations on collage technique. While literary elements contribute to the poem's effects, any attempt to determine a consistent narrative progress in the work can only yield frustration, "a wave of nausea," or loss of critical identity. It is a dangerous undertaking; its inevitable failure, however, makes a certain case for the poem as well, insofar as the extreme dislocations and garbled multiplicities within yield an almost monolithic sense of boredom, a critical anaesthesia in which any idea of organic development cedes to one of ironic inertia. From this standpoint, each section of the poem provides another chamber of noise in a hopeless series. The parts, even the subtlest components, have a kind of primary indistinguishability, a tendency to go nowhere but to the next in the series, to "funnily" repeat what comes before and after in a way that produces a vast figure of entropic stasis.

THREE POEMS: "THE SKATERS," "THE NEW SPIRIT," "SELF-PORTRAIT IN A CONVEX MIRROR"

If "Europe" capitalizes on erasure and assemblage as primary poetic procedures, Ashbery's two long poems "The Skaters" and "The New Spirit" provide incipient commentaries on these procedures as a starting point for a more meditative direction in his subsequent work. In doing this, both poems provide insights into Ashbery's developing attitude toward the relation between poetry and the plastic arts as a function of their avant-gardism, as well as toward the changing nature of avant-gardism itself.

Ashbery's well-known opposition between "putting it all in" and "the leaving-out business" first appears in "The Skaters" and–like assemblage and erasure in "Europe"–generally characterizes his working approach in a poem that oscillates between collagism and a more ruminative mode. [58] Determining which one of

---

[58] This assessment is directly confirmed by Ashbery in an interview with Fred Moramarco: "Also, when you mention what I refer to in 'The Skaters' as 'this leaving-out business,' which seems to be a preoccupation of mine–it's also in *Three Poems* and a lot of other work–I see now that it is really a major theme in my poetry, though I wasn't aware of it as it was emerging. It's probably something that came from painting too. A lot of De Kooning's drawings are partly erased. Larry Rivers used to do drawings in which there are more erasures than there are lines.

these modes occupies the place of the putting-in and the leaving-out businesses is the impossible task the poem sets before the reader in the following lines–despite any rhetorical pretense at dispelling such ambiguity:

It is time now for a general understanding of
The meaning of all this. The meaning of Helga, importance of the setting, etc.
A description of the blues. Labels on bottles
And all kinds of discarded objects that ought to be described.
But can one ever be sure of which ones?
Isn't this a death-trap, wanting to put too much in
So the floor sags, as under the weight of a piano, or a piano-legged girl
And the whole house of cards comes dinning down around one's ears!

But this is an important aspect of the question
Which I am not ready to discuss, am not at all ready to.
This leaving-out business. On it hinges the very importance of what's novel
Or autocratic, or dense, or silly. [59]

The "collectibles"–Rousselesque bottle labels and Helga, the discarded objects and other plastic "phenomena" unceremoniously juxtaposed or catalogued in so many modernist poems–would seem to be the substance of this deadly inclusiveness that swamps the imagination. Or is it just the opposite?–the will to explain these phenomena, "the meaning of all this," yet a meaning that can only be all-inclusive through selective abbreviation. And if explanation is a way of putting it all in, aren't those "unexplained" catalogues a mode of "leaving-out" by virtue of not explaining themselves? Turning the problem around again: if catalogues and collages are plastic forms of putting-in, explanation becomes a form of leaving-out, a sort of convenient, summary, semiotic replacement for all that junkyard clutter. As such, explanation can assume either progressive or autocratic properties depending on the spirit of one's re-

---

Rauschenberg once asked De Kooning to give him a drawing so that he could erase it. I got to wondering: suppose he did erase it? Wouldn't there be enough left so that it would be something? If so, how much? Or if not, how much could be erased and still have the 'sense' of the original left? I always tend to think that none of the developments in painting rubbed off on me very much, but then, when it comes down to it, I see that, as in this case, a lot of it did." Moramarco, p. 454.

[59] Ashbery, "The Skaters" in *Rivers and Mountains* (New York: Ecco Press, 1977), p. 39.

placements. Ironically, the most devastating effects of the explanatory mode (as it assumes the business of leaving-out) come in the
guise of modern revolutions of discourse symbolized in the poem
by invisible winds of change that trash everything in order, ostensi-
bly, to celebrate trash. This vast cultural purge is filtered through
language evoking modernist and avant-garde experiments–not to
mention more sinister, political ones that were being undertaken at
the same time. Yet the absolutist tenor of the windy rhetoric goes
surprizingly well with a variety of ideological positions, whether
from the right or left, whether originating in high modernist techniques or low dadaist ones, whether in the heroic self-expression of
a Pollock or in the group ethics of process artists–all of whom risk
everything in pursuit of prescribed forms of modernity:

> A great wind lifted these cardboard panels
> Horizontal in the air. At once the perspective with the horse
> Disappeared in a *bigarrure* of squiggly lines. The image
>   with the crocodile in it became no longer apparent.
> Thus a great wind cleanses, as a new ruler
> Edits new laws, sweeping the very breath of the streets
> Into posterior trash. The films have changed–
> The great titles on the scalloped awning have turned dry
>   and blight-colored.
> No wind that does not penetrate a man's house, into the
>   very bowels of the furnace,
> Scratching in dust a name on the mirror–say, and what about letters,
> The dried grasses, fruits of the winter–gosh!
>   Everything is trash!
> The wind points to the advantages of decay
> At the same time as removing them far from the sight of men.
> The regent of the winds, Aeolus, is a symbol for all earthly potentates
> Since holding this sickening, festering process by which
>   we are cleansed
> Of afterthought. (pp. 36-37)

With this sarcastic invalidation of sweeping cultural decrees
(identified with that Joycean windbag, Aeolus), Ashbery distances
himself from any energetic program of change. Yet the distance is
only by half, a measure of self-abnegation, insofar as his own past
experiments also made vigorous "editorial" use of trash. And although it seems a pity to blow the very breath out of the streets,

certain effects of the potentates' decrees have a definite appeal to Ashbery's sense of novelty. But in the end, it is novelty–not revolution–that is recommended here, as much for retaining certain qualities of the exquisite as for its own effects of surprise.

> The answer is that it is novelty
> That guides these swift blades o'er the ice
> Projects into a finer expression (but at the expense
> Of energy) the profile I cannot remember. (p. 34)

If "The Skaters" offers an image of this "finer expression" in the form of lines cut in ice, crisscrossing in ways that suggest overlapping and transparent collagist edges, "The New Spirit" blurs those edges even further by dissolving collagism itself in a matrix of abstract prose. Ironically, the medium traditionally associated with "explanation" is virtually ubiquitous in this poem, with only occasional lapses into the graphic modulations of free verse. Yet in no sense is Ashbery resorting to mere explanation or even traditional narrative by way of prose: he is appropriating it for avant-garde purposes, or at least those of an idiosyncratic avant-garde. [60] Thus the medium of explanation is drained of didactic potential while avant-garde poetry itself is deprived of graphic energy, the visible disjunctions that formerly signaled novelty. Ashbery also reduces the imagery of the visible, including those catalogues of concrete phenomena that proliferate in "The Skaters." They are expressed only as things outside expression: natural elements to be "reclaimed" through the action of art or to reclaim art in turn. [61]

Interestingly, this movement away from the conspicuous physicality and randomness that were indicative of an aesthetics of medium in the painting of the 1950s parallels a certain movement away from visual media and toward verbal discourse in the art of the 1960s, in particular, conceptual and minimal art. In the context of avant-garde poetry, however, any such resumption of discursivity comes provocatively close to resuming the narrative strategies of an

---

[60] Of course the prose poem itself, as David Lehman says, is "a form invested with modernity" by way of Baudelaire's *Spleen de Paris,* Rimbaud's *Illuminations,* and Max Jacob's *Le Cornet à dés.* See Lehman, *The Last Avant-Garde: The Making of the New York School of Poets* (New York: Doubleday, 1998).

[61] See pages 36 and 29, respectively, in Ashbery's "The New Spirit" in *Three Poems* (New York: Viking Penguin, 1986).

older poetics. The old and the new, then, seem to overlap here in the narrow, conditional interests of something even newer (if less presumptuous than its "contributors"). Within these confines, Ashbery's new spirit is conceived. Finding a kind of freedom in circumstances of diminished options is the ironic premise concerning the expressive "self" in this poem: "One is aware of it as an open field of narrative possibilities. Not in the edifying sense of the tales of the past that we are still (however) chained to, but as stories that tell only of themselves, so that one realizes one's self has dwindled and now at last vanished in the diamond light of pure speculation" (p. 41).

A recurring, escalating dialectics of "self" and "other" provides the structural movement of "The New Spirit." The fusion, separation, and mannered variation of these meditative categories are the formal modes of the new spirit in its perpetual task, once again, of either putting it all in or leaving it out in the process of going forward. [62] The poem describes the task in the opening lines, initially calling the leaving-out business the "truer" way, but quickly remembering that "forget as we will, something soon comes to stand in their place. Not the truth, perhaps, but–yourself" (TP, p. 3). While "they" represent everything omitted, the "you" is the domain of everything that puts itself in against the "I's" intention of leaving it out. Thus "The New Spirit" seems to be the subject's coming to terms with a tendency–exemplified by the Avant-Garde on one hand and democracy on the other–toward greater inclusion in expressive media that traditionally operate through a process of elimination. Both resignation and a futile bravado characterize the discursive voice of the poem that can only know itself through another but defines itself against that other. Consequently, it is virtually impossible to know whether the "I" and "you," subject and object of the poem, are distinct entities or internalized divisions representing the construction of the self through identification–in a sort of Lacanian mirror-stage–with the object. A strange, hostile complicity surrounds them, like that between the leaving-out and the putting-in. It is a numbing, confused complicity necessitated by perpetually

---

[62] While David Lehman discusses *Three Poems* in *The Last Avant-Garde* as a Kierkegaardian quest for spiritual salvation, I see it more as a quest to determine the spirit of the age, a perpetual search for the new in the spirit of Baudelaire's "Le Voyage." See *The Last Avant-Garde*, pp. 354-357.

advancing on the future: "I can only say that the wind of the change as it has happened has numbed me, to the point where the false way and the true way are confounded, where there is no way or rather where everything is a way, none more suitable nor more accurate than the last, oblivion rapidly absorbing their outline like snow filling footprints" (p. 17).

Despite its fresh appearance, the title of Ashbery's poem is self-consciously outdated, duplicating in English the original phrase from an essay by Apollinaire, itself laden with traditional, quasi-religious overtones. The new, then, seems almost weary in this poem for its evocations of both the recent, "playful" past and a more archaic one, fraught with eschatology:

> The visitation, was it more or less over? No, it had not yet begun, except as a preparatory dream which seemed to have the rough texture of life, but which dwindled into starshine like all the unwanted memories. There was no holding on to it. But for that we ought to be glad, no one really needed it, yet it was not utterly worthless, it taught us the forms of this our present waking life, the manners of the unreachable. And its judgments, though harmless and playful, were yet the form of utterance by which judgment shall come to be known (pp. 7-8).

The preparatory dream, harmless though it may have been, potentially assumes a more sinister, judgmental aspect in keeping with the long, salvific tradition out of which it grew. As ironic heir of *l'esprit nouveau,* the voice of "The New Spirit" seems oppressed by this potential and convinced of the necessity—for the sake of its own future—of sustaining a radical avant-garde vision only in the realm of speculation (where the judgments resulting from that vision of inclusion are less irrevocable). "The New Spirit" is avant-garde, then, primarily as a meditation on the meaning of the Avant-Garde and the new; it does not repeat the original action of the Avant-Garde—otherwise its own newness would be at risk, especially given its partial dependency on elements of a tradition that are presumably crushed by the success of the Avant-Garde. Such success is, for Ashbery, the Avant-Garde's self-undermining, whereby it becomes a ubiquitous, Faustian endeavor, signalled through obsessive, sweeping *action* to remake the world, to "change life" (again, in Rimbaud's phrase), but using methods that increasingly resemble those

of venture capitalism: " . . . there never was a day like this for getting things done, and action pursues its peaceful advance on the
lethargic, malarial badlands of the day, draining swamps, clearing
scrub forests, putting the hygienic torch to the villages, planting
ground-cover crops such as clover, alfalfa, colza, buckwheat and
cowpeas." (p. 36)

In the context of the sort of poetic speculation that characterizes Ashbery's version of the Avant-Garde, this sweeping force remains mysteriously docile, the poem's disquisitions providing a
more constrained influence in the interest of a conditional future.
Like the convulsive Bretonian image of a stilled locomotive in the
jungle, the mythic Avant-Garde goes into dormition here preparatory to a form of reverse engineering by which the poem secures alternative futures, personal avant-gardes:

> The wind is now fresh and full, with leaves and other things fly-
> ing. And to release it from its condition of hardness you will
> have to take apart the notion of you so as to reconstruct it from
> an intimate knowledge of its inner workings. How harmless and
> even helpful the painted wooden components of the Juggernaut
> look scattered around the yard, patiently waiting to be reassem-
> bled! So ends the first lesson: that the concave being, enfolding
> like air or spirit, does not dissolve when breathed upon but
> comes apart neatly, like a watch, and the parts may be stocked or
> stored, their potential does not leak away through inactivity but
> remains bright and firm, so that in a sense it is just as much *there*
> as if it were put back together again and even more so: with
> everything sorted and labeled you can keep an eye on it a lot bet-
> ter than if it were again free to assume protean shapes and sens-
> es, the genie once more let out of the bottle, and who can say
> where all these vacant premises should end? No, it is far better
> to keep this potential dry, even at the risk of having its immobili-
> ty come to seem a reproach, the mute appeal of the saber hung
> up on the wall. [. . .] Why, its imperfections are just a token of
> how life moves along, haltingly but somehow always getting
> there in time, in our time (pp. 19-20).

The Juggernaut of the Avant-Garde must be analyzed and, in a
sense, tamed. Yet there is also a sense of its fragility, a fear of it
evaporating under the breath of discursive expression. Hence, so
many precautions about it: as well as "taming" it, the tactful analyt-

ics of the poem provide a way of preserving its power. The task, of course, seems merely custodial and suggests a narrowing of ambition for the author of this change, who exists in a state of "erect passivity . . . free to come and go within a limited area, a sort of house-arrest of the free agent intentionally cut off from the forces of renewal" (pp. 20-21). There can be little doubt, however, that the agent has imposed these limits for the sake of the new tradition he has inherited and thus may find genuine "happiness within the limitations" (p. 27). For all its apparent narrowness and inertia, the situation still offers compensations that make it preferable to what went before (i.e., insofar as the latter is construed as simply moving without variation along its projected path toward successful ubiquity). Its space is aerated, protective, more "elevated" than before. Funnily, it has all the earmarks of a new Manhattan apartment where the poet can comfortably take in the life of the streets that sustains his project—only: at a remove, the poet perversely marginalized even as circumstances require that his efforts be somehow broadly encompassing. Only by way of a certain "outward-hanging, ledge over the pitfalls of mankind" (p. 10) is this broadness to be attained. The temptation "to retreat again into the hard dark recesses of yourself" (p. 44) can be difficult to resist when one looks from that ledge into the throng below, described with Eliotic horror as a flood or snake pit (p. 44). The need to think things out, however, is maintained and a workable, compromise solution is found, one that even seems beautiful from the right perspective:

> He thought he had never seen anything quite so beautiful as that crystallization into a mountain of statistics: out of the rapid movement to and fro that abraded individual personalities into a channel of possibilities, remote from each other and even remoter from the eye that tried to contain them: out of that river of humanity comprised of individuals each no better than he should be and doubtless more solicitous of his own personal welfare than of the general good, a tonal quality detached itself that partook of the motley intense hues of the whole gathering but yet remained itself, firm and all-inclusive, scrupulously fixed equidistant between earth and heaven, as far above the tallest point on the earth's surface as it was beneath the lowest outcropping of cumulus in the cornflower-blue empyrean. Thus everything and everybody were included after all, and any thought that might ever be entertained about them; the irritating drawbacks each

possessed along with certain good qualities were dissolved in the enthusiasm of the whole, yet individuality was not lost for all that, but persisted in the definition of the urge to proceed higher and further as well as in the counter-urge to amalgamate into the broadest and widest kind of uniform continuum (pp. 48-49).

But true to "time's way of walking sideways out of the event, at the same time proceeding in a straight line toward an actual vanishing point" (p. 23), Ashbery, at the end of the poem, assumes yet another perspective–this time outside the above "liberal" solution. The apartment block the reader has been imaginatively occupying with the poet is now seen from across the parking lot, as it were, and what he discovers is a new tower of Babel, "perfect in its vulgarity" (p. 50) and strangely reminiscent of the Juggernaut of before, only fully reassembled and arrogantly occluding the sky. The compromise one was so pleased to have negotiated now seems an embarrassing surrender to the vast social project of total cultural assimilation. The poet's efforts to establish an idiosyncratic middle way between tradition and anti-tradition have an ironic success or "acceptance" from which he wants to dissociate himself. The only alternative now–again unsatisfactory–is one of absolute negation, of turning one's back on the whole business of assimilation to behold the impassive, uncompromising constellations one had thought were lost to view. New oppositions are posited and the process resumes with the Archer (Ashbery's symbolic self-caricature?) challenging those constellations by "aiming at a still higher and smaller portion of the heavens" (p. 51).

As if in fulfillment of this final image, Ashbery's next long poem is the famous "Self-Portrait in a Convex Mirror" in which his poetic sights are representationally focused on a specific historico-aesthetic object: a truly "smaller portion of the heavens" that, nevertheless, possesses "total" reflecting powers (in keeping with the nature of convex mirrors [63]). In this work, Francesco Parmigianino and his own self-portraiture have replaced the slippery, amorphous "you" of "The New Spirit." The fact that Ashbery has selected a well-known mannerist painting [fig. 24] in which the highest Renaissance ideals are both confirmed and questioned with singular suavi-

---

[63] See Stephen Paul Miller, "'Self-Portrait in a Convex Mirror,' the Watergate Affair, and Johns's Crosshatch Paintings: Surveillance and Reality-Testing in the Mid-Seventies" in *Boundary 2*, 20:2 (Summer 1993), pp. 84-115.

ty reveals his assumption that painting continues to offer the adequate correlative of any sustained poetic meditation on problems of artistic production in general. The painting becomes the focus of renewed speculation about the nature of artistic inclusion and exclusion, experimentation and consolidation, democratization and colonization. The boundaries of that speculative activity, however, have shifted to accommodate a broader tradition suggested by the cultural object represented in the poem. It is an object in which "the enchantment of self with self" [64] is unapologetically proclaimed in keeping with a certain Renaissance self-conception that is at odds with the modern aspiration toward the lowest common denominator and the self-abnegating character of such accommodation. What "spars" of otherness are retained in the painting ("eyebeams, muslin, coral") exist only to reinforce that enchantment, a kind of rigorous narcissism bolstered by the most sophisticated illusionistic techniques. Gone are the piano-legged girls, the bottle-labels and other discarded objects that betoken dada and surrealist influences and assume the rough texture of assembled fragments, the marvelous sheen of chimerical juxtapositions, or the cacophonous jangle of simultaneous interdiscursivities. In its most uncompromising formulation, Parmigianino's art is one of intention, reproduction, and discrimination: "The record of what you accomplished by sitting down/ 'With great art to copy all that you saw in the glass'/ So as to perfect and rule out the extraneous/ Forever" (p. 72).

Round like the globe and drawing everything onto its surface, the convex mirror provides the model for this reduction of experience to a "magma of interiors," a deathly, homogenous substance, as the self organizes otherness into self-affirming uniformity. Ashbery, for whom the "strewn evidence ... the small accidents and pleasures of the day as it moved gracelessly on" (p. 71) still mean something, is nevertheless mesmerized by this exquisite, though "warped" putting-in business by which inclusion becomes ruthless self-expansion. But later in the poem, the idea of the city as the backing or support of this artistic enterprise predominates and, far from being sucked up into that enterprise, city life–at least on the scale of metropolitan New York–works to "siphon off the life of the studio ..." (p. 75). The city and its dynamism become an almost dogmatic force of cultural change in themselves, pushing relentless-

[64] Ashbery, "Self-Portrait in a Convex Mirror" in *Self-Portrait in a Convex Mirror* (New York: Viking Press, 1975), p. 72.

ly, yet thoughtlessly toward something new: "... a new preciosity/ In the wind. Can you stand it,/ Francesco? Are you strong enough for it?/ This wind brings what it knows not, is/ Self-propelled, blind, has no notion/ Of itself. It is inertia that once/ Acknowledged saps all activity, secret or public" (p. 75). As a negative force, it sweeps all initiative to the suburbs of the mind where imagination languishes in a state of private entropy. But, once again, Ashbery offers an alternative response to these sweeping changes that tend to stifle creative energy: they also divulge new, unexpected values from the more "reticent" aspects of the past (such as mannerist painting) which acquire an unlikely and provocative vitality and which become a part of the change itself.

With the creation and critical success of *Self-Portrait in a Convex Mirror* a particular parameter of the continuum between "tradition" and "other tradition" (as Ashbery broadly and provisionally defined them) had been set. And although this more traditionally discursive poem, written in iambic pentameter, may have ultimately satisfied Bloom's definition of a counter-sublime as a way of explaining Ashbery's precarious assimilation to the American romantic tradition, it more accurately reflects the poet's cautious assimilation of the latter to his own avant-garde inclinations. The poem "Self-Portrait in a Convex Mirror" is the furthest Ashbery goes—poetically and ideologically–toward realigning his experimentalist propensities with a refulgent, "Stevensian" tradition, but only on the assumption that both categories are in need of revision. The consequence is that avant-gardism becomes less of a practice than an object of sustained meditation, while traditional forms and themes are perversely experimented with. "Self-Portrait" does not set the standard for Ashbery's subsequent poetry, which often vigorously reincorporates the experimental plasticities of collagist, juxtapositional, and other disjunctive strategies (the long, double-columned poem "Litany" from *As We Know* represents the most visually conspicuous instance). But it does reveal the limits of his renunciation of the tradition and a certain "nostalgia for nostalgia" (O'Hara's phrase) that emerges in the work of a number of late avant-garde poets. Such a tendency, however, is sanctioned by Ashbery's own, somewhat idiosyncratic investigations of the French and American Avant-Gardes–both literary and artistic–which are shown to be always less monolithic and less radically anti-artistic than their respective manifestos suggest.

CONCLUSION

NONE of the poets in this study were selected on the basis of a necessary literary influence, but for a collective responsiveness to another art. This responsiveness was the medium, as it were, of their poetic genealogy. Furthermore, their literary adaptations of plastic strategies reveal a quality of critical emulation between the two arts themselves, arts that seem to reflect and comment upon each other's ironic predicament vis-à-vis modernity. As media, painting and poetry are mostly out of step with modern experience, hence their modern forms involve a technical re-mastering of any appearance of obsolescence. Yet it is also a way of preserving the expressive subject even as he or she submits to the necessary mortifications of this re-mastering.

The critical emulation of another art, then, turns out to be a strategy of mutual seduction, a dissolving of aesthetic borders in a way that appears to point to the future, but which actually embraces an alternative future mostly already obviated by the one of mass production and consumption that we know. It is a way of masking the low-tech nature of the poet's and painter's traditional media by manufacturing unexpected forms and functions for them that have an aura of cultural provocation. This provocation arises from the paradoxical autonomy both poetry and painting demand even in the process of obscuring their boundaries with each other. But it is the painter that provides the model for this autonomy through an initial emphasis on the function of seeing—of seeing while trying not to formalize seeing and therefore of seeing sight itself, as it were. Increasingly the medium of paint is seen apart from any function of resembling, and by this example, the poet's way of seeing language as its own, similarly autonomous process is accelerated. But at the same time, the poet, like the painter, persists in using his medium to establish continuities with the external world without resorting to mere mimesis. Instead, it is a kind of media diegesis: by insinuating itself as an enunciative fragment or synecdoche of the world rather than a symbolic substitute, the medium of language becomes witness to the world by being only itself. In this way, poetry, like painting, achieves a kind of parity with the real, as Pierre Reverdy and William Carlos Williams have argued.

For the modern poet, painting represented its wordless other, a kind of alien twin that occupied—with a sense of adventure and physical tenacity—a silent, unknown terrain, not unlike the future itself. But it was a future that still included the poet, the self-allegorizing subject with a special, but increasingly limited public role to play with words. The material basis and conspicuous (if narrow) economic viability of painting implied a certain proximity to the most advanced aspects of material culture. Thus, the literary adaptation of these techniques involved both an acceleration of the poetics of autonomy and a transgressive crossing of borders not only between media, but also between the categories of art and life themselves: life not as nature, but as the human body enmeshed in modern techno-industrial society and its systems of exchange. In attempting to fuse these categories, avant-garde techniques promised to vastly extend human powers of expression on the model of technology itself, but also to eclipse the very autonomy its own modernity simultaneously implied.

Such techniques suggested a commitment to recuperating much that was threatened with cultural irrelevance in the process of modernization (a process that ironically involved the over-valuation of aesthetic tradition, as if the art could be inoculated from the contagion this process initiated). Yet for some in the early part of the last century (and especially in France), painting seemed ontologically accommodated to the work of recuperation insofar as its own plasticity aligned it with material contingency itself, and thus with everything that was strangely antithetical to art but which remained vehicles and facilitators of it. Modern artists made this alignment conspicuous through the use of untraditional, "degraded" materials in works of art that subsequently, "miraculously" yielded high prices on the market. The avant-garde painter's reuse of such cultural waste products drew attention to the necessity of an art that operated on the margins of advanced society, that resuscitated the material discards of the dominant culture by enhancing their symbolic value for a modern audience. But it was a new, anti-mimetic symbolism, calling for provisional allegories, but never specifying any single interpretation. The relations between these plastic signifiers and the things or ideas they represented had become ambiguous in a way that not only challenged assumptions about painting's necessary iconic resemblance to its models (both physical and cultural), but also the absolutism of many other regimes of signification. Verbal and visual signs were being increasingly seen for themselves–for their material basis and connotative instability in anticipation of future interpretands. With this critical re-examination of the forms and functions of representational art in modern times, the future looked both exhilarating and forbidding, both redemptive and destructive. The new art seemed to aestheticize the world while de-aestheticizing itself, dissolving into non-art as distinctions between such categories became hopelessly relativistic, a function of ideological perspective. Avant-garde practice at the beginning of the Twentieth Century was inherently schizoid in its impulse toward both utopian recuperation of everything and nihilistic self-mortification that implied its own disappearance.[1]

For the poets, the stakes involved in this revolution of expression had to be deliberated through another medium of comparison: art criticism. It is in their art criticism–or art writing–that poets could set forth a range of aesthetic and mediumic regroupings, establishing a commodious, proto-poetic space that both facilitated the formulation of an individual poetics, but also concretized the recuperative, interdisciplinary impulse of the Avant-Garde. In a sense, the poem-paintings, calligrams, and other concrete, or neo-ekphrastic poetry that eventually emerged from this veritable mirror-stage of modern poetic development could only have occurred in the context of a critical probing of the actual art objects helping to form the new poetic subject.

As a poet, Apollinaire vacillated between wanting a poetic medium purified of denotative functions and wanting a poetic medium that preserved such functions for the interpretive frameworks they afforded. This poetic vacillation was conditioned by shifting critical allegiances to Cubism, Futurism and Orphism as expressed

---

[1] Antoine Compagnon, *The Five Paradoxes of Modernity*, trans. Franklin Philip (New York: Columbia University, 1994), pp. 31-32.

through his art writing. While analytic Cubism initially inspired him to promote the idea of pure structure in poetry in basic conformity with his earlier Symbolist principles, he soon became dissatisfied with such a posture because it precluded too many of the pleasures of mimesis and sentiment: pleasures he could never entirely abandon and which seemed to acquire relevance in the Twentieth Century because of their degraded status with the Symbolists of the previous century. Apollinaire's continuing ambition to create a broadly encompassing poetics that synthesized yet transcended all the other arts led him to embrace Futurism and simultaneism—at first openly yet superficially, and later more obscurely yet profoundly. In turning from these movements to Orphism, he simply combined simultaneist practice with Symbolist residues in a way that accommodated his lyrico-synthetic aspirations more fully. But the closest he finally came to capturing the *esprit nouveau* he had once proclaimed for his century was in his calligrams, brilliantly inventive hybrids that exploited the visual properties of printed language to achieve poetic effects. "Lettre-Océan" remains the calligram par excellence of his oeuvre, combining an abstract, geometric layout with a concrete, collagist inclusiveness. It is a verbo-visual map (indeed two maps!) of the modern world with the Eiffel Tower at its center and a cacophony of elements extending out to the margins in a way that simultaneously implies the unchartability of that double world.

If this cacophony of simultaneism seems to reach critical mass in the work of Apollinaire, it collapses to an icy hush in the poetry of Reverdy. Reverdy's poems convey—in their careful integration of word and pause, type and void—a much firmer, elemental control than Apollinaire's and in this way seem closer to the sensibility of Reverdy's one-time friend and collaborator, the painter Juan Gris. Indeed, the juxtapositioning of poetic elements—the emphasis on word placement and line breakage—at first suggests a decisive concern with the visual dimension of poetry. Furthermore, this visual articulation of elements combines with their connotative resonance in a way that seems to detach the linguistic sign from its conventional meaning and realign it with its physical basis—not just as enunciative voice, but as cold, hard copy. Thus, like the elements of cubist painting whose interrelations Reverdy helped clarify in his art writing, the elements of Reverdian poetry refuse to accommodate the anecdotalism of traditional expression, turning the work

into a labyrinth of fractured sentences that point in different directions and condense multiple perspectives. But this was as far as
Reverdy went in condoning visual poetry, since his own exhibits a
relative fidelity to the conventions of print. The rigor of his philosophical treatment of painting prevented him from indulging any
laxity in his own medium, a laxity he associated with Apollinaire's
calligrams. Such experiments were misconceived in his view, confusing distinct spheres of art and deleteriously affecting their autonomy in different media. In this way, Reverdy continued to adhere
to Symbolist precepts, fending off the radical encroachments of
chance, non-art, and life, in order to ensure parity among the autonomous members of a sort of republic of arts. But consistent with
the paradoxes of modernism, this autonomy was conditioned by a
theoretical parallelism that enabled Reverdy to make unexpected
connections between the arts and thus identify his poetics with
avant-garde impulses.

With the Surrealists, the pendulum of culture swung back the
other way—only higher and faster. Chance and speed were the
methodological watchwords of the new aesthetic that pretended
not to be one. André Breton's insistence on this last point allowed
him to dismiss Apollinaire's calligrammatic experiments as overly
preoccupied with art and having little to do with the workings of
"objective chance" that the Surrealists tried to manifest in their
own activities. As they saw it, the products of their investigations
were not art at all, but the simple verbal residues of an otherwise in-
expressible collective reality only discoverable by abandoning all
formal control of expression. Because of this last requirement, Breton was skeptical of the surrealist qualifications of visual art, an art
that he believed relied too much on formal technique and academic
training. Images required iconic resemblance, which in Breton's
view prevented them from even approximating immediacy because
of the conscious intervention required to achieve such resemblance.
Language was different, however, and even if such controls as the
consistent use of syntax persisted in surrealist poetry, the mechanisms were virtually automatic and thus natural, or *un*-conscious.
Nevertheless, Breton gradually accommodated his theories of expression and immediacy to painting and poem-objects because of
their ability to capture the look and feel of eidetic images (or, "interior models") that occurred spontaneously in the brain during sleep
and at other times. Surrealism's program was too broad not to take

political advantage of such a tool for training the world how to forget all its training and live spontaneously. Breton's art writing, then,
provided a means of coming to terms with a medium for which he
initially had grave misgivings, but which exemplified the temptations of modernity in the face of theoretical principle, temptations
that in the end proved irresistible to Breton's school of desire–its
graduates and dropouts.

The merging of art with everyday experience (or "life praxis")
was an inevitable effect of what Peter Bürger has identified as the
institutional self-criticism of art, not to be confused with Clement
Greenberg's notion of the self-definition of art, which draws the
two apart. And yet the products of this merger represented
supreme acts of bad faith, since mere life-products could never exhibit any consciousness of formal arrangement or quality of performance. If Breton and the Surrealists, in emphasizing the unconscious, attempted to disavow any aesthetic impulse behind their
productions, they, too, managed to create enduring works, texts,
performances. It was this element of bad faith that the New York
poets overcame–in a sort of Wildean way–by simply yielding to it,
by abandoning the programmatic aspect of avant-garde adventures
in reality and unapologetically retaining the private pleasures art afforded. In this way both Cubism and Surrealism could be admired
without compromising anyone's categorical imperatives simply because no such imperatives were ever articulated in New York and
everyone felt compromised already simply for being there. Thus,
action art and chance operations became high art, and a certain
species of realist art (such as the paintings of Fairfield Porter and
Jane Freilicher) became respectable genres tolerated for their
"avant-garde" refusal to do the "fashionable" thing. Like the New
Realist and Pop artists they admired, the New York poets were no
longer rhetorically allergic to aspects of the tradition that radical
modernism had tried to destroy. Painting could be illusionistic and
poetry rhetorical without having to adhere to the letter of the law of
illusionism or rhetoric. With the New York poets, the Avant-Garde
had come full circle, only to end up somewhere else: a sort of wry
anachronism, celebrated as cutting-edge.

And yet in the work of the two most important figures of the
New York school–John Ashbery and Frank O'Hara–the same para-
doxes of modernity emerge, only double- and quadruple-layered.
O'Hara's apparent triviality masked a hyper-sophistication that in

turn concealed a painful vulnerability that was expiated through poetic seriousness. But like the painter Jackson Pollock he so esteemed, O'Hara's inspiration chiefly concerned the poetic subject's immediate, if self-allegorizing, but fundamentally sincere interaction with the world around his body. Narcissistic, surely, but it was also a definitively avant-garde compulsion (a form of "spiritual clarity") to which O'Hara's instincts perfectly conformed. Thus, even in O'Hara's most abstract poems, in which meaning itself seems "under erasure," the recognizable vestiges of a real, if socially hectic life, help frame discussions about the discursive deformations being enacted.

John Ashbery's instincts, on the other hand, demanded sustained self-concealment behind a complex of cryptic word games, formal discourses and banal asides. No exhibitionist impulse here–though the verbal subterfuges undertaken often made the reader's curiosity about the writing subject all the more acute. Not surprisingly, the artists to whom Ashbery most persuasively responded as an art critic were those such as Yves Tanguy and Jasper Johns, whose way of disappearing into or onto interior landscapes and ordinary signs created a parallel sense of absence. Ashbery had a talent for emptying even the most refulgent signs of meaning, but in a way that gave them a borrowed air of mystery. After going to exasperating extremes in such poems as "Europe" and "Leaving the Atocha Station," Ashbery veered toward a more ruminative mode, taking as his perennial object the very paradox his poetry exemplified: what it means to become an avant-garde tradition (the recurring question of his best art writing). In becoming part of a tradition of breaking with tradition and thus risking, by accepting, his own place within it (indeed one could not presume to be in it unless one were always trying to circumvent it), Ashbery assumed a posture of sly insouciance toward his avant-garde status and subjects, establishing an alternative criteria for them. In this way, both art and anti-art became poetic options, thus making it perfectly feasible to intercalate the aesthetic positions of Parmigianino, Tanguy, Pollock, Johns, and even Warhol in a single poetic corpus. All history, narrative and discourse seemed to flatten themselves out at this late hour of the Avant-Garde in which the self-deconstructing language of Ashbery's poetry craftily strung the reader along, only to bring him to the center of nowhere: our postmodern home. Yet while such surprising convexities, densities and sudden aporias became the hallmark of his poetry, Ashbery retained the sense of painting as a distinctive medium with a range of formal procedures he could harness or simply refer to as cultural road-signs to the destination he had in mind. Even nowhere could be made beautiful through the evocation of visual art.

The mutually reinforcing fascination between poets and painters, poems and paintings, is an index of avant-gardism itself. As mutual surrogates for the twin abysses of politics and non-art, the two arts sustain each other while seeming to dare each other to jump. If the Avant-Garde can be reduced to a series of fads, as David Lehman, quoting Renato Poggioli, has observed, [2] (Lehman 286) these fads partly consist in the way language and image interact, and in this way transcend the merely fashionable. The interactive space of poetry and painting established an experimental ground between two technologically marginalized media, a ground richly mined by the French and American Avant-Gardes to yield new insights into the fusion and divergence of visual and verbal signs through the neuro-sensory networks of integrated human perception. Many of these experiments were anticipated by the technical process of integrating print, photography, audio and film media, media that were superceded in turn by television, video and finally digitalization. Yet in maintaining a space through which the capacity for social mobilization remained limited (precisely because of the technical obsolescence of the media involved), that space also became relatively free as a zone of ideologico-intellectual exchange. Although the expressive methods might be appropriated or subsumed by other, larger media forces (as those of the Concrete Poets were, it would seem, by commercial advertising), [3] they cannot be entirely secured against future counter-appropriation and re-utilization. The combined, yet far-ranging efforts of the French and American Avant-Gardes offered a formal resource for the unmotivated examination of semiotic play between verbal and plastic signs. Insofar as this resource may have succumbed to an epistemological dispersion among a wider range of optico-auditory media testifies to the importance of those early investigations.

---

[2] David Lehman, *The Last Avant-Garde: The Making of the New York School of Poets* (New York: Doubleday, 1998), p. 286.

[3] Marjorie Perloff, *Radical Artifice: Writing Poetry in the Age of Media* (Chicago: University of Chicago, 1991), pp. 118-120.

BIBLIOGRAPHY

Adorno, Theodor W. "On Lyric Poetry and Society" in *Notes to Literature*. New York: Columbia University, 1991, pp. 39-53.

Alloway, Lawrence. "Rauschenberg's Development" in *Robert Rauschenberg*. Washington, D.C.: National Collection of Fine Arts, Smithsonian Institution, 1976.

Altieri, Charles. "John Ashbery and the Challenge of Postmodernism in the Visual Arts" in *Critical Inquiry*. Vol. 14, no. 4 (Summer 1988), pp. 805-830.

———. *Self and Sensibility in Contemporary American Poetry*. Cambridge: Cambridge University Press, 1984.

Amossy, Ruth. "Délire paranoïaque et poésie" in *Europe: Revue littéraire mensuelle*. No. 743 (mars 1991), pp. 40-54.

Apollinaire, Guillaume; Greet, Anne Hyde, trans. *Alcools*. Berkeley: University of California, 1965.

———; Breunig, Leroy C., ed.; Suleiman, Susan, trans. *Apollinaire on Art: Essays and Reviews 1902-1918*. New York: Da Capo, 1988; Viking, 1972.

———. *Calligrammes*. Paris: Éditions Gallimard, 1966.

———; Greet, Anne Hyde, trans. *Calligrammes: Poems of Peace and War (1913-1916)*. Berkeley: University of California, 1980.

———; Breunig, L-C. *Chroniques d'art: 1902-1918*. Paris: Éditions Gallimard, 1960.

———; Breunig, L-C. and Chevalier, J-C., eds. *Méditations esthétiques: Les Peintres cubistes*. Paris: Hermann, Collection Savoir, 1980 [1965].

———; Shattuck, Roger, trans. "The New Spirit and the Poets" in *Selected Writings of Guillaume Apollinaire*. New York: New Directions, 1948, pp. 227-237.

Artaud, Antonin. *L'Ombilic des Limbes*. Paris: Éditions Gallimard, 1968.

Ashbery, John. *Houseboat Days*. New York: Viking, 1977.

———. *Reported Sightings: Art Chronicles 1957-1987*. New York: Alfred A. Knopf, 1989.

———. "Reverdy en Amérique" in *Pierre Reverdy: 1889-1960*. Paris: Mercure de France, 1962, pp. 109-112.

———. *Rivers and Mountains*. New York: Ecco Press, 1977.

———. *Selected Poems*. New York: Viking/Penguin, 1986.

———. *Self-Portrait in a Convex Mirror*. New York: Viking Press, 1975.

———. *Three Poems*. New York: Viking/Penguin, 1986.

Balakian, Anna. *André Breton: Magus of Surrealism*. New York: Oxford University Press, 1971.

———. Introduction to *André Breton Today*. Eds. Anna Balakian and Rudolf E. Kuenzli. New York: Willis, Locker & Owens and *Dada/Surrealism*, 1989.

Balakian, Anna. "Breton in Light of Apollinaire" in *About French Poetry from Dada to "Tel Quel": Text and Theory.* Ed. Mary Ann Caws. Detroit: Wayne State University Press, 1974.

———. *Surrealism: The Road to the Absolute.* Chicago: University of Chicago, 1986.

Barr, Alfred H. *Cubism and Abstract Art.* New York: Museum of Modern Art, 1986.

Barthes, Roland; Miller, Richard, trans. *The Pleasure of the Text.* New York: Farrar, Straus & Giroux, 1975.

Bataille, Georges; Stoekl, Allan, ed. and trans. *Visions of Excess: Selected Writings, 1927-1939.* Minneapolis: University of Minnesota, 1986.

Baudelaire, Charles; Charvet, P. E., trans. *Baudelaire: Selected Writings on Art & Artists.* Cambridge: Cambridge University, 1972.

Baudrillard, Jean; Lotringer, Sylvère, ed. *Forget Foucault.* New York: Semiotext(e), 1987.

———; Foss, Paul and Pefanis, Julian, eds. and trans. *Revenge of the Crystal: Selected Writings on the Modern Object and its Destiny.* Concord, Massachusetts: Pluto Press, 1990.

Behar, Henri. "La Saveur du réel" in *Europe: Revue littéraire mensuelle. Cubisme et littérature.* Nos. 638-641 (juin-juillet 1982), pp. 101-108.

Benjamin, Walter. "The Work of Art in the Age of Mechanical Reproduction" and "On Some Motifs in Baudelaire" in *Illuminations: Essays and Reflections.* New York: Harcourt, Brace, and World, Inc., 1968.

Berenson, Bernard. *The Italian Painters of the Renaissance.* Revised Edition. Oxford: Clarendon Press, 1930.

Bergson, Henri; Mitchell, Arthur, trans. *Creative Evolution.* New York: Random House, 1944.

Blasing, Mutlu Konuk. *Politics and Form in Postmodern Poetry.* Cambridge: Cambridge University, 1995.

———. "Frank O'Hara: The Speech of Poetry," in *Frank O'Hara: To Be True to a City.* Ed. Jim Elledge. Ann Arbor: University of Michigan, 1990, pp. 301-320.

Bloom, Harold. "John Ashbery: The Charity of the Hard Moments" and introduction in *John Ashbery.* Ed. Harold Bloom. New York: Chelsea House, 1985, pp. 49-79.

Boccioni, Umberto, et al.; Apollonio, Umbro, ed.; Brain, Robert and Flint, R. W., trans. *Futurist Manifestos.* New York: Viking, 1973.

Bohn, Willard. "Circular Poem-Paintings by Apollinaire and Carrà" in *Comparative Literature.* Vol. 31, no. 3 (Summer 1979).

———. "Semiosis and Intertextuality in Breton's 'Femme et oiseau'" in *Romanic Review.* Vol. 76, no. 4 (November 1985), pp. 415-428.

Bonnet, Marguerite. *André Breton: Naissance de l'aventure surréaliste.* Paris: Librairie José Corti, 1975.

Bordat, Denis and Veck, Bernard. *Apollinaire.* Paris: Hachette, 1983.

Breton, André; Soupault, Philippe. *Les Champs magnétiques.* Paris: Gallimard, 1971.

———. *Clair de terre.* Paris: Gallimard, 1966.

———; Parinaud, André; Polizzotti, Mark, trans. *Conversations: The Autobiography of Surrealism.* New York: Paragon House, 1993.

———; Zavatsky, Bill and Rogow, Zack, trans. *Earthlight.* Toronto: Coach House Press, 1993.

———; Eluard, Paul; Melville, Antony, intro; Graham, Jon, trans. *The Immaculate Conception.* London: Atlas Press, 1990.

———. *Je vois, J'imagine: Poèmes-objets.* Paris: Gallimard, 1991.

———; Caws, Mary Ann, trans. *Mad Love.* Lincoln: University of Nebraska, 1987.

———. *Manifestes du surréalisme.* Paris: Gallimard, 1987.

Breton, André; Bonnet, M., Bernier, P., Hubert, E-A., Pierre, J., eds. *Les Pas perdus* in *Oeuvres Complètes I*. Paris: Gallimard, 1988.

———; Cauvin, Jean-Pierre and Caws, Mary Ann, trans. *Poems of André Breton*. Austin: University of Texas Press, 1982.

———. *Point du jour*. Paris: Gallimard, 1970.

———. *Signe ascendant*. Paris: Gallimard, 1968.

———; Taylor, Simon Watson, trans. *Surrealism and Painting*. New York: Harper & Row, 1972.

———. *Le Surréalisme et la peinture*. Paris: Éditions Gallimard, 1965.

———; Rosemont, Franklin, ed. *What is Surrealism?* New York: Monad Press, 1978.

Breunig, Leroy C. "Apollinaire et le Cubisme" in *La Revue des Lettres Modernes*. Nos. 69-70 (printemps 1962), pp. 7-24.

———. "From Dada to Cubism: Apollinaire's 'Arbre'" in *About French Poetry from Dada to "Tel Quel": Text and Theory*. Ed. Mary Ann Caws. Detroit: Wayne State University Press, 1974, pp. 26-39.

Bryson, Norman. *Vision and Painting: The Logic of the Gaze*. New Haven: Yale University, 1997 [1983].

Bürger, Peter; Shaw, Michael, trans. *Theory of the Avant-Garde. Theory and History of Literature, Vol. 4*. Minneapolis: University of Minnesota, 1984.

Carrier, David. *Principles of Art History Writing*. University Park, Pennsylvania: Pennsylvania State University, 1991.

Carroll, Paul. *The Poem in its Skin*. New York: Follett Publishing Co., 1968.

Caws, Mary Ann. *The Poetry of Dada and Surrealism*. Princeton: Princeton University Press, 1970.

Chénieux-Gendron, Jacqueline. "Toward a New Definition of Automatism: *L'Immaculée conception*," in *André Breton Today*. Eds. Anna Balakian and Rudolf E. Kuenzli. New York: Willis, Locker & Owens and *Dada/Surrealism*, 1989, pp. 74-88.

Chevalier, Jean-Claude. "G. Apollinaire. Role de la peinture et de la poésie dans l'élaboration d'une poétique" in *La Revue des Lettres Modernes*. Nos. 217-222 (1969), pp. 97-113.

Clark, J. G. "Delaunay, Apollinaire, et 'Les Fenêtres'" in *La Revue des Lettres Modernes. Apollinaire 7*. Nos. 183-188 (1968), pp. 100-112.

Collot, Michel. *Horizon de Reverdy*. Paris: Presses de l'École Normale Supérieure, 1981.

Compagnon, Antoine; Philip, Franklin, trans. *The Five Paradoxes of Modernity*. New York: Columbia University, 1994.

———. *La Seconde Main, ou le travail de la citation*. Paris: Éditions du Seuil, 1979.

Cook, Albert. "Expression Not Wholly Abstract: John Ashbery" in *American Poetry*. Vol. 2, no. 2 (Winter 1985), pp. 53-70.

Culler, Jonathan. *Structuralist Poetics*. Ithaca: Cornell University, 1982.

Dalí, Salvador. "Autour de la méthode paranoïaque-critique: La Conquête de l'irrationnel" and "Nouvelles considérations générales sur le mécanisme du phénomène paranoïaque du point de vue surréaliste," in *Oui*. Paris: Éditions Denoël, 1971.

———. *Le Mythe Tragique de l'Angelus de Millet*. Paris: Pauvert, 1978.

Danto, Arthur C. *The Philosophical Disenfranchisement of Art*. New York: Columbia University Press, 1986.

De Méredieu, Florence. *André Masson: Les Dessins automatiques*. Paris: Blusson Éditeur, 1988.

De Costa, René. "Juan Gris and Poetry: From Illustration to Creation" in *Art Bulletin*. Vol. 71, no. 4 (December 1989), pp. 674-692.

Debon, Claude. *Guillaume Apollinaire après "Alcools."* Paris: Minard, 1981.

Decaudin, Michel and Hubert, Étienne-Alain. "Petite Histoire d'une appellation: 'Cubisme littéraire'" in *Europe: Revue littéraire mensuelle. Cubisme et littérature.* Nos. 638-641 (juin-juillet 1982), pp. 7-25.

Delaunay, Robert. *Du Cubisme à l'art abstrait.* Paris: S.E.V.P.E.N., 1957.

Deleuze, Gilles and Guattari, Félix; Sweet, David. L., trans. "Capitalism: A Very Special Delirium" in *Chaosophy.* Ed. Sylvère Lotringer. New York: Semiotext(e), 1995.

———. *Nomadology: The War Machine.* New York: Semiotext(e), 1986.

Derrida, Jacques. "Restitutions" in *The Truth in Painting.* Trans. Geoff Bennington and Ian McLeod. Chicago: University of Chicago, 1987.

Dijkstra, Bram. *Cubism, Stieglitz, and the Early Poetry of William Carlos Williams.* Princeton: Princeton University, 1969.

Eberz, Ingrid. "Kandinsky, Breton, et le modèle purement intérieur" in *Pleine Marge.* No. 1 (mai 1985), pp. 69-80.

Eichbauer, Mary E. *Poetry's Self-Portrait: The Visual Arts as Mirror and Muse in René Char and John Ashbery.* New York: Peter Lang Publishing, 1992.

Eliot, T. S. "The Metaphysical Poets" in *Selected Prose of T.S. Eliot.* Ed. Frank Kermode. New York: Harcourt, Brace, Jovanovich, 1975.

Ernst, Max. *Beyond Painting.* New York: Wittenborn, Schultz Inc., 1948.

Feldman, Alan. *Frank O'Hara.* Boston: G. K. Hall, 1979.

Fenollosa, Ernest; Pound, Ezra, ed. *The Chinese Written Character as a Medium for Poetry.* San Francisco: City Lights, 1983.

Ferguson, Suzanne. "Crossing the Delaware with Larry Rivers and Frank O'Hara: The Post-Modern Hero at the Battle of Signifiers" in *Word & Image.* Vol. 2, no. 1 (January-March 1986), pp. 27-32.

Fink, Thomas A. "'Here and There': The Locus of Language in John Ashbery's 'Self-Portrait in a Convex Mirror'" in *Contemporary Poetry.* Vol. 4, no. 3 (1982), pp. 47-64.

Foucault, Michel; Smith, A. M. Sheridan, trans. *The Archeology of Knowledge.* New York: Tavistock Publications Limited, 1972.

———. *Ceci n'est pas une pipe.* Paris: Fata Morgana, 1973.

Fowlie, Wallace. *Mallarmé.* Chicago: University of Chicago, 1953.

Freud, Sigmund; Strachey, James, trans. *The Interpretation of Dreams.* New York: Avon Books, 1965.

———; Tyson, Alan, trans. *The Psychopathology of Everyday Life.* New York: W. W. Norton, & Co., 1965.

Fried, Michael. "Art and Objecthood" in *Aesthetics Today.* Eds. Morris Philipson and Paul J. Gudel. New York: New American Library, Meridian, 1961, pp. 214-240.

Fumet, Stanislas. "La 'poésie plastique' de Pierre Reverdy" in *Pierre Reverdy: 1889-1960.* Paris: *Mercure de France,* 1962, pp. 31-47.

Gavronsky, Serge. *Culture Ecriture: Essais Critiques.* Rome: Bulzoni editore, 1983.

Golding, John. *Cubism: A History and Analysis 1907-1914.* Boston: Boston Book & Art Shop, 1968.

Gombrich, E. H. *Art and Illusion.* Princeton: Princeton University, 1969.

———. "Image and Code: Scope and Limits of Conventionalism in Pictorial Representation" in *Image and Code.* Ed. Wendy Steiner. Ann Arbor: University of Michigan Studies in the Humanities, No. 2, 1981.

Gooch, Brad. *City Poet: The Life and Times of Frank O'Hara.* New York: Alfred A. Knopf, Inc., 1993.

Goodman, Nelson. *Languages of Art.* Indianapolis, Indiana: Hackett Publishing, 1988.

Gray, Christopher. *Cubist Aesthetic Theories.* Baltimore: Johns Hopkins, 1953.

Greenberg, Clement. "The Crisis of the Easel Picture," in *Art and Culture.* Boston: Beacon Press, 1965, pp. 154-157.

Greene, Robert W. *The Poetic Theory of Pierre Reverdy. University of California Publications in Modern Philology.* Vol. 82. Berkeley: University of California, 1967.

Guiney, Mortimer. *La Poésie de Pierre Reverdy.* Geneva: Librairie de l'Université, Georg & Cie., S.A., 1966.

———. *Cubisme et littérature.* Geneva: Librairie de l'Université, Georg et Cie., S.A., 1972.

Hoeppner, Edward H. "Visual Gestalt and John Ashbery's 'Europe'" in *Concerning Poetry.* Vol. 20 (1987), pp. 87-96.

Hubert, Étienne-Alain. "Pierre Reverdy et la 'poésie plastique' de son temps" in *Europe: Revue littéraire mensuelle: Cubisme et littérature.* Nos. 638-641 (juin-juillet 1982), pp. 109-126.

Jameson, Fredric. *Postmodernism.* Durham, North Carolina: Duke University Press, 1992.

Jean, Raymond. *La Poétique du desir.* Paris: Éditions du Seuil, 1974.

Jenny, Laurent; Trezise, Thomas, trans. "From Breton to Dali: The Adventures of Automatism" in *October.* Vol. 51 (Winter 1989), pp. 105-114.

Jouffroy, Alain. "Le Premier rendez-vous de la peinture surréaliste" in *XXᵉᵐᵉ siècle.* No. 38 (juin 1972), pp. 15-22.

Kahnweiler, Daniel-Henry. "Reverdy et l'art plastique" in *Pierre Reverdy: 1889-1960.* Paris: *Mercure de France,* 1962, pp. 169-176.

———; Cooper, Douglas, trans. *Juan Gris: His Life and Work.* New York: Curt Valentin, 1947.

Knox, Israel. *The Aesthetic Theories of Kant, Hegel, and Schopenhauer.* New York: Columbia University, 1936.

Koch, Kenneth. "All the Imagination Can Hold" in *Frank O'Hara: To Be True to a City.* Ann Arbor: University of Michigan, 1990, pp. 31-37.

Koethe, John. "The Metaphysical Subject of John Ashbery's Poetry" in *Beyond Amazement: New Essays on John Ashbery.* Ithaca: Cornell University, 1980, pp. 87-100.

Kostelanetz, Richard. "Frank O'Hara and his Poetry: An Interview with Kenneth Koch" in *American Writing Today.* Ed. Richard Kostelanetz. Troy, N.Y.: Whitston Publishing Company, 1991, pp. 201-209.

Krauss, Rosalind. *The Optical Unconscious.* Cambridge: MIT Press, 1993.

———. *The Originality of the Avant-Garde and Other Modernist Myths.* Cambridge, Massachusetts: MIT Press, 1989.

Kuspit, Donald. "Cubist Hypochondria: On the Case of Picasso and Braque" in *Artforum.* Vol. 28 (September 1989), pp. 112-116.

———. "Dispensable Friends, Indispensable Ideologies" in *Artforum.* Vol. 22 (December 1983), pp. 56-63.

Lacan, Jacques. *The Four Fundamental Concepts of Psycho-Analysis.* New York: W. W. Norton & Co., 1981.

Latimer, Dan, ed. *Contemporary Critical Theory.* New York: Harcourt, Brace, Jovanovich, 1989.

Lautréamont, Comte de. *Oeuvres complètes: Les Chants de Maldoror, Lettres, Poésies I et II.* Paris: Éditions Gallimard, 1973.

Lawler, James R. *The Language of French Symbolism.* Princeton: Princeton University, 1969.

Lebel, Robert. "André Breton et la peinture," in *L'Oeil.* No. 143 (November 1966), pp. 10-19.

Lehman, David. *The Last Avant-Garde: The Making of the New York School of Poets.* New York: Doubleday, 1998.

———. "The Shield of a Greeting" in *Beyond Amazement: New Essays on John Ashbery.* Ed. David Lehman. Ithaca: Cornell University, 1980, pp. 101-127.

Lemaitre, Georges. *From Cubism to Surrealism in French Literature.* New York: Russell & Russell, 1967.

Libby, Anthony. "O'Hara on the Silver Range" in *Frank O'Hara: To Be True to a City.* Ed. Jim Elledge. Ann Arbor: University of Michigan, 1990, pp. 131-155.

Lockerbie, S. I. "'Les Fenêtres' et le poème créé" in *Revue des Lettres Modernes. Apollinaire 5.* Nos. 146-149 (1966), pp. 6-22.

Lowney, John. "The 'Post-anti-aesthetic' of Frank O'Hara" in *Contemporary Literature.* Vol. 32, no. 2 (Summer 1991), pp. 244-262.

Lucie-Smith, Edward. "An Interview with Frank O'Hara" in *Standing Still and Walking in New York.* Ed. Donald Allen. San Francisco: Grey Fox Press, 1983, pp. 3-24.

Mallarmé, Stéphane; Caws, Mary Ann, ed. *Selected Poetry and Prose.* New York: New Directions, 1982.

———. "Crise de vers" in *Oeuvres Complètes.* Eds. Henri Mondor and G. Jean-Aubry. Paris: Bibliothèque de la Pléiade, Gallimard, 1945.

———. "Crisis in Verse" in *Symbolism: An Anthology.* Ed. and trans. T. G. West. London: Methuen, 1980.

———. "The Impressionists and Edouard Manet" in *Mallarmé, Manet, and Redon* by Penny Florence. Cambridge: Cambridge University, 1986.

———. *Correspondance.* Paris: Gallimard, 1985.

Marinetti, F. T.; Flint, R. W. and Coppotelli, A. A., eds. and trans. *Marinetti: Selected Writings.* New York: Farrar, Straus & Giroux, 1972.

Mathews, Timothy. *Reading Apollinaire: Theories of Poetic Language.* Manchester: Manchester University, 1987.

Matthews, J. H. "André Breton and Arshile Gorky" in *André Breton Today.* Eds. Anna Balakian and Rudolf E. Kuenzli. New York: Willis, Locker & Owens and *Dada/Surrealism,* 1989, pp. 40-44.

———. *André Breton: Sketch for an Early Portrait. Purdue University Monographs in Romance Languages. Vol. 22.* Philadelphia: John Benjamin Publishers, 1986.

———. *André Breton.* New York: Columbia University, 1967.

Meyer, Thomas. "Glistening Torsos, Sandwiches, and Coca-Cola" in *Frank O'Hara: To Be True to a City.* Ed. Jim Elledge. Ann Arbor: University of Michigan, 1990, pp. 85-102.

Milhau, Denis. "Lecture du Cubisme par deux poètes: Apollinaire et Reverdy" in *Europe: Revue littéraire mensuelle. Cubisme et littérature.* Nos. 638-641 (juin-juillet 1982), pp. 44-48.

Miller, J. Hillis. "William Carlos Williams" in *Poets of Reality.* Cambridge, Massachusetts: Belknap Press, 1966, pp. 285-359.

Miller, Stephen Paul. "'Self-Portrait in a Convex Mirror,' the Watergate Affair, and Johns's Crosshatch Paintings: Surveillance and Reality-Testing in the Mid-Seventies" in *Boundary 2.* Vol. 20, no. 2 (Summer 1993), pp. 84-115.

Mitchell, W. J. T. *Iconology: Image, Text, Ideology.* Chicago: University of Chicago, 1986.

Moramarco, Fred. "John Ashbery and Frank O'Hara: The Painterly Poets" in *Journal of Modern Literature.* Vol. 5, no. 3 (September 1976), pp. 436-462.

Motherwell, Robert, ed. *The Dada Painters and Poets.* Cambridge, Massachusetts: Belknap Press, 1989.

Mundy, Jennifer. "Surrealism and Painting: Describing the Imaginary," in *Art History.* Vol. 10, no. 4 (December 1987), pp. 492-508.

Munn, Paul. "An Interview with John Ashbery" in *New Orleans Review*. Vol. 17, no. 2 (Summer 1990), pp. 59-63.

Myers, John Bernard. *The Poets of the New York School*. Philadelphia: University of Pennsylvania, 1969.

Nadeau, Maurice; Howard, R., trans. *The History of Surrealism*. Cambridge, Massachusetts: Belknap Press, 1989.

O'Hara, Frank. *Art Chronicles 1954-1966*. New York: George Braziller, Maureen Granville-Smith, 1975.

———. *The Collected Poems of Frank O'Hara*. Ed. Donald Allen. Berkeley: University of California, 1995.

———. *The Selected Poems of Frank O'Hara*. New York: Random House/Vintage, 1974.

———. *Jackson Pollock*. New York: George Braziller, 1959.

———; Berkson, Bill. "Reverdy" in *Pierre Reverdy: 1889-1960*. Paris: Mercure de France, 1962, pp. 97-98.

———. Statement in *The New American Poetry 1945-1960*. Ed. Donald M. Allen. New York: Grove Press, 1960.

Parker, Alice C. *The Exploration of the Secret Smile: The Language of Art and Homosexuality in Frank O'Hara's Poetry*. New York: Peter Lang, 1989.

Pater, Walter. "The School of Giorgione" (excerpt) in *Victorian Poetry and Poetics*, Second Edition. Eds. W. Houghton and G. R. Stange. Boston: Houghton Mifflin, 1968.

Peirce, C. S. "Logic as Semiotic: The Theory of Signs" in *The Philosophy of C. S. Peirce: Selected Writings*. New York: Harcourt, Brace and Company, 1950.

Perloff, Marjorie. "Frank O'Hara and the Aesthetics of Attention" in *Frank O'Hara: To Be True to a City*. Ed. Jim Elledge. Ann Arbor: University of Michigan, 1990, pp. 156-188.

———. *Frank O'Hara: A Poet among Painters*. New York: George Braziller, 1977.

———. *The Futurist Moment*. Chicago: University of Chicago, 1986.

———. *The Poetics of Indeterminacy: Rimbaud to Cage*. Princeton: Princeton University, 1981.

———. "From 'Poetry Chronicle: 1970-71,'" in *Frank O'Hara: To Be True to a City*. Ed. Jim Elledge. Ann Arbor: University of Michigan, 1990, pp. 59-63.

———. *Radical Artifice: Writing Poetry in the Age of Media*. Chicago: University of Chicago, 1991.

Pierre, José. *André Breton et la Peinture*. Lausanne, Suisse: Éditions d'Homme, 1987.

Pleynet, Marcelin. "Painting and *Surrealism and Painting*" in *Comparative Criticism*. Vol. 4 (1982), pp. 31-53.

Py, Françoise. "L'Oeil sauvage" in *Europe: Revue littéraire mensuelle*. No. 743 (mars 1991), pp. 135-142.

Renaud, Philippe. *Lecture d'Apollinaire*. Lausanne: Éditions l'Âge d'Homme, 1969.

Restany, Pierre. *Art in America*. Vol. 51 (February 1963), pp. 102-104.

Reverdy, Pierre. *Nord-Sud, Self Defence et Autres Écrits sur l'Art et la Poésie (1917-1926)*. Paris: Flammarion, 1975.

———. *Plupart du temps, I (1915-1922)*. Paris: Gallimard, 1969.

———. *Au Soleil du plafond et autres poèmes*. Paris: Flammarion, 1980.

Rexroth, Kenneth. Introduction to *Pierre Reverdy: Selected Poems*. New York: New Directions, 1972.

Riffaterre, Michel. "Semantic Incompatibilities in Automatic Writing" in *About French Poetry from Dada to "Tel Quel": Text and Theory*. Ed. Mary Ann Caws. Detroit: Wayne State University Press, 1974, pp. 223-236.

Rimbaud, Arthur; Fowlie, Wallace, trans. *Rimbaud: Complete Works, Selected Letters*. Chicago: University of Chicago, 1966.

Rivers, Larry; Weinstein, Arnold. *What Did I Do? The Unauthorized Autobiography*. New York: HarperCollins Publishers, 1992.

Rizzuto, Anthony. *Style and Theme in Reverdy's "Les Ardoises du toit."* University, Alabama: University of Alabama Press, 1971.

Rosenberg, Harold. "The American Action Painters" in *The Tradition of the New*. York: Horizon Press, 1959, pp. 23-39.

Rosenthal, Mark. *Juan Gris*. New York: Abbeville, 1983.

Ross, Andrew. "The Death of Lady Day" in *Frank O'Hara: To Be True to a City*. Ann Arbor: University of Michigan, 1990.

————. *The Failure of Modernism*. New York: Columbia University, 1986.

Rothwell, Andrew. "Cubism and the Avant-Garde Prose-Poem: Figural Space in Pierre Reverdy's *Au Soleil de plafond*" in *French Studies: A Quarterly Review*. Vol. 42, no. 3 (July 1988), pp. 302-319.

Roussel, Raymond. *Comment j'ai écrit certains de mes livres*. Paris: Pauvert, 1963.

————. *Locus Solus*. Paris: Gallimard, 1979.

Rubin, William; Lanchner, Carolyn. *André Masson*. New York: Museum of Modern Art, 1976.

Rubin, William. *Dada, Surrealism, and their Heritage*. New York: Museum of Modern Art, 1977.

————. *Picasso and Braque: Pioneering Cubism*. New York: Museum of Modern Art, 1989.

Russell, Charles. *Poets, Prophets, and Revolutionaries: The Literary Avant-garde from Rimbaud to Postmodernism*. New York: Oxford University Press, 1985.

Russell, John. *Max Ernst: Life and Work*. New York: Harry N. Abrams, 1960.

Sacks-Galey, Pénélope. *Calligramme ou Ecriture Figurée: Apollinaire inventeur de formes*. Paris: Lettres Modernes, Minard, 1988.

Salusinsky, Imre. "The Genesis of Ashbery's 'Europe'" in *NMAL: Notes on Modern American Literature*. Vol. 7, no. 2 (Fall 1983), item #12.

Sartre, Jean-Paul; Turnell, Martin, trans. *Baudelaire*. New York: New Directions, 1950.

————; Sturm, E., trans. *Mallarmé or the Poet of Nothingness*. Philadelphia: Pennsylvania State University, 1988.

Saussure, Ferdinand; Baskin, Wade, trans. "Nature of the Linguistic Sign" in *Critical Theory*. Ed. Dan Latimer. New York: Harcourt, Brace, Jovanovich, 1989.

Sayre, Henry. *The Visual Text of William Carlos Williams*. Chicago: University of Illinois, 1983.

Schapiro, Meyer. "The Nature of Abstract Art" in *Modern Art: Nineteenth and Twentieth Centuries, Selected Papers*. New York: George Braziller, 1978, pp. 185-211.

Sellin, Eric. "The Esthetics of Ambiguity: Reverdy's Use of Syntactical Simultaneity" in *About French Poetry from Dada to "Tel Quel": Text and Theory*. Ed. Mary Ann Caws. Detroit: Wayne State University Press, 1974, pp. 113-121.

Shapiro, David. *John Ashbery: An Introduction to the Poetry*. New York: Columbia University Press, 1979.

Shattuck, Roger. *The Banquet Years*. New York: Random House, Vintage, 1968.

Shklovsky, Viktor. "Art as Technique" in *Twentieth-Century Literary Theory*. Ed. K. M. Newton. London: Macmillan, 1997.

Shoptaw, John. *On the Outside Looking Out: John Ashbery's Poetry*. Cambridge: Harvard University Press, 1994.

Shroeder, Jean. *Pierre Reverdy*. Boston: Twayne, 1981.

Smithson, Robert. "A Tour of the Monuments of Passaic, New Jersey" in *The Writings of Robert Smithson.* New York: New York University, 1979.

Sontag, Susan. "Against Interpretation" in *Against Interpretation.* New York: Farrar, Straus, Giroux, 1966.

Spate, Virginia. *Orphism: The Evolution of Non-figurative Painting in Paris 1910-1914.* Oxford: Clarendon Press, 1979.

Stamelman, Richard. "Critical Reflections: Poetry and Art Criticism in Ashbery's 'Self-Portrait in a Convex Mirror'" in *New Literary History.* Vol. XV, no. 3 (Spring 1984), pp. 607-630.

Steegmuller, Francis. *Apollinaire: Poet Among the Painters.* New York: Viking Penguin, 1963.

Steinberg, Leo. "The Polemical Part" in *Art in America.* March/April 1979, pp. 114-127.

———. *Other Criteria: Confrontations with Twentieth-Century Art.* Oxford: Oxford University, 1972.

Steiner, Wendy. *The Colors of Rhetoric: Problems in the Relation Between Modern Literature and Painting.* Chicago: University of Chicago, 1982.

Taylor, Charles. *Hegel.* New York: Cambridge University Press, 1975.

Thompkins, Calvin. *The Bride and the Bachelors: Five Masters of the Avant-Garde.* New York: Penguin, 1976.

Tzara, Tristan. "Dada Manifeste sur l'amour faible et l'amour amer" in *Sept Manifestes Dada, Lampisteries.* Paris: Société Nouvelle des Éditions Pauvert, pp. 53-76.

Verlaine, Paul; MacIntyre, C. F., trans. *Verlaine: Selected Poems.* Berkeley: University of California, 1948.

Warren, Rosanna. "Orpheus the Painter: Apollinaire and Robert Delaunay" in *Conversant Essays: Contemporary Poets on Poetry.* Detroit: Wayne State University, 1990, pp. 549-563.

Williams, William Carlos. "Introduction to *The Wedge*" in *Poetics of the New American Poetry.* Eds. Donald Allen, Warren Tallman. New York: Grove Press, 1973, pp. 137-139.

———. Selections from *Kora in Hell* and *Spring and All* in *The William Carlos Williams Reader.* Ed. M. L. Rosenthal. New York: New Directions, 1962.

———. *Paterson.* New York: New Directions, 1992.

———. "Prologue to *Kora in Hell*" in *Selected Essays of William Carlos Williams.* New York: Random House, 1954, pp. 3-26.

———. "The Work of Gertrude Stein" in *Selected Essays of William Carlos Williams.* New York: Random House, 1954, pp. 113-120.

Wolf, Leslie. "The Brushstroke's Integrity: The Poetry of John Ashbery and the Art of Painting" in *Beyond Amazement: New Essays on John Ashbery.* Ed. David Lehman. Ithaca: Cornell, 1980, pp. 224-254.

ILLUSTRATIONS

Fig. 1. Giorgio de Chirico. *The Double Dream of Spring.* 1915. © 2002 Artists
Rights Society (ARS), New York/SIAE, Rome

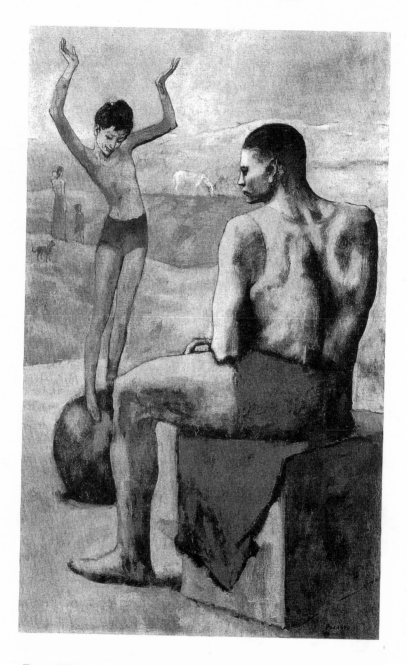

Fig. 2. Pablo Picasso. *Acrobat on a Ball.* 1905. © 2002 Estate of Pablo Picasso/
Artists Rights Society (ARS), New York

Fig. 3. Umberto Boccioni. *Simultaneous Visions*. 1911

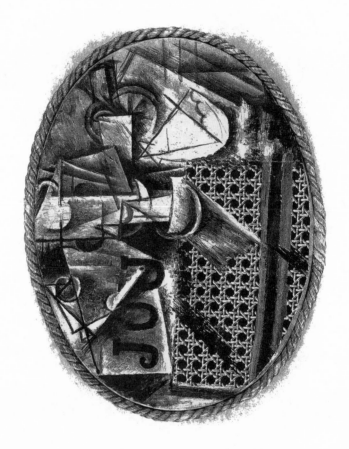

Fig. 4. Pablo Picasso. *Still Life with Chair Caning*. 1911. © 2002 Estate of Pablo
Picasso/Artists Rights Society (ARS), New York

Lettre-Océan

Je traverse la ville net en avant
et je la coupe en **2**

J'étais au bord du Rhin quand tu partis pour le Mexique
Ta voix me parvient malgré l'énorme distance
Gens de mauvaise mine sur le quai à la Vera Cruz

Les voyageurs de *l'Espagne* devant faire
le voyage de Coatzacoalcos pour s'embarquer
je t'envoie cette carte aujourd'hui au lieu

Juan Aldama

Correos
Mexico
4 centavos

YPIRANGA

REPUBLICA MEXICANA
TARJETA POSTAL

11 45
29 - 5
14
Rue des Batignolles

de profiter du courrier de Vera Cruz qui n'est pas sûr
Tout est calme ici et nous sommes dans l'attente
des événements.

U. S. Postage
2 cents 2

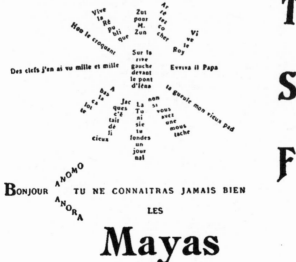

T
S
F

Vive
la
Ré
pu
bli
que

Zut
pour
M.
Zun

Ar
ré
tes
co
cher

Vi
ve
le
Roy

Hou le croquant

Des clefs j'en ai vu mille et mille

Sur la
rive
gauche
devant
le pont
d'Iéna

Evviva il Papa

la gueule mon vieux pad

A
bas
ca
lot
te

Jac
ques
c'é
tait
dé
li
cieux

La
Tu
ni
sie
tu
fondes
un
jour
nal

non
si
vous
avez
une
mous
tache

BONJOUR

ANOMO
ANORA

TU NE CONNAITRAS JAMAIS BIEN

LES

Mayas

Fig. 5. Guillaume Apollinaire. "Lettre-Océan" (page 1)

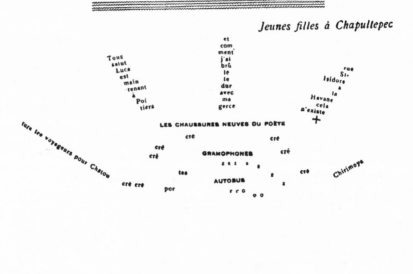

Fig. 6. Guillaume Apollinaire. "Lettre-Océan" (page 2)

Fig. 7. Juan Gris. *Still Life with Poem.* 1915. © 2002 Artists Rights Society (ARS),
New York/ADAGP, Paris

Fig. 8. Max Ernst. *Two Ambiguous Figures*. 1919-1920. © 2002 Artists Rights Society
(ARS), New York/ADAGP, Paris

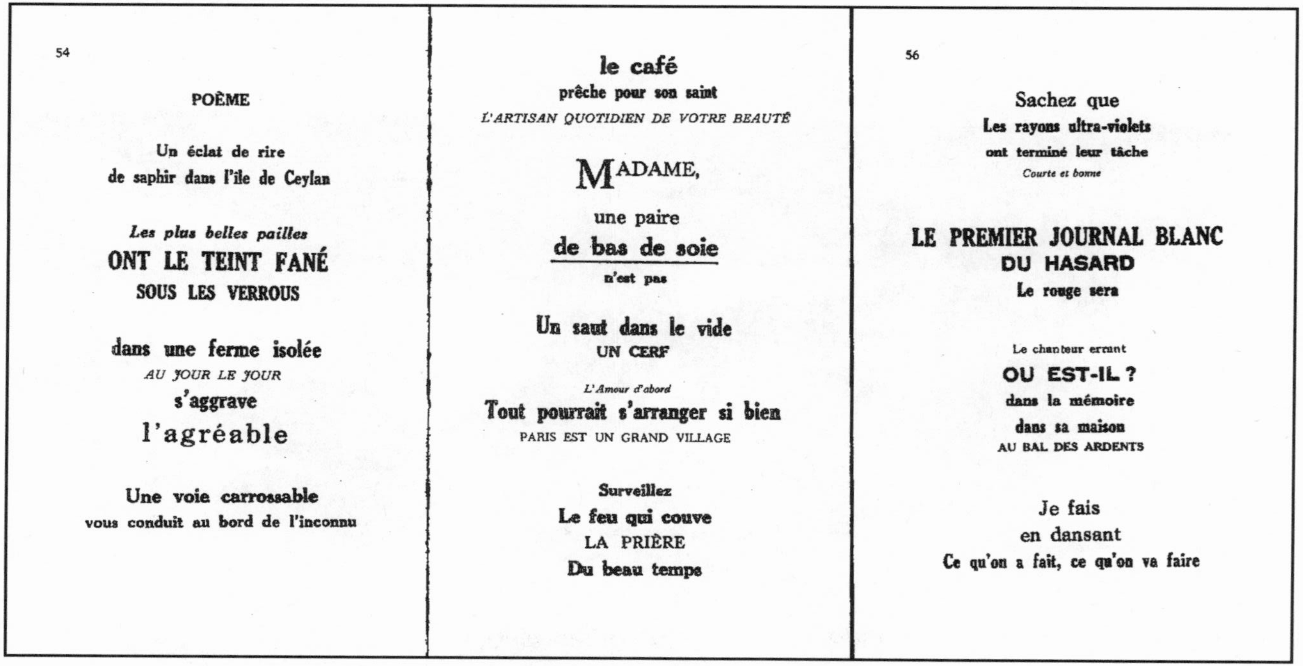

54

POÈME

Un éclat de rire
de saphir dans l'île de Ceylan

Les plus belles pailles
ONT LE TEINT FANÉ
SOUS LES VERROUS

dans une ferme isolée
AU JOUR LE JOUR
s'aggrave
l'agréable

Une voie carrossable
vous conduit au bord de l'inconnu

le café
prêche pour son saint
L'ARTISAN QUOTIDIEN DE VOTRE BEAUTÉ

MADAME,
une paire
de bas de soie
n'est pas

Un saut dans le vide
UN CERF

L'Amour d'abord
Tout pourrait s'arranger si bien
PARIS EST UN GRAND VILLAGE

Surveillez
Le feu qui couve
LA PRIÈRE
Du beau temps

56

Sachez que
Les rayons ultra-violets
ont terminé leur tâche
Courte et bonne

LE PREMIER JOURNAL BLANC
DU HASARD
Le rouge sera

Le chanteur errant
OÙ EST-IL ?
dans la mémoire
dans sa maison
AU BAL DES ARDENTS

Je fais
en dansant
Ce qu'on a fait, ce qu'on va faire

Fig. 9. André Breton. "Poème" (in *Manifeste du Surréalisme*). 1925. © Pauvert département des éditions Fayard 2000

Fig. 10. Max Ernst. *The Repose of Death* (from *Natural History*). 1925. © 2002 Artists Rights Society (ARS), New York/ADAGP, Paris

Fig. 11. André Masson. Automatic drawing. 1925. © 2002 Artists Rights Society
(ARS), New York/ADAGP, Paris

Fig. 12. Salvador Dalí. *Metamorphosis of Narcissus*. 1936-1937. © Salvador Dalí, Gala-Salvador Dalí Foundation/Artists Rights Society (ARS), New York

Fig. 13. André Breton. Symbolically-functioning object. 1931

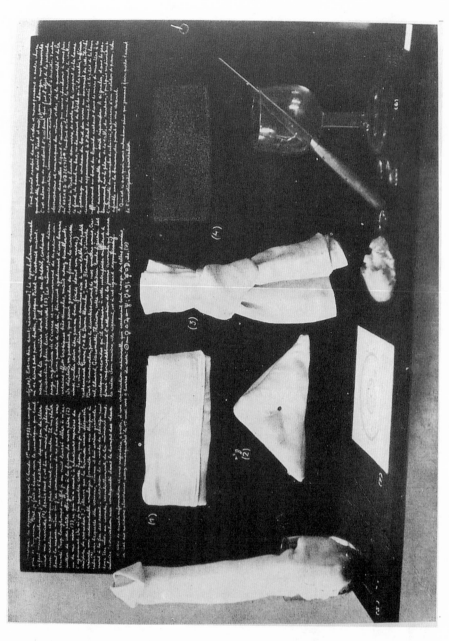

Fig. 14. André Breton, Poem-object, 1931

Fig. 15. Joan Miró. *The Beautiful Bird Revealing the Unknown to a Pair of Lovers* (from *Constellations*). 1941. © 2002 Successió Miró/Artists Rights Society (ARS), New York/ADAGP, Paris

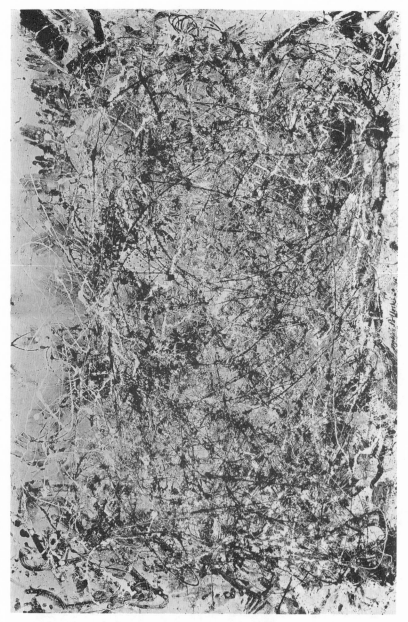

Fig. 16. Jackson Pollock. *Number 1, 1948*. 1948. © 2002 The Pollock-Krasner Foundation/Artists Rights Society (ARS), New York

Fig. 17. Willem de Kooning. *Woman I.* 1950-1952. © The Willem de Kooning
Foundation/Artists Rights Society (ARS), New York

Fig. 18. Larry Rivers. *Second Avenue with THE*. 1958. © Larry Rivers/Licensed
by VAGA, New York, NY

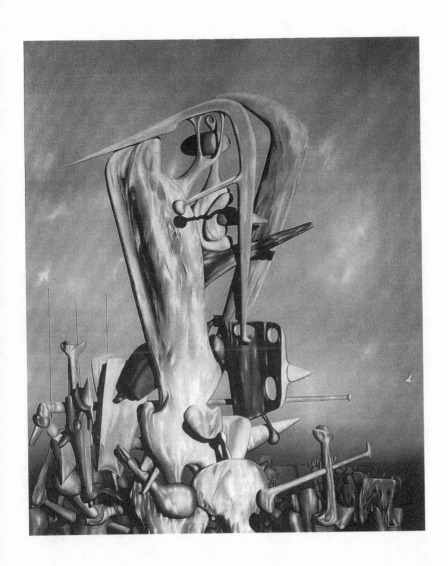

Fig. 19. Yves Tanguy. *My Life, White and Black*. 1944. © 2002 Estate of Yves
Tanguy/Artists Rights Society (ARS), New York

Fig. 20. Jasper Johns. *Liar.* 1961. © Jasper Johns/Licensed by VAGA, New York, NY

Fig. 21. Jasper Johns. *Map.* 1962. © Jasper Johns/Licensed by VAGA, New York, NY

Fig. 22. Robert Rauschenberg. *Monogram.* 1955-1959. © Robert Rauschenberg/
Licensed by VAGA, New York, NY

Fig. 23. Robert Rauschenberg. *Winter Pool.* 1959. © Robert Rauschenberg/
Licensed by VAGA, New York, NY

Fig. 24. Il Parmigianino. *Self-Portrait in a Convex Mirror.* 1524

NORTH CAROLINA STUDIES IN THE ROMANCE LANGUAGES AND LITERATURES

I.S.B.N. Prefix 0-8078-

Recent Titles

THE RAVISHMENT OF PERSEPHONE: EPISTOLARY LYRIC IN THE *SIÈCLE DES LUMIÈRES*, by Julia K. De Pree. 1998. (No. 258). *-9262-9.*

CONVERTING FICTION: COUNTER REFORMATIONAL CLOSURE IN THE SECULAR LITERATURE OF GOLDEN AGE SPAIN, by David H. Darst. 1998. (No. 259). *-9263-7.*

GALDÓS'S *SEGUNDA MANERA*: RHETORICAL STRATEGIES AND AFFECTIVE RESPONSE, by Linda M. Willem. 1998. (No. 260). *-9264-5.*

A MEDIEVAL PILGRIM'S COMPANION. REASSESSING *EL LIBRO DE LOS HUÉSPEDES* (ESCORIAL MS. h.I.13), by Thomas D. Spaccarelli. 1998. (No. 261). *-9265-3.*

'PUEBLOS ENFERMOS': THE DISCOURSE OF ILLNESS IN THE TURN-OF-THE-CENTURY SPANISH AND LATIN AMERICAN ESSAY, by Michael Aronna. 1999. (No. 262). *-9266-1.*

RESONANT THEMES. LITERATURE, HISTORY, AND THE ARTS IN NINETEENTH- AND TWENTIETH-CENTURY EUROPE. ESSAYS IN HONOR OF VICTOR BROMBERT, by Stirling Haig. 1999. (No. 263). *-9267-X.*

RAZA, GÉNERO E HIBRIDEZ EN *EL LAZARILLO DE CIEGOS CAMINANTES*, por Mariselle Meléndez. 1999. (No. 264). *-9268-8.*

DEL ESCENARIO A LA PANTALLA: LA ADAPTACIÓN CINEMATOGRÁFICA DEL TEATRO ESPAÑOL, por María Asunción Gómez. 2000. (No. 265). *-9269-6.*

THE LEPER IN BLUE: COERCIVE PERFORMANCE AND THE CONTEMPORARY LATIN AMERICAN THEATER, by Amalia Gladhart. 2000. (No. 266). *-9270-X.*

THE CHARM OF CATASTROPHE: A STUDY OF RABELAIS'S *QUART LIVRE*, by Alice Fiola Berry. 2000. (No. 267). *-9271-8.*

PUERTO RICAN CULTURAL IDENTITY AND THE WORK OF LUIS RAFAEL SÁNCHEZ, by John Dimitri Perivolaris. 2000. (No. 268). *-9272-6.*

MANNERISM AND BAROQUE IN SEVENTEENTH-CENTURY FRENCH POETRY: THE EXAMPLE OF TRISTAN L'HERMITE, by James Crenshaw Shepard. 2001. (No. 269). *-9273-4.*

RECLAIMING THE BODY: MARÍA DE ZAYA'S EARLY MODERN FEMINISM, by Lisa Vollendorf. 2001. (No. 270). *-9274-2.*

FORGED GENEALOGIES: SAINT-JOHN PERSE'S CONVERSATIONS WITH CULTURE, by Carol Rigolot. 2001. (No. 271). *-9275-0.*

VISIONES DE ESTEREOSCOPIO (PARADIGMA DE HIBRIDACIÓN EN EL ARTE Y LA NARRATIVA DE LA VANGUARDIA ESPAÑOLA), por María Soledad Fernández Utrera. 2001. (No. 272). *-9276-9.*

TRANSPOSING ART INTO TEXTS IN FRENCH ROMANTIC LITERATURE, by Henry F. Majewski. 2002. (No. 273). *-9277-7.*

IMAGES IN MIND: LOVESICKNESS, SPANISH SENTIMENTAL FICTION AND *DON QUIJOTE*, by Robert Folger. 2002. (No. 274). *-9278-5.*

INDISCERNIBLE COUNTERPARTS: THE INVENTION OF THE TEXT IN FRENCH CLASSICAL DRAMA, by Christopher Braider. 2002. (No. 275). *-9279-3.*

SAVAGE SIGHT/CONSTRUCTED NOISE. POETIC ADAPTATIONS OF PAINTERLY TECHNIQUES IN THE FRENCH AND AMERICAN AVANT-GARDES, by David LeHardy Sweet. 2003. (No. 276). *-9281-5.*

AN EARLY BOURGEOIS LITERATURE IN GOLDEN AGE SPAIN. *LAZARILLO DE TORMES, GUZMÁN DE ALFARACHE* AND BALTASAR GRACIÁN, by Francisco J. Sánchez. 2003. (No. 277). *-9280-7.*

When ordering please cite the *ISBN Prefix* plus the last four digits for each title.

Send orders to: University of North Carolina Press
P.O. Box 2288
Chapel Hill, NC 27515-2288
U.S.A.
www.uncpress.unc.edu
FAX: 919 966-3829